THE NATIONAL INSTITUTE OF
ECONOMIC AND SOCIAL RESEARCH

Economic and Social Studies

XXXII

INDUSTRIALISATION
AND THE
BASIS FOR TRADE

2 DEAN TRENCH STREET, SMITH SQUARE, LONDON, SW IP 3HE

The National Institute of Economic and Social Research is an independent, non-profit-making body, founded in 1938. It has as its aim the promotion of realistic research, particularly in the field of economics. It conducts research by its own research staff and in cooperation with the universities and other academic bodies. The results of the work done under the Institute's auspices are published in several series, and a list of its publications up to the present time will be found at the end of this volume.

INDUSTRIALISATION
AND THE
BASIS FOR TRADE

R. A. BATCHELOR
R. L. MAJOR
A. D. MORGAN

CAMBRIDGE UNIVERSITY PRESS

CAMBRIDGE

LONDON   NEW YORK   NEW ROCHELLE
MELBOURNE   SYDNEY

Published by the Press Syndicate of the University of Cambridge
The Pitt Building, Trumpington Street, Cambridge CB2 1RP
32 East 57th Street, New York, NY 10022, USA
296 Beaconsfield Parade, Middle Park, Melbourne 3206, Australia

First published 1980

Filmset by Keyspools Ltd, Golborne, Lancs

Printed in Great Britain at
the University Press, Cambridge

British Library Cataloguing in Publication Data
Batchelor, R A
Industrialisation and the basis for trade. –
(Economic and social studies; 32).
1. Commerce 2. Industrialization
I. Title II. Major, R L III. Morgan, A D
IV. Series
382   HF1007   79-41582
ISBN 0 521 23302 X

CONTENTS

v

viii

LIST OF TABLES

ix

LIST OF CHARTS

Conventions in the text and tables

.. not available
n.a. not applicable
— nil or negligible
Mha megahectares (million hectares)
log used for natural logarithms throughout
Germany means West Germany unless stated

PREFACE

In 1963 the National Institute published *Industrial Growth and World Trade* by Alfred Maizels. It was thought that Britain's economic future, and especially its export prospects, would be very much influenced by the long-term changes in production and trade taking place in the outside world. A mass of statistical material was presented showing the development of production and trade for many countries from the beginning of the twentieth century up to 1959. The relationships between production and the trade of advanced countries with primary producing countries and with one another were studied, and these relationships were used to project the likely future developments in the following ten or fifteen years. Mr Maizels' book has come to be regarded as a classic. It was reprinted in 1965, and again, with some revisions, in 1969. On neither occasion, however, was the attempt made to bring up to date the numerous time-series of trade and production.

The starting point of the present book is precisely the extension of the statistical record to the early 1970s. Mr Maizels had taken the view that the very rapid rise of world trade during the 1950s was, in the main, a catching up from the depression of trade during the 1930s and the second world war. He anticipated, therefore, that during the coming decade the growth of trade would cease to be faster than the growth of production. In the event the disparity between the growth of trade and the rapid growth of production became greater and a second objective of the present book has been to seek explanations of this unexpected development.

The fact that events did not follow the course charted for them means that the analytical sections of the present study differ from those originally used, so that the book has become much more than a revision of the earlier volume. In the light of the analysis we have not attempted to repeat a detailed projection of trade for the coming decades, but the concluding chapter reviews a number of such projections which have been made elsewhere and comments upon the principal factors which are likely to determine the growth of trade in the future.

We should like to express our thanks to Mr Alfred Maizels, who acted as Consultant to the project, to Mr David Worswick, the Director of the

National Institute, and Mrs Kit Jones, its Secretary, for encouraging and helping us to carry out the study, and to the Leverhulme Trust Fund which financed it. We are also grateful to Professor Richard Caves of Harvard University, Professor Christopher Saunders of the Centre for European Studies at Sussex University, and Mrs Sheila Page and Mr George Ray of the National Institute, who read and commented on a number of draft chapters, and to Mr Laszlo Campbell-Boross for advice on statistics included in the earlier book.

Mrs Sarah Adler, Mr Stewart Lansley and Mrs Darinka Martin helped to organise the extraction of particular sections of the data, in the processing of which Mrs Martin also took a major part, together with Mr Richard Berman, Mr Paul Clark, Miss Alison Corfield, Miss Lois Dines, Mr Daniel Ellis, Miss Susan Johnson, Mr Jeremy Posen, Miss Catherine Till, Mr Gerard Walsh and Mr David White. Mrs Joan Dare, Mrs Muriel Hill and Mrs Pamela Watts collated most of the appendix tables, as well as carrying out many of the calculations embodied there and elsewhere in the book. Mr Hassan Feisal was also responsible for some of the computing. Most of the drafts were typed by Miss Lesley Hart and Mrs Rita Leach. Miss Gillian Little prepared the text for the printer and Mrs Alison Rowlatt compiled the index. To all of them we must express our grateful thanks.

London
October 1979   R.A.B., R.L.M., A.D.M.

INTRODUCTION AND SUMMARY

by *R. A. Batchelor* and *R. L. Major*

INTRODUCTION

Objectives and methods

The maintenance of growth in developed economies, and the transmission of the lessons and benefits of this growth to less developed economies, have in recent decades become matters of conscious planning by national governments and supranational agencies. The demand for a coherent approach to growth and development, which is associated particularly with the names of Myrdal and Prebisch, originated partly in the traumatic experiences of depressed trade and output suffered by the developed economies in the 1930s and partly in the aspirations of the new sovereign states created in the 1950s as Britain, France and Belgium divested themselves of colonies in Africa, Asia and the Caribbean. Understandably, a major theme in the economic policies of the developed countries has been the application of demand management strategies suggested by Keynes' analysis of the depression. The developing economies, on the other hand, have sought to imitate the sort of structural transformations characteristic of the early development of richer countries, the most striking feature of which was the progressive industrialisation of consumption and production.[1] The full enjoyment of growing income per head clearly entailed the consumption of a growing proportion of manufactured goods and, since productivity growth in manufacturing appeared to exceed that in agriculture and services, the future growth of income per head seemed likely to be faster the more manufactured goods could be provided by a domestic industrial sector.

Given this dynamic interaction between growth and industrialisation, important positive and normative questions arise about the basis for international trade in manufactures as industrialisation advances, which

---

[1] A few of the more recent commentators on growth in developed economies have also emphasised supply constraints – labour shortages in the case of C. P. Kindleberger, *Europe's Postwar Growth*, London, Oxford University Press, 1967, inadequate resources in manufacturing in N. Kaldor, *Causes of the Slow Rate of Economic Growth of the United Kingdom*, Cambridge University Press, 1966, and, more recently, R. W. Bacon and W. A. Eltis, *Britain's Economic Problem: too few producers*, London, Macmillan, 1976.

in a given country will depend partly on the policies pursued. If consumption of manufactures runs continuously ahead of domestic supply, a need will be created for export promotion to generate foreign exchange earnings sufficient to cover desired imports, so that a continuous expansion of trade relative to output is likely to result. At the other extreme, protection of domestic producers against import competition at early stages of their growth may set in train a process of import substitution which continues unchecked until imports of manufactures are rendered completely redundant. Alternatively, some equilibrium relationship between trade and output growth may be established when the benefits from further import substitution are outweighed by the costs – in terms of lost exports or lower productivity growth – of switching more resources into meeting domestic demand.

By the mid-1950s the growth of manufacturing industry in the primary-producing countries, to which at that time about three fifths of British export trade was directed, had already modified the character of this trade very substantially and it seemed clear that its longer-term prospects depended crucially on the kind of relationships between output and trade which would in fact evolve as industrialisation proceeded. A detailed study of the question was accordingly undertaken at the National Institute of Economic and Social Research. This, in the event, expanded into a more general examination of the mutual adjustments which would be necessary between developed and developing economic areas and of their varying implications for the United Kingdom and the other main industrial countries.[1]

The author of the study, Alfred Maizels, deliberately framed his work as an extension to the statistical studies of trade and industry carried out by the League of Nations between 1940 and 1945, and his method of analysis was inspired by Chenery's formal descriptions of the process of industrialisation and other systematic changes in economic structure which occurred during development.[2] In two respects, however, Maizels' study proved path-breaking. The first lay in the broadening of the League of Nations' data base into a set of trade network tables, involving not only the industrial countries of Western Europe, North America and their satellites, but also several large developing countries; in addition, Maizels considered not only the behaviour of production and trade in manufactures as a whole, but also the behaviour of various classes of semi-finished and finished products within the manufacturing

[1] A. Maizels, *Industrial Growth and World Trade*, Cambridge University Press, 1963.
[2] For early studies of trade and growth see League of Nations, *Europe's Trade*, Geneva, 1941, *The Network of World Trade*, Geneva, 1942, and particularly *Industrialization and Foreign Trade*, Geneva, 1945; these were mostly the work of Folke Hilgerdt. On the formal description of growth patterns see H. B. Chenery, 'Patterns of industrial growth', *American Economic Review*, vol. 50, September 1960.

sector. The second main contribution of Maizels' study was a set of estimates for the same countries of gross domestic product (GDP), net output of manufactures and gross value of consumption of non-food manufactures. All these statistics covered selected years over the whole period 1899–1959. Finally, projections were added, by region and product, of world trade in manufactures up to the early 1970s. These were derived, on stated assumptions about rates of growth of population and income per head, from the empirical regularities observed in the historical data.

One purpose of this book is to update Maizels' statistics on trade and output and to revisit the analytical parts of his study where the basic relationships between the level and pattern of trade and industriali-sation are established. Viewed in his longer perspective, the rates of growth of trade during the 1950s seemed to him artificially high, as he found about half of the increase in imports of manufactures into the industrial countries to be attributable to a return to more normal levels of the ratio of imports to total absorption after this ratio had been artificially depressed by trade and currency restrictions. On the assumption that 'normality' had been restored by 1959, he envisaged for the 1960s and early 1970s a return to a more normal relationship with output growth, which in the event did not materialise. One of our aims has been, therefore, to identify the reasons for this, as well as to indicate what inferences about interactions between trade and growth can properly be drawn from the data available.

The balance of our study is, however, different from that of its predecessor. The increased flow of figures and commentary on trade and development has made the basic facts relatively familiar and our new data less intrinsically interesting than Maizels' reconstruction of early twentieth century trends.[1] We have accordingly given much less attention to detailed accounts of individual manufactured products and individual industrialising countries. This same improvement in the quality and quantity of the data available has, however, enabled us to pay much more attention to formal testing of theories about the impact of industrialisation on growth and trade, which have changed radically in the fifteen years or so since the earlier book was published.

Industrialisation is not now regarded as a necessary and sufficient

---

[1] Detailed figures on output, trade and expenditure are published annually by the United Nations: Department of Economic and Social Affairs, *The Growth of World Industry*, and Statistical Office, *Yearbook of International Trade Statistics* and *Yearbook of National Accounts Statistics*, respectively. Commentaries on industrialisation and trade in manufactures are published annually in United Nations Industrial Development Organization (UNIDO), *Industrial Development Survey*. Figures relating specifically to the performance of less developed countries are published in United Nations Conference on Trade and Development (UNCTAD), *Handbook of International Trade and Development Statistics* and a corresponding commentary is given in its annual review of *Trade in Manufactures of Developing Countries and Territories*.

condition for development. Many developing countries have been impatient to achieve the consumption patterns of advanced economies, but the satisfaction of these demands by rapid internal industrialisation has involved high social costs and has failed to trigger the economic benefits of sustained productivity growth. One reason for this is that technological changes in developed countries have increased the minimum internationally competitive plant size in many sectors of manufacturing. Sometimes too there has been a failure to adapt the new technology to local needs; there may, for example, be a wide gap between the skills required to operate new machines effectively and the skills actually available in developing countries. Most programmes of accelerated industrialisation have therefore entailed protectionist commercial policies and these, in turn, have removed the competitive pressures for improved productivity in the new industries. In more advanced countries there has been a certain disenchantment with industrialisation stemming from its environmental repercussions, both locally – in terms of the accumulation of waste products, some non-degradable – and globally – in terms of the demands which industry makes on limited supplies of mineral resources. The social fabric of advanced economies has also been damaged by the advance of large-scale mechanised production technologies as individuals find it progressively harder to obtain fulfilment from work.

Theories of trade have been responsive to these new conditions and explanations of trade in manufactures based on interdependent demand patterns, technological gaps and labour skills have supplanted earlier explanations based on the comparative costs of homogeneous products manufactured by economies differing only in their endowments of a few basic factors of production. Even more significant for our present exercise are the implications of these conditions for theories of development. Chenery's approach explicitly assumes the existence of stable laws of growth, relating broad features of economic structure to the income level and size of the developing country. However, the above discussion suggests that paths to growth open to today's developing countries are by no means independent of history and the current state of development elsewhere in the world economy. Patterns of growth may change because of the demonstration effects of advanced economies on consumer demand, the unrepeatable nature of growth based on the exploitation of some natural or inventive resource and the trend towards centrally planned growth encouraged by social, environmental and technological pressures.

In our opinion, these problems do not invalidate the search for patterns in trade and growth, nor the usefulness of such patterns in making medium-run projections. They emphasise, however, the need to explore thoroughly the limits to any generalisations which do emerge, by a statistical appraisal of the stability through time and across countries of the parameters of such growth models and by the application of a little commonsense.

The plan of the book

In chapters 2, 3, and 4 we describe the broad relationships, particularly over the fifteen years or so prior to the recession of the mid-1970s, between the growth of manufacturing output and the growth of trade in manufactured goods (chapter 2) and hence between consumption and imports of manufactures (chapter 3); we seek also (in chapter 4) to identify the institutional and other factors responsible for the exceptional buoyancy in this period of the trade sector in particular and for the individual successes or failures in world markets of the industrial countries, of whose exports international trade in manufactures is predominantly composed. We then turn in chapters 5, 6 and 7 to more fundamental questions of causation. We seek to establish relationships between economic structure and economic growth, especially in the form of industrial expansion (chapter 5); we then try to identify the factors which mainly influence the character and extent of a country's participation in international trade (chapter 6) and to assess the feedback from such participation to domestic demand and income (chapter 7); finally, in chapter 8 we discuss the prospects for output and trade in the remainder of the twentieth century and particularly for the manufacturing sector in the comparatively near future.

To keep the statistical data manageable, the analysis in chapters 3 and 4 is conducted in terms of the individual years 1963, 1967 and 1971. Thus a four-yearly sequence is established between the last years which Maizels covered in detail (1955 and 1959) and 1971, the last year before the already difficult task of constructing constant price series for international trade which could be considered even moderately reliable was rendered almost impossible by the abandonment of the Bretton Woods system of relatively stable exchange rates and the advent a little later of galloping inflation in the industrial world.

Again in the interests of statistical continuity, we have followed in chapters 2, 3 and 4 the classification of countries which Maizels adopted, dividing them into three categories (industrial, semi-industrial and non-industrial) on the basis of the value of their production of manufactures per head of population and the proportion of finished manufactures in their total exports.[1] For the purposes of chapters 5, 6

---

[1] The categories are: *industrial*, United States, United Kingdom, Japan, France, Germany (West), Italy, (large); Canada, Belgium-Luxembourg, Netherlands, Norway, Sweden, Switzerland, plus (for some purposes) Austria, Denmark, Finland (small); *semi-industrial*, Australia and New Zealand

and 7, however, we found it advantageous to take account of a wider range of economic and demographic characteristics and adopted a system of grouping countries into seven 'clusters' based on similarity with respect to seven criteria: income per head, population size and density, the shares of gross fixed investment and of the foreign sector in total output, the share of manufactures in total exports and the share of the agricultural labour force in the whole economically active population. The composition of each cluster is given in full in table 5.6 on page 112 but can be briefly summarised as follows: one cluster includes the three richest countries (in terms of income per head) which we have distinguished (the United States, Canada and Kuwait) and a second the bulk of the developed countries with the next highest incomes per head; a third cluster mainly comprises island economies, a fourth metal exporters and a fifth the poorest countries; of the two remaining clusters, which include most of Maizels' 'semi-industrial' group, one tends to be distinguished from the other mainly by a much smaller population and substantially higher income per head.

SUMMARY OF FINDINGS

Recent trends in trade and output

It is the semi-industrial countries whose imports of manufactures showed the most striking acceleration between the 1950s and the 1960s; the annual rate of increase in volume terms went up from about 2 per cent between 1950 and 1959 to about 9 per cent over the next twelve years. But even the latter figure was relatively low by the standards of the time. For the non-industrial countries (other than the centrally planned economies) the rate of rise from 1959 to 1971 was also about 9 per cent, compared with 4 per cent between 1950 and 1959, but for the industrial countries it was $13-13\frac{1}{2}$ per cent compared with $9\frac{1}{2}$ per cent, with the biggest countries continuing to show the fastest increase of all. Total exports of manufactures by the eleven major countries rose at an annual rate of $10\frac{1}{2}$ per cent, compared with $6\frac{1}{2}$ per cent in the previous nine years, and the volume of trade in manufactures trebled during the twelve years, while the volume of output of manufactures doubled.

The growth of manufacturing output was itself exceptionally rapid in the period prior to the recession. The rate of increase from 1957–9 to 1966–8 and again from 1966–8 to 1972–4 had been exceeded during the present century only in the periods of recovery from the first world war and from the great depression of the early 1930s. But in the latest period the growth of trade was exceptionally high even in comparison with the

(Oceania), South Africa, India, Pakistan, Argentina, Brazil, Chile, Colombia, Mexico, Greece, Ireland, Portugal, Spain, Yugoslavia, Israel, Turkey; *non-industrial*, all other market economies.

growth of output. The normally stable medium-term relationship between the two was thus seriously disrupted for only the second time in the century (the first being in the 1930s, when restrictive policies prevented a revival in trade in parallel with that in manufacturing production). The decline during the interwar period in the ratio of manufacturing trade to output was consequently reversed and by 1977 the ratio was once more close to its 1913 level.

For primary products also trade increased much faster than output. But the share of manufactures in world trade rose both in volume and, until 1972–4, even more markedly in value. The big increases between 1971 and 1974 in the price of oil and, to a lesser extent, other primary products, more than reversed the previous movement of the terms of trade in favour of manufactures which had taken place during the interwar period and since the Korean war. But even so, in 1977 manufactures accounted for a considerably higher share than in 1959 of the value of world trade, the shares of foodstuffs and basic materials slumping (especially those exported by the non-industrial countries), while that of fuels approximately doubled. Thus the industrial countries maintained their share of world exports in terms of value and increased it in terms of volume, even though exports of manufactures from some of the non-industrial countries were growing at a spectacular pace.

Recent trends in consumption of manufactures

The rapid growth of output and, more especially, of trade in manufactures has naturally reflected the scale and pattern of their consumption (or, more strictly, absorption by consumers and investors). This almost doubled between 1959 and 1971 in the market economies, increasing at the record rate for a period of such length of nearly 6 per cent per annum. Consumption per head rose by about 50 per cent; there was also a rapid growth of population in the developing countries, where consumption per head of manufactures probably rose less than in the developed countries, though their share of total consumption of manufactures in the market economies seems to have been maintained. As between the industrial, semi-industrial and non-industrial groups, shares in total consumption of manufactures were fairly stable, but within the first two groups, where consumption per head appears to rise about 50 per cent faster than income per head in annual terms, the Western European and Latin American countries and, more especially, Japan raised their shares at the expense of the others, in particular, India and Pakistan.

With trade growing faster than output, the total volume of 'supplies' of manufactures available to the industrial and semi-industrial countries, that is to say their production plus their imports, naturally increased more rapidly than their consumption, and their imports increased more rapidly still. This was contrary to the assumption made by Maizels that the reversal after 1950 (except in the semi-industrial countries) of the previous downward trend in the share of imports in total 'supplies' would prove to be shortlived. Even in the semi-industrial countries import substitution was being reversed by 1971 and in the industrial countries the whole of the substitution between 1913 and 1950 had been reversed by 1963. This mainly accounts for Maizels' under-projection of the growth of trade in manufactures, though incomes also increased faster than he was assuming. His assumption that 'supplies' of manufactures would in general grow annually about 1.2 times as fast as incomes was fairly close to the mark except in the semi-industrial countries, where the ratio was substantially higher, whereas he under-projected the import–'supply' growth ratio in all groups of countries, though most markedly in the United States.

While the United States had perhaps the fastest rise among the industrial countries in the ratio of imports to supplies of manufactures, this also increased very rapidly in the United Kingdom, France, Germany (after 1963) and Italy (before 1963), though it did not change significantly in Japan. Of these countries, the United Kingdom was in 1959 the only one apart from Japan in which the import ratio was still substantially lower than it had been in 1937, but France and Germany also had ratios which were low in relation to the size of their economies. In all three countries the ratios increased to what could perhaps be regarded as more 'normal' levels as protection was reduced in Western Europe by the formation of the European Economic Community (EEC) and the European Free Trade Association (EFTA), as well as through the geographically more extensive tariff cuts of the Dillon and Kennedy Rounds. The latter may have affected United Kingdom and United States imports more than most, because until the Kennedy Round both countries had a significant proportion of tariffs which were so high as to be almost if not quite prohibitive. The Ottawa Agreement on free trade in automotive products between Canada and the United States also had a major impact on each of these countries' imports, particularly from its partner.

Altogether, tariff reductions appear to explain a large part of the increases in import ratios between 1963 and 1971; although in the United Kingdom, the United States and Germany (after the Deutsche-mark was revalued in 1969) lack of competitiveness and supply shifts may have been no less important. Other factors were the development of multinational companies (which were particularly well placed to take advantage of tariff reductions), the related exploitation of economies of scale, particularly in marketing the 'new' and more diversified products which technological advances have generated, and utilisation of the skilled but initially cheap labour forces available in the Far East.

Shares in exports of manufactures

With exports of manufactures from Hong Kong, South Korea and Taiwan rising extremely rapidly, nine out of eleven of the major industrial countries for which data are available increased their imports of manufactures faster from the rest of the world than from one another between 1963 and 1971. The exceptions were the United States and the Netherlands. Japan remained the only major industrial growth centre outside North America and Western Europe, but was able on its own and with little participation by the multinationals to make massive inroads into the markets of the traditional industrial areas, particularly in the fields of transport equipment, machinery and semi-finished chemical and metal products. The United States and the United Kingdom suffered widespread losses of share in world trade in manufactures, which for the United States were concentrated in the second half of the period and for both countries were particularly marked in the faster-growing commodity groups. The original members of the EEC gained trade in each others' markets but lost elsewhere.

Price changes accounted for part of the competitive success or failure of individual countries; a rank correlation of share changes with price changes produces statistically significant coefficients of 0.855 for 1963–7 and 0.719 for 1967–71. Technological progress and flexibility of export patterns appear to have been other important factors. The latter in particular helps to explain Japan's emergence as the outstanding example of trade-promoting growth, while its absence may explain the United Kingdom's conspicuous forfeiture of that distinction during the present century.

The size and composition of the manufacturing sector in national economies

Despite the well-known fact that the richer countries are usually those which concentrate on the production of manufactures, while mainly agricultural countries are likely to be poorer, the tendency of the manufacturing sector to raise its share in total national output as the standard of living improves appears not to continue indefinitely. Though stable over time apart from a tendency to fall in the least developed countries, the income elasticity of the manufacturing sector's share declines with increasing individual wealth among the larger developing countries, and in the smaller semi-industrial countries the share of primary production does not fall systematically as incomes rise. A point appears to come, moreover, though not many countries have attained it yet, when the manufacturing sector begins to lose ground to services even in periods of normal overall economic growth. Otherwise the share of services is remarkably stable except among the very poorest countries, where it is low.

Our average elasticity of the manufacturing sector's share with respect to income per head is about 0.5, though it falls to 0.2 for the advanced countries. The share appears to be positively related also to size of population, though our calculated elasticity in this case is only 0.16. The shares of investment and of the trade sectors in the national economy appear to have little influence on the level of industrialisation in most cases, though both show a positive relationship with it among the more advanced countries.

Within the manufacturing sector the relative sizes of the various branches are naturally influenced by the composition of demand as well as by income and population size. Not surprisingly, high output of machinery and transport equipment (with a tendency to concentrate also on the earlier stages of metal processing) is normally associated with a high share of investment in GDP; being relatively specialised it also tends to be associated with a high ratio of trade to output. The most obvious general tendency as incomes increase is for these engineering branches to expand at the expense of the food, drink and tobacco industries, but our 'clusters' show considerable variations in the pace at which these changes occur. At intermediate levels of income the process seems to be much slower in the smaller countries than in the bigger ones, where, however, the normal switch away from production of textiles is less marked than in the other groups of countries.

The growth of total output and output per head in the manufacturing sector

Since the mid-1950s the centrally planned economies have consistently achieved the fastest rates of growth in the manufacturing sector. The rate of increase in productivity had, however, slowed down in Eastern Europe by the 1960s, whereas it was tending to accelerate in the market economies, especially the developing countries, where the growth of manufacturing output was consistently faster than in the more advanced market economies even though productivity increased on the whole somewhat faster in the latter.

Although productivity is generally higher in manufacturing than in agriculture, especially, it would seem, in the developing countries, differences in overall productivity between the more advanced economies and the less advanced cannot be attributed to any great extent to differences in the composition of output. In a typical developing country a shift in the balance between manufacturing and agriculture to that typical of a developed Western European country (implying a sevenfold increase in the manufacturing–primary production ratio) would raise output per worker outside services only from a third to a half of that in Western Europe; a similar structural switch within manufacturing industry would leave output per manufacturing worker virtually unchanged. As between manufacturing and services there is virtual parity in output per head in the most productive economies, but a more variable relationship among the least productive.

In developing economies at least, the degree of industrialisation appears to be the main factor in different levels of productivity for manufacturing as a whole and for most of its branches. A high ratio of trade to output is also associated with high productivity, notably in the small semi-industrial countries, perhaps because it stimulates efficiency. The age of the capital stock probably plays a part in explaining variations in rates of improvement in productivity, particularly in heavy industry. The contribution of differences in the quality of labour, to the limited extent that they can be measured, seems to vary widely from country to country.

The scale and pattern of manufacturing trade

While the ratio of trade to production tends overall to be higher in small countries than in big ones, whether the definition is in terms of area, population or output, there are important exceptions to this generalisation. Statistical criteria suggest that it is true of physical size only in medium to large developed economies, of population only in the most and least developed groups, and of output only in the island economies and the other small developing countries.

Colonial status appears to raise the ratio of trade to output, among the least developed countries at any rate, but to depress the share of manufactured goods in total exports and of chemicals and capital goods in imports. Achievement of independence more than reverses this effect on the composition of the least developed countries' exports, but does not seem to change the relationship between total trade and output, although a weakening of trading links with the former colonial power follows the weakening or severance of political links.

A big population is associated with a high share of manufactures in total trade, as, on the export side, is high density of population among the developed countries. Moreover, a big population accelerates achievement of a balance of trade in manufactures in relation to the level of industrialisation. In all branches of manufacturing except textiles and clothing, which the largest semi-industrial countries import hardly at all, deficits usually persist up to quite a high level. But in the later stages of industrialisation the share of manufactures in total exports increases very rapidly, whereas the share of manufactures in total imports appears to be affected by the level of industrialisation only in the large developing countries, where it declines as the share of manufactures in total exports grows.

There is a more general tendency for industrialisation to reduce the share of capital goods in total imports, particularly in the larger countries, where this share is initially higher than in smaller countries. Overall, however, though exports are more concentrated than imports throughout the process of development, this has much less effect on the structure of imports than of exports of manufactures, as there is a massive switch from textile to machinery exports. This enables mature economies to achieve earlier and bigger surpluses on trade in machinery than the general pattern would suggest.

The upward trend in the share of machinery exports in the most fully developed countries is accompanied by a sharp fall in the share of basic metals. This contrasts with the early stages of industrialisation, when the share of basic metals in total exports of manufactures rises except in the least developed countries, while that of machinery falls. This is consistent with the view that during industrialisation a transition takes place from a trading pattern based on factor-endowments towards one based on technological progress.

The feedback from trade to output

Exports were a major factor in economic growth in the 1960s in Western Europe and Oceania, where exports increased relatively fast, and Africa, where they increased particularly slowly but had accounted at the beginning of the decade for an exceptionally high proportion of total demand. Experience varied widely from country to country however. In Western Europe a high ratio of exports to output tended to be associated with a slow rate of output growth, perhaps because it meant that the share of resources devoted to investment was inadequate. For the advanced countries generally, however, exports appear to be equally significant with investment as an explanation of differences in growth performance. This is true also of the least developed countries, where, probably because of foreign exchange constraints, capital imports are strongly correlated with export receipts. In the bigger semi-industrial countries investment emerges as the more important factor, but in the smaller ones it is exports – manufactured exports in particular. In this last group an increase of 2 per cent per annum in exports seems to be sufficient to generate an increase of 1 per cent in total output. But in the bigger semi-industrial countries, as in the most developed and the least developed groups, to achieve such growth in total output through exports would seem to require an implausibly high rate of export expansion, whereas the investment route to growth appears perfectly viable.

Even where fast export growth and fast domestic growth are found to have been closely associated, it does not necessarily follow, of course, that the latter has been generated by the former; the direction of causation could have been the other way round, and in some cases it probably was. Nevertheless there appear to be grounds for believing in two types of export-led growth: the first, where expansion beyond domestic needs of a resource-based industry in a developing country has helped to make available supplies of labour and capital required for parallel development of a more advanced type; the second, where in fully employed mature economies rapid export expansion has generated additional investment and so raised productivity, whether as a normal function of output growth or because export success is especially conducive of confidence and encourages expansion of sectors of the economy in which productivity is particularly high.

On the other hand, a high share of manufactures in total exports appears to encourage the growth of productivity only in the large semi-industrial countries; in the smaller ones it is actually associated with low growth rates. A high share of capital goods in imports does appear to benefit the smaller semi-industrial countries (more obviously than the larger ones), but we have not been able to find any such effect in the advanced countries.

Product concentration seems to lead to instability in exports in all our country groups but, perhaps rather surprisingly, it provides less explanation of such instability in underdeveloped countries than in the semi-industrial and industrial groups. In any case the scope for increasing growth by export diversification appears to be small in less developed countries generally, though there are certain semi-industrial countries in which it could have important effects.

Prospects for output and trade

While the share of manufacturing output in the economies of the semi-industrial and non-industrial countries can be expected to go on rising for some time yet, many industrial countries are probably approaching the point at which the trend will turn downward. There are, moreover, a number of grounds for believing that their overall rates of economic growth will be slower in the remainder of this century than in the ten to fifteen years preceding the recession. These include the diminished scope for switching labour from less to more productive fields of employment (in terms not only of economic sectors, but, in Western Europe, of geographical areas also), the likelihood for demographic reasons of a markedly slower rate of increase of the total labour force by the 1980s and of changes in its composition less favourable to improvements in output per head, and the probability that for a time at least a significant proportion of investment will not be directed to improving productivity or expanding total productive capacity, but to pollution control, energy saving and the development of the energy-producing sector. Total business investment has been slow to recover after falling sharply in the recession and, despite the overall surplus of capacity, shortages could well develop in some areas as the huge increases in the relative cost of energy have intensified the normal process of structural change in the pattern of demand and may well have reduced the productivity of capital relative to that of labour.

One of the initial effects of the massive transfer of purchasing power to the oil-producing countries was a big rise in their imports of manufactures, which probably increased between 1972 and 1977 from about 4 to 10 per cent of total world trade in manufactures. The absorptive capacity and the purchasing power of the individual countries are, however, ill-matched and the rate of rise in their imports has slowed greatly after the early spurt; though much depends on the relative prices of oil and of the products they import, their aggregate surplus on current account could well remain very high at least through the 1980s. Moreover, while aid which they give to other developing countries either directly or through the international organisations has become very substantial, the reinvestment of their surpluses has been heavily concentrated in a few countries, especially the United States and, to a lesser extent, the United Kingdom. The strain which the surpluses thus impose on the balances of payments of the rest of the world is one of the causes of a growing trend towards restriction of imports during the last few years.

In assessing future trends in trade in manufactures among industrial countries, and between industrial and semi-industrial, two conflicting sets of arguments must be weighed. On the one hand the basis for trade has become more dynamic. Traffic in manufactured goods is attributable less and less to differences in national endowments of labour and capital, and more and more to differences in technologies and similarities in demand patterns. Unlike factor-endowments these features of the economy can be rapidly changed, by borrowing foreign inventions and by international marketing operations. On the other hand, the resurgence of protectionism could cause industrial countries' mutual trade in manufactures to rise more slowly in future than it did in the 1960s and 1970s, even in relation to a growth of output which itself is unlikely to gain its former momentum.

On balance, we consider that the opportunities for increased exchanges among industrial countries can hardly continue to be created on the scale of the past twenty years, given the substantial lowering of tariffs and other barriers to transfers of goods and technology which has already occurred. It is, however, harder to form a judgement about the prospects for trade in manufactures between the developed and the developing countries, or indeed about the pace of industrialisation of the latter. Much depends on their political will to develop and carve for themselves a niche in the international economy and on the political will of the developed countries to allow them to do so.

A study conducted under the auspices of the United Nations suggests that the developing countries' share of world manufacturing output could approximately treble between 1970 and 2000, with the volume of their imports increasing at $8-8\frac{1}{2}$ per cent per annum from about a sixth to nearly a third of the total. But, barring dramatic movements in the terms of trade of which there is little prospect, this can happen only if there is a massive rise in the aid which the developed countries give them or the volume of manufactured imports which they take from them. At present there is no real sign of the former and policies in respect of the latter have become more rather than less restrictive. This has adverse implications for the exports and, because of the loss of efficiency which protectionism entails, for the output and incomes of the industrial countries themselves.

2

RECENT TRENDS IN WORLD TRADE
IN MANUFACTURES

by *R. L. Major*

THE GENERAL COURSE OF OUTPUT AND TRADE

This chapter gives a brief account of the main features of trade in manufactures since the 1950s in relation to world trade, to output, both in the short run and in the longer term, and to the projections for the early 1970s with which Maizels concluded his work. Particular aspects of the relationships involved will be discussed in more detail in later chapters.

The fifteen years with which this book is mainly concerned – those immediately prior to the world recession of the mid-1970s – are notable for the fact that they brought a rate of expansion in production, and still more in trade in manufactures, which is without parallel over a period of comparable length for at least a hundred years. Per head of population world output of manufactures doubled and world trade in manufactures trebled in volume during this period (see table 2.1). Moreover, the disparity which these increments imply between the respective rates of growth of output on the one hand and trade on the other became more pronounced as the period proceeded. In the second half the normal relationship between these growth rates was in fact seriously disturbed for only the second time in the present century.[1]

While trade in manufactures tends to fluctuate more widely than their production, the relationship between their respective rates of growth has been relatively stable over long periods.[2] As can be seen

---

[1] It is, however, likely that the official statistics exaggerate the recent change in the relationship because of the growing importance for both output and trade of more sophisticated products. These tend not to be fully represented in output statistics; on the other hand, the unit values attributed to them when estimates of the volume of trade are derived from the value figures are probably too low, particularly in periods of rapid inflation. This is because the unit values are in fact based on the prices of a narrower range of homogeneous products and these have probably been more stable. A comparison of the unit value prices for German exports with a series based on invoice prices shows that between 1962 and 1970 the fomer rose by only $6\frac{1}{2}$ per cent for processed goods but the latter by $16\frac{3}{4}$ per cent. For capital goods, which account for a particularly high share of German exports, the relationship changed in the course of the period; between 1962 and 1968 the unit value index rose by $13\frac{1}{34}$ per cent and the price index by $10\frac{1}{2}$ per cent, but in the next two years the rise was 5 per cent for unit values and 13 per cent for prices (see General Agreement on Tariffs and Trade (GATT), *International Trade 1970*, Geneva, 1971, pp. 10–13).

[2] J. Knapp, 'Pragmatism and the British *malaise*', *Lloyds Bank Review*, no. 90, October 1968, p. 15.

Table 2.1. *World trends in population, production and trade, 1900–77*

Indices, 1913 = 100

	Popu-lation[a]	Manufactures[b]			Primary products		
		Output volume	Trade volume	Trade unit value	Output volume[a]	Trade volume[b]	Trade unit value[b]
1900	94	60	52	100	76	70	81
1911–13	99	98	94	100	93	96	100
1926–30	111	145	123	135	123	132	119
1931–3	117	122	87	97	120	130	60
1934–5	120	150	91	114	125	128	79
1936–8	124	193	110	116	135	135	87
1948–50	145	289	141	226	156	125	250
1951–3	151	360	191	246	176	146	273
1954–6	158	420	246	241	191	168	256
1957–9	166	493	299	250	203	189	251
1960–2	173	591	377	256	219	223	237
1963–5	184	720	483	261	237	265	242
1966–8	195	880	632	274	263	310	242
1969–71	208	1058	858	300	284	382	255
1972–4	221	1275	1128	409	301	469	454
1975–7	235	1422	1332	565	316	488	767

[a] Figures taken so far as possible from Maizels. Centrally planned countries excluded from population from 1948 and from output of primary products from 1971.
[b] Figures taken so far as possible from UNCTAD, *Handbook*. For the later periods the volume series are substantially higher than those derived by Maizels from various sources; this applies particularly to manufacturing production, where his series was taken from W. A. Lewis, 'World production, prices and trade 1870–1960', *Manchester School of Economic and Social Studies*, vol. 20, May 1952, in which the USSR is excluded.
SOURCES: Maizels, *Industrial Growth and World Trade*; UNCTAD, *Handbook of International Trade and Development Statistics 1972*, New York, 1972; United Nations Statistical Office, *Statistical Yearbook* and *Monthly Bulletin of Statistics*, New York; NIESR estimates.

from chart 2.1 it broke down for a time in the period immediately preceding the second world war, when trade in manufactures increased at well under half the rate which the normal relationship would imply. After the war this relationship was, broadly speaking, restored, although even in the 1950s and early 1960s the growth of trade was somewhat above its norm. Subsequently, however, it broke down once more, with growth in trade accelerating rapidly until the onset of the recession, even though the rate of growth of output remained unchanged.

The failure of trade in the 1930s to respond fully to the exceptionally rapid growth of output in the years of recovery from the depression can clearly be connected with the restrictive international trading policies then in operation. The converse also applies to the period since the mid-

Chart 2.1. *Annual rates of growth in the volumes of manufacturing output and trade, 1900–74*

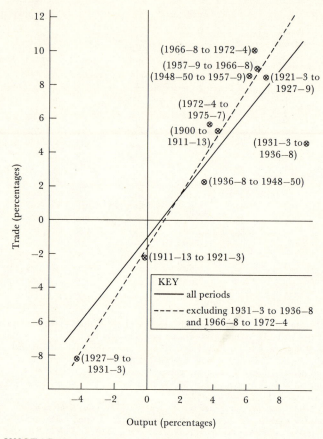

SOURCES: UNCTAD, *Handbook of International Trade and Development Statistics 1972*, New York, 1972; table 2.1.

1950s, in which trade has been boosted by the progressive relaxation of quantitative restrictions, particularly on dollar-costing goods, the creation of the EEC, EFTA and other limited free-trading areas, and the worldwide and very substantial Dillon and Kennedy Rounds of tariff reductions.[1] At the same time both the growth of international companies and the increasing sophistication of manufactured products have encouraged specialisation and international trade. The latter may well have been stimulated also by the accelerated pace of change in the

---

[1] An analysis by GATT shows that the proportion of the trade of parties to the Agreement which was transacted under preferential tariff arrangements increased from 10.1 per cent in 1955 and 17.2 per cent in 1961 to 24.3 per cent in 1970. UNCTAD estimates it at 32 per cent by 1973.

Table 2.2. *Value and volume of exports from industrial and other countries, 1950–71*

	1950	1955	1959	1963	1967	1971
	($ billions)					
Value of exports						
From industrial countries[a]						
Manufactures[b]	20.1	33.9	45.3	64.8	99.4	174.1
Other	11.3	15.8	17.7	25.0	30.7	45.0
Total	(31.4)	(49.7)	(63.0)	(89.9)	(130.1)	(219.1)
From other countries[c]	24.0	33.0	36.7	45.0	58.6	91.6
Total value	55.4	82.7	99.8	134.8	188.7	310.7
	(Indices, 1955 = 100)					
Volume of exports						
From industrial countries[a]						
Manufactures[b]	72	100	126	176	260	416
Primary products	76	100	117	164	217	313
Total	73	100	123	172	247	384
From other countries[c]	71	100	120	140	173	235
Total volume	73	100	122	158	216	323
Unit value of exports						
From industrial countries[a]						
Manufactures[b]	83	100	105	109	113	124
Total	86	100	103	105	106	115
From other countries[c]	102	100	92	98	104	119
Unit value of total	92	100	99	103	106	116

[a] Belgium-Luxembourg, Canada, France, Germany (West), Italy, Japan, Netherlands, Sweden, Switzerland, United Kingdom, United States.
[b] From 1963, includes United Kingdom exports of diamonds and re-exports, also United States exports of some items removed from the 'special' category in 1965 (the total value under these three headings was $1.5 billion in 1963). Other 'special' category exports from the United States are excluded.
[c] Other market-economy countries calculated as a residual.
SOURCES: Maizels, *Industrial Growth and World Trade*; United Nations Statistical Office, *Yearbook of International Trade Statistics, Statistical Yearbook* and *Monthly Bulletin of Statistics*; OECD, *Statistics of Foreign Trade* series C, Paris, annual; NIESR estimates.

competitive positions of individual countries which has been brought about by the instability of exchange rates and the wide variation in national rates of inflation. A country which has suffered a serious loss of competitiveness will tend to increase its imports faster than usual in relation to the strength of internal demand (whereas the extent to which the converse applies to a country gaining in competitiveness will depend on its capacity to expand production), while a country which has become ultra-competitive may be able to open up export markets which have previously been domestic preserves. The effects of factors such as these will be discussed in greater detail in chapter 4. Here it may be sufficient to state that by 1977 the decline during the interwar period in the ratio of manufacturing trade to production had been reversed and the 1913

Chart 2.2. *Changes in relative unit value and volume of world trade in manufactures and primary products, 1900–74*

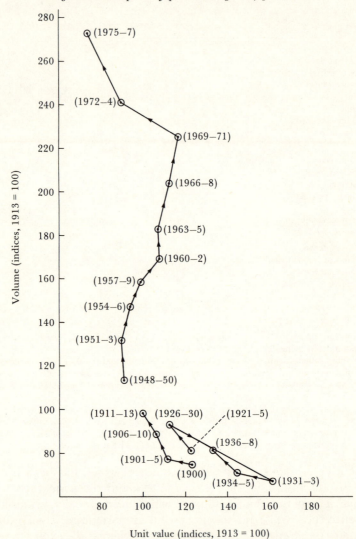

Unit value (indices, 1913 = 100)

Note: Both unit value and volume indices given as (index for manufactures)/(index for primary products).

SOURCES: as chart 2.1.

relationship restored – within the sort of limits by which such things can be measured. The official United Nations indices suggest that by 1974 the ratio had returned to about 95 per cent of its 1913 level from a low point of 57 per cent in 1937.

For primary products the period of downward movement in the trade–output ratio was briefer than for manufactures in peace-time, although for primary products this spanned the second world war. But for trade as well as output the increase in volume has been slower for primary products than for manufactures both during and since the 1950s. This again has been normal during the present century. However, the opposite relationship applied during the 1920s and early 1930s, and in almost every period up to the second world war volumes and prices were inversely related (see table 2.2 and chart 2.2), the share of manufactures in the total volume of world trade increasing only when manufactures were becoming cheaper in comparison with primary products and declining when they were becoming relatively more expensive. After the war the relationship was reversed for a quarter of a century. Up to 1971 the Korean war period was the only one in which the terms of trade did not move in favour of manufactures, with only the briefest of interruptions, at the same time as the manufacturing component of world trade accounted for a rising share of its total volume.

TRADE IN PRIMARY PRODUCTS

The main reasons for the relative weakness of demand for primary products in the middle and late 1950s and earlier 1960s were described by Maizels[1] and are by now too well known to call for lengthy discussion. As incomes rise the proportion spent on the necessities of life tends naturally to decrease, and this applies not only to food and drink but to some extent also to clothing and other textile products. These have a much higher raw material content than the more sophisticated products of the engineering and chemical industries and, as will be shown in chapter 5, it is on the latter that the rise in demand for goods tends to be concentrated as incomes increase. Between 1959 and 1977 world output expanded at annual rates of over 7 and 8 per cent in metal products and chemicals respectively, but only at 4 per cent in the textile and clothing industries. At the same time technological progress meant that within individual sectors of industry natural materials and products with a high natural material content were extensively displaced by man-made equivalents or substitutes – synthetic rubber and fibres, plastics, detergents and so on. Excise duties too have had substantial effects on consumption of two major products, coffee and tobacco, which in the latter case have been reinforced by the mounting campaign against smoking.

Demand for petroleum was strongly maintained until the last few

---

[1] Maizels, *Industrial Growth and World Trade*, pp. 83–4, 112–17 and 394–7.

years, the volume of international trade in crude oil and oil products increasing during the 1960s at an annual rate of 11 per cent. But prices were held down during this period by a potential excess of supply over demand. Output developed rapidly in nine new producing countries and the world's proved reserves increased from about 40 to 65 billion tons between 1960 and 1969.

A number of factors nevertheless emerged during this period which tended to stimulate trade in primary products. One such development of some importance was the growing dependence of the metal industries in the advanced countries on imported ores. This was partly due to depletion of domestic deposits, but it was also associated with the rapid development of the Japanese steel industry, which, in common with Japanese industry generally, depends particularly heavily on imported materials. GATT estimates suggest, for example, that in 1970 Japan's imports of industrial materials were a half greater than those of the United States and accounted for 20 per cent of the total for all industrial countries, whereas Japan was responsible for only $12\frac{1}{2}$ per cent (and the United States for $42\frac{1}{2}$ per cent) of OECD members' total manufacturing output. This figure of $12\frac{1}{2}$ per cent represented a doubling of the Japanese share in only five years and in the case of the steel industry this share rose over the same period from $7\frac{1}{4}$ to $15\frac{3}{4}$ per cent.

After about 1967 the movement of the terms of trade in favour of manufactures first slowed down, and then was sharply reversed between 1970 and 1974, with little subsequent change up to 1977. The period 1967–74, and more particularly 1970–3, was one in which industrial production was growing rapidly, while accelerating wage and price inflation in the developed countries was creating a distrust of paper assets generally, which violent fluctuations in rates of exchange reinforced periodically in respect of particular currencies. These conditions encouraged speculative buying of commodities at a time when demand for consumption was strong, stocks were initially low in some instances and in others crop failures had helped to create shortages.

Apart from these pressures on supply, at the same time rising import prices were adding to inflationary pressures in producing countries and so increasing output costs. There has, moreover, been an increasing tendency for governments of producing countries to intervene in markets with a view to securing higher export prices. In some cases (wool and rubber, for example) this intervention has taken the form of support buying; in others (copper, tea, hard fibres) export quotas have been fixed under formal or informal arrangements between producing countries (apart from those negotiated with the participation of consuming countries under the international agreements on coffee, tin and, though not as yet effectively, cocoa).

While the effects of these policies may have been significant in some cases, they have for the most part been unspectacular. But there is, of course, an outstanding exception in the case of petroleum, where mainly as a result of unilateral decisions O P E C (the Organisation of Petroleum Exporting Countries) more than trebled its prices within a few months at the end of 1973.

The United Nations index of developing countries' mineral export prices (in terms of United States dollars) thus increased more than fivefold between 1970 and 1974 and the index for all exports of primary commodities rose by nearly 175 per cent over the same period. Although prices of manufactures were also increasing very rapidly (by about 60 per cent on the United Nations index), the terms of trade between primary products and manufactures changed dramatically: previously they had been the most favourable to manufactures of the whole period since the second world war, but since 1974 they have favoured primary products to a greater extent than at any time in the present century. Though manufactures have continued to increase their share of world trade at constant prices, thereby restoring the inverse price–volume relationship which had prevailed before the war, the rise in the value of the market economies' exports has been substantially faster for primary products than for manufactures. In dollar terms it rose about 250 per cent for primary products between 1971 and 1976 (well over 400 per cent for fuels and more than 100 per cent for both food and raw materials) compared with about 160 per cent for manufactures.[1]

Despite the reversal in the early 1970s of the previous trend, manufactures still accounted in 1977 for a substantially higher proportion of the value of world trade than in 1959. As shown in table 2.3, their share in the total increased from about $52\frac{1}{2}$ per cent to over 60 per cent over the eighteen years. This gain was at the expense of food and materials, food's share falling by nearly a third (from 19 per cent to $12\frac{1}{2}$ per cent) and that of materials by over three fifths (from $16\frac{1}{2}$ to $6\frac{1}{2}$ per cent). Fuels (19 per cent of the total in 1977) nearly doubled their share over the same period.

These differences in commodity patterns are reflected in a change in the relative shares of the industrial countries and the rest in exports of primary products. Although the industrial countries' exports of both food and materials declined as a proportion of world trade, the fall was much less steep in their case than in that of the non-industrial countries. Partly because of slow growth in demand for tropical beverages and

[1] The rise in prices over this period is somewhat exaggerated by the use of the United States dollar as the unit of value, because it depreciated in terms of other currencies (weighted in proportion to the importance in world trade of the countries concerned) by about 5 per cent between 1971 and 1976.

Table 2.3. *Network of trade, 1959, 1970 and 1977*

Exports to:	Industrial countries[a]	Other market economies	Total[b]	Industrial countries[a]	Other market economies	Total[b]
	($ billions[c])			(percentages[d])		
Manufactures exported from:						
Industrial countries:						
1959	28.8	17.4	47.9	25.5	15.4	42.4
1970	120.9	38.6	166.1	38.7	12.4	53.2
1977	367.7	150.1	545.3	32.8	13.4	48.6
Centrally planned countries:[e]						
1959	0.8	0.6	7.7	0.7	0.5	6.8
1970	3.3	3.1	21.1	1.1	1.0	6.8
1977	11.1	11.2	66.9	1.0	1.0	6.0
Other countries:						
1959	2.5	1.3	3.9	2.2	1.2	3.5
1970	10.6	5.0	16.2	3.4	1.6	5.2
1977	40.5	21.8	64.0	3.6	1.9	5.7
All countries:						
1959	32.0	19.4	59.4	28.3	17.2	52.6
1970	134.8	46.7	203.3	43.2	15.0	65.2
1977	419.3	183.1	676.2	37.4	16.3	60.3
Primary products exported from:						
Industrial countries:						
1959	16.0	4.0	20.5	14.2	3.5	18.1
1970	37.8	7.1	46.4	12.1	2.3	14.5
1977	117.1	23.5	146.2	10.4	2.1	13.0
Centrally planned countries:[e]						
1959	1.6	0.4	6.1	1.4	0.4	5.4
1970	4.0	1.3	10.4	1.3	0.4	3.3
1977	17.7	5.3	39.0	1.6	0.5	3.5
Other countries:						
1959	18.5	5.5	25.1	16.4	4.9	22.2
1970	34.8	8.9	46.4	11.1	2.8	14.9
1977	176.8	54.3	242.2	15.8	4.8	21.6
All countries:						
1959	36.1	9.9	51.7	32.0	8.8	45.8
1970	76.5	17.2	103.2	24.5	5.5	33.1
1977	311.6	83.1	427.4	27.8	7.4	38.1

[a] North America, Western Europe (excluding Gibraltar and Malta in 1959) and Japan.

[b] Includes also exports to the centrally planned economies (see note e).

[c] Valued f.o.b.

[d] Of a total value including exports not distinguished by commodity.

[e] Albania, Bulgaria, China (mainland), Czechoslovakia, East Germany, Hungary, Poland, Romania and USSR, *plus* (except in 1959) Mongolia, North Korea and North Vietnam, apart from the trade of these three countries with one another and China, which is excluded.

SOURCES: GATT, *International Trade 1960, 1973/74* and *1977/78*.

hard fibres, which are among the major exports of the developing countries, by the mid-1950s the industrial countries had become the main exporters of food and were also responsible for more than half the world's exports of materials. But their relatively small initial share in fuel exports received only a minor boost from the rapid expansion of this trade, whereas other countries' exports of fuels accounted by 1977 for 16 per cent of world trade, compared with only $7\frac{1}{2}$ per cent eighteen years earlier. Thus, total primary products exported from non-industrial countries accounted for almost the same proportion of world trade in 1977 as in 1959, whereas the primary exports of the industrial and centrally planned economies had diminished considerably in relative importance.

THE GROWTH IN VALUE OF TRADE IN MANUFACTURES

Some non-industrial market economies have also achieved spectacular increases in their exports of manufactures. This applies particularly to the three Far Eastern territories of Hong Kong, South Korea and Taiwan. In 1959 their combined manufactured exports had been worth well under $500 million, but by 1976 the value had risen to 14\frac{1}{2}$ billion for Hong Kong and South Korea alone. The addition of Taiwan, for which the United Nations has ceased to publish trade data, would probably raise this figure to at least $20 billion. Total exports of manufactures from the non-industrial market economies also increased relatively fast, though they still accounted for less than 6 per cent of world trade in 1977 (table 2.3).

By 1973 manufactures accounted for almost a third of trade between developing countries, compared with a fifth at the beginning of the 1960s. The proportion fell subsequently because of the rise in the price of oil, but in 1977 nearly half of trade between the developing countries which do not export oil consisted of manufactures. Even so, in 1977 as in 1959, some two thirds of the developing countries' exports of manufactures still went to the industrial countries despite substantial changes in their commodity composition. In value terms, miscellaneous manufactures, mainly consumer goods, have been overtaking the traditional textiles and clothing (though the latter have increased their share in manufactured exports to the industrial countries); exports of engineering goods have also increased rapidly in relative importance, while the position of non-ferrous metals has varied with their price. Differential price movements have probably made other important contributions to these changes in share. In volume terms the International Bank for Reconstruction and Development (IBRD) estimates that between 1970 and 1975 the developing countries increased their exports of manufactures to all destinations at annual rates of $20\frac{1}{4}$ per cent for clothing and for machinery and transport equipment, $17\frac{3}{4}$ per cent for textiles and $16\frac{1}{2}$ per cent for chemicals, but only 10–11 per cent for iron and steel and for other manufactures. The overall rate of increase in the volume of their exports of manufactures is put at 15 per cent a year over this period.[1]

Exports from the centrally planned countries have risen comparatively slowly, particularly to one another and to the non-industrial countries. Whereas in 1959 their exports of manufactures had represented twice the value of those of the non-industrial countries, by the mid-1970s they were of a similar order of magnitude.[2] This can be attributed partly to the worsening in political relations between mainland China and countries of Eastern Europe. Total Chinese trade in both directions in 1976 was worth only about two thirds of the 1960 figure of $\$2\frac{1}{4}$ billion, whereas with Japan it rose from almost negligible proportions to over $\$3$ billion and with Western Europe quadrupled to more than $\$2\frac{1}{2}$ billion over the same period.

This situation has helped the industrial countries to raise their exports of manufactures to the centrally planned countries as a proportion of world trade. But the figure remains a low one at $2\frac{1}{2}$ per cent in 1977 and the relative importance of industrial countries' exports to the rest of the world of both manufactures and primary products has diminished quite sharply.

Industrial countries' mutual trade in primary products has also risen comparatively slowly, though under the influence of the CAP (Common Agricultural Policy) the value of trade in foodstuffs within the EEC increased at an annual rate of about 15 per cent in the 1960s. But their intra-trade in manufactures has soared. Its dollar value rose about thirteenfold between 1959 and 1977, at an annual rate of over 15 per cent, and as a proportion of world trade it increased from a quarter to a third. Of the main manufacturing trade flows included, the fastest growing were Japanese trade in both directions with the other industrial countries and trade within the original Six of the EEC.

From 1959 to 1972, after which the Community's membership was increased by the adhesion of Denmark, Ireland and the United Kingdom, the annual rate of increase in the dollar value of its intra-trade in manufactures was nearly 18 per cent. Over the same period Japanese exports of manufactures to the other industrial countries rose at an annual rate of over 20 per cent and their exports to Japan at a

---

[1] IBRD, *World Development Report*, Washington (DC), 1978.
[2] This is so even with the changes of definition in table 2.3, whereby the coverage of the centrally planned countries is slightly increased and that of the non-industrial countries slightly reduced between the two years in question.

rate of over 15 per cent. These increases were achieved in the face of substantial obstacles to trade in both directions. Japan has from time to time been obliged to enforce 'voluntary' restrictions on exports to other industrial countries of various classes of goods (perhaps most important, exports of steel to the United States and the EEC) under the implicit or explicit threat that otherwise quotas would be introduced. And there have been repeated complaints of non-tariff barriers of an administrative character to imports of manufactures into Japan.

Largely because of the relatively slow growth of British imports and exports, the manufacturing trade of EFTA increased much less rapidly – both between members (at an annual rate of 13 per cent) and with the Six, the United States and Canada (at rather under 11 per cent). Trade between the United States and Canada rose faster than this (at an annual rate of $12\frac{1}{2}$ per cent), but a high proportion of the increase was attributable to the Ottawa Agreement of 1965 on free trade in automotive products. Transport equipment in fact accounted for practically half of the total increase in the two countries' manufactured exports to each other between 1959 and 1972, and for an even higher proportion in the second half of the period.

PROJECTED AND ACTUAL RISES IN THE VOLUME OF TRADE IN MANUFACTURES

Our estimates of the growth of the major industrial countries' exports of manufactures at constant prices present a similar pattern of relative rates (table 2.4). They suggest that the total volume of these exports more than trebled over the period 1959–71, increasing at an annual rate of $10\frac{1}{2}$ per cent. For intra-trade the rate of rise comes out at 12 per cent. For exports to semi-industrial countries and the rest of the world the rates are lower, but still of the order of $6\frac{1}{2}$ per cent and 9 per cent respectively.

All these results involve an acceleration as compared with the annual rates of increase in trade between 1950 and 1959. Those were 9–$9\frac{1}{2}$ per cent for the major countries' intra-trade, $1\frac{1}{2}$ per cent for their exports to the semi-industrial countries and 5–$5\frac{1}{2}$ per cent for their exports to the rest of the world. The particularly spectacular increase in trade with the semi-industrial countries reflects the fact that in 1959 their imports were reacting to the fall in their export earnings resulting from the 1958 recession. (The volume of imports of manufactures into Australia, New Zealand and South Africa, for example, was substantially lower in 1959 than in 1955.)

This outcome contrasts strongly with the projections made by Maizels, who envisaged a slowing-down in the rate of growth of trade in

Table 2.4. *Industrial countries'[a] exports of manufactures by destination,*
1950–71

$ billion[b]

	1950	1955	1959	1963	1967	1971
Intra-trade						
UK – Western Europe[c]	1.6	2.1	2.5	4.0	5.0	7.6
Intra-Western Europe[c]	3.0	5.7	8.5	15.4	22.2	39.1
Intra-North America	2.5	3.7	4.0	4.4	8.3	11.7
W. Europe – N. America	2.6	3.8	5.8	7.4	10.9	15.6
Japan – W. Europe and N. America	0.3	0.7	1.6	3.0	6.2	13.7
Total	(10.0)	(16.0)	(22.3)	(34.3)	(52.6)	(87.8)
To semi-industrial countries[d]	5.9	6.7	6.8	8.2	10.4	14.6
To rest of world	8.4	11.2	13.8	17.2	25.2	38.6
TO ALL COUNTRIES	24.3	33.9	42.9	59.6	88.2	141.0

[a] As in table 2.2 (Norway included as a destination of intra-trade). Commodity coverage as in table 2.2.
[b] At 1955 prices.
[c] Continent only.
[d] Argentina, Australia, Brazil, Chile, Colombia, India, Israel, Mexico, New Zealand, Pakistan, South Africa, Turkey, Yugoslavia.
SOURCES: Maizels, *Industrial Growth and World Trade*; United Nations Statistical Office, *Yearbook of International Trade Statistics* (and related data); OECD, *Statistics of Foreign Trade*, series C; NIESR estimates.

manufactures, fairly heavily concentrated on imports into the United States, but extending also to trade with the other industrial countries. While he correctly foresaw an acceleration in imports into the semi-industrial countries, its magnitude greatly exceeded his projections and he envisaged little if any increase in the rate of growth of imports into the non-industrial countries. Moreover the comparison does not appear to be distorted, at any rate in the aggregate, by the difference in the periods considered. According to United Nations statistics the rate of rise in the total volume of the major industrial countries' exports of manufactures was virtually the same from 1959 to 1971 as from 1959 to the average for the period 1970–5, as a further acceleration of trade between 1971 and 1973 compensated for the effect of the subsequent recession.

Table 2.5 shows that part of the difference between projection and outcome was attributable to unduly pessimistic assumptions about rates of growth of income (in effect of income per head, since the assumptions about population were generally close to the mark). This applies particularly to the small industrial countries and the semi-industrial countries and to a lesser extent to the larger industrial countries other than the United States. But for the semi-industrial countries the rate of growth of 'imports' of manufactures was about twice as high in relation

Table 2.5. *Growth rates of incomes and 'imports' of manufactures, projected[a] and actual*

Percentages p.a.

		Real incomes				Real 'imports' of manufactures[b]	
		Assumed 1959 to 1970–5		Actual 1959 to 1971		Projected 1959 to 1970–5	Actual 1959 to 1971
		Per head	Total	Per head	Total		
Industrial countries							
Large							
United States	II	2.5	3.9⎱	2.4	3.7	⎰4.4–5.1⎱	12.7
	III	2.0	3.4⎰			⎱3.1–4.4⎰	
Other	II	4.0	4.9⎱	4.8	5.9	⎰8.0–9.1⎱	16.1
	III	4.5	5.4⎰			⎱8.6–9.4⎰	
Total	I	3.0	4.1⎲			⎧5.7–6.8⎫	
	II	3.0	4.1⎬	3.4	4.5	⎨6.6–7.6⎬	14.7
	III	2.5	3.6⎳			⎩6.6–7.6⎭	
Small		3.0	3.9	3.8	4.9	5.3–5.9	11.1
Semi-industrial							
countries	I	2.0	4.3⎱	3.0	5.3	⎰1.8–4.3⎱	8.9
	II	3.0	5.3⎰			⎱3.1–5.4⎰	
Non-industrial							
countries	I	2.0	4.1⎱	2.3	5.4	⎰2.9–4.8⎱	8.7
	II	3.0	5.1⎰			⎱3.4–5.7⎰	

[a] The roman figures in the first column refer to Maizels' alternative assumptions for growth in real income per head (see source, pp. 387 ff).
[b] Based on exports from eleven major countries (see footnote *a* to table 2.2) up to 1963, but on imports from all sources 1963–71 (see chap. 3, p. 32 and appendix C).
SOURCES: Maizels, *Industrial Growth and World Trade*; United Nations Statistical Office, *Yearbook of National Accounts Statistics*; appendix A.

Table 2.6. *Major industrial countries' exports of manufactures by commodity group, projected and actual*

					Rates of increase	
	Actual levels				Projected 1959 to 1970–5	Actual 1959 to 1971
	1959	1963	1967	1971		
	($ billion, 1955 prices)				(% p.a.)	
Metals	6.2	7.9	10.9	15.1	4.7	7.7
Machinery	9.7	14.3	20.1	31.1	6.9	10.3
Transport equipment	6.9	9.9	16.1	28.5	6.9	12.5
Chemicals	5.7	8.8	14.9	24.7	7.2	12.9
Textiles and clothing	4.9	6.5	8.5	14.8	–2.1	9.6
Other manufactures	9.4	12.3	17.7	26.7	4.7	9.1
All manufactures	42.9	59.6	88.2	141.0	6.2	10.4

SOURCES: Maizels, *Industrial Growth and World Trade*; appendix A.

to the growth of income as the projections imply; for the United States the rate of rise in income was within the range which Maizels considered plausible, but imports rose at about two and a half times the maximum rate envisaged. In general, the main source of difference was clearly the relationship between total demand and imports – a subject which is considered in the next two chapters.

Maizels correctly foresaw that, in terms of the major countries' exports of manufactures, chemicals would continue to be the fastest-growing commodity group, followed, as had been the case from 1950 to 1959, by transport equipment and machinery. He was right also in suggesting that the exports of the other commodity groups would, as before, increase more slowly than the total. But the share of machinery in the total did not maintain until 1971 the rising trend which he projected and, whereas the magnitude of the fall in share was of the order projected for metals and miscellaneous manufactures, the textiles and clothing group maintained its share of trade far more successfully than Maizels envisaged. His projection for the volume of exports of this group was a fall of the order of 2 per cent a year (after a rise of 3 per cent a year between 1950 and 1959), but our estimates in table 2.6 suggest that the volume actually increased between 1959 and 1971 at an annual rate of about $9\frac{1}{2}$ per cent. This represents the greatest acceleration achieved in any of the commodity groups, probably because the stimulus provided by the formation of the EEC appears to have been particularly important in this case.

3

CONSUMPTION AND IMPORTS OF MANUFACTURES

by *R. L. Major*

INTRODUCTION

Our more detailed analysis of developments in the 1960s and early 1970s, which is initiated in this chapter, is based on the three years 1963, 1967 and 1971. This establishes a four-yearly progression from the last two years, 1955 and 1959, on which Maizels concentrated particular attention, but at some sacrifice of his principle of selecting years in which the world economy was relatively buoyant; 1971 was in fact rather below trend in this respect, notably in the United States, where manufacturing output was virtually unchanged from 1970. In comparison with the years immediately following, however, trade in 1971 was still for the most part relatively unaffected by the distortions introduced by violently fluctuating rates of exchange, and it can in other respects be considered more representative than the outright boom years of 1972 and 1973 (or, of course, the recession years of 1974 and 1975).

We have followed the classification of countries used by Maizels,[1] but have taken advantage of the improved range of statistics which has become available since he was writing to change some of the methods of estimation which he was constrained to employ. This applies to both output and trade but more especially to the former.[2]

In order to facilitate comparison between output and trade statistics we have followed Maizels in calculating production of manufactures gross, that is to say in including the whole value of manufactured products (other than food, drink and tobacco, the exclusion of these items again being dictated by the need for consistency with the trade statistics). This is in contrast with conventional output statistics, which cover only net value added and not the value of materials or components incorporated in the manufacturing process.

---

[1] See footnote to pp. 5–6.
[2] These differences are described more fully and their significance discussed in appendix C. It should be noted also that we have followed Maizels in not attempting to exclude petroleum products from the output series. This implies an overstatement of output in relation to trade, which for most countries is fairly trivial. We have also taken over unchanged the purchasing power parity rates of exchange which he employed. These points too are dealt with in more detail in appendix C.

The main point at which we part company with Maizels is in our use of revised factors for the conversion from net to gross values. The new factors tend on the whole to yield higher values for gross output, particularly in the developed countries (see appendix C). Probably the most important difference is for Japan, where our conversion factor is about 75 per cent higher than that used by Maizels, though there is an even wider disparity in the case of Pakistan. In the latter case Maizels was obliged to depend on analogies with a limited range of other countries, whereas we have had the use of actual input–output data. On the trade side we have abandoned the simplification adopted by Maizels of basing the figures for imports of manufactures solely on the export statistics of the major supplying countries; this is because other trade in manufactures is now both more important and better documented than it was formerly.

In both cases the general effect is, of course, to give higher figures for consumption of manufactures. As a result our estimate of consumption in 1963 is in aggregate about 10 per cent above the figure at which we

Table 3.1. *Estimates of total apparent consumption of manufactures,[a] 1955–71*

$ *billion, 1955 prices*

	1955[b]	1959[b]	1963[b]	1963	1967	1971
Industrial countries						
Western Europe[c]	100	118	157	177	212	267
North America	182	200	236	253	332	367
Japan	5	10	18	28	45	66
Total	*287*	*328*	*411*	*458*	*589*	*699*
Semi-industrial countries						
Western Europe[d]	10	14	21	25	34	47
Oceania, S. Africa	11	13	16	17	22	27
India, Pakistan	5	6	8	8	10	11
Latin America[e]	14	17	21	21	26	38
Total[f]	*42*	*52*	*69*	*74*	*96*	*129*
Non-industrial countries	*16*	*22*	*26*	*26*	*34*	*43*
WORLD[g]	345	402	506	558	719	871

[a] Excludes food, beverages and tobacco.
[b] Calculated on the original basis; the differences between this and the revised basis (in the other columns) are explained briefly in the text and in more detail in appendix C.
[c] Includes Austria, Denmark, Finland and Norway in addition to countries usually classified as industrial – Belgium-Luxembourg, France, Germany, Italy, Netherlands, Sweden, Switzerland and United Kingdom.
[d] Greece, Ireland, Portugal, Spain and Yugoslavia.
[e] Argentina, Brazil, Chile, Colombia and Mexico.
[f] Includes also Israel and Turkey.
[g] Excludes centrally planned economies.
SOURCES: Maizels, *Industrial Growth and World Trade*, table 6.1; NIESR estimates.

arrive by employing the methods which Maizels used (table 3.1). On the other hand the differences tend to cancel out when the share of imports in consumption or total supplies comes under review; they would in any case have little effect on rates of change as opposed to levels and, in order to provide a link between the two sets of data, we have calculated them for 1963 on the system followed by Maizels as well as on our own. This link provides the basis for any textual statements in this chapter in which periods both before and after 1963 are involved.

CONSUMPTION OF MANUFACTURES

Within this framework our estimates suggest that consumption of manufactures in the market economies almost doubled between 1959 and 1971.[1] This represents an annual rate of increase of between $5\frac{1}{2}$ and 6 per cent. Consumption per head appears, however, to have risen by rather over 50 per cent (table 3.2), or about $3\frac{1}{2}$ per cent a year. This means a somewhat higher rate of expansion than Maizels believed to have been achieved between 1950 and 1959.

Table 3.2. *Estimates of apparent consumption per head of manufactures,[a]*
        1955–71

$, 1955 prices

	1955[b]	1959[b]	1963[b]	1963	1967	1971
Industrial countries						
Western Europe[c]	410	465	599	672	774	950
North America	1000	1025	1133	1213	1515	1604
Japan	55	105	188	292	446	625
Total	*560*	*605*	*725*	*807*	*992*	*1137*
Semi-industrial countries						
Western Europe[d]	165	200	295	353	462	620
Oceania, S. Africa	450	485	525	552	627	695
India, Pakistan	10	12	14	15	15	16
Latin America[e]	105	125	128	122	140	190
	58	*70*	*83*	*85*	*101*	*124*
Non-industrial countries	*30*	*35*	*38*	*38*	*44*	*49*
WORLD[g]	190	210	242	262	311	344

Notes: see notes to table 3.1.
SOURCES: as table 3.1.

[1] We have followed Maizels in using the term 'consumption' in a broad sense in which a word like 'absorption' might be considered more strictly accurate. That is to say 'consumption' for our purposes includes additions to fixed assets in the form of capital goods as well as consumption more narrowly defined and is regarded as equivalent to production plus imports (free of duplication) less exports. No allowance is made for stock movements.

There was no very marked change between 1959 and 1971 in the shares of total consumption accounted for by the industrial, the semi-industrial and the non-industrial countries as defined in table 3.1. The industrial countries' share probably fell a little, but on our reckoning they were still responsible in 1971 for about 80 per cent of the total, though they contained only 23 per cent of the world's population. North American consumption, though still much the highest per head of population, declined in relative terms from all but half the total in 1959 to about 42 per cent in 1971. But industrial Western Europe maintained its share and Japan seems to have nearly quadrupled its consumption per head. By 1971 Japan had on our estimation achieved parity in this respect with the semi-industrial countries of Western Europe, though still lagging a long way behind their more fully industrialised neighbours.

Semi-industrial Europe itself increased its consumption per head very rapidly, probably by about 150 per cent, but the semi-industrial non-European countries fared a good deal less well and the rate of increase for the group as a whole was depressed in particular by the slow expansion of India and Pakistan, especially the former. These countries, which contain over two thirds of the total population of the group as Maizels defined it, appear by 1971 to have been consuming manufactures at only about 1 per cent of the North American rate per head.

The semi-industrial countries of Latin America seem to have raised their consumption per head by about 60 per cent between 1959 and 1971, but for Australia, New Zealand and South Africa the aggregate rise per head was probably only 35–40 per cent. For the non-industrial countries, at their very much lower level, it seems to have been of a similar order. In all, the developing countries probably raised only marginally their share of total consumption despite the rise in their share of the world's population.

Rates of consumption of manufactures are, not surprisingly, closely related to levels of income. Maizels found (a) that 'the industrial countries generally consume considerably greater quantities in relation to income than do the semi-industrial countries', but (b) that 'in the early stages of industrialization the demand for manufactures increases at a faster rate, in relation to income, than it does at a more mature phase'.[1] The latter conclusion was based on regression equations, using both time-series and cross-country comparisons, of consumption per head of manufactures on real incomes per head; the time-series gave income coefficients for consumption of 1.4 for the industrial countries and 1.7 for the semi-industrial, while the cross-country series gave 1.2 and 1.4.

[1] Maizels, *Industrial Growth and World Trade*, pp. 132–4.

Our own calculations for 1971, the results of which are illustrated in chart 3.1, lend support to (a), though the close conformity of Australia and New Zealand with the pattern set by the industrial countries suggests that the level of incomes rather than the degree of industrialisation is the determining factor. The position of South Africa is also consistent with this view, though the wide disparity in incomes between the black and the white populations in that country may make it an unreliable guide. As regards (b) the 1971 results again provide confirmation to the extent of giving income coefficients similar to those which Maizels obtained, 1.5 for the industrial countries and 1.6 for the

Chart 3.1. *GDP per head and consumption of manufactures per head, 1971*

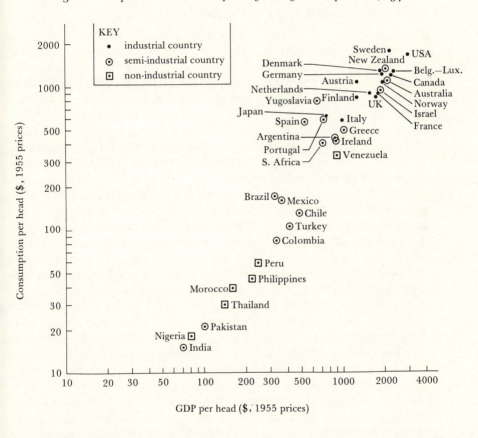

SOURCES: Maizels, *Industrial Growth and World Trade*, appendix table E.1; United Nations, *Yearbook of National Accounts Statistics* and *Monthly Bulletin of Statistics* (various issues); appendix table C.2.

semi-industrial if Yugoslavia is excluded. The relationships are fairly erratic so far as the industrial countries are concerned.[1] The income coefficient for the semi-industrial countries comes down to 1.5 if we include Yugoslavia, which appears to have an exceptionally high ratio of consumption of manufactures to output, possibly because of the high proportion of resources devoted to investment in its state-controlled economy. For the non-industrial countries we get an income coefficient of 2.5 where Maizels had only 1.0, but as we managed to cover only six countries our result may be unrepresentative, though it is more consistent than Maizels' own result with his proposition (b) above.

IMPORT DEPENDENCE

The overall picture in the industrial and semi-industrial countries

As the figures in chapter 2 would seem to imply, exports of manufactures have increased even faster than consumption. Those of the industrial countries more than trebled in volume between 1959 and 1971, while those of the semi-industrial countries probably rose at much the same rate and those of the non-industrial countries even faster. Including goods which were exported as well as those consumed at home, the total supply of manufactures disposed of by the large industrial countries just about doubled, for the smaller industrial countries supplies increased even more and for the semi-industrial groups they came nearer to trebling.

Maizels showed that for all these groups the share of imports in total supplies of manufactures, defined as in the last paragraph, had fallen sharply during the first half of the century. This decline had continued between 1950 and 1959 for the semi-industrial countries, but had on the whole been reversed for both the other groups. Indeed the only industrial country where the import content of supplies was lower in 1959 than in 1950 was France, where imports were depressed in 1959 by devaluations of the franc during the two previous years and by other measures which had followed the return to power of General de Gaulle. The recovery in the ratio of imports to supplies in the industrial countries was on a fairly modest scale however, particularly in the large countries. It left industrial countries' total imports of manufactures more than 12 per cent lower in 1959 than they would have been if they had increased in line with demand from 1913. But in the semi-industrial countries import substitution was on a far bigger scale and actual imports reached only 45 per cent of the level at which they would have

---

[1] R^2 is 0.72 for the fourteen industrial countries covered, whereas it is 0.99 for the non-industrial countries and 0.83 for the semi-industrial countries (0.91 for the other sixteen if Yugoslavia is excluded).

stood if constant relationships with demand had been maintained.

Maizels took the view that, for the larger economies at any rate, the rise in the industrial countries' import ratios in the 1950s probably represented a recovery from an abnormally low level at the beginning of the decade – possibly to something like a trend position – brought about by the relatively severe restrictions which Western European countries had maintained on their trade with one another until the mid-1950s and on their imports from the Dollar Area until the closing years of the decade. On this hypothesis it seemed reasonable to suppose that trade would have been likely to grow more slowly in relation to output during the 1960s had trading conditions remained unaltered. The establishment of the EEC and EFTA appeared, however, to point to a 'rather faster' rate of growth in the industrial countries' inter-trade than would have been expected on the basis of past trends alone.[1]

In fact the recovery in the industrial countries' import ratios has not only continued but greatly accelerated. For the larger countries as a group the ratio comfortably exceeded its 1899 level by 1971 and for the United States it was nearly trebled. From the more limited data on the smaller industrial countries which are presented in table 3.3. it seems probable that in their case also imports were higher in relation to total supplies than they had been at the beginning of the century. The effects of these changes on actual imports are evaluated in table 3.4. This indicates that the whole of the industrial countries' import substitution between 1913 and 1950 had been reversed by 1963. And over the next eight years expansion of demand accounted for only a third of the increase in their manufactured imports. The change, though universal among the industrial countries, has on the whole been most marked in the big ones where the import content of supplies is particularly low (the United States, the United Kingdom and Germany). The exception in this respect is Japan, where, as in Italy, the recovery in import content has been relatively slow.

For the semi-industrial countries the story is rather different, in that import substitution continued between 1959 and 1963. Nevertheless its scale was considerably diminished and a subsequent recovery probably brought the ratio back to about the 1959 level by 1971, although Pakistan's imports in the latter year were severely depressed as a result of the war which followed the declaration of independence by Bangladesh.

It is not easy to judge what significance should be attached to the movements in the import ratios of the semi-industrial countries. This is partly because of their widely varying characteristics. Apart from India, which we were unable to fit into any of the 'clusters' on which our own

[1] Maizels, *Industrial Growth and World Trade*, pp. 153–4.

Table 3.3. *Import content of 'supplies' of manufactured goods,*[a] *1899–1971*

Percentages, *1955 prices*

	Original basis					Revised	
	1899	1913	1950	1959	1963	1963	1971
Industrial countries							
United Kingdom	16	17	4	6	7	9	16
France	12	13	7	6	12	12	19
Germany[b]	16	10	4	7	10	9	17
Italy	11	14	8	8	13	13	15
United States	3	3	2	3	3	3	8
Japan	30	34	3	4	6	4	5
Total large	*9*	*8*	*3*	*4*	*6*	*6*	*11*
Belgium-Luxembourg	26	24	14	15	24	25	34
Netherlands	..	..	33	33	39	35	44
Norway	..	35	33	34	34	35	44
Sweden	8	14	12	17	17	18	22
Canada	20	23	16	20	18	22	32
Total small	..	..	*18*	*21*	*24*	*25*	*33*
TOTAL INDUSTRIAL	..	10–11	5	6	8	8	14
Semi-industrial countries							
Australia	..	39	25	15	16	20	26
New Zealand	..	46	32	19	21	27	23
South Africa	..	97	33	..	27	28	30
India	} 58	61	{ 22	20	20	20	14
Pakistan			{ 80	24	33	25	17
Argentina	..	81	16	17	14	13	11
Brazil	..	..	21	..	7	9	13
Chile	..	..	23	20	23	31	29
Colombia	..	..	49	..	36	34	32
Mexico	..	..	27	20	19	21	16
Israel	..	..	..	29	30	27	42
Turkey	..	..	33	..	26	27	18
Yugoslavia	..	..	7	6	7	6	11
TOTAL SEMI-INDUSTRIAL	..	55–60	23	17–18	17	17	18

[a] Defined as gross value of production of non-food manufactures free of duplication, plus c.i.f. value of imports of 'finished' manufactures (goods not normally subject to further processing). See also appendix C.
[b] West Germany from 1950.
SOURCES: Maizels, *Industrial Growth and World Trade*, table 6.4; NIESR estimates.

classification is based (see pages 110–15), the countries in question are distributed over five of the seven 'clusters'. As in the case of the industrial countries, there certainly seems to have been an upward shift in the trend of import ratios in the latest period. But the great majority of the semi-industrial countries still maintained relatively strict control over imports in 1971.

Table 3.4. *Effects of import substitution^a and of expansion in demand on imports of manufactures in selected periods 1913–71*

$ billion, 1955 prices

	1913–29	1929–37	1937–50	1950–9	1959–63	1963–71
Industrial countries						
Import substitution	−2.2	−5.1	−2.0	+6.1	+5.4	+46.0
Demand expansion	+4.5	+1.9	+4.1	+6.3	+7.2	+24.3
Total	+2.3	−3.2	+2.1	+12.4	+12.7	+70.3
Semi-industrial countries						
Import substitution	−1.9	−1.8	−2.1	−3.1	−0.3	+1.1
Demand expansion	+3.0	+1.1	+3.7	+3.9	+1.9	+7.5
Total	+1.1	−0.7	+1.5	+0.8	+1.6	+8.6

^{a} Defined as the difference between actual imports of manufactures at the end of the period and what they would have been if, during the period, imports of finished manufactures had changed at the same rate as domestic consumption of manufactures and imports of semi-manufactures had changed at the same rate as domestic consumption plus exports if significant. A minus sign denotes substitution.
SOURCES: Maizels, *Industrial Growth and World Trade*, table 6.11; NIESR estimates.

Individual countries

Especially perhaps in the Latin American countries, which constitute an important element in the semi-industrial group, the level of the group's imports at any particular time has tended to be governed to a great extent by the current state of the balance of payments. In 1971 both Brazil and Mexico received exceptionally large net inflows of capital and in Chile, where a major redistribution of income in favour of wage-earners led to a big increase in imports of consumer goods, a massive rise in foreign exchange reserves between end-1967 and mid-1971 provided the means of financing this. Even so it is noteworthy that after the share of agriculture in GDP had fallen between 1965 and 1970 from 16.0 to 13.5 per cent in Argentina, from 23.4 to 19.1 per cent in Brazil, from 10.2 to 9.6 per cent in Chile, from 31.1 to 29.7 per cent in Colombia and from 14.8 to 12.2 per cent in Mexico, three of the five countries (Argentina, Brazil and Colombia, which are all heavily dependent on agricultural exports) had higher import ratios for manufactures in 1971 than in 1967 and only Mexico had a lower one.

More generally, it is clear that, as Maizels put it, 'countries which have large export sectors in relation to their total economies will tend to rely more heavily on imports for their supplies of manufactures than will countries where exports provide only a small part of the national income'. Apart from the need for some degree of equilibrium in the balance of payments, it is of course fairly obvious that income generated

Table 3.5. *Import content of 'supplies' of manufactures in relation to export content of GDP,[a] 1955 and 1971*

	Import content of 'supplies'				
	Under 10%	10–19%	20–29%	30–39%	40%+
Export ratio:					
Under 10%					
1955	United States	Brazil Chile India	—	—	—
1971	United States	Argentina Brazil India Mexico Pakistan	—	—	—
10–19%					
1955	France Italy Japan	—	Australia Mexico	Israel	—
1971	Japan	France	Australia Chile	Colombia	—
20–29%					
1955	Germany United Kingdom	Sweden	Canada	New Zealand	
1971	—	Germany Italy United Kingdom Yugoslavia	New Zealand Sweden	Canada South Africa	—
30–39%					
1955	—	Belgium- Luxembourg	South Africa	—	—
1971	—	—	—	—	—
40%+					
1955	—	—	—	Netherlands Norway	—
1971	—	—	—	Belgium- Luxembourg	Netherlands Norway

[a] Includes exports of services.

SOURCES: Maizels, *Industrial Growth and World Trade*, table 6.7; United Nations Statistical Office, *Yearbook of National Accounts Statistics, 1974*, New York, 1975; NIESR estimates.

from production for export is not matched by an addition to domestically available supplies from domestic sources and hence must be expected to create an addition to import demand. Maizels suggested on the basis of data for 1955 that after the export ratio (that is the share of exports in GDP) exceeded about 25 per cent in the industrial countries the import content of supplies of manufactures (otherwise less than 10 per cent) tended to rise with the export ratio and that a similar positive relationship existed for the semi-industrial countries.[1] The average import content for a given export ratio tended, however, to be higher in the industrial than in the semi-industrial countries. Indeed, whereas Japan and all the industrial countries of Western Europe had export ratios exceeding the import content of their supplies of manufactures, the reverse was true of all the semi-industrial countries except South Africa.

While supporting the main proposition, our estimates for 1971 point to a marked narrowing of the distinction between the industrial and semi-industrial countries. Table 3.5 shows that of the industrial countries Canada had by then an import content exceeding the export ratio, in France, Sweden and Norway the two were approximately equal, and Germany, the Netherlands and the United Kingdom had also raised the import content of their manufactured supplies without changing their export ratios to a significant extent (while Italy and Belgium-Luxembourg had increased both). In the non-industrial countries, on the other hand, the direction of change in the relationship had varied. South Africa had reduced its export ratio and increased its import content and Chile had raised both, but New Zealand had brought the two into line, while Mexico had reduced both to a similar extent and Australia showed no change. Of the countries whose relationships Maizels did not analyse in this particular context, Argentina, Pakistan and Colombia conformed in 1971 with the general pattern for the semi-industrial countries, namely an import content higher than the export ratio (substantially higher for Colombia), but this was reversed in Yugoslavia.

The main reason why import content has tended to rise in relation to export ratios in the industrial countries but not in the semi-industrial countries is presumably that the movement of the terms of trade in favour of the former, which between 1955 and 1971 was of the order of 11 per cent, made it possible for them to increase the ratio of import to export volumes at a given balance of payments. While the result was on the whole to reduce inter-country disparities in import content, these remained extremely wide, and to show that they were positively related to disparities in export ratios does not, of course, explain why both should be high or low. The factors which influence the extent of a country's overall participation in international trade are, however, considered in some detail in chapter 6. It may be sufficient here, therefore, to say merely that the main determinant of self-sufficiency is size, whether defined in terms of area, population or output.

---

[1] Ibid, pp. 144–5.

Individual commodity groups

A study by UNCTAD covering the United States, Japan, the United Kingdom and the original six members of the EEC, which are responsible between them for about three quarters of consumption of manufactures in the market economies, indicates that the share of imports in these nine countries' consumption more than doubled between 1959–60 and 1973–4 and was rising even faster at the end of the period. In particular it suggests that for all commodity groups the import content rose much faster after than before 1971–2 in the United Kingdom, and that it increased rapidly in Japan in 1973–4 after an initial fall. Even so the rise over the whole period was much less marked in Japan than in the other countries. In the Six the import share nearly doubled between 1959–60 and 1973–4 and in the United Kingdom it increased even faster; the EEC and EFTA tariff reductions must obviously have contributed to this outcome. But the rise in the United States import share was more rapid still. Moreover the study excluded United States imports of road motor vehicles from Canada because of the way in which they were affected by the Automotive Products Agreement of 1965 (see page 54).

In spite of this exclusion, the import content of the nine countries' consumption of transport equipment had more than doubled by 1971–2 and approximately trebled by 1973–4. This is true also of textiles and clothing and, up to 1971–2, of 'machinery and other' (table 3.6), of which the main component is machinery though it also includes some semi-manufactures and a wide range of consumer goods. Particularly spectacular rises were recorded both for textiles and clothing in Japan and for transport equipment in the United Kingdom and, to a lesser extent, the United States. In both the latter countries import content also rose relatively fast for 'machinery and other', whereas in the EEC countries (as in Japan) it was textiles and clothing that set the pace – in their case principally clothing, for which the import content rose from $6\frac{1}{2}$ per cent in 1959–60 to 28 per cent in 1973–4.

Falls in import content were recorded only in Japan, for chemicals and metals up to 1971–2, for transport equipment subsequently and for machinery in both periods. There was, however, a general tendency towards comparatively slow rises in the groups consisting mainly of intermediate products. Even so, metals maintained the highest import share, followed, as before, by chemicals. Indeed the only change in the ranking order was that the group comprising products of rubber, wood and miscellaneous minerals fell from third to bottom place.

The recession of 1975 brought a change in this picture. Import content continued to rise in all groups both in the Six and in the United Kingdom. In the latter indeed the rate of increase was even faster than

Table 3.6. *Shares of imports in consumption^a by commodity group, 1959–60 and 1971–5*

Percentages^b

	United Kingdom	EEC Six	United States	Japan	Total of these
Metals					
1959–60	23.4	29.6	6.0	17.9	15.1
1971–2	31.7	39.4	11.3	11.5	21.6
1973–4	40.8	42.0	12.5	18.9	25.5
1975	47.5	43.8	13.0	19.3	26.8
Machinery and other ^{c}					
1959–60	10.4	15.3	2.3	6.1	6.2
1971–2	24.4	26.7	7.3	5.6	13.9
1973–4	32.5	28.2	8.7	5.2	15.4
1975	41.5	31.8	8.1	4.6	16.1
Transport equipment^d					
1959–60	3.4	12.4	2.6	3.0	4.4
1971–2	13.9	25.1	6.4	3.5	11.3
1973–4	17.2	27.2	8.0	3.0	13.1
1975	18.9	28.4	8.2	3.1	14.6
Chemicals					
1959–60	16.1	23.2	2.4	10.8	8.9
1971–2	25.7	36.8	4.5	10.0	16.0
1973–4	34.2	45.5	6.3	13.8	22.0
1975	43.5	45.8	6.0	12.7	21.3
Textiles and clothing					
1959–60	11.8	11.1	4.3	1.1	7.0
1971–2	24.5	28.8	11.3	8.9	18.7
1973–4	30.6	32.8	11.8	12.5	21.6
1975	31.7	35.6	11.5	7.9	22.2
Rubber, wood and other mineral products					
1959–60	17.7	12.6	4.4	1.2	7.2
1971–2	18.7	16.8	5.8	2.1	9.3
1973–4	22.1	19.9	6.2	3.9	11.1
1975	22.4	20.7	4.9	3.1	10.3
All manufactures^{cd}					
1959–60	13.0	16.5	3.4	6.1	7.6
1971–2	22.4	27.2	7.3	5.6	14.0
1973–4	28.7	30.5	8.5	7.0	16.6
1975	33.2	32.4	7.9	5.7	16.8

^{a} Consumption here defined as gross output *plus* imports *minus* exports. Because imports of intermediate as well as finished goods are included, it tends to yield lower estimates than ours of the import shares. Our estimates for all manufactures in 1971 at 1955 prices are 20.8 per cent for the United Kingdom, where the share rose sharply in 1972, 27.6 per cent for the EEC Six, 8.6 per cent for the United States and 6.2 per cent for Japan.
^{b} At current prices. ^{c} Excludes food, drink and tobacco, and coal and petroleum products.
^{d} For United States excludes imports of road motor vehicles from Canada.
SOURCES: UNCTAD, *Handbook of International Trade and Development Statistics, 1976* and *Supplement 1977*, New York, 1976 and 1977.

before. But import content fell slightly in the United States and there was a steeper decline, to about the 1971–2 level, in Japan, where textile imports suffered particularly severely. For the nine countries together import content rose only marginally and imports failed to keep pace with consumption of chemicals, textiles (excluding clothing) and wood products (including paper and printing).

PROJECTED AND ACTUAL RELATIONSHIPS

As we showed in chapter 2, the volume of world trade in manufactures more than trebled during the twelve years from 1959 to 1971. The exports of the eleven major countries probably increased at an annual rate of about $10\frac{1}{2}$ per cent in total, or 8 per cent per head of the world's population. The latter figure compares with a maximum of about $4\frac{1}{2}$ per cent in the projections which Maizels adopted.

The method which Maizels employed was to make assumptions about the rate of growth in income per head – alternative assumptions in most cases – and to derive from these projections first of supplies per head and then of imports per head, largely on the basis of past relationships. We showed in chapter 2 that the initial assumptions about rates of growth in incomes had set them too low, except on one alternative for the United States, and that this had made some contribution to the wide gap between the projected and actual growth of imports; this gap, however, was mainly attributable to an incorrect assessment of the relationship between incomes and imports. We have now to consider, therefore, at what stage or stages these expectations were falsified – in the transition from incomes to supplies, the transition from supplies to imports, or both.

So far as supplies are concerned, Maizels assumed for the most part that the ratio of the annual growth rates per head for these to the corresponding rates for incomes would be about 1.2 to 1. This applied without qualification to the small industrial, semi-industrial and non-industrial countries. It was also true of the separate projections made for the United States on the one hand and the other large industrial countries on the other. But because the United States was given both a rather lower ratio and a substantially lower income growth rate, this implied a somewhat higher ratio than 1.2 for the large industrial countries collectively. These expectations as regards the ratios proved not to be very far wide of the mark. If anything the relationship for supply growth to income growth proved to be rather lower than expected for the large industrial countries. For the remaining groups, however, the errors went the other way, the actual elasticities probably ranging between about 1.4 for the smaller countries and 2.0 for the

Table 3.7. *Rates of change in supplies and imports of manufactures per head,[a] projected and actual relationships*

		Projected growth rates[b] 1959 to 1970–5			Actual growth rates 1959 to 1971		
		Supplies[c]	Imports	Imports/ supplies	Supplies[c]	Imports	Imports/ supplies
		(% p.a.)	(% p.a.)		(% p.a.)	(% p.a.)	
Industrial countries							
Large							
United							
States	II	3.0	3.4	*1.1* ⎫	3.3	11.3	*3.3*
	III	2.2	2.6	*1.2* ⎭			
Other	II	4.9	7.4	*1.5* ⎫	6.8	14.9	*2.2*
	III	5.6	8.0	*1.4* ⎭			
Total	I	4.4	5.3	*1.2* ⎫			
	II	3.8	5.8	*1.5* ⎬	4.9	13.6	*2.7*
	III	3.8	6.0	*1.6* ⎭			
Small		3.5	5.6	*1.6*	5.4	9.9	*1.8*
Semi-industrial countries							
	I	2.4	1.0	*0.4* ⎫	5.9	6.5	*1.1*
	II	3.5	2.1	*0.6* ⎭			
Non-industrial countries							
	I	2.5	1.6	*0.6* ⎫	3.9	5.4	*1.4*
	II	3.6	2.5	*0.7* ⎭			

[a] At 1955 prices.
[b] The roman figures in the first column refer to Maizels' alternative assumptions for growth in real income per head (see source, pp. 387 ff).
[c] Ratios of growth rates of supplies/income can be calculated from these data and the figures for incomes in table 2.5.
SOURCES: Maizels, *Industrial Growth and World Trade*, tables 15.1 and 15.2; NIESR estimates.

semi-industrial group. (It should be noted that, on the definition of 'supplies' which we have followed Maizels in adopting, a faster growth of trade in relation to output will in itself tend to increase the ratio of 'supplies' to income, since goods which have been traded internationally are treated as supplies available to both the exporting and the importing country.)

By far the largest source of error was the relationship between supplies and imports of manufactures. Maizels projected the growth ratios of imports to supplies as ranging between about 0.5 to 1 for the semi-industrial countries and 1.6 to 1 for the small industrial ones. But while the latter projection proved reasonably accurate, the former was much too low and the elasticities for the large industrial countries, which

Maizels put at 1.1 to 1.2 for the United States and 1.4 to 1.5 for the rest, in fact lay further outside his range – on our estimation at 3.3 and 2.2 respectively. In the next chapter, in which patterns of trade are looked at in greater detail, we examine some of the possible explanations for this unexpected development.

4

EXPORT COMPETITION AND IMPORT SUBSTITUTION: THE INDUSTRIAL COUNTRIES 1963 TO 1971

by *A. D. Morgan*

SHARES IN 'WORLD' EXPORTS OF MANUFACTURES

In his discussion of the effects of competition and import substitution on the exports of the main industrial countries, Maizels drew attention to 'the secular decline in Britain's share [of world exports of manufactures] from one third in the period prior to 1914 to one sixth by the end of the 1950s',[1] with a corresponding increase in the United States share up to 1950 and of the German share in the late 1950s. Between the time he wrote and 1971 Britain's share continued to fall almost without interruption, but it was joined as a loser by the United States; the German share stabilised and Japan, which even by 1959 had not fully recovered its prewar position in world markets, dramatically increased its share – by 1971 ranking third in the list of major industrial exporters. The only other country that managed to secure a significantly larger share in world trade during the 1960s was Italy, though an initial decline in Canada's share was later sharply reversed; for the remainder, share changes since 1959 were generally small (table 4.1). For the most part these comments apply equally to trade measured at current and at constant prices. Share changes in constant price terms were usually more pronounced, since falling shares were associated with more than average price rises and vice versa. However, between 1967 and 1971 German shares at current and constant prices moved in opposite directions. The former rose slightly, sustained by the very sharp rise in German export prices (in terms of dollars) following the appreciation of the Deutschemark, while the price rise depressed Germany's export share in volume terms.

Analysing changes in market shares at constant prices, Maizels concluded that: 'Changes in shares due to variations in the area and commodity pattern of trade have been in general the least important element in the period since 1913.'[2] Changes in 'competitiveness' – that is changes in market share after making allowance for the effect on exporting countries of differential rates of growth in demand by commodities and areas – were the major element. The pattern of such

[1] Maizels, *Industrial Growth and World Trade*, p. 188.

[2] Ibid, p. 199.

Table 4.1. *Shares in the total exports of manufactures from industrial countries,*
1959–71

Percentages

	Shares at current prices				Shares at 1963 prices		
	1959	1963	1967	1971	1959	1967	1971
Exports from:							
United States	21.4	20.8	20.4	17.0	20.8	20.1	16.1
United Kingdom	17.9	15.4	12.2	10.9	18.3	11.7	10.8
Japan	6.6	7.6	9.8	13.0	5.8	10.6	14.7
E E C Six	42.5	45.0	45.2	46.8	43.7	45.3	46.1
France	(9.1)	(9.0)	(8.5)	(8.8)	(9.4)	(8.3)	(8.7)
Germany	(19.0)	(19.9)	(19.6)	(20.1)	(20.0)	(19.9)	(19.2)
Italy	(4.4)	(6.0)	(7.0)	(7.3)	(4.3)	(7.2)	(7.5)
Belgium-Luxembourg	(5.9)	(5.9)	(5.8)	(5.9)	(5.8)	(5.6)	(5.8)
Netherlands	(4.1)	(4.2)	(4.3)	(4.7)	(4.2)	(4.3)	(4.9)
Canada	5.2	4.4	5.8	5.9	5.0	5.9	5.8
Sweden	3.0	3.4	3.3	3.3	2.9	3.3	3.3
Switzerland	3.4	3.4	3.2	3.0	3.5	3.1	2.9
Total of above	100.0	100.0	100.0	100.0	100.0	100.0	100.0

Note: In this and subsequent tables United States exports include certain special category exports in 1959 and 1963 and United Kingdom exports include re-exports and diamonds throughout. Hence the figures are not comparable with Maizels' previous series, which excluded these items. SOURCE: appendix A.

changes varied from time to time but two countries showed a consistent tendency: barring the 1940s, Japan gained and Britain lost competitively. During the 1950s the United States joined Britain among the losers, while Germany secured a big increase in its competitive residual. The constant market share analysis is extended to the 1960s in the next section. Here it is sufficient to say that its most striking feature is the overwhelming increase in Japan's competitiveness, especially during the latter part of the decade.

A parallel analysis by Maizels of the influence of import substitution on exports of manufactures to industrial and semi-industrial countries showed Britain, once again, as the chief loser, particularly in semi-industrial markets. In the latter, Maizels suggested, 'import substitution ... reflects the growth of domestic secondary industries', but in industrial countries it 'tended to be more a reflection of import restrictions'[1] and so with the liberalisation of trade in the 1950s it was reversed. Writing before the Kennedy Round of tariff reductions, Maizels thought that the trend towards lower protection would continue, but that it would be less important in the future than in the

[1] Ibid, p. 229.

recent past. In the event import penetration in the industrial countries has accelerated. Maizels' prediction that the intra-trade of the industrial countries would be the most dynamic element in world trade has been abundantly borne out by events.

In broad terms, Maizels' analysis of the factors influencing exports of manufactures from the industrial countries has been confirmed by the events of the last fifteen years, but the development of this trade has been profoundly affected by the emergence of Japan as the world's third largest and most expansionary industrial exporter, by major tariff changes and by the increasing import dependence of the largest of the mature industrial economies. It may also have been much influenced by the growing activities of multinational enterprises, though it is hard to determine what the direction, let alone the scale, of their influence has been.

SHARES BY COMMODITY AND MARKET 1963–71

Following Maizels we have made a constant market share analysis of exports of manufactures from the industrial countries for the periods 1963–7 and 1967–71. This method of organising trade data is designed to distinguish the influence of the growth of the world market and of trade in particular commodities with particular countries from other factors affecting a country's export performance during a specified period. The average performance of a group of countries is taken as the norm. Thus to calculate the effect of the growth of the world market on a given country's exports, it is assumed that they grow at the same rate as the group's total exports or, in other words, that each country maintains a constant share in the group's export market. To distinguish commodity or area effects, it is assumed that each exporting country maintains a constant share in the exports of each commodity supplied by the group and of exports to each market area distinguished in the analysis. A country with exports concentrated in commodities (or areas) where the group's exports have risen faster than its total exports will, if it maintains a constant share in each trade flow distinguished, show a gain in its trade from the commodity (or area) effect. Correspondingly, a country with exports concentrated on slow-growing commodities and market areas will show a loss. Any difference between the sum of these effects and the actual change in the value of a country's exports during the period reflects changes in market shares; it is often referred to as the competitive residual.

The analysis summarised in table 4.2 is based on a grouping of commodities and market areas broadly similar to that employed by Maizels. The grouping of markets in both text and tables has, however,

Table 4.2. *Changes in the volume of exports of manufactures attributable to changes in the size of the world market, the pattern of world trade and market shares, 1963–7 and 1967–71*

$ million, 1963 prices

	Base-year exports	Changes due to:					Actual change
		World market growth[a]	Commodity pattern[a]	Area pattern[a]	Market share		
					Current-weighted	(Of which base-weighted)	
1963–7 exports from:							
United States	13,503	5,500	127	606	−710	(−538)	5,523
United Kingdom	9,984	4,578	71	−217	−3,299	(−2,144)	1,133
Japan	4,949	2,275	−149	253	2,692	(1,820)	5,071
EEC Six	29,168	13,554	−58	−462	712	(870)	13,746
France	5,841	2,637	8	−278	−382	(−258)	1,985
Germany	12,910	6,029	193	−39	−197	(169)	5,986
Italy	3,877	1,870	−71	−64	1,253	(896)	2,988
Belgium-Luxembourg	3,830	1,769	−180	−58	−96	(−43)	1,435
Netherlands	2,710	1,249	−8	−23	134	(106)	1,352
Canada	2,830	1,265	−100	607	946	(162)	2,718
Sweden	2,195	1,026	−22	16	−56	(−9)	964
Switzerland	2,196	1,030	−13	14	−289	(−179)	742
1967–71 exports from:							
United States	19,026	10,373	−39	−1,241	−3,728	(−2,464)	5,365
United Kingdom	11,117	6,421	8	−484	−1,037	(−509)	4,908
Japan	10,019	5,741	56	−457	6,605	(4,022)	11,945
EEC Six	42,914	23,766	−99	2,881	−746	(−547)	25,802
France	7,826	4,441	29	437	195	(104)	5,102
Germany	18,895	10,109	−38	823	−1,188	(−823)	9,706
Italy	6,865	3,918	41	552	−118	(−39)	4,393
Belgium-Luxembourg	5,265	2,983	−187	549	25	(−6)	3,370
Netherlands	4,063	2,315	56	520	340	(217)	3,231
Canada	5,548	3,276	−84	767	−843	(−426)	3,116
Sweden	3,159	1,829	−116	−167	208	(155)	1,754
Switzerland	2,938	1,678	2	140	−456	(−230)	1,364

[a] Base-weighted calculations with weights (shares in world markets, commodity and area pattern of trade) of initial years 1963 and 1967. Current-weighted estimates are not shown; they are rarely significantly different for commodity and area effects.

SOURCE: NIESR calculations based on data in appendix A.

been altered to permit the analysis of the effects of the creation of the EEC and EFTA on the pattern of trade. Further, the present analysis distinguishes between the effects of differential rates of growth in commodity groups and market areas, whereas Maizels in effect treated them as one. Maizels' analysis followed the formula:

$$\Delta x = s^0 \Delta X + (\sum_{ij} s_{ij}^0 \Delta X_{ij} - s^0 \Delta X) + \sum_i \sum_j X_{ij}^1 \Delta s_{ij}$$

where X stands for the value of 'world' exports at constant prices (the world being the eleven major non-Communist industrial countries), x for a given country's exports and s for its share in 'world' exports; the i and j subscripts refer to commodity groups and market areas, and o and I superscripts to the initial (base) and terminal (current) years of the period for which the analysis is being performed. Thus the first term on the right-hand side of the equation measures the effect of world market growth; the second term measures a combined commodity and area effect; the final term measures the effect of changes in shares, the changes being weighted by current (terminal year) world export values. In the present analysis the middle term of the equation is divided into:

$$(\sum_i s_i^0 \Delta X_i - s^0 \Delta X) + \sum_i (\sum_j s_{ij}^0 \Delta X_{ij} - s_i^0 \Delta X_i)$$

In addition, besides calculating commodity and market effects weighted by product and country shares in the base years 1963 and 1967, giving current-period weights to the competitive residual, an alternative formula was used to calculate commodity and area effects with current-period weights. Comparison between the two sets of calculations indicates whether the pattern of a given country's exports has become more or less favourable during the period – whether, that is, it has obtained a larger or smaller share of fast-growing commodities and markets – according to whether any gain is greater or less when weighted with current rather than base-year shares. It should be remembered, however, that an improvement during one period does not necessarily imply that the country in question starts the next period more advantageously placed as an exporter; for the relative rates of growth of demand by commodity groups and areas may vary (and indeed have done so) between periods.

Calculations using current weights for commodities and markets have a base-weighted competitive residual $(\sum_i \sum_j X_{ij}^0 \Delta s_{ij})$ which measures the 'pure' share effect, that is the effect on the value of a country's exports of changes in shares related to the value of world exports at the beginning of the period. By deducting this term from the current-weighted residual, it is possible to arrive at a figure $(\sum_i \sum_j \Delta X_{ij} \Delta s_{ij})$ for the effect of changes in a country's share of changes in the value of world exports during the period. The difference between the current-weighted and base-weighted residual thus gives some indication of a country's performance in expanding markets.

It should be added that in interpreting the results of these calculations, not too much reliance should be placed on the movement of the different terms, since such analysis is extremely susceptible to differences in levels of aggregation by commodity and market areas and to the order in which these effects are calculated. A high degree of aggregation, for example, will minimise commodity and market effects and maximise the competitive residual. Again, the results will differ for a given country depending on the number of exporters deemed to represent the 'world'. More seriously perhaps, the form of the analysis implicitly suggests that the commodity and market effects are due to autonomous demand factors and the competitive residual is the outcome of influences on the supply side. If, for example, world trade in a particular commodity grows exceptionally rapidly because of innovation in one country, this will show up partly as an advantageous commodity effect for the country in question rather than as the result of competitive innovation. Nevertheless, the method is a useful and suggestive way of analysing the data.[1]

In practice differences in commodity patterns of trade and changes for individual countries during the two periods analysed proved to be of little importance to the total increase in a given country's exports save in one or two instances. In relation to the increase in exports implied by the growth of the world market, the commodity composition of trade had a significantly unfavourable effect on Japan, Belgium-Luxembourg and Canada from 1963 to 1967 and on Belgium-Luxembourg and Sweden from 1967 to 1971 but, save in the cases of Belgium-Luxembourg and Sweden, adverse commodity effects were equivalent to under 5 per cent of the increase in trade actually achieved. Belgium-Luxembourg appears to be uniquely unfavourably placed because of the relatively small shares of intermediate chemicals and transport equipment, both fast-growing commodity groups, in its exports; while Swedish exports from 1967 on were, on this analysis, handicapped by the large share of intermediate metals and other intermediate goods, both slow-growing groups. However, the 'fast-growing' and 'slow-growing' groups each span a range of items with very different growth rates, so that at the more disaggregated level discussed in the next section the effects of the commodity composition of trade and of changes in composition appear in rather a different light.

---

[1] For a full account of the problems associated with constant market share analysis see S. P. Magee, 'Prices, incomes and foreign trade' in P. B. Kenen (ed.), *International Trade and Finance*, Cambridge University Press, 1975.

Differential rates of growth by market area show up in the analysis as being of much greater significance than differential rates of commodity growth. Though exports to industrial areas as a whole grew more rapidly than exports to semi-industrial areas and the rest of the world both from 1963 to 1967 and from 1967 to 1971, only exports to the United States grew much faster than world exports in both periods. Canada, Japan and the United Kingdom were relatively fast-growing markets only in the first period, the EEC Six only in the second, while EFTA countries other than the United Kingdom increased their imports from the 'world' at much the same rate as the non-industrial areas in both periods. The growth of the United States market was particularly important to Canada during 1963–7, but the area effect proper is exaggerated by the influence of trade covered by the United States–Canadian Automotive Agreement on the growth of United States 'demand'; the area effect on United States exports was similarly exaggerated. During 1967–71 the growth of the EEC market benefited its members substantially, more than offsetting their combined loss in competitiveness. Britain's trade was unfavourably affected throughout because of the high proportion of its exports still going to markets outside the industrial areas, especially the semi-industrial countries. Unlike Japan it had no offset in the form of unusually high dependence on the United States market.

The most remarkable feature of table 4.2 is the Japanese gain in competitiveness, which contributed more to the increase in Japanese exports than did the growth of the world market. From 1963 to 1967 the shift in market shares for all exporters was equivalent to about $5 billion worth of trade measured at constant prices; out of this Japan secured nearly $2.7 billion – 54 per cent. Its gain in 'established' trade as measured by the change in its base-weighted market share was larger proportionately as well as absolutely than its gain in 'new' trade. It accounted for 57 per cent of all positive shifts in base-weighted market shares, but only 43 per cent of positive shifts in shares of additional exports. From 1967 to 1971 Japan secured no less than 90 per cent of the $7.3 billion shift in market shares, and its gains were proportionately as large in 'new' as in 'established' trade.

The main thrust of Japanese competition was concentrated on the United States and the non-industrial countries, and on transport equipment and machinery, with intermediate metals and intermediate chemicals also figuring largely. These four commodity groups accounted for almost three quarters of Japan's total competitive gains during 1963–7 and for 90 per cent in 1967–71. The pattern of these developments is illustrated in table 4.3. Unfortunately the rather broad commodity grouping obscures the tendency to concentrate sales of

Table 4.3. *Japan's competitive gains, 1963–7 and 1967–71*

$ *million, 1963 prices*

	Change 1963–7 due to:			Change 1967–71 due to:		
	Market growth[a]	Market share		Market growth[a]	Market share	
		Estab-lished[b]	New trade[c]		Estab-lished[b]	New trade[c]
Exports of:						
Intermediate metals	350	149	92	536	899	379
(to United States)	(183)	(82)	(66)	(190)	(108)	(37)
(to non-industrials)	(139)	(68)	(28)	(252)	(365)	(159)
Machinery	553	437	216	1099	1332	705
(to United States)	(313)	(53)	(69)	(462)	(366)	(252)
(to non-industrials)	(195)	(210)	(104)	(417)	(523)	(247)
Transport equipment	359	562	253	1146	1043	989
(to United States)	(120)	(11)	(26)	(289)	(509)	(711)
(to non-industrials)	(181)	(252)	(98)	(573)	(351)	(201)
Intermediate chemicals	179	151	133	481	366	256
(to non-industrials)	(104)	(84)	(84)	(294)	(196)	(151)
All other commodities	938	521	178	2078	412	254
Total	2379	1820	872	5340	4022	2583

[a] Sum of change in exports calculated from growth of world exports to the market, and from commodity and area effects.
[b] Value of changes in market shares during the period in relation to value of 'world' exports in the initial year.
[c] Value of changes in market shares during the period in relation to the increase in the value of 'world' exports during the period.
SOURCE: NIESR calculations based on data in appendix A.

products new to the Japanese export list (other than sophisticated consumer goods) initially on markets in developing countries, only later mounting an export drive in the developed countries.[1] But traces of this pattern can be discerned in the shift of geographical emphasis in sales of transport equipment from the non-industrial countries to the United States and in the concentration of trade gains in intermediate chemicals in non-industrial areas.

Of the two other countries that secured significant gains during the period 1963–7, Italy increased its market share mainly in 'established' trade, particularly trade in machinery. The Canadian case is interesting, for it illustrates the effect of the 1965 Automotive Agreement with the United States: Canada increased its share of United States imports of transport equipment from 16 to 54 per cent. Out of its total increase of $1645 million of exports of transport equipment to the United States, $903 million was 'new' trade and $373

[1] On this point see, for example, GATT, *International Trade 1968*, p. 50.

million a share gain in 'established' trade. But even its privileged position did not wholly insulate it from the blast of Japanese competition thereafter; in 1967–71 it suffered a loss on 'established' exports of transport equipment of $184 million.

In the reverse direction, the Automotive Agreement helped to shore up American exports of transport equipment, as did the United States' predominance in the market for aircraft. Because of these two factors, the United States actually secured a larger share of world export markets for transport equipment in 1967 than it had enjoyed in 1963, but this gain was more than outweighed by heavy losses in machinery, metals and chemicals. From 1967 on the United States was a loser in all commodity groups and in almost all market areas, reflecting widespread loss of competitiveness and also, possibly, increasing trade diversion in

Table 4.4. *Changes in EEC exports, 1963–7 and 1967–71*

$ million, 1963 prices

	Change 1963–7 due to:			Change 1967–71 due to:		
	Market growth[a]	Market share		Market growth[a]	Market share	
		Estab-lished[b]	New trade[b]		Estab-lished[b]	New trade[b]
Exports to EEC from:						
France	731	44	38	2,428	300	266
Germany	1,765	191	98	4,223	43	93
Italy	628	415	179	2,249	95	88
Belgium-Luxembourg	860	104	37	2,448	96	88
Netherlands	587	107	47	1,862	210	214
Total Six	4,571	861	399	13,210	744	749
Exports to EFTA from:						
France	346	−80	−25	598	−18	−9
Germany	1,411	−256	−105	2,343	−206	−98
Italy	227	112	46	519	−62	−38
Belgium-Luxembourg	173	−56	−20	285	2	−19
Netherlands	221	−53	−7	363	72	6
Total Six	2,378	−333	−111	4,108	−212	−158
Exports to all other areas from:						
France	1,290	−222	−137	1,881	−178	−166
Germany	3,007	234	−359	4,328	−660	−360
Italy	880	369	132	1,743	−72	−129
Belgium-Luxembourg	498	−91	−70	612	−104	−38
Netherlands	410	52	−12	666	−65	−97
Total Six	6,085	342	−446	9,230	−1,079	−790

[a] Sum of change in exports calculated from growth of world exports to the market, and from commodity and area effects.
[b] For definitions see table 4.3.
SOURCE: NIESR calculations based on data in appendix A.

the EEC. United Kingdom exports had shown a similarly widespread loss of share, affecting all commodity groups and almost all markets from 1963 to 1967. After 1967, however, there was a marked turn for the better. It continued to lose very heavily in transport equipment, and also in intermediate chemicals and intermediate metals, but shares in all other commodity groups stabilised or even rose. At the same time it managed to regain ground lost in some market areas, notably EFTA, but also and more surprisingly in the non-industrial countries, where sales of finished goods other than transport equipment were doing well.

Changes in the competitive residuals of the EEC Six member countries are interesting for the stark contrast in their behaviour in intra-Community trade and elsewhere. This is illustrated in table 4.4. The Six gained trade in each other's markets without exception; they lost almost as uniformly in EFTA; and, while as a group they more or less maintained their position in the rest of the world from 1963 to 1967, they lost heavily, both individually and collectively, thereafter. It is clear that the formation of the customs union and of EFTA had a marked influence on trade, though of course these figures are no guide to its magnitude. The other noteworthy features of table 4.4 are the

Table 4.5. *Changes in EFTA countries' exports, 1963–7 and 1967–71*

$ *million, 1963 prices*

	Change 1963–7 due to:			Change 1967–71 due to:		
	Market growth[a]	Market share		Market growth[a]	Market share	
		Estab-lished[b]	New trade[b]		Estab-lished[b]	New trade[b]
Exports to EFTA from:						
Sweden	424	83	19	499	264	156
Switzerland	186	57	14	312	35	21
United Kingdom	449	−59	−23	650	68	44
Exports to EEC from:						
Sweden	196	−70	−31	459	−38	−34
Switzerland	397	−192	−90	856	−188	−182
United Kingdom	790	−478	−193	1609	−262	−227
Exports to all other areas from:						
Sweden	400	−22	−35	588	−71	−69
Switzerland	448	−44	−34	652	−77	−65
United Kingdom	3193	−1607	−939	3686	−315	−345

[a] Sum of change in exports calculated from growth of world exports to the market, and from commodity and area effects.
[b] For definitions see table 4.3.
SOURCE: NIESR calculations based on data in appendix A.

phenomenally large increases in demand within the EEC from 1967 to 1971 and the weakening in Germany's competitive strength during the same years. The loss of potential German trade outside the EEC was relatively little larger in proportionate terms than the loss sustained by most other members, but Germany notably failed to secure significant gains in intra-EEC trade.

Table 4.5 shows comparable figures for the three major EFTA exporters – Sweden, Switzerland and the United Kingdom. Except for the United Kingdom in its period of extreme competitive weakness before 1967, they all gained trade in EFTA markets, but they all lost both in the EEC and in the rest of the world. Thus the dismantling of tariffs on intra-EFTA trade did not affect their total exports to anything like the same extent as the EEC customs union affected the trade of member countries, but the results were not negligible, especially for Sweden, which was more dependent on EFTA markets than Britain or Switzerland.

COMPETITION IN PRICES AND PRODUCTS

In his discussion of the influence of price on competition, Maizels pointed out the many practical and conceptual problems involved in measuring it,[1] problems that have not been resolved since he wrote. The most formidable practical difficulty is to calculate reliable indicators of price changes for broad commodity groups. It is generally known that the available export unit value index numbers are seriously deficient, but the consequences are not perhaps sufficiently appreciated. Two in particular concern us here. First, differences in weighting and construction may impart a consistent bias to the series available for different countries and seriously impair international comparability. Following Maizels' example, the available price indicators have been reweighted with current export weights so far as is possible, but the component series used in this exercise themselves differ in construction and coverage, so that although they are more nearly comparable than official unit value index numbers, they may still be biased and impart a contrary bias to figures of trade values at constant prices when used as deflators.[2] Secondly, the use of current weights means that the figures intended to measure changes in price are also picking up the effect of changes in the composition of trade, which may themselves be an element in competition independent of price.

Our indices of 'export unit values' in dollar terms are shown in table

---

[1]   Maizels, *Industrial Growth and World Trade*, pp. 203–6.
[2]   See appendix D for some illustrations of the effect of using different weighting systems, as well as for a description of the construction of the series used in this chapter.

Table 4.6. *Unit values of exports of manufactures, 1955–71*

	Unit value indices (1963 = 100)				Relative price indices[a]	
	1955	1959	1967	1971	1967	1971
Exports from:						
United States	87	100	107	122	102	103
United Kingdom	88	95	109	119	104	102
Japan	108	111	97	103	92	86
France	95	94	108	119	104	103
Germany	89	92	103	122	98	106
Italy	105	100	102	112	97	97
Belgium-Luxembourg	95	98	109	119	104	104
Netherlands	93	96	105	111	102	100
Canada	99	101	106	121	100	101
Sweden	90	100	105	117	99	98
Switzerland	93	95	108	121	104	108
Average	*92*	*98*	*105*	*117*	..	..

[a] Country export prices (1963 = 100) divided by index of competitors' export prices (1963 = 100) weighted by reference country's commodity pattern of exports.
SOURCE: appendix D.

4.6 linked to Maizels' figures for 1955 and 1959, together with relative prices for 1967 and 1971. Some of the long-term price trends observed by Maizels persisted throughout the 1960s, notably the decline in Japanese relative export prices. The deterioration in American price competitiveness, whose beginning in the 1950s Maizels had noted, accelerated during the 1960s, particularly after 1965. On the other hand, the rise in British relative export prices was arrested by the 1967 devaluation, while the French devaluation in the following year had a similar effect. The biggest change, however, was in Germany's price competitiveness. The long-term downward trend in relative price was easily maintained until the last years of the decade, but the exchange rate changes that culminated in 1971 abruptly reversed this tendency. By 1971, German export prices relative to competitors' prices had risen more than those of any other major industrial country.

Maizels found the smaller industrial economies of Western Europe to be generally and increasingly competitive. Since he wrote their fortunes have been mixed. Italy, the Netherlands and Sweden have maintained or improved their position *vis-à-vis* their competitors. Switzerland has lost ground badly. Belgium-Luxembourg also lost ground in the early and middle 1960s but subsequently stabilised its position.

Maizels used his price data, which spanned the period 1899–1959, to calculate export price elasticities for the major countries; save for

Germany and Japan the calculations produced coefficients that were in the range -1 to -2, though not always significant; the Japanese figure was much higher (-2.7), but the German results were indeterminate, possibly because of defective data.[1] It is difficult to compare these with later calculations because of differences in the particular elasticity concept used, in time periods, in coverage and in degree of aggregation. Maizels' calculations yielded price substitution elasticities measuring the effect of relative price changes on a given country's volume of exports relative to those of its competitors. The most nearly comparable estimates come from two studies by Junz and Rhomberg. In the first they calculated elasticities of different kinds for industrial countries over the period 1956–63. The results varied widely from country to country and from market to market, but they suggest rather larger elasticities than those found by Maizels and markedly larger elasticities in the long run than in the short run. 'With regard to exports of manufactures by industrial countries to industrial markets, the findings of this study suggest that, in a longer-run context, a value for the price elasticity in the range of -3 to -5 may be a more appropriate assumption [than the] -2 often used as a rule of thumb.'[2] Their second study supported this view of the magnitude of the average elasticity for industrial countries, demonstrated the lag in the response of trade to price changes – they found the effect to be at a maximum after three years – and confirmed the view that reactions to 'pure' price changes and changes induced by exchange rate changes do not differ in the long run though the immediate impact on trade may differ.[3] They also pointed out that relative price changes explain a small part of changes in exports (a view confirmed by other studies), but are much more effective in explaining deviations from constant market shares; prices 'explain' around 40 per cent of such deviations averaged over periods of four years.

In view of the somewhat tenuous links between our price series and those used by Maizels, it was not considered appropriate to extend his calculations into the 1960s, while the limited number of observations available and the known deficiencies of the data implied that the results of independent regression analysis for recent years would hardly be worth the effort involved. Nonetheless, a simple comparison of deviations from constant market shares with changes in relative prices gives strong support to the view that prices and competition are intimately linked. For this purpose the competitive residuals of the constant market share analysis in the previous section were expressed as

[1] Maizels, *Industrial Growth and World Trade*, p. 214.
[2] H. B. Junz and R. R. Rhomberg, 'Prices and export performance of industrial countries, 1953–63', *IMF Staff Papers*, vol. 12, July 1965.
[3] H. B. Junz and R. R. Rhomberg, 'Price competitiveness in export trade among industrial countries', *American Economic Review*, vol. 63, May 1973.

a percentage of the potential trade (measured at constant prices) of each country. A rank correlation of these percentages with relative price changes produced statistically significant coefficients of 0.855 for 1963–7 and 0.719 for 1967–71. The matching of prices and performance is greatly improved in both periods by the elimination of two problem countries – Belgium-Luxembourg and Canada in 1963–7 and Germany and Britain in 1967–71. This done, the rank correlation coefficients rise to 0.933 and 0.979 respectively, both significant at the 1 per cent level.

It is not surprising that Canada was out of line in 1963–7 because of the overwhelming influence of the Automotive Agreement on its exports, while Belgian exports were benefiting from structural changes that are discussed below, so that both countries put up a better showing in trade than the movement of relative prices would suggest. That Germany did better, Britain worse than might be expected from relative price changes during the period 1967–71 is harder to explain, but may follow from differences in demand elasticities for different commodities. It is reasonable to suppose that standardised products have a higher elasticity than more complex products where design and performance are more important to the purchaser and where there is a longer time-lag in the response to price changes. Thus a price change for an intermediate product or a fairly standardised finished good would have more impact on trade than a change in the price of sophisticated machinery. German machinery prices soared between 1967 and 1971, but prices of several intermediate groups and of transport equipment did not move too far out of line with those of competitors. In Britain it was machinery prices that fell most, prices of transport equipment fell only slightly and prices of some intermediates rose relatively to changes in competitors' prices.

Price changes, then, explain part, but only part, of the competitive success or failure of industrial exporters from 1963 to 1971. Some of the factors involved in non-price competition – vigorous marketing, prompt delivery, effective after-sales service – are not susceptible to direct measurement, but it is probable that competitiveness in these respects is commonly associated with competitive prices; certainly this is so in the case of Japan. One element in a country's competitiveness, however, could be largely independent of apparent price changes, that is the ability to supply new, high-technology products or, more loosely, the ability to adapt the range of goods offered to the changing pattern of market demand. Maizels himself stressed the 'pervasiveness' of this aspect of competition – 'the development of quite new products, the emergence of which enables a wider range of goods to be offered for export'.[1]

[1] Maizels, *Industrial Growth and World Trade*, p. 217.

Maizels was writing in the context of growth, but subsequently the idea of technological advance or technological leadership was largely used to explain the comparative advantage of the United States in research-intensive industries and in the development of the product-cycle theory of trade. In relation to competition the theory has been used most fully and successfully to explain Japan's performance in export markets. One study attributes 35 per cent of the growth of Japanese exports from 1961 to 1971 to the introduction of 'new products', adopting Kojima's estimate that trade in such items grew by $6.8 billion more than might have been expected from the growth of world demand during the period.[1] Other writers have tended to emphasise the importance of the switch to more capital-intensive products (and sometimes research-intensive products also) in Japan's exports since the 1950s, rather than their 'newness' as such.[2]

Though a switch towards new or more sophisticated products implies a change in the composition of exports, the reverse is not necessarily true. A country can change the structure of its exports by concentrating more resources on products already established for which demand is growing and less on declining industries, or industries whose cost structure is increasingly unsuited to its factor-endowments. Flexibility may be as important as technological advance; ideally the two should be treated as making independent contributions to export performance. Unfortunately it is not possible to test these hypotheses precisely, but there is sufficient evidence to suggest that both flexibility and technological progress were important elements in competition during the 1960s.

Flexibility – the change in a country's export pattern – can be roughly measured by summing all increases, over a given period, in the proportion of exports supplied by particular products or product groups. For present purposes we have summed all increases of 0.1 per cent or more in the share of any four-digit item in the SITC (Standard International Trade Classification) in a country's exports valued at current prices; the change in commodity composition is thus measured at a more detailed level than in the aggregate figures of the constant market share analysis. The resulting totals reflect not only changes arising from a switch to new products and the expansion of successful industries, which is what they are intended to measure, but also statistical quirks such as the reallocation of products from one trade heading to another, the effect of divergent price movements and

---

[1] L. B. Krause and S. Sekiguchi, 'Japan and the world economy' in H. Patrick and H. Rosovsky (eds.), *Asia's New Giant*, Washington (DC), Brookings Institution, 1975.
[2] See, for example, H. Kanamori, *Economic Growth: the Japanese experience since the Meiji era*, Homewood (Ill.), Irwin, 1968.

changes arising from the decline of leading trades rather than the emergence of new ones. The first two defects are probably not of great importance in the present instance, especially as prices for the same product in different countries tend to move in a similar fashion. The third problem could be more serious. If the share of any product in exports falls, the share of all other products must increase and if the declining product is of sufficient importance in trade then there could be significant share increases elsewhere. However, it is to be expected that share increases which are purely the counterpart of the decline of staple industries would, with a diversified industrial structure, be spread over a considerable number of products and so individually be small. Thus the exclusion of increases of less than 0.1 per cent in calculating the indicator limits the risk of getting a false reading.

Table 4.7. *Indicators of flexibility[a] in export composition*

	1963–7	1967–71
Exports from:		
United States	21.9	10.2
United Kingdom	11.0	10.6
Japan	20.1	18.5
France	12.7	12.1
Germany	8.9	8.9
Italy	16.2	12.2
Belgium-Luxembourg	16.4	14.9
Netherlands	16.1	14.0
Canada	33.7	19.4
Sweden	12.1	10.9
Switzerland	8.1	10.5

[a] Calculated by summing all increases of more than 0.1 per cent in the share of each four-digit SITC item in exports at current prices. The larger the indicator the greater the change indicated in the composition of exports.

SOURCES: OECD, *Statistics of Foreign Trade*; United Nations, Statistical Office, *Commodity Trade Statistics*.

The indicators thus calculated, shown in table 4.7, for the most part confirm the association expected between 'competitiveness' and flexibility. Japan and Canada, for example, show a high degree of flexibility. In Japan share increases were spread across a considerable number of products; in Canada, as might be expected, they were concentrated on motor vehicles and components. At the other extreme, Britain, Switzerland and Germany show a relatively inflexible pattern of exports. Belgium-Luxembourg shows a fairly high degree of flexibility, which helps to explain why the negative deviation in its market share was smaller than might have been expected on grounds of price behaviour; conversely, competitive Swedish prices were partially offset by rather low flexibility. There are one or two instances where the pattern breaks down, but it does so seriously only in the United States from 1963 to 1967, where very flexible exports apparently did nothing to improve competitiveness. There are faint indications in the statistics of weakness in staple industries, but share increases were unusually concentrated and were moreover principally in 'growth' products, especially motor vehicles (like Canada because of the Automotive Agreement) and aircraft. On the other hand, it appears that in many growth industries United States performance was poor and that it lost ground by failing to develop trade on a wider front in 'new' products with a mass market.

For the purpose of analysing the contribution of 'new' and growth products to trade more precisely than was possible on the broad classification adopted by Maizels, a new classification based on four-digit SITC categories was devised, which started from the contribution made to the growth of a given country's exports rather than the growth of world exports. For any country, those commodities whose share in exports increased over the period 1963 to 1971 necessarily contributed more to the growth of its exports than those whose share diminished, so that the initial selection of commodities was made on this criterion. In order to limit the number of commodities involved and to exclude fast-growing commodities whose contribution to world exports in absolute value is minimal, the items in our selected groups include only those whose share in the exports of any one country rose by not less than 0.3 per cent. The items thus chosen were divided into five categories:

(1) General growth products, where the share in world trade and in the trade of a majority of the eleven exporters (excluding countries with less than 1 per cent of world exports in 1971) is increasing. This covers a great variety of products including certain types of steel and machinery and such unexpected items as 'non-knit outerwear' and furniture, but it is dominated by three products or product groups: cars, including engines, and commercial vehicles; synthetics, including not only organic chemicals and plastics but textiles; and computers and similar products. These three together accounted for over 27 per cent of the increase in world exports from 1963 to 1971; other Group 1 products supplied 19 per cent.

(2) Specialist growth products are distinguished from those in Group 1 by the fact that their share of trade is increasing only in a minority of exporting countries. They supplied a small part of the increase in world exports from 1963 to 1971, something over 2 per cent.

Table 4.8. *Indicators of performance by product groups,[a] 1971*

Ratios

	Group[b]					Total
	1	2	3	4	5	
Exports from:						
United States	0.82	0.84	1.26	0.66	0.77	0.81
United Kingdom	0.59	0.90	0.61	0.84	0.78	0.70
Japan	2.35	1.22	1.74	2.12	1.34	1.77
France	0.95	0.84	0.87	1.04	1.04	0.98
Germany	0.87	1.00	0.86	1.07	1.11	0.97
Italy	1.02	1.10	1.23	1.76	1.17	1.17
Belgium-Luxembourg	1.42	1.13	0.33	1.01	0.99	1.07
Netherlands	1.17	1.08	0.67	1.22	1.17	1.11
Canada	4.54	0.70	0.93	0.95	0.94	1.55
Sweden	0.89	1.46	0.62	1.40	1.11	0.96
Switzerland	0.77	1.04	0.93	1.01	1.02	0.94

[a] Ratios of actual to hypothetical trade; hypothetical trade is calculated on the assumption that exports by each country in each product group grew at the same rate as 'world' exports in that group from 1963 to 1971. A performance indicator less than unity shows that a country's exports grew less rapidly than 'world' exports, an indicator greater than unity that they grew more rapidly.
[b] Groups 1, 2 and 3 are growth products (1 = general, 2 = specialist, 3 = single-country); group 4 = competitive shift; group 5 = other. For detailed definitions see text.
SOURCE: as table 4.7.

(3) Single-country growth products are those where a commodity's share in world trade is increasing but the gains accrue to one country; for other suppliers as a group the growth of exports is below the world average for manufactures. Aircraft and ships each accounted for about one third of the total increase in this group, equivalent to 9 per cent of the growth of world trade. Other items are such specialities as Italian footwear and Japanese motor cycles.

(4) In this group, which is designated competitive shift, the share of individual commodities in world exports has fallen, but their share in the exports of some countries has nevertheless risen significantly. It includes some chemicals, steel and a fair range of machinery, as well as some miscellaneous items; it accounted for 15 per cent of world export growth.

(5) All other products are allocated to this residual group.[1]

For each of the groups performance indicators by country were calculated by dividing actual exports in 1971 by hypothetical exports, that is what exports would have been had they grown at the average rate of world exports in the group. The results are shown in table 4.8.

[1] For a cross-classification of trade according to Maizels' ten commodity classes and the five groups specified above, see appendix B.

They demonstrate that, while the United States was fully competitive in single-country growth products (Group 3), it performed poorly in all other groups, particularly in 'competitive shift' products (Group 4), where it bore the brunt of Japan's competitive challenge. (In fact, United States leadership in terms of trade performance was even more circumscribed than the Group 3 indicator suggests; the indicator exceeds unity because, and only because, of the export performance of the aircraft industry.) Clearly technological leadership in a narrow range of specialised products is an inadequate foundation for successful competition in international trade.

As is to be expected the United Kingdom had an even worse record than the United States, with ratios below unity in every group, but its weakness was most apparent in the growth-product groups. In single-country growth products (Group 3) it could not withstand American competition in the aero-industry (though its performance was better here than in most others), nor Japanese competition in shipbuilding. It was not, of course, alone in this. But equally, and in this unlike the Italians or the French, there was no other single-country growth product in which it achieved a highly successful performance. Although British exporters put up their most dismal performance in Group 1, there was a marked discrepancy in the behaviour of the three leading industries – motors, synthetics and computers – and the remainder. The average performance indicator for the first three was 0.50, for the rest 0.77.

The United Kingdom was not alone in putting up a worse performance in the three leading growth industries than in other Group 1 products. Germany, France and Italy likewise did worse in these three industries, even though their performance was very much better than Britain's. For the most part the loss of share followed from their inability to withstand Japanese competition – Japan's performance indicator for the three industries was 3.25 – though the figures are also influenced by Canadian gains, thanks to the Automotive Agreement, in motor vehicle exports, which account for the very high Canadian performance indicator in Group 1. The two other EEC countries, however, both achieved high performance in the major growth industries – the Netherlands because of the development of synthetic chemicals and textiles, Belgium-Luxembourg because of the growth of motor vehicle assembly as well. They owed their success jointly to new technology, new raw material supplies, and excellent communications and foreign capital which combined to create new export industries.

Japan's success in Group 1 has already been mentioned. In Group 3, its performance rested on shipbuilding and motor cycle manufacture – losers for other countries but winners for it – and in Group 4 principally on a range of machinery and on iron and steel. Italy, too, owed its success in 'competitive shift' products to these groups, though the importance of machinery was much greater.

Apart from the United States and the United Kingdom (and Canada which is as always a special case because of the effect of the Automotive Agreement) no country had a performance indicator less than unity in both Groups 4 and 5; they were all at least reasonably competitive in non-growth products. Their average ranking was determined by their performance in growth industries covered by Groups 1, 2 and 3. Those countries with average performance indicators less than unity – Germany, France, Sweden and Switzerland – also had indicators below unity in at least two out of the three groups, while those with average indicators above unity had at least two out of the three above unity. A high or low proportion of exports in growth products, broadly defined, at the beginning of the period (or indeed at the end) was not necessarily associated either with good or bad trade performance overall, or with competitive success in these sectors of trade. On the other hand, no country that lost ground in the market for growth products managed to maintain or increase its share of the world market for manufactures as a whole and, with few exceptions, the competitive gain or loss in exports of growth products exceeded that in other goods.

TARIFF REDUCTIONS AND IMPORT PENETRATION

We turn now to consider the increase in the ratio of imports to total supplies of manufactures in industrial countries. It had begun to rise in the late 1950s, towards the close of the period surveyed by Maizels, in response to import liberalisation. It continued to rise rapidly from 1963 to 1971, particularly after 1967 and particularly in four of the larger industrial countries – the United States, Britain, Germany and France.[1] In most countries a small but potentially significant part of this increase was due to imports of manufactures from outside the group of eleven industrial countries. Table 4.9 compares indices of the volume of total imports of manufactures, based on actual imports, and of the volume of imports from other industrial countries, based on the exports of industrial countries to the import market in question. Save in the United States and the Netherlands these figures suggest that imports from the non-industrial areas rose faster than imports from the industrial areas between 1963 and 1971. Because of the different basis of the two sets of indices, not too much weight should be put on small differences in the rate of growth. Nonetheless, there is discernible a shift in the locus of production and in competitive strength that has

---

[1] See chapter 1, p. 6 above.

Table 4.9. *Imports of manufactures into the industrial countries, 1967 and 1971*

Volume indices, 1963 = 100

	Total imports[a]		Imports from industrial countries[b]	
	1967	1971	1967	1971
Imports into:				
United States	189	338	194	339
United Kingdom	168	234	152	224
Japan	181	278	154	240
France	164	281	162	268
Germany	145	316	139	289
Italy	115	188	106	173
Belgium-Luxembourg	144	249	145	248
Netherlands	143	236	147	239
Canada	175	248	168	225
Sweden	140	193	108	142
Switzerland	130	216	123	200

[a] Calculated from import data.
[b] Calculated from data on exports by the industrial countries to other industrial countries.
SOURCES: appendix A; appendix table C.3.

influenced trade patterns. But by far the greater part of the rise in industrial countries' import ratios followed from the more than proportionate increase in imports from industrial countries relative to the growth of total supplies of manufactures. Here too the locus of production was shifting to economies with high rates of output growth and, initially at least, low labour costs, primarily of course to Japan.

Table 4.10 shows the 'additional' imports (from both industrial and other countries) attributable to rising import ratios as a percentage of hypothetical imports, the latter being calculated on the assumption that the ratio of imports to supplies of manufactures remained constant in real terms from 1963 to 1971. This assumption is obviously unrealistic, since import ratios, even in a highly stable trading situation, fluctuate from year to year in response to the level of world economic activity and other short-term influences. Moreover, some of the increase in import ratios deriving from liberalisation in the 1950s may have occurred *after* 1963. But the figures serve to indicate the general order of magnitude of the additional trade arising from import penetration. For most of the smaller industrial countries the increase ranges from around 20 to 40 per cent over hypothetical imports by 1971, with Italy and Sweden recording smaller rises. For the larger countries apart from Japan, the increase ranges from 60 to 132 per cent. In the last two columns of table 4.10 the percentages are related to actual imports from the industrial

Table 4.10. *'Additional' imports due to rising import ratios*

	Excess/ hypothetical imports		'Additional' from industrial countries	
	1967	1971	1967	1971
	(percentages)		(1963 $ billion)	
Imports into:				
United States	44	132	4.1	12.7
United Kingdom	46	81	1.0	2.6
Japan	9	5	−0.2	−0.3
France	26	60	1.2	3.4
Germany	21	83	0.9	5.4
Italy	−9	16	−0.7	0.4
Belgium-Luxembourg	13	36	0.5	1.8
Netherlands	9	23	0.5	1.6
Canada	24	42	1.1	2.0
Sweden	5	12	−0.5	−0.6
Switzerland	10	36	0.1	0.9

Note: Hypothetical imports were calculated on the assumption that the ratio of manufactured imports to supplies (as defined in chap. 3, p. 33, where the calculations are at 1955 prices) remained constant at the 1963 level in 1967 and 1971. 'Additional' imports are actual imports less hypothetical imports.

countries (as measured by exports from the industrial countries to other industrial countries) to give some idea of the amount of trade involved. To the extent that the growth of imports from non-industrial countries exceeded the growth of imports from industrial countries, or vice versa, these figures overestimate, or underestimate, the effect of rising import ratios on purchases from industrial countries.

Two further comments should be made on the figures in table 4.10. First, although the rate of import penetration generally increased after 1967, this does not necessarily imply that the increase was induced by events occurring after 1967. The rate of response to changing circumstances can vary widely and, as noted already, is susceptible to short-term influences. Secondly, and more importantly, a rising import ratio is in part a mirror image of declining competitiveness in world export markets and is a direct consequence of the developments discussed in relation to exports in the previous section. That the United States, Britain and Germany all purchased large 'additional' imports, while Japan did not, follows from the same competitiveness or lack of it in prices and products that influenced their relative performance in export markets. It is against this background that the effect of tariff reductions must be considered.

Almost all the major tariff-cutting exercises of the postwar years fall within the period under review or immediately preceding it, including the Dillon and Kennedy Rounds, the formation of the original EEC and EFTA, and the Canadian–United States Automotive Agreement. Only the effects on trade of the EEC, and to some extent EFTA, have been extensively studied and, although it is fairly widely accepted that both induced trade creation in manufactures and that trade creation exceeded diversion, there is little agreement as to the size of the effect.

The earliest studies of the EEC relating to trade in the early 1960s failed, not surprisingly, to pick up any significant integration effects. By 1962 the measurable effects on trade were still fairly small, but thereafter they rose rapidly. A most convenient summary description of the methods employed and the results achieved, together with their own estimates of the integration effect, has been published by Williamson and Bottrill;[1] a similar summary covering later estimates has been published by Balassa.[2] In table 4.11 we reproduce estimates, derived from studies relating to the effects of integration in 1967 and subsequent years, of the ratio of trade creation (that is 'additional' imports) to hypothetical trade in a non-integrated world, together with some indication of the methods employed in making them. The results range from 5 to 60 per cent of hypothetical trade, with the median estimate in the neighbourhood of 30 per cent of EEC countries' imports of manufactures.

The range of effects tabulated is large principally because of differences in the period chosen as the basis for calculation and differences in methods of estimation implying different views of the effect of tariff reductions. Most of the authors attempt to estimate hypothetical trade by projecting past experience into the future, taking as their starting point the ratio of imports to consumption. Similar approaches are based on the share of EEC intra-trade in total imports or on changes in income elasticities. Where small trade flows and one major institutional change are concerned such a method may give reasonably reliable results, but where the entire foreign trade of a country is powerfully influenced by various institutional changes (and, through trade, the entire economy) the results vary from the doubtful to the seriously misleading. It is unfortunate that many of the studies listed in table 4.11 project the trading experience of the 1950s into the 1960s when calculating hypothetical trade, without analysing the influences underlying that experience. The 1950s were, after all, a period of extensive trade liberalisation for all the countries concerned, which

[1] J. Williamson and A. Bottrill, 'The impact of customs unions on trade in manufactures', *Oxford Economic Papers*, vol. 23 (new series), November 1971.
[2] B. Balassa, 'Trade creation and diversion in the European Common Market' in B. Balassa (ed.), *European Economic Integration*, Amsterdam, North-Holland, 1975.

Table 4.11. *Estimates of trade creation in manufactured goods in the EEC Six*

Author	Year	Base or estimation period	Method	'Additional'/ hypothetical trade (%)
(1) EFTA	1967	1954–9	Actual share of imports in consumption less shares derived from projected trend	8
(2) Major & Hays/Truman	1968	1960	Actual share of imports in consumption less base-period shares	60
(3) Truman	1968		Actual share of imports in consumption:	
		(a) 1960	(a) less base-period shares	35
		(b) 1953–60	(b) less predicted shares[a]	8
(4) Resnick & Truman	1968	1953–68	Actual imports less imports predicted from import function	5
(5) Verdoorn & Schwartz	1969	1956–69	Actual imports less imports predicted from cross-section import function:	
			(a) without separate tariff variable	14
			(b) with separate tariff variable	41
(6) Williamson & Bottrill	1969	1954–69	Actual less predicted EEC share in imports[b]	35–42[c]
(7) Kreinin	1969–70	1959/60– 1969/70	Actual share of imports in consumption less share predicted by:	
			(a) analogy with changes in US share	15
			(b) applying assumed income elasticity to actual growth in GNP	21
(8) Prewo	1970	1959	Actual share of imports in consumption less base-period share[d]	52
(9) Balassa	1970	1953–9	Increase in imports attributable to post-integration rise in income elasticity of imports	27

[a] Shares were predicted by reference to a time trend and to the pressure of domestic demand.
[b] Predicted EEC share of imports was estimated by reference to performance in third markets; trade creation was assumed to bear a fixed relation to the increase in share.
[c] This was the preferred estimate; an alternative estimate gave a range of 40–48 per cent.
[d] Calculations were made in an input–output framework.
SOURCES: (1) EFTA, *The Trade Effects of EFTA and the EEC 1959–67*, Geneva, 1972; (2) and (6) Williamson and Bottrill, 'The impact of customs unions on trade in manufactures'; (3), (4), (8) and (9) Balassa, *European Economic Integration*; (5) P. J. Verdoorn and A. N. R. Schwartz, 'Two alternative estimates of the effects of EEC and EFTA on the pattern of trade', *European Economic Review*, vol. 3, October 1972; (7) M. E. Kreinin, 'Effects of the EEC on imports of manufactures', *Economic Journal*, vol. 82, September 1972.

certainly stepped up the rate of growth both of total imports and of intra-European trade. To assume that trade would have grown as fast in the 1960s without further reductions in trade barriers gives too high a figure for hypothetical trade and hence an underestimate of the effects of integration. The EFTA study is clearly biased in this fashion; so too probably is the second Truman study. On the other hand, estimates that assume there would have been no increase in the ratio of imports to consumption during the 1960s in a non-integrated world, such as those by Major and Hays or Truman and Prewo, are probably biased upwards, as are those (the majority) which ignore the effects on imports of the Dillon and Kennedy Rounds or other tariff changes.[1]

Calculations based on regression analysis of time-series are made under more severe constraints. They still rely on experience in determining 'normal' behaviour in a non-integrated world, but experience is treated more analytically. However, in most cases such calculations assume that reactions to tariff changes are identical in character to reactions to other changes in relative import prices and that the price elasticity of imports is therefore an adequate tool to measure the effects of integration on trade. A case can be made out for this view, especially if one is prepared to ignore the problem of determining what caused the increase in import ratios if it was not primarily caused by reduced protection, but a theoretical case that is at least equally strong can be made out for the opposing view – that responses to tariff changes differ from responses to price cuts because traders and producers see them as permanent, because they are well publicised and because they usually involve the reduction or abolition of near-prohibitive duties to which imports react very sharply.[2] In support of this view there are the results of the analyses based on import shares referred to in table 4.11 and the Verdoorn–Schwartz findings. Their regressions without a 'prohibitive tariff variable' show a relatively small trade creation effect for the EEC, but with it they conform reasonably closely to the results of independent calculations based on a shares approach.

It is generally accepted that integration helped to encourage the phenomenon of intra-industry as opposed to inter-industry specialisation in production and trade. The former entails the exchange between countries of products of the same industry, the latter of products of

---

[1] It should be noted that in R. L. Major and S. Hays, 'Another look at the Common Market', *National Institute Economic Review*, no. 54, November 1970, the rise in the import ratio is *not* attributed to the creation of the EEC. Williamson and Bottrill used its data to update an earlier estimate by Truman.

[2] For an extended discussion of this view see A. D. Morgan, 'Tariff reductions and UK imports of manufactures: 1955–1971', *National Institute Economic Review*, no. 72, May 1975. Balassa, in the article mentioned above, also stresses the promotional effect of tariff cuts.

different industries. When the EEC was established it was easier for existing firms to adapt and develop their existing product range in order to exploit the new trading arrangements rather than to launch into the manufacture of entirely new products in the light of *national* comparative advantage, which might have given rise to inter-industry specialisation. Firms were in fact trading on their own accumulated advantage in the production of differentiated goods. Other things being equal, intra-industry trade entails a higher ratio of imports to output than inter-industry trade. The exchange of Renaults as well as French perfumes for Volkswagens as well as specialised German optical equipment will lead to more trade both ways than if France exports perfume but not cars to Germany and Germany only optical equipment to France. This effect would be captured by studies based on changes in import ratios, import market shares or income elasticities, but not by those based exclusively on price elasticities.

So it may be accepted, if with reservations, that trade creation in the EEC Six was on average of the order of 25 to 35 per cent of hypothetical trade and that integration was a major influence on import growth. Equally, of course, it was of major importance for exports, with trade diversion as well as trade creation promoting an abnormal rise in the exports of EEC countries to the rest of the Community, as our earlier constant market share analysis of exports suggested. The effect on the trade of individual states varied widely because of differences in pre-integration tariffs, in costs and in the size of their economies. The Benelux countries, too small to supply the full range of goods required by a modern industrialised economy, were fairly specialised in production and had been less heavily protected throughout the postwar years than other members, so that trade creation arising from the removal of tariffs was less proportionately than in the other member countries. France and Germany were able, with protection, to behave like large economies and develop a wider range of industries, so that import ratios were artificially reduced to a much greater extent. With protection reduced, import ratios rose more sharply to a 'normal' level.

Studies of the 'EFTA effect' made by various methods uniformly show a relatively smaller amount of trade created than in the EEC, though the total effect was sometimes found to be larger because of greater trade diversion. Williamson and Bottrill estimate trade creation at about 25 per cent of hypothetical trade in the late 1960s for EFTA as a whole. Much smaller figures were found by Truman, the EFTA secretariat and, more surprisingly, by Verdoorn and Schwartz, who put trade creation at less than 5 per cent of hypothetical trade. A lowish average figure for trade creation, though not as low as 5 per cent, is consistent with the behaviour of Swedish imports – Sweden was one of the most open markets in Europe prior to the formation of EFTA – and also with that of Swiss imports if the deterioration in Swiss price competitiveness in the late 1960s is taken into account. Nor does the big rise in the United Kingdom's import ratio imply a larger average EFTA effect, for it is clear that there were other influences at work tending to increase the ratio, while the scope for trade creation was restricted by the relatively small share of other EFTA countries in United Kingdom imports and their limited capacity to supply additional goods. An average figure of perhaps 10 to 15 per cent additional imports as a result of trade creation in EFTA may be a plausible estimate.

On the other side of the Atlantic there appears to have been significant trade creation arising from regional free trade in the context of the Canadian–United States Automotive Agreement. The effects here were particularly interesting because they show so clearly the reaction of multinational enterprises to the opportunities created by free trade. If it is assumed that, in the absence of the Agreement, Canadian and United States imports from each other would have grown at a similar rate to their imports from the rest of the world, then Canadian imports of motor vehicles and related products were some $0.9 billion and United States imports some $1.4 billion higher in 1967 than they would otherwise have been. (With little change in prices between 1963 and 1967 the figures differ little in current and constant values.) On similar assumptions, United States affiliates in the transport equipment industry in Canada raised their export sales to the United States by almost the same amount. The figures are not precisely comparable because of differences in coverage and valuation, but the near coincidence of the two is impressive. If these estimates are accepted, then the Automotive Agreement accounted for almost two thirds of 'additional' Canadian imports in 1967 and around 30 per cent of 'additional' United States imports. In fact these estimates do not cover all the trade in automotive parts falling under the Agreement and it may have boosted trade even more. An econometric study of its effects put the increase in Canadian imports in the region of $1.4 billion by 1967, which would account for the whole of the rise in the import ratio since 1963, while the rise in United States imports was estimated at around $1.7 billion, approaching 40 per cent of additional United States imports.[1]

Import ratios were also affected during the period 1963–7 by the Dillon Round of tariff reductions. In Europe its influence was probably small, and anyway not readily distinguished from EEC and EFTA

[1] Canada, Economic Council, *An Econometric Analysis of the Canada, United States Automotive Agreement* by D. A. Wilton, Ottawa, 1976.

effects on trade; in the United States it may have been quite pronounced. Examining the effect of earlier tariff reductions on a sample of United States imports of manufactures excluding resource-oriented products, Krause found that the long-run tariff elasticity of the ratio of imports to domestic shipments was about three times the size of the comparable import price elasticity; he concluded that 'large tariff changes applicable "across the board" ... do seem to cause large relative changes in the import ratios', even allowing for the fact that the method he employed could not take into account the effect of reductions in prohibitive tariffs.[1] Assuming that the tariff elasticity for all manufactures was close to that for the products in Krause's sample, the Dillon Round cuts could have contributed 10 to 15 per cent of 'additional' United States imports.

By 1967–71 formal tariff-cutting programmes in the EEC and EFTA had been completed, though their effects were still working through into trade. Meanwhile the Kennedy Round gave a further boost to import ratios. In terms of proportionate tariff reductions and products affected, the changes in all the major participating countries were very similar; the average duty on manufactures was reduced by about 35 per cent of its base level over a period of four years, with the biggest cuts, 50 per cent of the base level, falling on machinery and vehicles. Very high rates (many of them probably prohibitive or near-prohibitive) were largely eliminated, so that the dispersion of tariff rates in all participating countries was reduced. It is estimated that the proportion of non-agricultural products other than mineral fuels attracting tariffs of 15 per cent or less rose in the United States from 53.6 per cent of four-digit product groups to 85.2 per cent, in the United Kingdom from 37.7 per cent to 84.7 per cent and in the EEC from 71.5 per cent to 96.6 per cent.[2] Before the Kennedy Round both the United States and the United Kingdom had had a fair proportion – 7 per cent or more – of very high rates which almost wholly disappeared. If tariff elasticities were similar across countries the effect on import ratios would likewise have been similar, though more pronounced in the United States and the United Kingdom than in the EEC because there were more high and very high tariffs to be reduced.

However, the magnitude of the effect must have been greatly influenced by the openness of the economy prior to the Kennedy Round, and also by the persistence of widespread non-tariff barriers thereafter, which helps to explain why the Japanese import ratio reacted so little to cuts in import duties. Before the Kennedy Round cuts were agreed, the EEC countries had already abolished tariffs on

---

[1] L. B. Krause, 'United States imports, 1947–1958', *Econometrica*, vol. 30, April 1962.
[2] E. H. Preeg, *Traders and Diplomats*, Washington (DC), Brookings Institution, 1970.

imports from many of their main competitors. Hence only part of their trade was directly affected by the Kennedy Round, limiting the scope for trade creation following the cuts. (The Kennedy Round may have offset some of the trade-diverting effects of integration, but this would not have raised the import ratio; it would merely have affected the source of imports.) The same is true of the three EFTA members – the United Kingdom, Sweden and Switzerland – though to a much more limited extent. In the United States in contrast, by far the greater part of its imports of manufactures from other industrial countries attracted tariff reductions and the effect on the import ratio was therefore correspondingly greater.

Unfortunately, no reliable general estimates of the effects of the Kennedy Round on imports into the industrial countries have been made. Those that are available rely solely on price elasticities and the results are implausibly small. If it is accepted that the effect of tariff cutting in the EEC and EFTA was greater than the 'pure' price effect on imports, then a similar reaction must be allowed for in response to the Kennedy Round.

Calculations by the present author of the effect on imports of manufactures of tariff reductions in the United Kingdom during the period 1959–72, using dummy variables to capture the 'tariff' as opposed to the 'price' reaction, suggest that altogether they led to an increase in imports of 32 per cent over and above the level of trade had tariffs not been reduced, of which the Dillon Round accounted for 3 per cent, the EFTA cuts for 13 per cent and the Kennedy Round for 16 per cent.[1] The British reaction to the Kennedy Round tariff cuts was probably larger than that of other European countries because of the higher tariff, so an additional 15 per cent of imports might be taken as the upper limit of their response, with the likelihood being that it was somewhat below this figure. In the United States however, the rise in imports could have been several times larger, not only because it affected *all* imports of manufactures but also because, judging by the reaction to earlier tariff-cutting exercises, the United States 'tariff elasticity' was much larger than in Europe.

If these rather rough and ready estimates of the effects of various tariff cuts are added together, they explain for all except three (or perhaps four) countries most of the increase in the import ratio between 1963 and 1971. Any unexplained residual is usually commensurate with the change in their price competitiveness indicated by the change in their relative export prices. Thus, for example, 'additional' Belgian imports between 1963 and 1971 were equivalent to 36 per cent of hypothetical

---

[1] A. D. Morgan, 'Commercial policy' in F. T. Blackaby (ed.), *British Economic Policy 1960–74*, Cambridge University Press, 1978.

trade, additional Dutch imports to 22 per cent. The combined effect of EEC integration and the Dillon and Kennedy Rounds was to add between 25 and 30 per cent to hypothetical imports. Belgian relative prices rose, taking its imports up further; Dutch prices were stable or falling, so reducing the rise in imports. Similarly, rising relative prices help to explain excess French, Swiss and Canadian imports, and falling prices the estimated shortfall in Japanese, Swedish and perhaps Italian imports. But the shift in relative prices cannot alone explain the rise in the import ratio over and above the rise induced by tariff reductions in the United States, the United Kingdom and Germany unless the extent of their reaction to tariff changes has been seriously underestimated in all the studies previously referred to. Between a third and a half of their 'additional' imports remains unaccounted for.

Tariff reductions, then, were one of the most important influences on trade during the period. Cuts in duties came at a time when firms were growing, transport costs were falling relatively and incomes were rising rapidly, so that producers were increasingly able to exploit the new conditions to sell new and differentiated products to a growing mass market, thereby raising the proportion of intra-industry trade. In one instance certainly, and almost as certainly in others, these opportunities were most fully exploited by multinational enterprises.

THE ROLE OF MULTINATIONAL ENTERPRISES

When Maizels wrote *Industrial Growth and World Trade* he did not find it necessary to examine the activities of multinational enterprises; it is indicative of their changing role in the world economy that it should be necessary to do so now. Any assessment of the change and its consequences must, however, be qualified and tentative, for there are formidable difficulties, both practical and conceptual, in judging the influence of multinationals on world trade. For a start, data on true multinational enterprises – firms with facilities scattered across a number of countries, that organise their production as well as their sales in an international framework – are indistinguishable from the (highly imperfect) data published on all enterprises with foreign ownership. Most quantitative estimates of the growth and importance of multinationals rest, explicitly or implicitly, on the assumption that their development exhibits the same broad trends. It is true that the activities of both the wider and the narrower group have, over the last fifteen to twenty years, tended to be concentrated increasingly on industrial, more particularly West European, countries and on manufacturing, but how far other developments are similar is largely a matter of guesswork.

For example, it is widely believed that the business of multinationals is growing more rapidly than that of other firms and the fact that sales by American owned enterprises abroad have increased more rapidly than world GDP is quoted in support. Thereafter it is, all too often, a short step to a picture of world output and trade increasingly dominated by multinationals. For those who argue that such enterprises are an efficient means of transferring technology or improving the international division of labour this is a desirable outcome and, incidentally, promotes trade. For those who view them as enterprises so large and diverse that they can escape the web of government control (and unscrupulous to boot) the outcome is the very reverse; whether trade is promoted or not is largely irrelevant. However, the critics of the multinationals have also on occasion called on the pure theory of international trade to argue that since, in an abstract world, factor movements are a substitute for commodity movements, foreign investment and hence the multinationals reduce world trade.

To make a dependable estimate of the influence of multinationals on world trade it would be necessary to answer three questions: Does their overseas production replace trade or induce additional trade? What is their share of world output and exports and is it growing or diminishing? Do their trading activities distort trading conditions and reduce competition? To none of these questions, unfortunately, is it possible to give a precise answer.

How the growth of multinationals' activities is judged to influence world trade in manufactures depends critically on the assumptions made about what would have happened had they not increased their investment, as Hufbauer and Adler pointed out.[1] On what they designate 'classical' assumptions, foreign investment is made at the expense of domestic (home country) investment and adds to foreign (host) country investment. Production there replaces imports into the host country; international trade is reduced. On 'reverse classical' assumptions foreign investment neither reduces domestic investment nor increases host country investment, for if the foreigner does not invest the local entrepreneur in the host country will do so; import replacement is no greater in one case than the other provided it is assumed that new production in the host country always replaces imports rather than local output. On both sets of assumptions there is an offset to import replacement resulting from foreign investment in the shape of additional imports of capital goods, parts and components and 'associated exports' – that is imports of finished products produced by the investor in his home country but not in the host country. Hufbauer and Adler estimated that it would not be as large as import replacement on

[1] United States Treasury, *Overseas Manufacturing Investment and the Balance of Payments* by G. C. Hufbauer and F. M. Adler, Washington (DC), US Government Printing Office, 1968.

'classical' assumptions, while it would add to trade on 'reverse classical' assumptions, when foreign investment would normally increase international trade.[1]

Table 4.12. *Estimates of effects on trade of $1 of direct investment in American controlled manufacturing subsidiaries*

US cents

	On 'classical' assumptions[a]		On 'reverse classical' assumptions[a]	
	After 1 yr	After 10 yrs	After 1 yr	After 10 yrs
Canada	−59.6	−94.1	+2.5	+3.9
Western Europe	−6.5	−10.3	+7.8	+12.6
Latin America	−18.1	−30.2	+4.6	+7.7
Rest of world	−65.2	−147.5	−19.5	−44.3

[a] For details see text, p. 77.

SOURCE: United States Treasury, *Overseas Manufacturing Investment and the Balance of Payments* by Hufbauer and Adler.

When it came to calculating results, Hufbauer and Adler distinguished four host areas: Canada, Western Europe, Latin America and the rest of the world. The effects of foreign investment on trade vary not only according to the assumptions as to alternative developments, but also according to the area of investment because of varying import propensities, as the summary of their findings in table 4.12 shows. These figures indicate the possible order of magnitude of the trade effects of foreign investment in the early 1960s. They cannot, of course, be used to calculate the effects of foreign investment as such, for they relate only to American experience and are heavily influenced by the propensity of the host areas to import from the United States.[2] The assumption that the output of enterprises owned abroad replaces imports rather than local production is also critically important. Hufbauer and Adler have, indeed, been criticised for the narrowness of their assumptions and for ignoring secondary effects on incomes, productivity and prices in the economy as a whole. But if one takes a wider view, it simply extends the range of possible effects, generally in the direction of greater trade promotion, without increasing their reliability.

Though Hufbauer and Adler did not commit themselves to any single

[1] Estimates were also made on 'anti-classical' assumptions – that world investment increases, since investment in the host country is increased without any reduction in domestic investment. The direct effects on trade as calculated were identical to the effects on 'classical' assumptions; the results differ only for secondary (trade propensity and multiplier) effects.

[2] For an alternative estimate see W. B. Reddaway *et al.*, *Effects of UK Direct Investment Overseas: final report*, Cambridge University Press, 1968.

set of assumptions, they concluded that if United States investment overseas were curtailed, native firms in industrial countries would soon take advantage of the opportunities available, though a similar reaction was not to be expected in developing countries. Later American studies, such as the Tariff Commission report,[1] were less cautious and asserted that foreign manufacturing produced a net increase in United States exports. More recently, however, Glejser has estimated that, over the period 1953 to 1971, direct foreign investment in overseas manu-facturing facilities caused a fall of $6.3 billion in United States exports.[2] This estimate was based on a correlation between American owned capital stock and United States exports to selected host countries which, it should be noted, was positive in some cases, but strongly negative for Canada and Germany. But unless it can be shown that total imports into the market fell because of United States investment, this connection may simply reflect the inability of certain American industries to compete in that market – an inability that was a contributory factor in the decision to invest in order to maintain United States exports or at least to prevent them falling further. The evidence is insufficient to support a firm conclusion either way and in default of further empirical investigation there are strong grounds for assuming that native investors in industrial countries would have established production facilities if there had been no foreign investment.

Empirical studies tend of necessity to analyse the problem in terms of measurable variables such as capital stocks and flows. Yet it is increasingly clear that what is involved in 'foreign investment' in manufacturing is the transfer of firm-specific skills, especially techno-logical and marketing, rather than capital as such. Indeed capital transfers are only one element, and not by any means an essential element, in 'foreign direct investment' by multinational enterprises; much investment has in fact been financed by foreign borrowing and by reinvesting overseas earnings. Multinationals and their subsidiaries are not the only vehicle of technological transfers, as the Japanese experience abundantly demonstrates, but outside Japan they have been a very important (probably the most important) agent of such transfers. (It may be argued that they have only speeded up an inevitable process, but whether or not that is so is not relevant in the present context.) Secondly, it is apparent that the objectives of the investing firms will profoundly affect their influence on trade. The models reviewed above

---

[1] United States Senate, Committee on Finance, *Implications of Multinational Firms for World Trade and Investment and for U.S. Trade and Labor*, Washington (DC), US Government Printing Office, 1973.
[2] H. Glejser, 'The respective impacts of relative income, price and technology changes, US foreign investment, the EEC and EFTA on the American balance of trade' in H. Glejser (ed.), *Quantitative Studies of International Economic Relations*, Amsterdam, North-Holland, 1976.

relate essentially to defensive investment. There are other and increasingly important motives at work, which might be described as cost, regional and logistic. The first of these is probably more important in relation to investment in developing countries, the second and, in the period under review, the third to investment in industrial countries.

Table 4.13 summarises the trade effects of these types of investment, together with (for the sake of completeness) defensive investment and what is described as technical investment – that is in production facilities for bulky or perishable goods not entering into international trade. Secondary effects are again ignored, but it is assumed throughout that:

(a) the foreign entrepreneur uses resources more efficiently than would a domestic entrepreneur;

(b) the foreign entrepreneur purchases a higher proportion of manufactured inputs (capital equipment, parts and materials) outside the host country than would a domestic undertaking and also imports 'associated' finished goods that would not be imported by a native firm.

The first assumption is probably well justified in respect of American owned enterprises, which have almost invariably been found to achieve higher productivity thanks to superior technology and managerial skill than their local rivals, and equally well justified in most cases of investment in the developing countries.[1] It may, however, be invalid in respect of European investment in other European countries. But if the European owned foreign enterprise is to stay in business it must at least use resources as efficiently as local entrepreneurs, while there are major European firms – SKF for example – whose efficiency is certainly greater than that of local competitors. On balance then, the first assumption seems justified in respect of European owned as well as American enterprises. The second assumption is based not only on a fair amount of empirical evidence, but is implicit in the nature of the true multinational enterprise whose management is seeking to maximise sales worldwide and deliberately uses foreign affiliates to extend the range and quality of products traded in different countries.

Foreign investment primarily determined by cost-saving considerations is perhaps best exemplified by United States investment in Taiwan and Mexico, where a firm moves a major part of its operations outside the home country and a return flow of exports is generated from the host country to the home country. The kind of cost-saving investment that entails the relocation of production from country A to country B in order to supply third markets is ignored in the table since it will not affect the volume of trade. A's exports may fall but B's will rise.

[1] There are, however, some notorious instances where United States firms have come a cropper in Europe – for example, Raytheon in Sicily.

Table 4.13. *Effects on international trade of foreign direct investment*

Type of investment	Alternative: no domestic investment	Alternative: domestic investment
Technical	Small increase: associated trade	Negligible effect
Defensive	Reduction: import replacement not offset by associated trade	Small increase: associated trade
Cost-saving	Increase: return flow of exports to investing country and additional associated trade	Small increase: additional associated trade and possibly higher exports owing to greater efficiency
Regional	Uncertain: exports from regional base larger than direct exports but may be offset by net import replacement in host country	Increase: exports from host country by foreign investor larger than exports by domestic investor, and additional associated trade
Logistic	Large increase equivalent to all exports by parent company and affiliates net of direct exports of parent company	Does not apply: logistic investment cannot be domestic by definition

United States investment in the EEC is the best current example of regional investment, as United States investment in the United Kingdom to take advantage of Commonwealth Preference was the outstanding past example. Here the firm invests in production facilities primarily designed to serve a group of markets, rather than a national market. Facilities designed for a national market may, of course, also be used to produce for export, but the very fact that they are designed for a national market is likely to make them less effective promoters of trade. Nor is there any reason why domestic investors should not invest in facilities designed for a regional market, but it appears that they have been less ready to do so than foreign, especially American, enterprises. Most of the evidence on the share of exports in the output of American owned and native firms in Europe shows the former to be more export-oriented. The failure, on the part of several investigators, to find any connection between the creation of the EEC and the amount of American investment in Europe does not affect the issue, since it is the character rather than the amount that matters. One American owned plant in the Netherlands supplying the entire Community will generate more trade than three or four in the different member states, but it does not entail a larger total capital outlay.

Logistic investment is international investment *par excellence* – the location of production facilities each undertaking a different stage of the production process in different countries. The outstanding example of this type of investment is the European operation by International Business Machines, which has certainly contributed a great deal to the phenomenal growth of intra-European trade in computers and associated material. As with regional investment and technological transfer, foreign investment is not a necessary condition for trade of this kind, as demonstrated by Volvo's purchase of British engines for installation in cars then exported to the United Kingdom. (Indeed if foreign investment were a necessary condition of trade in intermediate products, the economist's ideal world in which only primary products and finished goods were traded would approximate to the real world.) The fact remains that the best known and, in terms of trade flows involved, the most important examples of this kind of undertaking are associated with foreign investment. In the end it may prove that logistic investment by multinational enterprises has been more significant as a catalyst than in itself, but in present circumstances it has certainly led to an increase in the volume of international trade.

For the purposes of this analysis, a sharp distinction has been drawn between different types of foreign investment. In practice a firm is likely to be influenced by a mixture of motives. But it is reasonable to conclude that over the past fifteen to twenty years there has been more trade-promoting than trade-reducing investment. Only where a host country is determined to exclude certain foreign products and local entre-preneurs either cannot or will not replace them by domestic production does investment in foreign production facilities unequivocally lead to a reduction in trade. All other types of foreign investment are likely to be neutral in their effects on trade or, more probably, to increase it to a greater or lesser degree. Those that lead to a significant increase in international trade do, however, depend on the special circumstances of the last twenty years – the reduction in tariffs on imports of manufactures into the industrial countries. Without it, neither cost-saving, regional nor logistic investment would have been possible to the same degree and the idea of making such investments might barely have developed.

This having been said, it must be admitted that it is impossible to determine how much of the foreign investment carried out in the period under review is of the trade-promoting kind and how much it has promoted trade. (Nor should it be forgotten that some past defensive investments may, in changed circumstances, have been converted into regional or even logistic undertakings. United States firms dominated the Canadian motor industry long before the Automotive Agreement, but exported little; once the Agreement was in force they became large exporters.) All that can be done is to present such evidence as there is on the scale of investment and the resulting pattern of trade.

Table 4.14 shows the growth and distribution of foreign assets in manufacturing for those investing countries for which reasonably reliable data are available. (It should be borne in mind that the figures,

Table 4.14. *Investment in overseas manufacturing enterprises: estimated book value of assets (investing country data),[a] 1963–71*

$ billion

				Host countries			
		North America	EEC	United Kingdom	Other EFTA	Other	Total
Investments by:							
United States	1963	5.29	2.38	2.59	0.21	3.23	13.70
	1967	7.56	4.73	3.70	0.45	6.09	22.53
	1971	9.94	8.00	5.24	0.82	9.44	33.44
United Kingdom	1963	0.92	0.40	n.a.	0.09	2.11	3.52
	1967	1.13	0.63	n.a.	0.11	2.73	4.60
	1971	1.79	1.32	n.a.	0.19	4.09	7.39
Germany[b]	1963	0.19	0.23	0.02	0.13	0.46	1.03
	1967	0.35	0.70	0.04	0.21	0.70	2.00
	1971	0.75	1.43	0.12	0.48	1.61	4.39
Canada	1963	0.85	..	0.28	..	..	1.52
	1967	1.03	..	0.37	..	..	1.93
	1971	1.39	..	0.43	..	..	2.59
Sweden	1963	0.12	0.24	0.04	0.05	0.09	0.54
	1967	0.16	0.42	0.07	0.09	0.17	0.91
	1971	0.22	0.55	0.09	0.12	0.22	1.20

[a] So far as possible adjusted to exclude investments in food, drink and tobacco industries.
[b] Transaction values excluding reinvested profits.
SOURCES: see appendix E.

though based on official sources, involve some degree of estimation in all cases and that they are not comparable from country to country owing to differences in the definition of assets and in methods of compilation.) For four of the five countries listed, the book value of assets more than doubled between 1963 and 1971 and in the fifth, Canada, they rose by 70 per cent. The rate of increase in asset formation rose between 1963–7 and 1967–71 in the United Kingdom, Germany and Canada; although it fell in the other two countries, Sweden alone showed a smaller absolute addition to assets in the second half of the period. Again in four of the five countries the major part of assets was located in other industrial countries in North America and Europe: the proportions were over 80 per cent for Sweden, over 70 per cent for Canada and the United States and, by 1971, over 60 per cent for Germany. Even for the United Kingdom, where more than half of all assets was located in the rest of the world, the share of industrial countries had risen to 45 per cent by 1971.

New investment – additions to assets – was more concentrated on European industrial countries, primarily the EEC but also the United

Kingdom and the rest of EFTA. Investment in North America by all five countries rose at less than the average rate over the period as a whole, although among the European investing countries the rate of asset formation in North America rose above the average from 1967 to 1971, reflecting their growing interest in establishing production facilities in the United States. At the same time the rate of increase in investment in Europe, other than investment by the United Kingdom, fell off as compared with 1963–7, though there was no decline in the absolute value of asset formation save by Sweden and perhaps Canada.

Table 4.15 shows the reverse side of the coin – the growth and ownership of foreign assets in host countries. Some features are similar: the value of foreign owned assets, except in Canada, more than doubled between 1963 and 1971; the great bulk is owned by other industrial countries, with the United States, as is to be expected, at their head.

Table 4.15. *Foreign owned assets in manufacturing by country of origin :*
estimated book value of assets (host country data),[a] 1963–71

$ *million*

		Investors					
		United States	United Kingdom	EEC	Switzer-land	Other	Total
Investments in:							
United States	1963	n.a.	0.74	0.44[b]	0.32	0.92[c]	2.42
	1967	n.a.	0.96	0.67[b]	0.50	1.22[c]	3.35
	1971	n.a.	1.53	1.35[b]	0.75	1.83[c]	5.46
United Kingdom	1963	2.31	n.a.	0.30	..	..	3.27
	1967	2.88	n.a.	0.44[d]	0.33	0.57	4.22
	1971	4.92	n.a.	0.94[d]	0.55	0.87[e]	7.28
Germany[f]	1963	0.50	0.07	0.33[g]	0.23	0.12	1.25
	1967	1.01	0.10	0.46[g]	0.32	0.18	2.07
	1971	1.97	0.19	0.77[g]	0.60	0.36	3.89
Canada	1963	5.10	0.76	..	..	0.23[h]	6.09
	1967	7.51	0.83	..	..	0.30[h]	8.64
	1971	8.83	0.75	..	..	0.81[h]	10.39

[a] So far as possible adjusted to exclude investments in food, drink and tobacco industries.
[b] Of which from the Netherlands, 0.21 in 1963, 0.29 in 1967 and 0.52 in 1971.
[c] Of which from Canada, 0.75 in 1963, 0.98 in 1967 and 1.41 in 1971.
[d] Of which from the Netherlands, 0.30 in 1967 and 0.34 in 1971; and from France 0.08 in 1967 and 0.11 in 1971.
[e] Of which from Canada 0.55.
[f] German asset data are very much more narrowly defined than those for other countries; by 1971 total foreign owned assets were probably at least $1\frac{1}{2}$ times as large as indicated in the table.
[g] Of which from the Netherlands, 0.16 in 1963, 0.22 in 1967 and 0.34 in 1971; and from France, 0.08 in 1963, 0.10 in 1967 and 0.22 in 1971.
[h] Includes investment by the EEC countries and Switzerland.
SOURCES: see appendix E.

The figures suggest, however, that the rate of investment in European countries may not have fallen between 1963–7 and 1967–71 and they underline the importance of Switzerland and EEC countries other than Germany as investors. Some 15 per cent of foreign assets in the United States and Germany were registered as in Swiss ownership and 8 per cent in the United Kingdom. Figures for Belgium and France were respectively 5 per cent in 1967 and 11 per cent in 1973, while some rather dubious data indicate that the Swiss share in foreign owned assets in Italy could have been as high as 25 per cent. It is probable that these percentages are inflated by indirect American participation via Swiss holding companies; nonetheless they indicate a sizeable Swiss stake, which is confirmed by such other evidence as is available. The EEC countries excluding Germany held 20 per cent of foreign owned assets in Germany in 1971. It was about the same proportion in Belgium in 1967 and France in 1973; both data from host countries and their own balance of payments statistics suggest that their investment in overseas manufacturing assets was rising briskly during the 1960s, if not as fast as Germany's.[1]

From these scattered indications, and from the figures in table 4.14, it is possible to make a crude estimate of the growth of total foreign investment in manufacturing from 1963 to 1971. It seems probable that investment by France grew rather rapidly, though not as fast as German foreign direct investment, while Swiss and Dutch investment grew more slowly, though faster than British. The two remaining European countries have relatively small overseas assets in manufacturing, while Japanese assets, though growing at phenomenal speed, were also small in 1971. Thus what happened in these three countries during the preceding decade does not much affect any estimate of the rate of growth of foreign owned assets.

Table 4.16 shows the estimated growth of the book value of foreign owned assets in manufacturing compared with the growth of exports of manufactures, measured at current prices. For the eleven major industrial countries as a group, assets grew slightly more rapidly than exports from 1963 to 1967, while from 1967 to 1971 exports grew more rapidly than assets. This broad comparison, however, is inappropriate because of the insignificant role of Japan as an investor during the 1960s, in contrast to its major role as an exporter. The two big investing countries, the United States and the United Kingdom, show a faster rise in assets than in exports throughout. Indeed, allowing for a possible understatement in the growth of assets due to time-lags in the revaluation of assets at current prices, the growth of assets may have exceeded the growth of exports by a wider margin than the figures

[1] See appendix E for sources of estimates in this paragraph.

Table 4.16. *Growth of exports of manufactures at current prices and estimated book value of assets, 1967 and 1971*

Indices, 1963 = 100

	1967		1971	
	Exports	Assets	Exports	Assets
United States	150	164	220	244
United Kingdom	121	131	191	211
Other Europe[a]	153	163[b]	275	298[b]
Total[c]	153	157[b]	269	240[b]

[a] E E C, Sweden and Switzerland.   [b] Estimated.
[c] Includes also Canada and Japan.
SOURCES: for exports – appendix A; for assets – table 4.15 and N I E S R estimates.

indicate. Other European countries as a group very probably also increased asset values faster than exports, but this was principally because of the high rate of German investment. For the remainder, the rate of asset growth on average was probably close to the rate of export growth, or only a little lower or higher. The United States nevertheless still accounted for more than half of all foreign owned assets in manufacturing, the E E C as a group probably for something over a fifth and the United Kingdom for more than a tenth at the beginning of the 1970s.

The value of sales by United States majority owned foreign affiliates grew at very much the same rate as assets from 1963 to 1967, rising from $28.3 billion to $46.2 billion. (These figures cover a slightly wider range of goods than export data for non-food manufactures; the coverage of asset data is also wider than that of sales data.) Thereafter the ratio of sales to assets rose, so that between 1967 and 1971 the growth of sales was faster; by 1971 the total was $84.8 billion. The rise in the sales–asset ratio was probably due to the coincidence of a falling rate of asset formation and the coming into full production of enterprises launched in the mid-1960s. Since the rate of asset formation quickened rather than fell in most other countries, a similar rise in the sales–asset ratio is unlikely. Even so, if the sales–asset ratio of their investments remained constant, the sales of all foreign owned enterprises, American and other, must have grown faster than assets and probably also faster than 'world' exports.

However, total sales by foreign owned enterprises in 1971 cannot, except on implausible assumptions, have equalled the value of exports of manufactures from the eleven industrial countries. Just as the sales–asset ratio is unlikely to have risen outside American overseas enterprises, so it is unlikely to have been as high as the American ratio. Moreover, the American sales figures include the resale by foreign owned affiliates of goods imported from their American parents and their own exports. Allowing for similar intra-company transactions and for exports by other countries' foreign owned enterprises, it appears that purely local sales of goods produced by foreign owned enterprises in host countries were less, possibly considerably less, than two thirds of the value of 'world' exports of manufactures. It was only in a handful of European countries – Britain, Switzerland, possibly the Netherlands – that the value of overseas manufacturing production approached or exceeded the value of exports and there is no evidence whatsoever that the relationship between the two approached the American pattern in any other country.

These estimates, of course, refer to all manufacturing. Since foreign manufacturing enterprises are concentrated in certain industries, the importance of their activities is considerably greater in some trades than it is relative to all manufacturing. Table 4.17 shows the distribution of assets or sales by broad industry groups for a number of investing and host countries. In almost every case three industries – chemicals, engineering and vehicles (in fact motor vehicles) – account for between 65 and 80 per cent of the total. Only Britain and Japan among investing

Table 4.17. *Distribution by broad sectors of industry of foreign direct investment in manufacturing[a] in the late 1960s and early 1970s*

Percentages

	Engineering	Vehicles	Chemicals	Other
Investments by				
United States (1971)	28	24	18	30
United Kingdom (1971)	27	3	24	46
Japan (1971)	21	13	7	58
Germany (1976)	29	10	30	31
Sweden (1970)	58	3	8	30
Investments in:				
United States (1974)	16	..	39	45[b]
United Kingdom (1970)	41	14	17	28
France[c] (1973)	34	13	22	31
Germany (1970)	33	11	21	35
Belgium (1967)	46		32	22
Canada[c] (1970)	25	40	12	23

[a] So far as possible adjusted to exclude investments in food, drink and tobacco industries.
[b] Includes vehicles.
[c] Based on sales data.
SOURCES: see appendix E.

countries and, probably, the United States among host countries show a different pattern.

The multinational companies influence trade indirectly through the development of overseas production facilities; they also exert great direct influence, since they are major exporters on their own account. Fairly comprehensive data are available for two countries – the United Kingdom and the United States. American multinationals accounted for 63 per cent of United States exports of manufactures in 1966 and 66 per cent in 1970; for imports the corresponding percentages were 35 and 38. (For details see appendix table E.2.) A sizeable part of this trade represented transactions with their majority owned foreign subsidiaries – 19 per cent of all United States exports of manufactures in 1966 rising to 21 per cent in 1970, and for imports 13 rising to 18 per cent. These figures, especially those for intra-company trade, are inflated by the transactions of the United States motor companies and their Canadian subsidiaries under the Automotive Agreement. If trade in transport equipment is excluded, intra-company trade accounted for only 18 per cent of 1970 exports and 10 per cent of imports. The composition of imports from affiliates is unknown, but data for a matched sample of United States firms in 1966 and 1970 showed that in both years 44 per cent of intra-firm exports consisted of goods for processing, while in 1966 47 per cent and in 1970 52 per cent were goods for resale by affiliates. The balance was made up of capital equipment. Implicit in these figures, and in the return flow of imports from affiliates, is a considerable and growing volume of intra-industry trade.

United Kingdom statistics are not available for imports, but exports of foreign owned enterprises located in the United Kingdom, as well as of British companies investing overseas, are distinguished. The former rose from 21 per cent of all exports in 1966 to 25 per cent in 1970, the latter from 45 to 47 per cent. The share of American owned firms in exports by all enterprises with foreign ownership was fairly closely in line with its share in assets. Exports to overseas affiliates by foreign owned enterprises rose from 10 to 12 per cent of total exports, while British investors' exports to affiliates remained steady at 12 per cent. In all, nearly a quarter of Britain's exports were shipped to related concerns (see appendix table E.3).

Further light on the role in trade of foreign owned enterprises is thrown by the ratio of exports by American majority owned foreign affiliates to total exports from industrial host countries, which is shown in table 4.18. Outside Japan the share of American owned enterprises rose from 1963 to 1971, as their exports rose faster than those of manufacturing industry in general. By 1971, majority owned United States enterprises in Canada supplied almost 50 per cent of Canadian

Table 4.18. *Shares of total exports of manufactures supplied by American owned enterprises*

Percentages

		Canada	United Kingdom	EEC Six	Total Europe[a]	Japan
1963[b]	Machinery	49.1	..	..	7.4	..
	Transport equipment	44.0	..	..	13.5	..
	Chemicals	73.1	..	..	8.5	..
	Other	42.6	..	..	2.8	..
	Total	45.2	13.3[c]	5.4[c]	6.3	..
1967A[b]	Machinery	44.7	..	..	10.6	..
	Transport equipment	89.3	..	..	11.3	..
	Chemicals	36.0	..	..	10.5	..
	Other	48.3	..	..	3.9	..
	Total	59.2	..	..	7.6	..
1967B	Machinery	36.3	20.5	10.5	11.1	3.0
	Transport equipment	85.5	20.7[c]	9.3[c]	11.6[c]	—
	Chemicals	43.3	19.7	9.8	10.6	7.9
	Other	20.6	12.0[c]	2.8[c]	4.1[c]	0.2
	Total	42.6	17.1[d]	6.7	7.8	1.3
1971	Machinery	45.4	25.4	11.6	12.8	1.7
	Transport equipment	83.2	19.6	13.3	13.4	—
	Chemicals	41.1	22.7	14.9	14.4	7.1
	Other	20.9	10.7	3.1	4.4	0.3
	Total	48.9	18.1[d]	8.6	9.3	1.0

[a] EEC, EFTA, Cyprus, Gibraltar, Greece, Iceland, Ireland, Malta, Spain, Turkey, Yugoslavia.
[b] 1963 and 1967A figures refer to shares supplied by enterprises where 25 per cent of total assets was held directly by United States firms; other figures refer to shares supplied by enterprises of which 50 per cent or more was United States owned directly or indirectly.
[c] Estimated.
[d] United Kingdom data for 1966 and 1970 suggest a slightly smaller share for United States enterprises – 14 and 16 per cent respectively.
SOURCE: appendix table E.1.

exports of manufactures; if United States enterprises' share in Canadian exports were calculated on the previous basis, that is including the exports of firms where the United States interest was 25 per cent or more, it would have been higher still. In Europe, United States firms made an exceptionally large contribution to exports from the United Kingdom; here, as in other European countries, their share in exports of chemicals, machinery and transport equipment is above the average for all manufactures. Shares in exports from the EEC Six as a whole are much smaller, but it is known that they conceal wide variations between individual countries. Unfortunately, data on exports by American majority owned affiliates from individual EEC countries are not published regularly, but from figures in the Tariff Commission report it is possible to calculate the share of American owned enterprises in the exports of three EEC countries in 1966 and 1970.[1] They were respectively 9.8 and 13.7 per cent in Belgium-Luxembourg, 6.5 and 8.0 per cent in Germany, and 6.5 and 9.7 per cent in France; while for the EEC Six as a whole in these years they were 6.9 and 8.5 per cent.

What proportion of these exports represented intra-firm trade is an open question, but in the light of the general pattern of behaviour by majority owned foreign affiliates it was probably high. (Intra-firm affiliate exports accounted for 54 per cent of affiliate exports other than transport equipment in 1970 according to the data reproduced in appendix table E.2; including transport equipment the proportion was 65 per cent. Once again, a large element of intra-industry trade is implied over and above the intra-industry trade between parents and affiliates already noted.) Exports from non-American foreign owned enterprises are also an unknown quantity, but judging solely by the share of such enterprises in all foreign owned assets they would be smaller than exports from American majority owned foreign affiliates, with a correspondingly smaller ratio of intra-firm exports by foreign owned enterprises to the total exports of the host countries. Exports by domestic firms with investments overseas to their affiliates would also in general be a smaller proportion of trade than in the United States and the United Kingdom because of the smaller scale of foreign investment by other countries. Swedish estimates, for example, show exports by Swedish parents to their overseas manufacturing subsidiaries to have been just under 9 per cent of all Swedish exports of non-food manufactures in 1970; their imports from affiliates were a bare 1.5 per cent of the total.[2]

From the various figures available it is possible to arrive at an approximate estimate of the share of intra-firm trade in world trade. The figures derived from United States data already quoted have to be adjusted upwards to allow for transactions involving minority owned affiliates and for exports by foreign owned enterprises located in the United States itself, and a similar adjustment is required for Sweden. Estimates for intra-firm exports of American owned affiliates in other industrial countries can be derived from the data in table 4.18. Adding in estimated exports of non-American foreign owned enterprises and parent firms located there, 15 per cent appears to be a reasonable figure for intra-firm exports from the EEC. Making generous allowance for Canadian intra-firm exports plus something for Switzerland and Japan and taking the United Kingdom as given, it appears that by the early 1970s intra-firm transactions accounted for at least 15 per cent and

---

[1] United States Senate, Committee on Finance, *Implications of Multinational Firms*.

[2] Derived from B. Swedenborg, *Den Svenska Industrins Investeringar i Utlandet, 1965–1970*, Uppsala, Almqvist & Wiksell, 1973, table 23, and Swedish trade statistics.

probably nearer 20 per cent of the industrial countries' exports of manufactures.[1]

The share of all exports by multinationals and their affiliates in world trade is of course very much larger, since it is almost invariably the case that those firms with foreign manufacturing subsidiaries are also major exporters to non-related firms. We know that multinationals based in the United States handled almost two thirds of total United States exports of manufactures (including intra-firm transactions) in 1970. United Kingdom parents supplied nearly half of United Kingdom exports of manufactures, Swedish parents some 55 per cent. It would not be surprising if firms that might reasonably be classified as multinationals handled as much as 50 per cent of all exports of manufactures from the industrial countries. Adding in the trade of affiliates, the share of multinationals, their subsidiaries and associates could approach two thirds of the total.

That the multinationals have so large a share in world trade must affect competitive conditions. It is sometimes implied that only through intra-firm trade, where transfer prices can theoretically be manipulated to maximise profits for the organisation as a whole, will the multinationals affect competition. However, it is equally possible that the existence of an intra-firm trading network affects the terms on which trade with outsiders is conducted. This is not to say that the behaviour of multinationals, whether in intra-firm or extra-firm trade, always differs from that of enterprises located in a single country. There are well known cases of high transfer prices, differential pricing and so forth which have created the impression that multinationals do behave differently. It can only be an impression; for what proportion of multinationals engage in such practices and, equally important, what proportion of non-multinationals do likewise is unknown.

Altogether, it is clear that the scale of activities of the multinationals is such that their potential influence on trade is very great. Some of their activities are trade-promoting, others the reverse. On balance we would conclude that their influence has been trade-promoting, partly because of the pattern of their investments, bearing in mind particularly their interest as major independent exporters in the growth of world trade and their engagement in intra-industry trade.

---

[1] An earlier estimate by Lall suggests a much higher figure: 'a quarter to a third of [developed countries'] trade in manufactured products takes place within MNEs' (S. Lall, 'Transfer pricing by multinational manufacturing firms', *Oxford University Bulletin of Economics and Statistics*, vol. 35, August 1973). The difference arises from three causes: Lall was using provisional data for American multinationals that suggested higher intra-firm shares in both exports and imports; he made a more generous allowance for the trade of foreign owned enterprises located in the United States; he assumed that the pattern of intra-firm trade in the United States and the United Kingdom was 'roughly representative of the pattern among developed countries as a whole'.

CONCLUSION

It appears, then, that the exceptionally rapid growth of trade in relation to output and consumption during the latter part of the 1960s may be attributed mainly to four factors: reductions in trade barriers, the activities of multinational enterprises, technological developments which created 'new' products where economies of scale are significant and which commanded a mass market, and the shift in the location of the major industrial growth centres to areas where labour was prepared and able to work as hard and skilfully as in the older industrial areas for a lower real wage.

The first two factors are clearly interrelated. Tariff reductions directly stimulated exports through the price mechanism. But they also created the conditions in which the trade-promoting activities of multi-national enterprises, especially of American enterprises in Europe, were as great as or greater than their trade-reducing activities. Nor would international subcontracting, the production of components in different locations, and the growth of intra-industry specialisation in trade have been practicable or profitable to the same extent without tariff cuts. The relative reduction in transport costs certainly had the same effect, as perhaps did (so far as consumer goods are concerned) the development of new retailing methods.

The development of 'new' products is in turn associated with the activities of multinational enterprises. They are leaders in the three general growth sectors identified earlier – motor vehicles, organic chemicals and related products, and computers. However, the Japanese case sufficiently demonstrates that the multinationals are not necessary for the development of technologically advanced, large-scale, mass-market industries. It is the character of the goods themselves rather than their production by multinational enterprises that has contributed to the exceptional growth of trade. Technology makes the new product with a high growth potential, economies of scale encourage production for international rather than national markets and mass consumption makes possible not only large-scale production but also a high rate of growth.

The fourth factor listed as promoting trade is of a different kind and in the period under review there was only one major example of its operation – in Japan. Japan was a special case, not perhaps so much because of the high quality of labour of all kinds combined with lower average real earnings (in this it is merely an extreme example of a process that promoted rapid expansion of industrial exports from the Netherlands and Italy also) as in its wholly exceptional dependence on imported raw materials and fuels. Had Japan been able to supply a higher proportion of its requirements, the pressure to export in order to finance imports essential to maintain a high rate of economic growth would have been much less. Shifts in the locus of industrial production and growth are bound to influence the development of trade, but whether trade will be promoted or reduced depends on the character of the economy which becomes a new growth centre. Japan is the outstanding twentieth century example, as Britain was the nineteenth century example, of trade-promoting growth and of international specialisation according to factor-endowments.

5

THE PROCESS OF INDUSTRIALISATION

by *R. A. Batchelor*

INTRODUCTION

Basic propositions

In this chapter we attempt to identify empirically some systematic relationships between industrialisation, economic growth and economic structure.

Maizels advanced two sets of hypotheses on these: first, that there is a tendency for the share of manufactures in GDP to increase at the expense of primary production as income per head increases and that similar uniform changes can be traced for the relative importance of individual industries within manufacturing; secondly, that the level and growth of labour productivity tend to be higher in manufacturing than in agriculture and the level to be higher in rich countries than in poor. Some precision was given to the first set by regressions of industry value-added shares on income per head, conducted on a cross-sectional sample of 30 countries and on time-series data on from seven to ten advanced economies; results from the two samples diverged in important respects, the time-series implying a more rapid decline of the textile industry and a more rapid growth in chemicals than was apparent in the cross-section. The propositions on labour productivity (value added per person engaged) were less rigorously tested and more diffidently stated. The main evidence consisted of scatter diagrams showing that some countries could achieve sharp increases early in industrialisation as skills were quickly developed or already existed in a handicraft sector prior to the institution of a factory system, but that in other countries the main growth in productivity occurred late in their industrialisation as initially diffuse production units were combined into large-scale plants.

The nature of the data

Our reappraisal of these propositions is based mainly on two sources – the industry census data in the United Nations series, *Growth of World Industry* and the aggregate data in the United Nations' *Yearbook of National Accounts Statistics*. Various supplementary national and international sources have also been canvassed.

While the sheer quantity of this data permits us to work with much larger samples than were at Maizels' disposal, several ineluctable problems concerning their quality remain. The relative importance of sectors within individual economies is ideally assessed only if their outputs can be clearly identified and measured under competitive market conditions, but the service sector is often hard to delimit and in many countries agriculture is heavily subsidised or protected by tariff barriers. In international comparisons of sector shares there are the further complications that the scope of the market economy and the terms of trade between sectors may differ systematically across countries and, in comparisons of production or consumption levels per head, official or market exchange rates are biased guides to the relative internal purchasing power of national currencies. Our problems are thus particularly acute when comparisons are made between centrally planned and market economies, or between advanced and less developed economies. Tables 5.1–5.5 are based on this admittedly imperfect data and show various summary statistics concerning regional and industrial patterns of production and labour productivity.

Table 5.1 confirms that high-income economies are characterised by relatively large manufacturing sectors and relatively small primary sectors, the ratio between total value added in each sector being around 3:1 in Western Europe and North America and 1:3 in Asia and Africa. Among the developed countries, Australia and New Zealand (Oceania) are exceptional in having large agricultural and mining industries and, among the developing countries, Latin America has approximately

Table 5.1. *Shares of primary production, manufacturing and services in GDP, 1963*

	GDP per head	Sector		
		Primary	Manufacturing	Other
	($)	(percentages)		
Developed market economies	1790	11	31	58
North America	3060	9	28	63
Western Europe	1340	12	34	54
Oceania	1510	20	27	53
Japan	711	15	34	51
Developing economies	150	38	16	46
Africa	140	42	13	45
Asia	120	45	14	41
Latin America	360	25	21	54
World[a]	660	15	28	57

[a] Excluding centrally planned economies.

SOURCE: United Nations Statistical Office, *Yearbook of National Accounts Statistics, 1972*, vol. III: *International Tables*, New York, 1974.

equal value added in the primary and secondary sectors. Individual developed countries all conform fairly well with the average pattern, only Ireland, Italy and Finland having unusually important agricultural sectors, the last because of forestry rather than farming. In the developing world there is a greater variety of structure, many countries in Africa and the Middle East relying on revenues from mineral extraction and oil production for the bulk of their national product.

Although the differences between developed and developing countries with respect to the importance of services appear much smaller than differences in agricultural or industrial activity, the figures conceal considerable dissimilarities in the nature of the services and in their importance for individual countries within the two groups. In 1963 Western Europe and Latin America received the same contribution to their GDP from the 'other' sector, but in Latin America only 17 per cent of this was infrastructure (construction, transport and communication) and 35 per cent was merchandising, whereas in Western Europe 27 per cent was infrastructure and 25 per cent merchandising; in Africa and Asia the breakdown of this sector was, however, closer to the European pattern. Among developed countries there is a striking contrast between the relative size of the sector in North America and in Western Europe. Its dominance in North America was achieved by a

Table 5.2. *Shares of major industries in manufacturing value added, 1963*

Percentages

	Food, etc.	Basic metals	Metal products	Chemicals^a	Textiles	Leather, etc.	Forest products^b	Mineral products
Developed market economies	12	8	37	14	6	5	12	5
North America	12	9	39	14	4	5	13	4
Western Europe	12	8	36	13	7	5	11	5
Oceania	16	9	30	12	6	6	15	5
Japan	9	12	35	15	8	2	11	5
Developing economies	27	6	16	15	14	6	9	5
Africa	26	7	18	12	12	6	11	5
Asia	24	5	13	13	18	7	9	7
Latin America	28	7	18	17	10	6	9	5
Centrally planned economies	16	9	39	9	5	5	7	7
USSR	16	9	40	8	4	5	7	5
World	14	8	36	12	6	5	10	5

^{a} Including products of petroleum and rubber.
^{b} Including printing.
SOURCE: United Nations, Department of Economic and Social Affairs, *The Growth of World Industry* (1969 edn), vol. II: *Commodity production data 1960–69*, New York, 1971.

Table 5.3. *Rates of growth of world manufacturing production, 1937–71*

	Shares in value added 1963[a]	Average annual growth rates				
		1937–50	1950–5	1955–60	1960–5	1965–71
	(%)	(percentages p.a.)				
Developed market economies	65	3.5	5.5	4.0	6.4	4.5
North America	(53)	5.2	4.5	2.2	5.9	2.8
Western Europe	(38)	1.7	7.1	5.7	5.4	5.1
Oceania	(2)	4.3	5.2	5.8	6.9	4.5
Japan	(6)	..	..	..	11.2	12.6
Developing economies	7	4.4	6.1	7.2	6.6	6.1
Africa	(14)	..	..	8.3	10.6	4.5
Asia	(34)	−0.6	12.4	8.5	6.9	5.2
Latin America	(52)	5.2	5.3	6.2	5.9	6.8
Centrally planned economies	29	5.0	..	10.7	8.5	8.3
USSR	(69)	7.3	13.0	..	8.2	8.4
World	100	..	..	6.0	6.9	5.9

[a] Total value added in 1963 was $481.3 billion.
SOURCES: Maizels, *Industrial Growth and World Trade*, table 1.2; as table 5.2.

rapid expansion in the 1920s and sustained by a further burst of growth in the 1950s.

Within manufacturing the chief difference between the developed and developing countries is, as shown in table 5.2, that the former concentrate on the engineering industries, but in the latter these are smaller than food, beverages and tobacco; textiles too are relatively much more important to the developing than the developed countries. The centrally planned economies are distinguished mainly by comparatively low shares for chemicals and forest products.

The growth of manufacturing output by region for the period 1937–71 is set out in table 5.3. The developing economies consistently outpaced the developed economies throughout the period. In view of their small industrial base this is not surprising, and the growth differential left their output in 1971 only 11 per cent of that of developed countries as against 8 per cent in 1937. More significantly, the centrally planned economies achieved more rapid rates of growth than even the developing countries, in spite of higher initial shares of world output and of manufactures in domestic output. There was, however, a continued deceleration in growth rates of centrally planned economies in the 1960s, from which only Bulgaria and Romania – the least industrialised members – were immune. In Western Europe growth in the same period, high by historical standards, did not follow a downward trend, but oscillated regularly around a basic rate of $5\frac{1}{2}$ per cent per annum, with peaks in 1950, 1955, 1960 and 1969; in the developing countries growth rates if anything increased and appear to have become progressively less sensitive to these fluctuations in advanced economies than in the 1920s and 1930s. These trends conceal much individual variation. The index for the developing economies is dominated by four large countries – Argentina, Brazil, India and Mexico – which account for over half of their total output. The index for the developed market economies is similarly dominated by its four largest members (with three quarters of their output) and the centrally planned economies' index by the USSR.

Among the developed countries, growth-rate rankings have been stable since 1950, with manufacturing output growing slower in the United Kingdom and Norway and faster in Germany and Italy than the general trend. These phenomena have been variously traced to differences in investment levels (over-investment in Norway) and to permissive labour-supply conditions (in Germany as a result of an influx of migrant workers and in France and Italy as a result of disguised unemployment in agriculture).

In the less developed areas large countries have expanded their industrial sector faster than small countries. During the 1960s growth in half of the developing countries with populations over twenty million exceeded 8 per cent per annum; only a third of the smaller developing countries approached such rates, among them several trading nations – Hong Kong, Singapore, Taiwan – which broke free from the constraints of their home market to outstanding but possibly inimitable effect.

Some estimates of value added per person engaged in three main branches of production are set out in table 5.4 and scatter diagrams of the relationships between these measures of productivity in the primary and tertiary sectors and in manufacturing are shown in charts 5.1 and 5.2. The impression given by the first chart is of an initial margin of productivity in manufacturing over agriculture steadily narrowing as efficiency increases generally. This could result from an increasing average product in agriculture as its labour surplus is tapped during a period of growth generated by high investment in manufacturing, or it could result from more direct industry–agriculture interactions, such as when high industrial productivity creates large, stable, geographically-concentrated markets for agricultural products, or when social benefits of efficiency – improved skills, appreciation of modern management principles – spill over into the primary sector. The second chart shows an approximate parity between labour productivity levels in manufacturing and services in the most efficient economies, with the relation becoming more diffuse at the other end of the spectrum. The positive

Table 5.4. *Value added per person engaged, 1963*

$, 1963 prices

	Sector		
	Primary[a]	Manufacturing	Other[b]
Developed countries			
United Kingdom	4103[c]	3441	2853
United States	9636[c]	9141	7341
Japan	664	1669	1932
France	1881	3444	3900
Germany	2118	3281	3699
Italy	1238	2162	2986
Belgium-Luxembourg	3757[c]	3722	3920
Denmark	2843	3624	3829
Finland	1779	3350	2953
Ireland	1046[d]	2590	2017
Norway	1980	3764	4636
Portugal	491	913	1327
Sweden	3278[c]	4397	5108
Australia	6221	4557	3457
Canada	5199	6925	5169
Developing countries			
Morocco	416	924	1119
Nigeria	171	763	218
South Africa	960[c]	2281	1664
India	129	279	452
Indonesia	161	403	377
Israel	1787	2889	2397
Pakistan	348	288	..
Philippines	177	644	1180
Turkey	267	1034	1419
Argentina	1447	1886	1340
Brazil	388	2115	991
Chile	616	2317	1133
Colombia	556	1451	1199
Mexico	534	1628	2630
Puerto Rico	1816	4061	4764

[a] Agriculture and mining.
[b] Construction; transport and communication; wholesale and retail trade; other services.
[c] In these countries value added per head in agriculture differs substantially from that in primary production as a whole: it is $2539 in the United Kingdom, $4867 in the United States, $3007 in Belgium-Luxembourg, $1911 in Sweden and $561 in South Africa.
[d] Agriculture only.

SOURCES: United Nations: Food and Agriculture Organization, *Production Yearbook 1972*, Rome, 1973; Statistical Office, *Yearbook of National Accounts Statistics 1973*; Department of Economic and Social Affairs, *The Growth of World Industry* (1969 edn), vol. II, table 9.

Chart 5.1. *Value added per person engaged in primary production and in manufacturing, 1963*

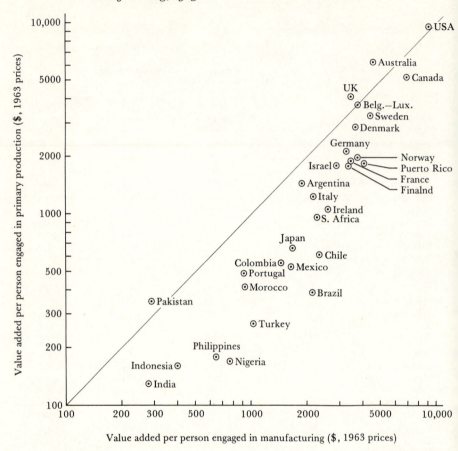

Value added per person engaged in manufacturing ($, 1963 prices)

Note: Population censuses in Nigeria have tended to overestimate the size of the labour force, so productivity outside manufacturing is probably understated (see S. A. Alecko, 'How many Nigerians?', *Modern African Studies*, vol. 3, October 1965).
SOURCE: table 5.4.

association between the two productivity levels can be rationalised by much the same two arguments as in the case of agriculture, the spillover being reinforced in this case by the fact that many services – transport, financial – are closely tied to manufacturing operations and may even fall under the same ownership. The diffusion at low levels occurs partly because in less developed countries much of the tertiary labour force is occupied in relatively unproductive domestic service, the exact proportion depending on the social *mores* of the country in question, and

Chart 5.2. *Value added per person engaged in the tertiary sector and in manufacturing, 1963*

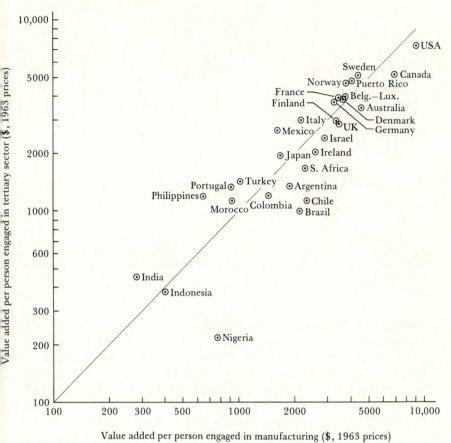

Value added per person engaged in manufacturing ($, 1963 prices)

Note: see note to chart 5.1.
SOURCE: table 5.4.

partly, perhaps, on the fact that in some countries there is employment provided in the government sector for members of an urban labour force which organised industry cannot fully absorb.

Rates of growth of labour productivity in manufacturing in the period 1955–71 are shown by region in table 5.5. While this growth has been generally slower in less developed countries than in the advanced economies of Western Europe, both these groups achieved some acceleration in the 1960s. In Eastern Europe, on the other hand, a marked deceleration brought the growth rate of labour productivity into line with that in Western Europe. This was not the result of any

Table 5.5. *Productivity growth in manufacturing, 1955–71*

	Value added per person engaged, 1963	Average annual growth rates		
		1955–60	1960–5	1965–71
	($)	(percentages p.a.)		
Developed market economies	4280	2.2	4.0	3.7
North America	8878	2.4	4.3	2.4
Western Europe	2930	3.7	3.8	4.7
Oceania	4342	3.8	4.3	2.7
Japan	1669	..	..	..
Developing economies	708	2.9	2.5	4.0
Africa	1323	..	..	..
Asia[a]	394	3.8	3.1	3.9
Latin America	1796	3.3	4.1	3.5
Centrally planned economies	4223[b]	6.9	4.7	5.6
USSR	4431[b]	..	..	..
World	3205	3.4	3.6	4.2

[a] Excluding Israel.
[b] Net material product at official exchange rates, which may be a misleading basis of comparison with market economies so far as actual values are concerned, but should be more reliable when applied to changes.
SOURCES: United Nations, *The Growth of World Industry* (1969 and 1972 edns), vol. II.

convergence in structure or techniques, however, as the centrally planned economies experienced the greatest deceleration in their major sector – engineering – while productivity growth in the West occurred mainly in chemicals, through improved plant design and increasing scale, and in textiles, through increased mechanisation and specialisation in high-quality products in the face of foreign competition in staple markets. The difference between the productivity growth rates in table 5.5 and the output growth rates of table 5.3 represents the part of growth due to changes in employment. Thus it can be deduced that employment in manufacturing rose by under 2 per cent per annum in the 1960s in developed market economies, as against 3 per cent in less developed and centrally planned economies. Indeed, in some advanced economies – Denmark, France, Sweden – industrial employment was stationary and the whole change in output was due to productivity gains. In many developing countries employment also increased much less than the average implied by the tables – in East Africa, Singapore and Argentina it actually declined – while in others – West Africa, Taiwan – annual growth rates were over 10 per cent.

The nature of the argument

Our inquiry in detail into the new data in the rest of this chapter is arranged as follows. First, we examine the intellectual basis for expecting uniformities in the relationship between economic structure and growth, and conclude that patterns common to most countries in our large sample should not be expected. The statistical techniques of cluster analysis are, however, applied to generate smaller, more homogeneous sets of economies within which similar development patterns might emerge. Secondly, the parameters of these patterns are estimated; it is concluded that, while Maizels' general assessment of manufacturing growth is valid, significant differences between large and small developing countries can be found in their rates of industrialisation. In tracing the evolution of individual branches of manufacturing little conflict between time-series and cross-sectional evidence occurs. Thirdly, labour productivity in manufacturing is formally analysed; it is concluded that differences between productivity at low and at high levels of industrialisation spring less from skill differences or organisational factors – as Maizels supposed – than from differences in natural resource-endowments. From a further inspection of productivity growth over time in branches of industry, the newness of the capital stock and an intermediate position in the development scale are also found to boost efficiency.

THE METHODOLOGY OF GROWTH PATTERNS

A general description

A substantial amount of empirical research on the relationships between economic structure and economic growth has accumulated in the past two decades, mainly from the efforts of Chenery and Kuznets.[1] Since this work superficially owes little to the contemporaneous burst of writings on the pure theory of economic growth,[2] and since the school has developed a distinctive style of investigation – one adopted by Maizels – it may be helpful before embarking on our own analysis to establish exactly what is entailed by this methodology, how it is informed by economic theory and why the schism with pure theory has occurred.

The empirical analysis of growth patterns generally starts from the observation of some strong contrast in the behaviour of two or more economic variables in the course of economic growth. The variables may come from any part of the national accounts, but Chenery and Syrquin distinguish three main classes of process – accumulation,

---

[1] Chenery, 'Patterns of industrial growth'; S. Kuznets, *Modern Economic Growth*, New Haven (Conn.), Yale University Press, 1966.
[2] As surveyed, for example, in F. H. Hahn and R. C. O. Matthews, 'The theory of economic growth: a survey', *Economic Journal*, vol. 74, December 1964.

resource allocation and demographic effects.[1] The first covers changes in human and non-human capital formation relative to consumption expenditures and the shifting balance between domestic and foreign sources of capital. The last covers the functional distribution of labour, the distribution of its rewards and trends in the urban–rural population balance. It is the second type of process which is of particular interest here, however, since it subsumes questions of how the shares of branches of productive activity move relatively to each other.

The criteria which have been used to define contrasting branches are quite varied. Some authors, like Chenery and Syrquin, Kuznets and Clark distinguish industries by type of output and so are led to gross comparisons between manufacturing and agriculture, or between manufacturing and services;[2] others – Chenery and Taylor, the United Nations and Maizels – on the same grounds make more detailed comparisons of movements in the relative shares of individual sectors of manufacturing.[3] Alternatively industries may be distinguished by their technology as heavy or light depending on whether they are more or less capital-intensive; comparisons of the growth patterns of such industry groups have been carried out by the United Nations.[4] Again, industries may be distinguished by the conditions of demand they face, as in the comparison of growth in consumer and capital goods by Hoffmann,[5] where absolute differences in income elasticities of demand are critical, or in the comparison of late and early industries by Chenery and Taylor,[6] where it is the relative shifts in these elasticities as income rises which are critical.

Some such contrast having been framed in qualitative terms – in all the pairs listed above, the first variable is presumed to outstrip the second in the course of development – the relationship is formalised by writing

$$X_1/X_2 = \phi(y)$$

$$\phi_y > 0 \qquad\qquad (5.1)$$

[1] H. B. Chenery and M. Syrquin, *Patterns of Development 1950–70*, London, Oxford University Press, 1975.

[2] Ibid; Kuznets, *Modern Economic Growth*; C. Clark, *The Conditions of Economic Progress* (3rd edn), London, Macmillan, 1975.

[3] H. B. Chenery and L. Taylor, 'Development patterns: among countries and over time', *Review of Economics and Statistics*, vol. 50, November 1958, Part III; United Nations, Department of Economic and Social Affairs, *A Study of Industrial Growth*, New York, 1963; Maizels, *Industrial Growth and World Trade*, chap. 2.

[4] United Nations, Department of Economic and Social Affairs, *The Growth of World Industry 1938–61*, vol. II, New York, 1965, chap. II.

[5] W. G. Hoffmann, *The Growth of Industrial Economies*, Manchester University Press, 1958.

[6] Chenery and Taylor, 'Development patterns', pp. 409–15.

where X_1 is the fast-growing variable, X_2 the contrasting slow-growing variable and $Y/N = y$ is income per head.[1] In practice only Hoffmann expresses his ideas in this ratio form, functions for X_1 and X_2 usually being calculated separately as

$$X_1 = \phi_1(y)$$
$$X_2 = \phi_2(y)$$
$$\phi_{1y}/\phi_{2y} > 1 \tag{5.2}$$

where the more positive response of the first sector to income growth is shown by the condition on the partial derivatives of ϕ_1 and ϕ_2.

The theoretical basis

It is at this point, before these propositions are confronted with the data in a proper statistical test, that theoretical considerations intervene. So far they have been involved only in the remote sense that in choosing to measure certain variables, such as industry output, and in choosing to draw certain contrasts rather than others, we must have held some preconceptions about what dimensions of economic life are of key importance. Two stronger questions can now be asked. First, how do the relations set out above arise and what causal significance can be attached to them? Secondly, what additional factors impinge on these simple relations and how should they be allowed for in the analysis?

The rationalisations usually offered for the dependence of structural characteristics on income per head are that most economies show a similar evolution of tastes as income rises; that there is a stable sequence of industrial expansion as increasing purchasing power permits the establishment of plants of optimum size; that human and physical capital formation develop in parallel, so that the technologies accessible to each country depend on its level of development. In a closed economy, industry output is simply the sum of domestic final and intermediate demands:

$$X_j = X_j^f + X_j^h \tag{5.3}$$

and, since the former is presumed to depend on income through systematic taste variations and the latter is determined by technological changes which are also governed by income, the dependence of industry output on income level is guaranteed. The relationship may not be unidirectional, however, since the pattern of resource-allocation by sector as determined by the ratio X_1/X_2 may in turn affect some accumulation

---

[1] The notation ϕ_y indicates the rate of change of ϕ with respect to y, that is the first partial derivative $\partial\phi/\partial y$.

processes which tend to stimulate or retard income growth, $g(y)$. The full model should then be written

$$X_1/X_2 = \phi(y)$$

$$g(y) = \psi(X_1/X_2) \tag{5.4}$$

One important instance of this interdependence between structure and growth is the notion that, because productivity levels are higher in manufacturing than in primary production, possibly because of its relative capital intensity, aggregate income is increased as industrialisation progresses and a cumulative process set in train.

Extensions of the model and some objections

The introduction of variables other than income into the simple growth-pattern model raises some doubts over the value of such exercises and the conduct of statistical tests. This is because such factors may not be simply additional to the relationship between structure and income, but may actually determine the response of sectoral growth rates to aggregate growth. In so far as this is true, and these factors differ across countries, no common growth patterns can be discussed. Suppose we write variables which have a simple additive effect as $\mathbf{U}$ and those which interfere with the relationship of X and Y (or X and $\mathbf{U}$) as $\mathbf{V}$; then equation 5.1 becomes

$$X_1/X_2 = \phi(y, \mathbf{U}, \mathbf{V})$$

$$\phi_y > 0$$

$$\phi_{y\mathbf{U}} = 0$$

$$\phi_{y\mathbf{V}} \neq 0 \tag{5.5}$$

where the last two derivative conditions express the differing roles of $\mathbf{U}$ and $\mathbf{V}$.

The variable included most frequently alongside income in an additive fashion is population size, on the grounds that this affects the optimum scale of production and the choice of technique, and hence influences intermediate demands X_j^h in the commodity-balance equation 5.3.[1] Other variables canvassed have been natural resource-endowments,[2] and the ratio of consumption (or investment) to output.[3]

---

[1] With this population feedback, relationships like 5.4 may exist in respect both of total population, which might grow faster as industrialisation gathers pace, and of its age profile and work participation rates. These demographic effects may be positive or negative.

[2] Chenery and Taylor, 'Development patterns', measures these as revealed by the share of manufactures in exports; in other studies population density is often taken as a proxy for scarcity of resources.

[3] See G. Fels, K.-W. Schatz and F. Wolter, 'Der Zusammenhang zwischen Produktionstruktur und Entwicklungsniveau', *Weltwirtschaftliches Archiv*, vol. 106, no. 2, 1971.

In contrasting manufacturing with primary production, we should, for example, expect the former to outpace the latter as population grew and, within manufacturing, we should expect mineral processing to be more prominent than finished manufacturing in resource-rich countries, and light industries to be more prominent than heavy in high-consumption societies.

A variety of factors **V** which might cause the parameters of the simple model to vary from country to country follow from criticisms of the adequacy of the commodity-balance equation 5.3 as a basis for speculation about growth.

The first criticism is that the equation relates to a closed economy and, if the products of sector j enter international trade so that the commodity-balance equation becomes

$$X_j = X_j^f + X_j^h + E_j - M_j \qquad (5.6)$$

where E_j and M_j are exports and imports, the simple dependence of output on income and other additional internal factors is credible only if exports are supply-determined and imports demand-determined.[1] Clearly this condition cannot be true for the world economy as a whole, since some countries' exports are others' imports; the growth-pattern framework gives at best a partial view of development in an open economy and one which may not generalise over time as the external environment changes, or across space as the character of trading patterns varies.

Equally damaging to the theoretical basis of the growth-pattern model are the objections that it ignores dynamic elements in internal development and gives no place to unique political or historical forces in individual countries. Dynamic problems arise from technological changes and changes in tastes, so that neither X_j^f nor X_j^h may be stable functions of income and size. Comparative advantage in certain lines of production is, for example, definable only against the prevailing state of the arts, but that state is constantly changing. Innovation tends to reduce costs in manufacturing by large-scale processes and so continuously expands the choice of techniques open to newly industrialised countries. Moreover, as Kuznets has observed, 'technological innovation is selective and its impact shifts over time from one branch of production to another'.[2] Thus the pattern of industrialisation followed by a particular country depends on how far it is prepared to

[1] M. D. Steuer and C. S. Voivodas, 'Import substitution and Chenery's patterns of industrial growth: a further study', *Economia Internazionale*, vol. 18, February 1965.
[2] S. Kuznets, *The Economic Growth of Nations*, Cambridge (Mass.), Harvard University Press, 1971, p. 325.

invest in capital-intensive plant,[1] on its ability to support a broad industry-mix given the increasing optimal scale in each sector and, above all, on the timing of its main development effort. The effects of differences in tastes on development patterns come about in a subtler way, through interactions between the sort of goods made available by local producers (and the environment of their production) and consumer preferences.

The self-validating nature of production is stressed by Kuznets, who notes that: 'Although changes on the production side do not necessarily affect the basic structure of human wants . . . they do affect the relative costs and varieties of specific goods that are comprised in those wants.'[2] Not only does availability stimulate consumption through the price mechanism and perpetuate consumption through habit formation, but the social *milieu* created by any particular industrial order generates distinctive kinds of secondary activities. These may involve supplying or servicing either major industries themselves or the employees of major industries in conurbations around industrial centres. In either case their presence locks the economy into a rigid development pattern by increasing the social costs of industrial transformation.

Political factors have already figured as determinants of the choice of technique and the readiness to accept change. There are instances of a deeper fault in the commodity-balance analysis of development patterns – its failure to embrace extra-market forces in economic growth. Catastrophe has obvious and not necessarily deleterious effects on industrialisation; for example, earthquakes, floods, famine and war have halted progress in Nicaragua, Honduras, Bangladesh and Nigeria in recent years – but the world wars actually promoted industrialisation in many countries, as Maizels argues,[3] through the encouragement of self-sufficiency and the diversion of resources into heavy industries. More sustained institutional pressures are also important, and several attempts have been made to explore empirically the effects of political systems and territorial status on growth patterns.

The United Nations, after running regressions of value added per head in thirteen industries on income per head, population size and a measure of general industrialisation, inspected deviations from normal

---

[1] This is a hard decision for developing countries. Investment in current best-practice methods, however capital-intensive, can be considered rational, since they can thereby compete against developed economies with older capital stocks and circumvent local shortages of skilled labour. But this implicitly gives priority to output over employment and the adoption of such investment criteria has historically aggravated unemployment in developing countries and in dual economies drawn the modern sector technologically further away from the traditional sector.

[2] Kuznets, *Modern Economic Growth*, p. 102.

[3] Maizels, *Industrial Growth and World Trade*, pp. 21–2.

levels in centrally planned economies.[1] Capital goods sectors were found to be substantially larger than those of market economies, though there were great variations among the countries studied. This technique assumes that the effects of planning are additive, but subsequently Gregory showed that for centrally planned East European economies the whole basis for growth patterns was shifted by the intrusion of planner preferences and military priorities.[2]

The colonial status of some countries has also been recognised as a distorting influence on the natural course of development. Myint has pointed to the rigidity and export-orientation of the production structure of countries in South East Asia, and their consequent inability to create a skilled labour force or to generate domestic investment or innovation.[3] Green has disputed the evidence of Hilgerdt on the fast growth of the larger Commonwealth countries in the first quarter of this century by noting that the growth was sustained only for the group as a whole, consisting of shortlived bursts of industrialisation in each member in turn.[4] Hong has documented the unbalanced character of industry in Taiwan and Korea during their periods of Japanese sovereignty and their subsequent return to normality in the 1950s.[5] And Girgis has pointed out that similarities between the productive structure of individual Arab countries and that of Western Europe multiply not with the prosperity of the country but with the time elapsed since the end of colonial rule.[6]

Enough has been said about the basic methods used in analysing growth patterns, and the controversies to which they lead, to explain the rift between growth theorists and empirical investigators. Growth theory has been concerned to solve in a deductive fashion puzzles arising from the existence of net investment in static Keynesian and neoclassical models of income determination. Work on growth patterns has been resolutely inductive in attempting to establish laws of growth or refute them; to the extent that the extra-market forces listed above have seemed unique or imponderable so has the value of simple general models of growth seemed slight to some researchers. Kuznets especially

[1] United Nations, Department of Economic and Social Affairs, *The Growth of World Industry 1938–61*.
[2] P. R. Gregory, 'Cross section comparisons of the structure of GNP by sector of origin: socialist and western countries', *Kyklos*, vol. 24, no. 3, 1971.
[3] H. Myint, *'South-East Asia's Economy: development policies in the 1970's'*, Harmondsworth, Penguin Books, 1972, chap. 1.
[4] R. H. Green, *Stages in Economic Development: changes in the structure of production, demand and international trade*, New Haven (Conn.), Yale Economic Growth Center, 1969.
[5] W. Hong, 'Industrialization and trade in manufactures: the East Asian experience' in P. B. Kenen and R. Lawrence (eds.), *The Open Economy*, New York, Columbia University Press, 1968.
[6] M. Girgis, 'Development and trade patterns in the Arab world', *Weltwirtschaftliches Archiv*, vol. 109, no. 1, 1973.

has been pessimistic on this count, whereas Chenery has consistently defended the concept of uniform development patterns.

An application of cluster analysis

Our own position is that, while the negative views have some force and while it may be futile to search for laws of growth applicable in every corner of the world economy, there may nonetheless exist identifiable groups of countries for which valid generalisations can be framed and common growth models constructed. This device of prior classification has previously been exploited by Chenery and Taylor,[1] who split their sample into large and small countries and the small countries further into primary and manufacturing-oriented; later Chenery and Hughes drew a basic distinction between countries like Venezuela and New Zealand, which can grow through exports of resource-based products, and large, poorly endowed countries like Taiwan, Korea and India, which must export manufactures very early in their development.[2] Maizels also found that classifying countries into industrialised, semi-industrialised and non-industrialised was helpful in analysing trading patterns.[3]

In all of these exercises countries were allocated to groups on the basis of only one or two criteria, but the many doubts about the existence of uniform growth patterns suggest that countries must be similar in many ways before the simple model can be applied. Since the number of categories to which countries might belong multiplies rapidly as the number of criteria by which they are classified increases, we have appealed for guidance to a branch of statistical theory – cluster analysis – which is concerned with grouping entities according to their similarity in certain measured characteristics.

The qualification that the characteristics must be measurable means that attention is confined to economic variables and, even in gauging these, proxy measures figure prominently.[4] Seven economic and demographic features for 116 countries were collected for use in the cluster analysis. These were – the level of income per head, population size, population density, the shares in GDP of gross fixed investment and total foreign trade in goods and services, the share of manufactures in total exports and the percentage of the economically active population engaged in agriculture. The relevance of these to the choice

[1] Chenery and Taylor, 'Development patterns'.
[2] IBRD, *The International Division of Labor: the case of industry* by H. B. Chenery and H. Hughes, Paris, 1972.
[3] Maizels, *Industrial Growth and World Trade*, pp. 60–4.
[4] A heroic attempt to score societies on non-economic criteria was made in I. Adelman and C. T. Morris, *Society, Politics and Economic Development: a quantitative approach*, Baltimore, Johns Hopkins University Press, 1967.

of growth model should be apparent. The first serves as a proxy for a particular composition of demand, the last two for the prevailing orientation of the production structure. The rest indicate the potential for change induced by growth in demand due to higher investment and by changes in specialisation within industry. This latter push towards a new industrial order can come about either through the realisation of economies of scale in the domestic market if the population is large, or through submission to the pattern of international division of labour if trade is important and freely entered, or in default of any alternative if natural resources are scarce.[1]

For each pair of countries a measure of economic 'distance' was calculated on the basis of these characteristics, very dissimilar countries generating large measures and very similar countries small measures. These distances were then used to build up clusters of homogeneous economies by hierarchical fusion. The exact way in which the distances were assessed and clusters formed is described in more detail in appendix F. Briefly, our method involved at each stage amalgamating the two individual countries, or clusters of countries formed at an earlier stage, which lay closest together. Thus the initial set of 116 clusters each containing one country was reduced to 115 clusters – made up of 114 one-country clusters and a cluster consisting of the two most similar countries in the sample – then to 114 clusters, and so on until some terminal number of clusters was reached.

Seven clusters were eventually identified by this method.[2] Their membership is shown in table 5.6; table 5.7 lists their economic characteristics. In addition to the mean value of each variable in the cluster, two statistics are given. One is a 't-statistic' which helps to identify formally the characteristics distinguishing any particular cluster from the rest of the population. The other is an 'F-statistic' measuring the internal homogeneity of the group with respect to each variable.[3]

There are two very distinctive clusters, III and V. The first of these consists mainly of the large, mineral-rich, sparsely populated states of North West and Central Africa, which all have very open economies, with revenues from the export of crudely processed metals sufficient to maintain very high rates of capital investment. The second consists mainly of 'island economies', small and densely settled, which rely on

---

[1] The use of population density as a proxy for resource scarcity was pioneered in D. B. Keesing and D. R. Sherk, 'Population density in patterns of trade and development', *American Economic Review*, vol. 61, December 1971.

[2] The computations were carried out using Wishart's CLUSTAN 1B package.

[3] These are not the t and F-statistics of normal distribution theory, but analogous measures applied to clusters regardless of their spatial distribution. The t-statistic is the difference between the mean of a variable in a cluster and its unweighted mean in the whole sample, divided by its standard error in the whole sample; the F-statistic is the ratio of the standard deviation of the variable in a cluster to its standard deviation in the whole sample.

Table 5.6. *An economic classification of countries by cluster analysis*

Cluster I	Afghanistan, Bolivia, Botswana, Burma, Burundi, Cameroon, Central African Republic, Chad, *Colombia*, Dahomey, Dominican Republic, Ecuador, El Salvador, Ethiopia, Gambia, Ghana, Guatemala, Guinea, Haiti, Honduras, Iran, Ivory Coast, Kenya, Liberia, Madagascar, Malawi, Mali, *Morocco*, Mozambique, Nepal, Nicaragua, Niger, *Nigeria*, Paraguay, *Philippines*, Rwanda, Senegal, Somalia, Sri Lanka, Sudan, Syria, Tanzania, Togo, *Turkey*, Uganda, Upper Volta, Vietnam
Cluster II	*Brazil, Egypt*, Greece, *Indonesia*, Korea, *Mexico, Pakistan*, Portugal, Sierra Leone, Spain, Thailand
Cluster III	Algeria, Congo, Gabon, Mauritania, Yugoslavia, Zaire, Zambia
Cluster IV	*Argentina*, Costa Rica, Cyprus, Fiji, Guadeloupe, Guyana, Iraq, *Ireland*, Jamaica, Jordan, Lebanon, Libya, Malaysia, Martinique, Mauritius, Panama, *Peru, Rhodesia, South Africa*, Tunisia, Uruguay, *Venezuela*
Cluster V	Barbados, *Luxembourg*, Malta, *Netherlands, Puerto Rico*, Singapore, Trinidad & Tobago
Cluster VI	*Australia, Austria, Belgium, Chile, Denmark, Finland, France, Germany*, Iceland, *Israel, Italy, Japan, New Zealand, Norway, Sweden, Switzerland, United Kingdom*
Cluster VII	*Canada*, Kuwait, *United States*

Notes: (i) For classification method see appendix F.
    (ii) Countries in italics both appeared in Maizels' study and are used for the time-series analysis on pp. 124–5 below.
   (iii) India and Hong Kong remained unclassified when the clusters in this table emerged.

exports of labour-intensive manufactures to buy both basic foods and capital equipment.

The economic structure of the other groups is less dependent on purely geographical features. Cluster I consists of small countries with low incomes per head; it includes most other African states and about half of the Asian and Latin American states for which adequate data could be obtained. It is distinguished from other less underdeveloped clusters, such as II and IV, by the extreme primary orientation of the labour force, the unimportance of manufactured exports and a failure to generate or attract investment. Cluster II contains countries rather larger in population and area than those in Cluster I, but is also marked by low incomes per head; foreign trade is an unimportant residual for most of the group, though the share of manufactures in exports is remarkably high and exceeded only among the less developed by the mainly mineral-rich economies of Cluster III. Conversely, Cluster IV contains small open economies which are richer than Cluster II in terms of incomes per head, but which have not succeeded to the same extent in promoting manufactured exports despite a more industry-biased labour force. Clusters VI and VII cover mainly the rich industrial countries; Canada, the United States of America and Kuwait are separated out by their extreme positions on the income scale.

Table 5.7. *Economic characteristics of the clusters, 1963 cross-section*

| | Income per head | Population | | | Ratio to GDP of: | | Share of manufactures in total exports |
		Size	Density	Propn. in agriculture[a]	Investment	Foreign trade[b]	
	($)	(millions)	(ooo/Mha)	(%)	(percentages)		
Mean value							
Cluster I	143.66	8.48	343.45	77.91	12.13	39.96	5.27
II	252.73	41.89	740.91	62.35	16.55	30.00	41.41
III	257.14	7.32	136.14	74.46	35.00	83.43	53.27
IV	453.64	4.55	700.86	44.80	18.64	65.77	12.39
V	823.43	2.58	3815.00	16.61	22.71	137.86	33.54
VI	1356.35	21.85	1043.06	19.47	24.53	48.71	67.35
VII	4338.00	69.52	155.67	7.07	17.33	44.00	36.00
t-statistic[c]							
Cluster I	−0.52	−0.19	−0.21	0.82	−0.74	−0.42	−0.68
II	−0.38	0.49	−0.09	0.26	−0.17	−0.69	0.53
III	−0.37	−0.22	−0.27	0.69	2.70	0.78	0.92
IV	−0.12	−0.27	−0.10	−0.38	0.09	0.30	−0.45
V	0.35	−0.31	0.87	−1.39	0.61	2.29	0.26
VI	1.04	0.08	—	−1.29	0.85	−0.17	1.39
VII	4.86	1.06	−0.26	−1.74	−0.07	−0.30	0.34
F-statistic[c]							
Cluster I	0.01	0.04	0.01	0.26	0.17	0.20	0.03
II	0.04	0.52	0.04	0.24	0.25	0.12	0.68
III	0.05	0.02	0.01	0.22	1.77	0.54	0.93
IV	0.07	0.01	0.08	0.20	0.34	0.41	0.20
V	0.22	0.01	0.96	0.06	0.49	1.39	0.90
VI	0.25	0.31	0.08	0.10	0.30	0.29	0.74
VII	0.50	3.04	—	0.03	0.14	0.77	0.75

[a] Of economically active population.
[b] Total trade in goods and services.
[c] See definitions in footnote on p. 111.

Clustering procedures such as hierarchical fusion are liable to throw up peripheral problems in the shape of 'albatrosses' – countries which have not been allocated to any larger groupings by the time the optimum breakdown has been effected – and 'cuckoos' – countries which are allocated to groups where intuition dictates they do not belong. Both Hong Kong and India were left unclassified in this exercise because they were so remote from other economies in population density and size respectively. Hong Kong is closest to Malta and Singapore and so has some affinity with Cluster V.[1] India is closest in size and structure to Pakistan and Indonesia; it can thus be considered an extreme member of Cluster II.

[1] Taiwan would probably also qualify for this cluster, but because of insufficient data it had to be excluded from the formal analysis.

The classification in several cases offends intuition. Sierra Leone is placed with the larger developing countries and Israel with the developed group; both obtained unjustifiably high scores for manufactured exports because of the high value of their trade in precious stones, which counted as manufactures for the purposes of this exercise. Yugoslavia also sits rather ill with the mineral exporters of Cluster III, this being due to the coexistence of a high rate of investment with low income per head, the result not of the exploitation of natural resources, but of forced saving under a centrally planned regime. Objections can also be raised to the inclusion of Luxembourg and the Netherlands in Cluster V, since both are closer in economic 'distance' to Belgium and Denmark in Cluster VI and come to be linked with the island economies only through a vague structural similarity between the Netherlands and Puerto Rico.

In spite of these problems of detail, the classification appears robust enough to support two important general propositions. The first is that differences in demographic features alone seem sufficient to cause economic structures to diverge. Table 5.7 shows that the clusters are generally most homogeneous with respect to factors like population size and density and the occupational distribution of the labour force. But they are not markedly different from each other in these respects; instead, they are most clearly distinguished in economic performance – particularly in their ratios for investment and manufactured exports. In other words, although countries exist on a continuum of demographic characteristics, such differences as emerge are associated with – and perhaps cause – sharp differences in economic structure.

The clearest illustration of this is the contrast between the export records of Clusters II and IV. Despite their higher incomes – and hence internal demand for more complex manufactures – and their considerable labour resources devoted to manufacturing, the countries of Cluster IV have failed to develop industrial exports to the same extent as those in Cluster II, presumably because the scale-advantages residing with the latter group are sufficient to outweigh the income differences.

At a superficial level, then, these tables support the proposition that the growth process is discontinuous. However, they confirm the presence only of systematic cross-sectional discontinuities; the more profound question of whether the dynamics of industrialisation and growth differ between groups remains to be explored below.

The second lesson to be drawn from this exercise is the danger of advancing generalisations based on extreme observations. The literature on growth economics is replete with studies of India and the United States, for example, while the cluster analysis suggests that both are so unlike other developing and advanced economies as to be removed entirely from the main classification.[1] In fact, two of the most important features of the growth patterns uncovered by Chenery and Taylor appear to derive entirely from the influence of such observations.[2] The first is the notion that for large countries the share of manufacturing reaches a maximum around income per head of $1500 and actually *declines* thereafter – based on the fact that Canada and the United States had proportionately smaller manufacturing sectors than Germany, France and the United Kingdom; the second is the notion that the share of agriculture in small industry-orientated countries falls at an increasing rate as GDP per head increases above $500 – based on the fact that Chile, Denmark and Australia had relatively less value added in agriculture than the poorer countries which formed the remainder of this subsample.[3] The cluster analysis shows that interpolation between the structures of Western European and North American economies is probably unwarranted and the connection between Australia or Denmark and a set of less developed countries, all but two of which fall into our Cluster I, is certainly tenuous.

THE EFFECTS OF GROWTH ON INDUSTRIALISATION

We now have the techniques to prepare our own estimates of what structural changes are induced by growth, and a classification of countries by which to judge how these structural changes vary from one type of economy to another. Two aspects of industrialisation are examined below: the behaviour of the manufacturing share relative to

---

[1] So large and cosmopolitan are India and the United States that attempts have been made to analyse their regional growth in terms of development patterns – see K. L. Gupta, 'Development patterns: an interregional study', *Quarterly Journal of Economics*, vol. 85, November 1971 – and to infer national development patterns from the results – R. N. Cooper, 'Growth and trade: some hypotheses about long-term trends', *Journal of Economic History*, vol. 24, December 1964.

[2] Chenery and Taylor, 'Development patterns', pp. 399–400.

[3] Using our data but Chenery and Taylor's samples and notation we find for the industry share X_m in large countries including Canada and the United States:

$$\log X_m = 2.58 + 1.49 \log y - 0.10 (\log y)^2 - 0.071 \log N$$
$$\quad\quad (3.07) \quad\quad (2.47) \quad\quad\quad (0.85)$$

Without these two countries it is:

$$\log X_m = -0.63 + 0.77 \log y - 0.03 (\log y)^2 - 0.061 \log N$$
$$\quad\quad (0.99) \quad\quad (0.49) \quad\quad\quad (0.64)$$

so that the significance of the non-linear term in income per head falls dramatically and the whole relationship looks less healthy; further investigation showed that only by introducing the investment ratio into this equation could differences in industrialisation among large countries be explained. Similarly, with small industry-oriented countries, omission of Denmark and Australia caused the regression for the share of agriculture to collapse and differences among the rest of the group were explicable only in terms of another variable Chenery and Taylor did not employ – the foreign trade ratio.

the primary share of domestic output as a whole and the behaviour of the shares of individual sectors within manufacturing.

Each is studied by means of simple logarithmic regressions of these shares on income per head and auxiliary variables, such as population size and density, and the investment and trade ratios. Initially, 1963 data for all 116 countries involved in the cluster analysis are used in estimating growth patterns, then separate regressions are calculated for each cluster in turn. The patterns found are then tested for stability over time by comparing them with results from 1971 data and with results from long time-series of data on selected industrial and semi-industrial countries covering the period 1899–1971. They are also tested for generality by statistical comparisons between the parameters found for related pairs of clusters and by comparing overall cross-section and time-series results with the growth paths followed by individual countries. Throughout our findings are checked against those established by Maizels and by the other studies in this field referred to earlier.

The share of manufactures in domestic output

The basic equation used to explain the evolution of broad sectoral shares in total output is

$$\log y_j = \alpha_0 + \alpha_1 \log y + \alpha_2 (\log y)^2 + \alpha_3 \log N \\ + \alpha_4 \log i + \alpha_5 \log t \tag{5.7}$$

where y_j = value-added share of sector (primary, manufacturing) in GDP

　　　y = income per head
　　　N = population size
　　　i = share of investment in GDP
　　　t = share of foreign trade (exports *plus* imports) in GDP

Table 5.8. *Primary and manufacturing shares: general growth patterns, 1963 cross-section[a]*

| | Coefficient | | | | | | $\overline{R}^2$ |
	α_0	α_1	α_2	α_3	α_4	α_5	
Primary sector[b]	6.87	−0.55	0.01	−0.01	0.04	−0.21	0.59
		(1.66)	(0.51)	(2.88)	(0.28)	(2.19)	
Manufacturing	−2.53	1.32	−0.08	0.16			0.57
		(4.02)	(2.89)	(6.09)			

[a] Equation 5.7 estimated on the full sample of 116 countries; t-statistics given in brackets.
[b] Includes mining.

The estimated equations of this form which best explain variations in the manufacturing and primary shares of GDP in all 116 countries in 1963 are presented in table 5.8. It can be seen that neither of the unconventional variables in equation 5.7 – the coefficients α_4 and α_5 on the investment and trade ratios – is important in determining the level of industrialisation, although in very open economies the primary share may be lower than in countries where foreign trade is a minor part of total economic activity. The manufacturing share is positively related to population size (α_3), whereas the primary share is negatively related to it. Similarly, the manufacturing share tends to rise and the primary share to fall with increasing wealth (α_1), the rise in the former becoming less pronounced at high income levels as shown by the negative coefficient α_2.

In chart 5.3 the growth patterns implied by these equations are plotted for a small country with ten million inhabitants and a large country with fifty million. This shows clearly the leading role of population size in fixing the level of industrialisation, the share of manufacturing being consistently 30 per cent higher in the large

Chart 5.3. *Growth patterns of primary and manufacturing shares for large and small countries*

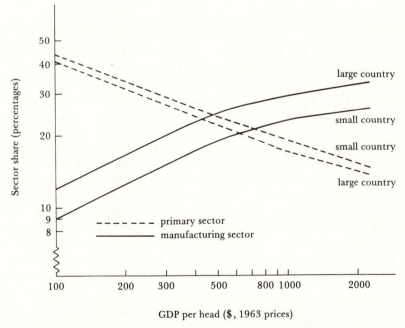

GDP per head ($, 1963 prices)

Note: Large country has population 50 million; small country has population 10 million.
SOURCE: calculated from table 5.8.

Chart 5.4. *Industrialisation and internal purchasing power in large and small countries*

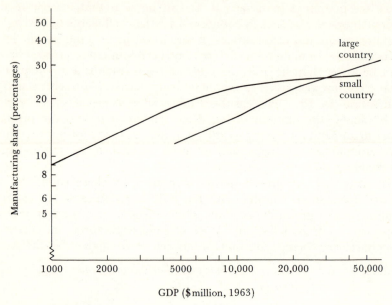

GDP ($million, 1963)

Note: see note to chart 5.3.
SOURCES: calculated from table 5.8 and chart 5.3.

country and reaching a saturation point at about 34 per cent of GDP as opposed to only 26 per cent in the small country.

Implicit in these patterns are three other features which deserve comment. First, since the effects of income per head on both primary and manufacturing shares are non-linear, for each there exists a turning point – a level of income above which the primary share starts to rise and another above which the manufacturing share starts to fall. For the primary share this point lies well outside the realms of experience; for the manufacturing share reversal is implied at incomes above $3800 per head in 1963, figures which had been experienced only by the rather atypical economies of Kuwait and the United States.[1] Secondly, since the effects of income growth and population growth are not symmetrical, a rather complex relationship exists between the degree of industrialisation and total internal purchasing power (population × income per head = GDP). As chart 5.4 shows, among economies with

[1] Manufacturing industry's output has, in fact, contracted in several industrial countries in recent years, but, except in the United Kingdom where the relative uncompetitiveness of the manufacturing sector appears to be responsible, this is probably due more to the greater stability in periods of cyclical weakness of the rates of growth of the primary and tertiary sectors than to any underlying change of trend.

GDP less than $30,000 million in 1963 smaller countries tend to have larger industrial sectors than larger ones, whereas above that figure the reverse is true. So while there is a general tendency for industry to exploit the scale-economies afforded by a large reservoir of domestic purchasing power – both curves rise with rising GDP – the extent of this exploitation depends on whether the economy consists of many consumers with low incomes or a few consumers with high incomes. The third interesting by-product of the growth patterns illustrated in chart 5.3 is the pattern it implies for the residual services sector of the economy. Because growth and size affect primary and manufacturing sectors in diametrically opposite ways, this component is practically constant at around 45–50 per cent of GDP for all but the very poorest and the very richest countries irrespective of their sizes.

Table 5.9 summarises the empirical results from six major studies which have appeared since 1963 and this table is used as a standard of reference throughout the rest of this section. For the moment we are interested in comparing our regression parameters with those from studies based mainly on cross-sections.[1] Our elasticity of the manu-facturing share with respect to income per head is about 0.5 on average;[2] with respect to population size it is 0.16. The former is slightly higher than that calculated by Maizels and appreciably higher than that found in the earlier United Nations study, but it does correspond with the sort of figure implicit in Kuznets' data; this last falls between Maizels' very low estimate and the surprisingly large effect estimated in the 1969 United Nations study. Apart from measurement errors, the discrepancies among these cross-sectional estimates can arise only from differences in the coverage of each sample – implying that the patterns are not truly general – or in the date at which the sample is drawn – implying that the patterns shift over time.

To test the first possibility our basic equation 5.7 was estimated for each cluster individually, with the results shown in table 5.10. The equations explaining the level of industrialisation are least successful in the extreme cases; in particular, differences in the structures of the advanced economies in Cluster VI owe little to size and income variations. The addition of the investment and trade ratios does, however, contribute something to the explanation here, in marked contrast to the irrelevance of these factors in all the less developed

---

[1] Maizels, *Industrial Growth and World Trade*: United Nations, Department of Economic and Social Affairs, *A Study of Industrial Growth*; UNIDO, 'The role of the industrial sector in economic development', *Industrialization and Productivity Bulletin*, no. 14, 1969; Kuznets, *The Economic Growth of Nations*.

[2] The income elasticity for equations including a term in $(\log y)^2$ is not constant; throughout this chapter such measures are calculated at the mean income for the sample (cluster) under consideration.

Table 5.9. *Effects of income and size on the share of manufacturing in GDP: a comparison of six major studies*

Study	Data		Countries		Elasticities[a]	
	Type	Period	No.	Type	Income	Size
Maizels (1963)	Cross-section	1955	48	Various	0.45	0.07
	Time-series	1899–1957	10	Industrial	0.27	—
United Nations (1963)	Cross-section	{1953 1958}	{53 42}	Various	0.37	0.25
Chenery and Taylor (1968)	Pooled	1950–63	54	Various	0.37	0.04
			19	Large	0.37[b]	0.10
			18	Small industrial	0.34[b]	0.06
			17	Small primary	0.34[b]	0.11
UNIDO (1969)	Cross-section	{1958 1964}	36	Various	0.59	0.11
Kuznets (1972)	Cross-section	1958	57	Various	0.53	
	Pooled	1953–65	32	{Rich Poor}	{0.31 1.55}	n.a.[c]
	Time-series	1850–1967	11	Mainly developed	0.39[d]	
Chenery and Syrquin (1975)	Pooled	1950–70	86	Various	0.09	0.02
			26	Large	0.08	0.01
			25	Small industrial	0.10	0.04
			35	Small primary	0.07	0.01

[a] Where the original equations were not linear in the logarithms of income per head and population, elasticities were computed at the sample means.

[b] This elasticity varies markedly with income per head: for the large countries it falls to zero at $1200 p.a. (1960 prices); for small industrial countries it declines but remains positive over the whole income range of the sample; for small primary countries it rises at high income levels.

[c] Kuznets only investigated average differences in industrialisation between large and small countries; he then excluded size from his analysis because, on his criterion, it had no discernible effects.

[d] Calculated from Kuznets' tables 1 and 21. It is an unweighted average of the following elasticities found for certain countries: Great Britain 0.43, France 0.09, West Germany 0.24, Belgium 0.26, Netherlands 0.47, Norway 0.34, Sweden 0.58, Italy 0.65, United States 0.56, Canada 0.15 and Australia 0.50. Construction is here included in the manufacturing sector.

SOURCES: Maizels, *Industrial Growth and World Trade*; United Nations, Department of Economic and Social Affairs, *A Study of Industrial Growth*; Chenery and Taylor, 'Development patterns'; UNIDO, 'The role of the industrial sector in economic development'; Kuznets, *The Economic Growth of Nations*; Chenery and Syrquin, *Patterns of Development*.

groups except Cluster II. Non-linearity in the relationship between the manufacturing share and income seems important only for the large countries of Cluster II, where the income elasticity declines at high income levels, and for the eccentric Cluster IV where it rises sharply. Most of the equations listed are necessarily based on small samples and the statistical problems this causes are exacerbated by the restricted spread of income per head encountered within each cluster. So we should hesitate to extrapolate any pattern for a cluster much outside the range of incomes of its members. With this reservation in mind, we can

Table 5.10. *Primary and manufacturing shares: growth patterns by cluster, 1963 cross-section[a]*

	Coefficient						$\bar{R}^2$
	α_0	α_1	α_2	α_3	α_4	α_5	
Cluster I							
Primary sector	5.13	−0.29		−0.01			0.39
		(5.30)		(0.25)			
Manufacturing	−0.28	0.49		0.09			0.40
		(5.20)		(1.54)			
Cluster II							
Primary sector	12.50	−2.18	0.15	−0.22	−0.02	−0.34	0.96
		(1.67)	(1.26)	(2.94)	(0.08)	(1.62)	
Manufacturing	−17.47	6.91	−0.60	0.24			0.74
		(2.41)	(2.23)	(2.47)			
Cluster III							
Primary sector	−0.80	1.39	−0.13	−0.02	−0.23	0.37	0.99
		(11.26)	(10.97)	(9.66)	(25.34)	(23.04)	
Manufacturing	38.42	−13.84	1.30	0.11			0.96
		(5.05)	(5.24)	(1.96)			
Cluster IV							
Primary sector	4.07	−1.18	0.10	0.05	0.06	0.62	0.38
		(0.20)	(0.20)	(0.70)	(0.15)	(2.60)	
Manufacturing	−0.50	0.48	0.19				0.45
		(2.54)	(2.71)				
Cluster V							
Primary sector	−187.95	57.20	−4.27	0.47			0.74
		(2.61)	(2.61)	(2.57)			
Manufacturing	96.09	−29.21	2.26	0.25			0.85
		(1.61)	(1.67)	(1.63)			
Cluster VI							
Primary sector	6.87	−0.55	0.01	−0.10	0.04	−0.21	0.59
		(1.66)	(0.51)	(2.88)	(0.28)	(2.19)	
Manufacturing	23.29	−6.42	0.46	0.11	0.44	0.17	0.34
		(0.77)	(0.78)	(1.60)	(1.30)	(0.60)	

[a] Equation 5.7 estimated on subsamples from 116 countries; t-statistics given in brackets.

see in charts 5.5 and 5.6 the growth paths over limited income ranges of the primary and manufacturing sectors for four major groups of countries; these paths are calculated from the equations of table 5.10 using the average population size and the investment and trade ratios appropriate to each cluster.

These charts highlight two clear departures from the smooth general growth patterns of chart 5.3. The large developing countries of Cluster II experience an early burst of industrialisation which falls off at quite modest levels of income per head and in the small semi-industrial countries of Cluster IV primary production persists so long as trade

Chart 5.5. *Primary shares : growth patterns by cluster*

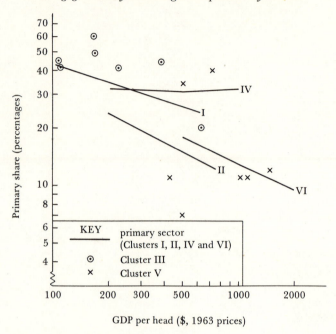

GDP per head ($, 1963 prices)

SOURCES: calculated from table 5.10; NIESR estimates.

persists and does not fall systematically with rising domestic incomes.[1] Size and autarky thus appear as substitutes for economic maturity, in the sense that manufacturing activity in large developing countries can expand readily to the sort of rates found in the advanced countries, large and small, which make up Cluster VI, but the process of agricultural transformation is likely to be inhibited in smaller countries if during development their economic structure is less sensitive to shifts in domestic demand towards manufactures than to the continuing foreign demand for their primary products.

Of the studies cited in table 5.9 only three investigate whether distinct growth patterns exist for subgroups of the countries they study.[2] All concur that in large rich countries the responsiveness of the share of manufacturing to income growth is lower than in small less developed countries, but they differ markedly in the exact figures put on these elasticities. Kuznets has the manufacturing sector outpacing income per

---

[1] Cf our comments on Chenery and Taylor's analysis of small industry-orientated countries on p. 115 above.
[2] Chenery and Taylor, 'Development patterns'; Kuznets, *The Economic Growth of Nations*; Chenery and Syrquin, *Patterns of Development*.

Chart 5.6. *Manufacturing shares: growth patterns by cluster*

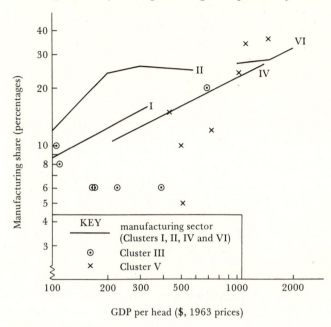

GDP per head ($, 1963 prices)

SOURCES: as chart 5.5.

head in poorer economies, an event which in our scheme occurs only with very large, very indigent countries and one which is ruled out altogether by other investigators. Even in the two related studies by Chenery and Taylor and Chenery and Syrquin average income elasticities of quite different orders of magnitude are obtained, 0.3–0.4 in the earlier work and 0.0–0.1 in the later. This phenomenon of a declining cross-sectional elasticity has also been observed for advanced countries by Gregory and Griffin in a statistical test of the compatibility of cross-sectional and time-series estimates of growth patterns.[1] It would arise if Kuznets' contention that poor countries industrialise faster than rich countries held good within each of the groups of countries distinguished and this in turn would mean that the groupings did not succeed in isolating distinct types of development pattern. Does our classification succeed any better? To test whether the industrialisation pattern found for each main cluster was stable over time the basic equation 5.7 was re-estimated on the basis of a 1971 cross-section and its

[1] P. R. Gregory and J. M. Griffin, 'Secular and cross-sectional industrialization: some further evidence on the Kuznets–Chenery controversy', *Review of Economics and Statistics*, vol. 56, August 1974.

Table 5.11. *Manufacturing share: growth patterns from time-series, whole sample and by cluster[a]*

	Coefficient				$\overline{R}^2$
	α_0	α_1	α_2	α_3	
Whole sample					
Including United States	−5.70	2.34	−0.16	0.13	0.54
and Canada		(7.74)	(6.50)	(6.61)	
Excluding United States	−1.90	1.22	−0.07	0.15	0.43
and Canada		(2.78)	(2.18)	(7.28)	
Cluster II	−11.73	4.11	−0.28	0.17	0.88
		(0.97)	(0.74)	(2.03)	
Cluster IV	−3.73	1.64	−0.10	0.12	0.26
		(0.43)	(0.33)	(1.10)	
Cluster VI	−1.90	1.22	−0.07	0.15	0.43
		(2.78)	(2.18)	(7.28)	

[a] Equation 5.7 with $\alpha_4 = \alpha_5 = 0$ estimated on a sample of 40 countries, or subsamples from it, with 1899–1971 pooled data; t-statistics given in brackets.

parameters tested for equality with the 1963 results shown in table 5.10. Only in the least developed group, Cluster I, was income elasticity found to fall (from 0.5 to 0.25); all other clusters exhibited very stable growth patterns indeed.

While this stability strengthens our faith in the value of the country classification produced by the cluster analysis, it is only a *necessary* condition for the regressions of table 5.10 to be interpreted as growth paths along which all the members of each cluster develop; a *sufficient* condition would be that in long time-series each country did in fact industrialise in the way the regressions indicate, so we next confronted our cross-sectional results with data on some 40 countries for all or part of the period 1899–1971.[1]

The patterns which emerge when all this data is pooled turn out to depend critically on whether North America is included in the analysis. Table 5.11 shows that with the complete sample a very curvilinear relation between industrialisation and income per head is obtained, with the implication that the share of manufacturing in GDP falls after $1900 is reached. But a cursory inspection of the history of economies which have passed that income level reveals that only in Canada and the United States has the manufacturing sector contracted.[2] If those countries are omitted the second equation appears, which is practically identical with the general cross-sectional pattern presented earlier. It is

[1] The countries involved appear in italics in table 5.6 above.
[2] See the footnote to p. 115 above for comments on this bias.

more difficult to establish whether the relationships we have estimated for individual clusters hold good for movements over time, as Cluster VI is the only group for which adequate data are available. We have nonetheless estimated paths for Cluster II using data on Brazil, Egypt and Mexico and for Cluster IV using data on Argentina, Ireland, Peru, South Africa and Venezuela. The resulting equations are also set out in table 5.11.

In chart 5.7, where the actual paths of industrialisation in representative developing countries are superimposed on their cross-sectional patterns, the implications of the equations stand out clearly. The large countries of Cluster II have experienced very rapid rates of industrialisation, but at incomes about 50 per cent higher than would be suggested by the cross-sectional pattern; the smaller countries have industrialised more slowly in a manner wholly consistent with their

Chart 5.7. *Manufacturing shares for developing countries: cross-sectional patterns and time-series*

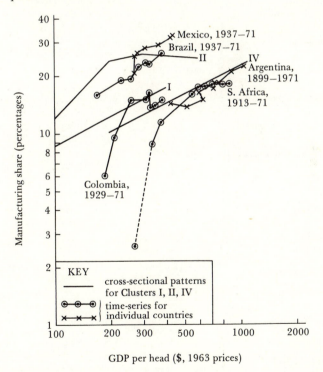

Note: Shares for individual countries are normalised to that appropriate to a country with the mean population for the relevant cluster in 1963, using the cross-sectional size elasticities in table 5.15.

SOURCES: United Nations, *The Growth of World Industry*; chart 5.6.

cross-sectional pattern. As to the advanced countries, the time-series data do not support the idea of an acceleration in the rate of industrialisation at high income levels as suggested by chart 5.6, but neither do they imply any contraction in the importance of the manufacturing sector except at impossibly high income levels. The average elasticity of the manufacturing share with respect to income is, at 0.2, identical in both time-series and cross-sectional regressions.

The shares of industries in manufacturing output

The basic equation used to explain the changing composition of the

Table 5.12. *The composition of manufacturing output: general growth patterns, 1963 cross-section[a]*

ISIC no.[b]		Coefficient						$\bar{R}^2$
		β_0	β_1	β_2	β_3	β_4	β_5	
311–14	Food, beverages, tobacco	1.43	−0.30 (1.38)		−0.37 (2.38)			0.10
371–2	Basic metals	−12.77	−0.95 (0.29)	0.09 (0.33)	0.78 (2.70)	2.08 (1.69)	0.96 (1.57)	0.32
382	Non-electrical machinery	−10.84	1.06 (8.09)		0.28 (2.87)			0.62
383	Electrical machinery	−12.13	0.44 (0.30)	0.02 (0.20)	0.53 (4.28)	0.56 (1.04)	0.53 (1.85)	0.58
384	Transport equipment	−13.60	1.85 (1.50)	−0.12 (1.20)	0.43 (3.77)	0.17 (0.36)	0.68 (2.19)	0.42
385	Other metal products	−6.12	0.39 (4.52)		0.24 (3.70)			0.41
351–2	Chemicals	−3.46	0.08 (1.05)		0.15 (2.54)			0.12
321	Textiles	−2.32	−0.08 (0.28)		0.17 (0.84)			0.01
322–4	Leather, clothing, footwear	−4.17	0.27 (0.94)		−0.25 (1.21)			0.05
331–2 341	Forest products	−3.47	0.11 (1.70)		0.04 (0.85)			0.05
361–9	Mineral products	−4.98	0.41 (0.64)	−0.04 (0.70)	0.05 (0.74)	0.08 (0.26)	0.17 (1.06)	0.03
355	Rubber products	0.58	−0.78 (0.59)	0.08 (0.77)	0.22 (1.66)	−1.16 (1.92)	−0.13 (0.34)	0.24
342 356 390	Other products	−5.32	−0.28 (0.40)	0.04 (0.65)	0.07 (1.13)	0.41 (1.45)	0.36 (2.31)	0.36

[a] Equation 5.8 estimated on samples of 86–116 countries; t-statistics given in brackets.
[b] Petroleum refining (ISIC 353–4) not included.

output of the industrial sector is

$$\log (Y_j/Y_m) = \beta_0 + \beta_1 \log y + \beta_2 (\log y)^2 + \beta_3 \log N \\ + \beta_4 \log i + \beta_5 \log t \tag{5.8}$$

where Y_j/Y_m is the share of some subsector j in total value added in manufacturing and all other variables have the same meaning as in equation 5.7 (page 116 above).

In all, thirteen branches of manufacturing were subjected to this analysis; their definitions appear in table 5.12 along with the overall patterns estimated from such data as were readily available for our large 116-country cross-section in 1963. The explanatory power of the model is greatest with respect to technologically sophisticated sectors such as machinery and transport equipment, and least with respect to labour-intensive or resource-dependent sectors like textiles, basic metal manufacturing and mineral products. In some of these awkward groups (basic metals and rubber products, for example) the level of investment is a better guide to the level of activity than income or size.

Table 5.13. *Effects of income and size[a] on the composition of manufacturing output[b]*

Percentages

| | \$100 | | \$500 | | \$1000 | | \$2000 | |
	Small	Large	Small	Large	Small	Large	Small	Large
				Income per head				
Food, beverages, tobacco	45	30	33	17	24	12	18	6
Basic metals	2	6	2	7	3	8	3	9
Metal products	10	15	20	28	26	36	33	44
Non-electrical machinery	(—)	(2)	(5)	(6)	(7)	(7)	(11)	(9)
Electrical machinery	(2)	(2)	(2)	(2)	(5)	(5)	(6)	(9)
Transport equipment	(3)	(6)	(8)	(14)	(8)	(15)	(9)	(16)
Other	(3)	(4)	(5)	(6)	(6)	(7)	(7)	(10)
Chemicals	6	8	7	9	8	10	8	10
Textiles	10	13	10	12	9	11	8	8
Miscellaneous	23	23	26	24	29	25	30	26
Leather, clothing, footwear	(4)	(2)	(5)	(3)	(7)	(4)	(7)	(4)
Forest products	(5)	(4)	(7)	(7)	(8)	(8)	(8)	(8)
Mineral products	(6)	(7)	(6)	(5)	(5)	(4)	(4)	(3)
Rubber products	(1)	(2)	(1)	(2)	(1)	(2)	(2)	(2)
Other products	(7)	(7)	(7)	(7)	(7)	(7)	(9)	(9)

[a] Small country with population 10 million; large country with population 50 million.
[b] Based on regressions of table 5.12. Columns may not add to 100, owing to rounding and the fact that additivity is not preserved in a system of logarithmic equations.

Table 5.14. *Effects of income and size on the composition of manufacturing output: elasticities compared*[a]

	Income elasticity			Size elasticity		
	Table 5.12	Maizels	UN	Table 5.12	Maizels	UN
Food, beverages, tobacco	−0.30	0.10	−0.39	−0.37	−0.14	−0.26
Basic metals	0.01	0.68	0.62	0.78	0.44	0.52
Metal products	0.39 to 1.85	0.97	0.62	0.24 to 0.53	..	0.19
Chemicals	0.08	0.31	0.18[b]	0.15	..	0.27[b]
Textiles	−0.08	−0.07	−0.16	0.17	..	0.21
Miscellaneous	..	0.50	..	..	..	..
Leather, clothing, footwear	(0.27)	(..)	(−0.48 to zero)	(−0.25)	(..)	(−0.27 to −0.16)
Forest products	(0.11)	(..)	(0.16 to 0.67)	(0.04)	(..)	(−0.09 to −0.01)
Mineral products	(−0.01)	(..)	(−0.21)	(0.05)	(..)	(−0.02)
Rubber products	(0.07)	(..)	(0.21)	(0.22)	(..)	(0.08)
Other	(0.14)	(..)	(0.48)	(0.07)	(..)	(0.21)

[a] Our estimates compared with Maizels, *Industrial Growth and World Trade*, table 2.5, and United Nations, Department of Economic and Social Affairs, *A Study of Industrial Growth*, table I, p. 7.
[b] Including petroleum refining.

The pattern implied by the complete set of equations generally confirms Maizels' picture of the evolution of industrial structure, in the sense that the initially dominant food processing and textile industries are overhauled by machinery and other metal manufacturing, as illustrated in table 5.13.[1] There are, however, some striking differences between the present estimates of the elasticities of industry shares with respect to income and size and those propounded by Maizels. The main points of disagreement are evident from table 5.14, where these estimates are tabulated; they are our finding of a pronounced negative income elasticity for food processing even in cross-sectional data, our failure to establish positive associations between income and the production of chemicals and basic metals, and our success in identifying scale-effects in metal manufacturing and chemicals. The first is probably explained by the greater number of low-income primary producers in our sample; the second by Maizels' omission of size from the equation for chemicals and investment from the equation for basic metals, both these factors dominating income effects in our analysis; the last by the wider coverage of our data.

[1] Maizels, *Industrial Growth and World Trade*, pp. 54–5.

If the explanations in terms of differences in country coverage are correct, we cannot regard the equations of table 5.12 as truly general patterns; so, as with the manufacturing sector as a whole, equation 5.8 was re-estimated on the basis of data for each cluster separately. The main results are summarised in table 5.15 in the form of income and size elasticities for each industry in each main cluster, and in table 5.16, where industry structures typical of each cluster are described. From the first table it is obvious why a study such as Maizels', which focuses mainly on advanced countries, will produce estimates of income elasticities for foodstuffs and basic metals which are biased upwards and estimates of scale-effects on chemicals which are biased downwards; in all these cases the elasticity observed for Cluster VI is quite different from that observed for less developed countries, and in only one sector – transport equipment – is there a uniform increase or decrease in importance during growth in the four clusters.

The complex shifts in industrial structure implied by the income elasticities can be appreciated if we consider what sectors contribute most to growth in output at the levels of development represented by the four main clusters. At the lowest income levels growth is mainly due to increased production of textiles and similar products at the expense of food processing and wood manufactures; mineral manufactures and basic metal production may also develop quickly, although their effects on total output or employment are circumscribed by their small initial base and, in the latter case, by local availability of raw materials. At intermediate income levels the pattern of expansion depends a great deal on population size. In the smaller countries of Cluster IV leather, clothing and footwear, and possibly electrical machinery, tend to develop fastest. In the large countries of Cluster II textile production persists at a high level and assembly of transport equipment may begin, these changes and the concomitant fall in the relative importance of the food and mineral processing industries being much more pronounced than any parallel changes in small developing countries. At high income levels the structure of production shifts away from traditional growth industries like textiles towards non-electrical machinery and chemicals.

As mentioned earlier, several generalisations have been advanced to explain such structural changes within manufacturing industry. Chenery and Taylor adopt a narrative similar to that of the last paragraph, describing sectors as 'early', 'middle', or 'late' according to the stage of development at which they matured and pointing to the more dramatic nature of changes in very large developing countries. Hoffmann and the United Nations use a broader brush, the former asserting that the whole pattern of change reflects simply the increasing demand for capital goods rather than consumer goods, the latter that it

Table 5.15. *Effects of income and size on the composition of manufacturing output : elasticities by cluster[a]*

	Income elasticity				Size elasticity			
Cluster:	I	II	IV	VI	I	II	IV	VI
Food, beverages, tobacco	−0.10	−1.58	−0.36	0.39	−0.26	−0.59	−0.27	−0.27
Basic metals	0.32	0.01	..	0.85	1.28	1.74	..	0.58
Non-electrical machinery	−0.42	..	0.33	0.86	−0.61	..	0.41	0.22
Electrical machinery	0.48	..	0.58	0.36	0.65	..	0.34	0.54
Transport equipment	0.50	1.48	0.85	0.46	0.55	0.83	0.52	0.26
Other metal products	0.57	0.50	..	0.06	0.83	0.27	..	0.08
Chemicals	0.22	..	−0.15	0.34	0.28	..	0.44	0.02
Textiles	0.18	1.79	0.31	−0.65	0.24	0.42	0.62	0.02
Leather, clothing, footwear	0.13	..	1.00	−0.69	0.14	..	−0.26	−0.24
Forest products	−0.40	−0.28	0.60	0.17	−0.13	−0.32	0.05	−0.09
Mineral products	0.28	−0.33	−0.40	−0.52	0.44	−0.28	−0.07	−0.02
Rubber products	−0.16	−0.86	1.07	−0.11	0.16	−0.39	0.63	0.21
Other products	0.08	1.66	0.84	0.19	0.09	0.53	0.08	0.01

[a] Evaluated at mean income of each cluster.

Table 5.16. *The composition of manufacturing output by cluster, 1963*

Percentages

	Cluster			
	I	II	IV	VI
Food, beverages, tobacco	40	18	30	12
Basic metals[a]	..	..	..	6
Metal products	7	27	9	40
Non-electrical machinery	(−)	(5)	(2)	(12)
Electrical machinery	(−)	(6)	(2)	(9)
Transport equipment	(5)	(12)	(5)	(12)
Other	(2)	(4)	(..)	(7)
Chemicals	4	..	10	10
Textiles	13	13	5	5
Miscellaneous	19	27	22	26
Leather, clothing, etc.	(3)	(..)	(3)	(5)
Forest products	(6)	(9)	(6)	(7)
Mineral products	(5)	(6)	(5)	(5)
Rubber products	(1)	(8)	(2)	(2)
Other	(4)	(4)	(6)	(7)

[a] Shares for Clusters I, II and IV vary over a wide range depending on resource-endowments.

reflects the increasing domination of light manufacturing by heavy industries. The logic of the former argument is powerful. The initial share of capital goods industries – essentially the 'metal products' of table 5.13 – is, as we have seen, small. The share of investment tends to grow rapidly early in development and, even when it slows at high income levels, in machinery and transport equipment it continues to increase and the share of capital goods in exports expands.

The two contrasts – between consumer and capital goods industries and between light and heavy industries – are closely related, since light industries are typically closer to the final demand of households than are heavy industries; also any distinction is further blurred by Hoffmann's dubious use of industry rather than product data to support his thesis. Lago has, however, successfully discriminated between the two by looking at the ratios of the contributions to United Kingdom manufacturing value added of final and investment demand, using a succession of input–output tables for years between 1907 and 1954.[1] This ratio does not decline systematically, although Hoffmann's own version – in effect the ratio of light to heavy manufacture – does fall. Subsequent investigations of the United States, Canada and Australia showed that the light–heavy industry ratio declined very rapidly early in their industrialisation from over $2\frac{1}{2}$ to about $1\frac{1}{2}$, but it then fell much more slowly and became stable at just over $\frac{1}{2}$.

Hoselitz has further noted that in several countries – El Salvador, Nicaragua, Iraq, Portugal – value added in the production of consumer goods has historically risen faster than value added in manufacturing as a whole;[2] he suggests that in gross comparisons of developed with less developed countries differences in the capital intensity of capital and consumer goods production may be more striking than differences in value-added shares. Both points may indicate that the contrast between development in industries differentiated by type of technology is more meaningful than that between industries differentiated by type of customer.

While the results of our cross-sectional model are not seriously at variance with any of these studies, some of which derive from the analyses of long time-series, the insights they give into past and potential structural changes are rather limited. Historically the rise and fall of industries within the broad sectors considered here are often more marked than the expansion or contraction of the sectors themselves. Sometimes these changes reflect stable trends in demand and production

---

[1] A. M. Lago, 'The Hoffmann industrial growth development path: an international comparison', *Weltwirtschaftliches Archiv*, vol. 103, no. 1, 1969.
[2] B. F. Hoselitz, 'Some problems in the quantitative study of industrialization', *Economic Development and Cultural Change*, vol. 9, April 1961.

possibilities, as with the displacement of basic foods by ice cream and confectionery in the foodstuffs sector of advanced economies or the displacement of soaps and pharmaceutical products by industrial chemicals and plastics in the chemicals sector of less developed countries.[1] This could in principle be remedied by further dis-aggregation of our model. Often, however, the intra-sectoral move-ments reflect technological factors specific to particular periods or geographical areas. In the United Kingdom, the United States and Japan the textile industry played a major role early in development; the initial expansion was confined in the United Kingdom to the cotton industry, where major inventions were introduced, and in Japan to the silk industry for similar reasons (although the innovations were more organisational than mechanical), while in the United States contraction in the interwar years was arrested by the production and processing of a new cellulose-based fibre, rayon. Most other sectors have had equally diverse histories, and the shortcomings of the growth-pattern method-ology when confronted with problems of specific resources, technical change and new goods should always be borne in mind. This applies especially in the context of judgements about the likely course of structural change in present-day developing countries, which could, with the aid of borrowed technologies, industrialise by unprecedented routes.

THE EFFECTS OF INDUSTRIALISATION ON GROWTH

The origins of changes in productivity

The idea that structural change may have a reciprocal effect on growth was touched upon in our discussion of the methodological foundations of growth-pattern studies. Some such relationship emerges naturally from this sort of approach, since the equations used to account for structural changes are, as we have seen, condensed forms of a more complex general equilibrium model and are ambivalent as regards direction of causation.

Structural change might rebound on aggregate growth in two distinct ways. First, the level of income might be increased simply because average product per head in expanding sectors exceeded that in stationary or declining sectors; secondly, the growth rate of income might be increased because the rate of growth of productivity in expanding sectors exceeded that in the rest of the economy. Evidence

---

[1] In Maizels' study this compositional change manifested itself as a discrepancy between a low growth coefficient for chemicals in regressions from a cross-section in which less developed countries were included and a high coefficient in regressions from time-series on advanced (non-tropical) economies only (*Industrial Growth and World Trade*, pp. 53–4).

Chart 5.8. *Growth of labour productivity in manufacturing and in the whole economy, 1964–71*

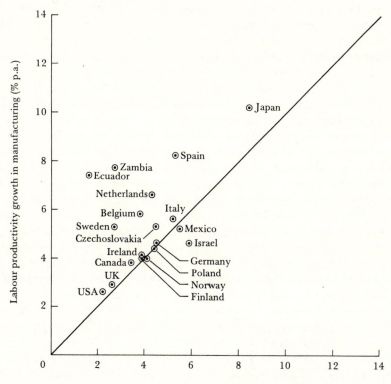

SOURCES: United Nations, Department of Economic and Social Affairs, *The Growth of World Industry*; Statistical Office, *Yearbook of National Accounts Statistics* (various issues); NIESR estimates.

that value added per man in one expanding sector – manufacturing – generally exceeds that in one declining sector – primary production – has already been presented (chart 5.1 above); although similar contrasts in productivity growth rates are harder to substantiate, it seems that manufacturing outpaces the rest of the economy in this respect also (chart 5.8).

Of these two mechanisms, that based on differential productivity growth is much more potent than that based simply on structural change. Calculation on the basis of data from tables 5.1 and 5.4 of what would happen in a typical developing country if the balance between manufacturing and agriculture were changed to that of a typical developed Western European economy, but productivity in each sector remained fixed, shows that output per worker outside services would be raised from a third to a half of that in Western Europe – a small return for such a drastic (sevenfold) increase in the manufacturing–primary production ratio. Even more striking is the parallel calculation that changing a developing country's industry profile within manufacturing to that of a West European economy would, with industry productivity levels unchanged, leave output per worker in manufacturing as a whole practically untouched.

How can these crucial inter-country differences in the level and growth of labour productivity in the industrial sector as a whole, and in its constituent branches, be explained? Most research on such topics has been carried out explicitly within the context of an aggregate or industry production function, although the degree of formality with which the concept is used varies greatly. In general, those studies dealing with productivity in aggregate terms are more faithful to the constraints it imposes than are studies dealing with productivity in individual plants or firms. Solow, for example, has exploited one type of production function – a Cobb–Douglas function with constant returns to scale and neutral technical progress – in which the contributions of labour and capital to output growth can be identified with their income shares and in which the contribution of technical change is independent of the growth of factor inputs. He shows that almost 90 per cent of the increase in private non-farm output in the United States between 1909 and 1949 was attributable to technical change.[1] Similarly, Arrow, Chenery, Minhas and Solow have attempted to describe inter-country productivity differences among nineteen countries in 24 industries in terms of relative factor-endowments, starting from a demonstration that the possibilities of substitution between labour and capital in each industry were common to all countries.[2] Three serious objections to the use of such methods in the analysis of productivity changes have, however, emerged.

First, the authors restrict their attention to labour and capital inputs only, whereas other factors of production – natural resources, managerial skills – have an obvious role in determining output per head. This has led to several constructive efforts – notably by Denison[3] – to eradicate Solow's residual by introducing additional factors (land, inventories, non-residential building, foreign assets) and by redefining the two basic factors to account for changes in the quality of labour (education, hours) and capital (utilisation). Any such extensions are,

---

[1] R. M. Solow, 'Technical change and the aggregate production function', *Review of Economics and Statistics*, vol. 39, August 1957.

[2] K. J. Arrow, H. B. Chenery, B. S. Minhas and R. M. Solow, 'Capital–labor substitution and economic efficiency', *Review of Economics and Statistics*, vol. 43, August 1961.

[3] E. F. Denison, *The Sources of Economic Growth in the United States and the Alternatives before Us*, New York, Committee for Economic Development, 1962.

however, destructive of the conclusion of Arrow *et al.*, since their assumption of internationally standard industry production functions requires the use of wage rates as a proxy for capital per man – a device which cannot be employed when, say, natural resources are involved, since wages would then reflect endowments of these as well as of capital.[1]

Secondly, the simplifying assumptions regarding technology cannot be supported. A corollary of our last point on common international production functions is that differences in technology rather than differences in factor-mixes within a given technology are not ruled out as the cause of international differences in labour productivity. It is possible also to challenge Solow's analysis for exactly opposite reasons – that technical changes might alter labour productivity not by increasing output for a given factor-mix, but rather by altering the factor-mix which would produce a given output at least cost. In other words, technical progress can be labour-saving or capital-saving rather than neutral.

A fruitful way of looking at a world with less stringent technology assumptions is to distinguish nations which are technologically advanced from those which are technologically backward. The former are typically highly developed and devote substantial resources to research and innovatory investment; the latter are typically less developed and borrow technological ideas from the advanced nations, this process being called technological diffusion.[2] To the extent that technical changes in mature economies have historically tended to raise output per man for any given capital–labour ratio, their immediate adoption by less developed countries would produce higher rates of labour and capital productivity growth than is feasible in mature economies where such techniques are already in operation. Moreover, productivity growth in countries only recently embarked on industrialisation would tend to exceed that encountered in the early stages of development of currently mature economies, since adoption is easier than invention.[3] We therefore expect an inverse relationship between productivity growth and maturity, subject to two qualifications. First, from a range of advanced technologies equally matched in terms of their total factor productivity, developing countries may choose processes of varying labour and capital intensities depending on their development

---

[1] For an elaboration of this point see R. R. Nelson, 'A "diffusion" model of international productivity differences in manufacturing industry', *American Economic Review*, vol. 58, December 1968.

[2] See the alternative growth model proposed by Nelson (ibid).

[3] The notion that growth opportunities expand according to the length of time a country has been undeveloped dates back to Veblen; it is treated in depth in A. Gerschenkron, *Economic Backwardness in Historical Perspective*, Cambridge (Mass.), Harvard University Press, 1962, chap. 1.

Chart 5.9. *Growth of labour productivity in manufacturing, 1964–71, and income per head, 1968*

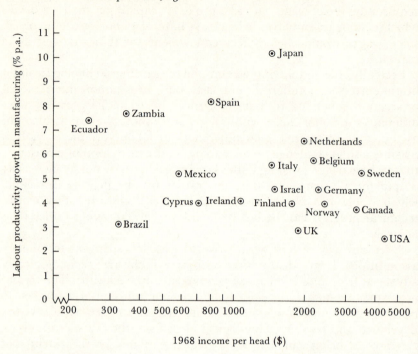

1968 income per head ($)

SOURCES: as chart 5.8.

priorities. Secondly, certain technologies generated in mature economies may be inaccessible to developing countries, either because they are biased towards the use of inputs characteristic of advanced economies, such as a skilled and experienced workforce, or because they are viable only in large markets.

Both qualifications have already figured as important constraints on the order in which industries can expand during development (page 132 above). Some consequences of the first can be traced if productivity growth is plotted against an index of maturity such as income per head. Chart 5.9 shows the generally negative relationship between productivity growth in manufacturing and maturity, with observations on lower-income countries noticeably more scattered than those on advanced countries in which technologies have converged. Within the low-income group the principal argument against the automatic adoption of labour-intensive techniques is that modern capital is necessary to offset skill disadvantages in open markets. If we now consider productivity growth in the economy as a whole, we should expect to find a less pronounced

Chart 5.10. *Growth of labour productivity in the whole economy, 1964–71, and income per head, 1968*

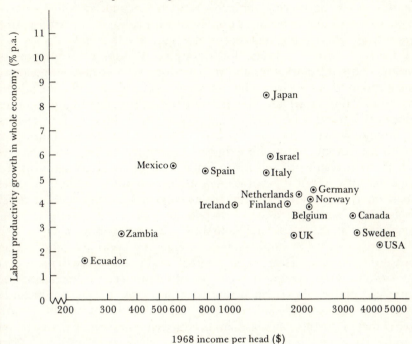

1968 income per head ($)

SOURCES: as chart 5.8.

negative relationship with maturity, since the output of manufacturing industry must, in the absence of protection, compete with internationally available substitutes. Chart 5.10 fulfils this expectation. Though alternative explanations for the humped relationship between the level and rate of growth of total GDP per head have been advanced,[1] some support for our rationale is found in a study by Diaz Alejandro, in which the margin of labour productivity in various United States industries over their counterparts in Argentina appeared strongly negatively correlated with the labour intensity of operations in each industry.[2]

The third fundamental objection to the analysis of productivity growth in a formal way is that the assignment of responsibility for output changes to individual factors breaks down in the presence of

[1] These are summarised in B. Horvat, 'The relation between rate of growth and level of development', *Journal of Development Studies*, vol. 10, April/July 1974.
[2] C. F. Diaz Alejandro, 'Industrialization and labor productivity differentials', *Review of Economics and Statistics*, vol. 47, May 1965.

static or dynamic increasing returns. By static increasing returns we mean the familiar economies of operating with large plants which occur mainly in an engineering context – as with pipelines or boilers, where costs vary with diameter but throughput with volume – or within large enterprises where the savings occur in a managerial context – from ease of access to credit sources, for example, or from co-ordination of production with marketing and distribution. Such economies generate an addition to output which has no connection with the efforts of labour or capital, but for which they are nonetheless compensated in relative amounts determined by bargaining power. The existence of such scale-economies is well documented.[1] By dynamic increasing returns we mean any productivity gains due to investment in new technologies when the investment itself is attributable to productivity gains at the most recently installed generation of plants. To initiate such economies there must already exist static scale-economies *in the benefits of which capital must participate* and to perpetuate such economies each new technology must itself be subject to static scale-economies.

The existence of dynamic scale-economies is supported by the finding of Verdoorn that in a linear regression of productivity growth on output growth in manufacturing in a sample of mature economies during the interwar period the coefficient on output growth was significantly greater than zero.[2] He inferred that any given rise in output growth generated a further increase in productivity growth. Our data on productivity growth confirm this result for the period 1964–71 (chart 5.11). Similar experiments on advanced economies only by Kaldor and by Cripps and Tarling for various postwar periods have demonstrated that this 'Verdoorn's law' does not hold outside the manufacturing and construction sectors.[3] Even within these sectors the statistical and logical foundations of the law have been challenged. Vaciago, for example, has found non-linear regressions which fit data on manu-facturing growth in the years 1950–69 rather better than linear regressions and suggest that the response of productivity growth to output growth is weakest in the fastest-growing economies.[4] A reworking of our regressions shows that Vaciago's preferred semi-log form does not describe our data particularly well, nor does eliminating

[1] A useful recent survey is C. T. Saunders, 'Industrial specialisation and trends in industrial policies' in United Nations Economic Commission for Europe, *Factors and Conditions of Long-Term Growth*, New York, 1974.
[2] P. J. Verdoorn, 'Fattori che regolano sviluppo della produttività del lavoro', *L'Industria*, no. 1, 1949.
[3] N. Kaldor, *Strategic Factors in Economic Development*, Ithaca (NY), Cornell University Press, 1967; T. F. Cripps and R. J. Tarling, *Growth in Advanced Capitalist Economies 1950–1970*, Cambridge University Press, 1973.
[4] G. Vaciago, 'Increasing returns and growth in advanced economies: a re-evaluation', *Oxford Economic Papers*, vol. 27, July 1975.

Chart 5.11. *Growth of labour productivity and of output in manufacturing,*
1964–71

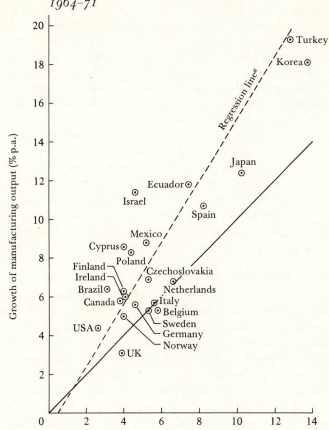

Growth of labour productivity in manufacturing (% p.a.)

[a] Regression line shown is:

$$g(Y_m) - g(L_m) = 0.53 + 0.64g(Y_m) \; (\overline{R}^2 = 0.79)$$
$$(9.14)$$

Alternatives (see p. 138) are:

$$g(Y_m) - g(L_m) = -5.24 + 12.66 \log [g(Y_m)] \; (\overline{R}^2 = 0.69)$$
$$(3.44)$$

or, with Korea and Turkey excluded:

$$g(Y_m) - g(L_m) = 1.41 + 0.51g(Y_m) \; (\overline{R}^2 = 0.49)$$
$$(4.20)$$

SOURCES: as chart 5.8.

outlying observations (Korea and Turkey) raise the coefficient on output (see footnote to chart 5.11).

More problematic than these statistical quibbles are the ambiguities of interpretation to which such regressions lie open. Verdoorn's law represents the 'anti-form' of the growth-pattern equations discussed at length above, in that it implies that output growth generates income growth rather than vice versa. Kaldor's reasons for adhering to this direction of causation are twofold: first, technical progress would otherwise be left wholly exogenous; secondly, productivity growth could generate output growth through demand expansion only in the presence of a flexible price mechanism and a set of price elasticities of demand exceeding unity. While for the whole economy this last condition is inconceivable, for manufacturing industry – precisely the sector for which Verdoorn's law is confirmed – neither possibility is absurd. Manufacturing is a natural target for spontaneous and imitative innovation, and the observed trends in its terms of trade *vis-à-vis* agriculture, as well as its tendency to expand its share of real output during development, would indicate that the demand conditions for sustained growth may well be met in practice.

Long-term patterns and short-term adjustments

As with the investigation of structural change, we have two bodies of data – cross-sectional and time-series – on which to test the strength of these hypotheses about the determinants of labour productivity. It seems reasonable to interpret the cross-sectional distribution of levels of value added per man as reflecting fundamental long-term factors – resource-endowments, wealth and size of market – and the distribution of rates of growth of labour productivity as reflecting short-term adjustments to trends in these basic circumstances, in particular trends in income growth and industrialisation. The debates arising out of classic production function exercises then make it clear that two separate types of model are required, since most of the complications uncovered – non-conventional factors of production, biased technical progress, increasing returns – are less germane to the analysis of productivity movements over short periods than to the analysis of long-run data on single countries or cross-sectional data drawn from countries with very disparate economic structures.

Our first model, designed to account for inter-country differences in productivity levels in manufacturing, is therefore entirely empirical. Observed variations in value added per head are supposed to depend on the amount of co-operating factors, on plant size and on the value of investment relative to total value added. The first item covers the volume of capital per worker – an increasing function of maturity and openness – and the volume of natural resources per worker; the last two items are intended to capture the potential for static and dynamic scale-economies. The model as estimated is

$$\log(Y_j/L_j) = \gamma_0 + \gamma_1 \log Y_m + \gamma_2 \log i + \gamma_3 \log t + \gamma_4 \log (N/A) + \gamma_5 \log (L_j/P_j) \quad (5.9)$$

where Y_j/L_j = value added per person engaged in industry j

Y_m = share of manufacturing in total output, a proxy for economic maturity

N/A = population density, a proxy for natural resource-endowments

L_j/P_j = average plant size, persons engaged per plant.

Our second model, designed to account for inter-country differences in labour productivity growth rates in manufacturing, is more closely tied to production theory. It differs from those of Solow and Arrow *et al.* in that output is produced by *three* factors – labour, capital and natural resources – and we have made 'vintage' assumptions – that new investment may involve a completely different technology from that of existing plants – to admit and explore the possibility of systematic differences in choice of technique among countries. If old plants are scrapped when they cease to make any return on capital and if natural resources used at new plants are a fraction ρ of their capital requirements, output growth in such a model is given by

$$g(Y_j) = \delta_0 g(N_j) + (\delta_1 + \delta_2 \rho)(I_j/Y_j) \quad (5.10)$$

where $g(Y_j)$ = rate of growth of output in sector j

$g(N_j)$ = rate of growth of labour input to sector j

I_j/Y_j = ratio of investment to output at new plants

$\delta_0, \delta_1, \delta_2$ = shares of wages, capital and natural resources in value added.[1]

---

[1] In any period the increments dY, dN, dR in output, labour and natural resources are the differences between output or factors used at new and scrapped plants; for example $dY = Y^n - Y^s$. Then

$$p\,dY - w\,dN - c\,dR = (pY^n - wN^n - cR^n) - (pY^s - wN^s - cR^s)$$

where p is output price, w is wage rate and c is unit cost of natural resources. The second term on the right-hand side represents profits at scrapped plants and so is zero by definition; the first term is rI, where r is the rate of return on investment in new plants. This can be rearranged to give:

$$\frac{dY}{Y} = \frac{wN}{pY} \cdot \frac{dN}{N} + \frac{cdR}{pY} + \frac{rI}{pY}$$

Now by assumption $dR = \rho I$, so we get for a particular industry j,

$$g(Y_j) = \delta_0 g(N_j) + (\delta_1 + \delta_2 \rho_j)(I_j/Y_j)$$

where $\delta_1 = c/p$ and $\delta_2 = r/p$.

Table 5.17. *Value added per person engaged: general growth patterns, 1963 cross-section*[a]

	Coefficient						$\bar{R}^2$
	γ_0	γ_1	γ_2	γ_3	γ_4	γ_5	
Food, beverages, tobacco	3.88	0.78 (4.77)	0.48 (1.81)	0.37 (2.30)	−0.23 (4.08)	0.01 (0.12)	0.64
Basic metals	2.89	−1.24 (1.28)	3.16 (2.06)	−0.88 (1.39)	−0.25 (0.86)	0.75 (2.82)	0.31
Metal products	1.20	0.93 (5.07)	0.87 (2.90)	0.38 (2.59)	−0.10 (1.10)	−0.01 (0.09)	0.69
Chemicals[b]	5.20	0.96 (6.47)	−0.10 (0.42)	0.07 (0.62)	−0.14 (2.64)	0.23 (3.01)	0.67
Textiles	3.10	1.23 (4.30)	−0.33 (0.76)	0.63 (2.93)	−0.11 (1.16)	−0.08 (0.55)	0.46
Leather, clothing, footwear[c]	0.05	0.56 (1.94)	1.35 (3.00)	0.41 (1.86)	−0.10 (1.06)	0.05 (0.38)	0.50
Forest products[c d]	0.63	0.92 (3.91)	0.75 (1.96)	0.70 (3.71)	−0.16 (1.98)	−0.12 (1.02)	0.61
Mineral products[c]	2.83	1.04 (5.56)	0.13 (0.43)	0.67 (4.43)	−0.17 (2.50)	−0.11 (1.19)	0.64
All manufacturing	2.41	0.97 (6.70)	0.52 (2.16)	0.44 (3.81)	−0.17 (3.19)	−0.03 (0.46)	0.74

[a] Equation 5.9 estimated on a sample of 44 countries; t-statistics given in brackets.
[b] Includes petroleum refining and rubber products, but major oil producers are excluded.
[c] Coverage of these sectors is incomplete.
[d] Wood and furniture only; paper, printing and publishing has coefficients
$\gamma_0 = 4.20$, $\gamma_1 = 0.87$, $\gamma_2 = 0.37$, $\gamma_3 = 0.24$, $\gamma_4 = 0.17$, $\gamma_5 = 0.04$, with $R^2 = 0.60$.
(5.09) (0.29) (1.67) (2.96) (2.11)

The growth in the labour input is composed of two parts – the growth $g(L_j)$ in the number of men engaged and the growth $g(Q_j)$ in their quality. This skill element, the microeconomic analogue of the 'residual' in long-term aggregate growth studies, can be isolated by rearranging equation 5.10 as:

$$\delta_0^{-1}[g(Y_j) - \delta_0 g(L_j)] = g(Q_j) + (\delta_1 + \delta_2 \rho)(\delta_0^{-1} I_j / Y_j) \qquad (5.11)$$

The main determinants of δ_1 can be identified as the modernity of the existing capital stock and the relative backwardness of the economy, and we can say that $\delta_2 \rho$ – the intensity of natural resource use – will depend on the country's resource-endowments. The model as estimated thus becomes

$$G = \overline{g(Q_j)} + [(\delta_{10} + \delta_{20}) + \delta_{11} g(Y_j) + \delta_{12}(Y_m) + \delta_{21}(N/A)](\delta_0^{-1} I / Y) \qquad (5.12)$$

where $\quad G = \delta_0^{-1}[g(\Upsilon_j) - \delta_0 g(L_j)]$

$\overline{g(Q_j)}$ = mean growth rate of labour quality in the sample
$g(\Upsilon_j)$ = past rate of growth of output, a proxy for the newness of the capital stock

and population density and the manufacturing share are again proxies for natural resource-endowments and relative maturity.

The results obtained from our model of inter-country differences in labour productivity levels (equation 5.9) are set out in table 5.17. The model works rather better for total manufacturing than for individual sectors; it is conspicuously unsuccessful in the basic metal and textile industries. Outside these two industries the factors which enter the model all play well defined roles in explaining the origins of differences in productivity levels. The extent of industrialisation itself has a coefficient just below unity in most sectors; a doubling in the relative size of the manufacturing sector almost doubles productivity. The pressure of international competition as represented by the trade ratio also raises productivity, particularly in food processing and other light industries. An abundant supply of land has a pervasive effect on labour productivity, the coefficients on population density mostly lying in the range -0.1 to -0.2; a country twice as densely populated as its neighbour will generally choose a factor-mix which leaves output per man some 10–20 per cent lower. Static scale-economies appear important only in the chemical industry; it may be, however, that such effects are swamped by the dependence of scale on other factors appearing in the regression, such as the level of industrialisation and the investment ratio.[1] Dynamic scale-economies, for which the investment ratio is admittedly an inadequate proxy, seem unimportant at the level of the individual industry (except in the large engineering branch), but appear very significant for manufacturing as a whole. This lends support to Allyn Young's observation that increasing returns are fundamentally macroeconomic phenomena.[2]

As with the models of development patterns, this model of productivity patterns was re-estimated from separate data on the four main types of economy; the results obtained are shown in table 5.18. The sample sizes involved are necessarily small and the only inferences that can safely be drawn from this table are that the effects of industrialisation on productivity are lower in developed economies than in less developed economies and that trade is a significant determinant

---

[1] See F. L. Pryor, 'The size of production establishments in manufacturing', *Economic Journal*, vol. 82, June 1972.
[2] The argument is expounded in N. Kaldor, 'The irrelevance of equilibrium economics', *Economic Journal*, vol. 82, December 1972.

of productivity differences mainly in the small semi-industrialised countries of Cluster IV.

Table 5.18. *Value added per person engaged: growth patterns by cluster, 1963 cross-section[a]*

	Coefficient						$\overline{R}^2$
	γ_0	γ_1	γ_2	γ_3	γ_4	γ_5	
Cluster I	5.37	0.96	−0.06	0.20	−0.38	0.23	0.59
		(2.21)	(0.12)	(0.58)	(2.48)	(0.99)	
Cluster II[b]	17.07	2.18	−2.72	−1.45	−0.13	−1.19	0.99
Cluster IV	−1.63	0.77	1.12	0.81	0.04	—	0.94
		(4.74)	(1.63)	(2.71)	(0.39)	(−)	
Cluster VI	8.74	0.34	−0.78	0.36	−0.11	0.03	0.83
		(1.09)	(2.32)	(2.19)	(3.27)	(0.18)	

[a] Equation 5.9 estimated on subsamples of 44 countries; t-statistics given in brackets.
[b] One degree of freedom; all coefficients significantly non-zero.

The results obtained from our productivity growth model (equation 5.12) are set out in table 5.19. This model is also obviously inadequate as a description of growth in several important sectors – textiles again and machinery – but it explains variations in productivity growth in

Table 5.19. *Growth in value added per person engaged: vintage model[a]*

	Coefficient					$\overline{R}^2$
	$g(Q_j)$	$(\delta_{10}+\delta_{20})$	δ_{11}	δ_{12}	δ_{21}	
Basic metals	7.41	1.17	−0.05	0.25		0.50
	(1.77)	(3.49)	(3.30)	(3.22)		
Machinery	−0.14	0.23		0.18	0.01	0.38
	(0.02)	(0.53)		(1.72)	(0.34)	
Transport equipment	3.09	−0.22			0.07	0.85
	(0.71)	(0.69)			(5.33)	
Other metal products	3.72	−0.23		0.08	0.04	0.87
	(1.20)	(0.89)		(1.49)	(2.95)	
Chemicals	13.86	−0.25		0.06	0.04	0.52
	(2.14)	(1.10)		(1.02)	(2.19)	
Textiles	2.33	−0.19	0.02	−0.04		0.16
	(0.42)	(0.91)	(1.53)	(0.51)		
All manufacturing	2.05	0.02		−0.06	0.06	0.83
	(0.63)	(0.12)		(1.61)	(3.52)	

[a] Equation 5.12 estimated on a sample of 20 countries; cross-section of growth rates 1964–71.

manufacturing industry as a whole reasonably well. Of the three factors which we speculated might determine the rate of return on new investment – age of capital stock, level of industrialisation and population density – only the first is significant in the aggregate equation and in heavy industries (transport equipment, other metal manufactures and chemicals); the others seem important only in basic metal processing, which is of course heavily dependent on natural resource-endowments. The mean values of the rates of improvement of labour quality come from residuals which are widely dispersed across countries and on average account for 30 per cent of the observed shift in labour productivity as measured by $g(Q_j)$ over the period 1964–71. None of the strictly economic hypotheses we investigated could account for this dispersion; in particular, past or current levels and rates of growth of output bore no relation to these implicit changes in labour quality. Using a similar model, Galenson and Pyatt have, however, found that within a group of 52 less developed countries some non-economic factors – educational attainment and nutrition – could explain much of this quality change.[1]

From all of these results we must conclude that, although we have gained considerable insight into the long-run determinants of productivity levels, the way in which economies converge towards these patterns in the short run is less clear. While some factors identified as important in the long run – population density, the state of industrialisation – have been found to affect the rate of return on investment in new plant, there remains in our vintage model a sizeable unexplained residual identified with the rate of improvement in the quality of labour.

---

[1] International Labour Office (ILO), *The Quality of Labour and Economic Development in Certain Countries* by W. Galenson and G. Pyatt, Geneva, 1964.

6

DEVELOPMENT PATTERNS AND THE BASIS FOR TRADE

by *R. A. Batchelor*

INTRODUCTION

In chapters 3 and 4 above relationships have been established between imports of manufactures and their production, and responsibility for concurrent changes in the fortunes of major exporters has been assigned to the general trade expansion implied by these relationships, to specialisation in fast-growing and slow-growing markets and to the price and non-price factors which constitute relative competitiveness. This is the limit of Maizels' empirical analysis, but his verbal argument often touches on the two more fundamental issues which concern us in this chapter. The first is the question whether links between import demand, export supply and home production are systematic enough to create stable patterns in the scale and structure of external trade which are amenable to description in terms of the growth patterns of chapter 5; the second is why the particular trading networks observed in the 1960s came into being and why they changed – that is, we are interested in the ultimate basis for trade which finds expression in the competitiveness elements isolated earlier and in the country and commodity composition of an economy's exports and imports.

On this second topic, the prime concern of trade theorists, Maizels is nowhere very explicit, though he seems to attribute links between countries largely to proximity and political encouragement and to view commodity specialisation mainly in terms of the impact of innovations in fast-growing sectors on unit costs of traded goods. A number of more specific hypotheses to explain the volume of bilateral trade have been advanced in the 1960s, and attempts have been made on a theoretical and empirical level to reconcile dynamic theories of specialisation with more traditional factor-endowment models. It seems important that these – often conflicting – views of the basis for trade should be put into perspective within the framework of this study, as they prove crucial to the question whether current patterns can be used to project the volume and nature of trade into the future. The first section of this chapter therefore gives a brief account of the development of trade theories and of the methods which have been found to test their validity and generality. We then examine recent trade structures within the framework of the more aggregative and more agnostic growth patterns, and end by speculating on the consistency of the results with those of more detailed tests of the basis for trade.

Maizels disputed the existence of simple relationships between the share of manufactures in exports or imports and the level of industrialisation because the systematic changes in the composition of domestic output and demand which occur are no guarantee of parallel changes in the composition of exports and imports. To the extent that early phases of industrialisation involve import substitution, the regular expansion of the metalworking and chemical industries noted in chapter 5 need not imply additional exports of their products; to the extent that the economy has a dual structure, high exports of manufactures from the factory system can co-exist with a low overall figure for value added per head in manufacturing when its output is averaged with that of the handicraft sector. On the import side, there are forces at work during industrialisation causing imports of both manufactures and non-manufactures to grow. The former result from increased household demands for consumer durables and increased industrial demand for capital goods; the latter result from increased demands for food by the urban population, which is growing while the agricultural population is diminishing, and for fuel and materials by industry.

Implicit in Maizels' discussion, however, is the further thought that, if account is taken of the effects of natural resources on the availability of exportable goods and the range of goods which must perforce be imported and if non-linear relationships are adopted to admit the possibility of successive inward-looking and outward-looking phases of development, some interesting patterns of trade can be identified. The basic contrast in his patterns is in fact not between manufactures and non-manufactures, but between manufactures which are finished or semi-finished; the first ratio is heavily dependent on resource-endowments – even comparatively poor countries may be rich in some minerals which, simply processed, may account for the bulk of their exports. Moreover, the most influential variable bearing on his chosen ratio is not necessarily the level of income or industrialisation, but the size of the economy, which determines how far it is possible to meet domestic demands from domestic resources and how far exports can be diversified given the minimum viable size of plant in certain industries and the skewed distribution of resources and skills in small countries.

Using this framework we can find in Maizels' work three nested statements about the progress of imports. First, during industrialisation the share of manufactured goods in total imports tends to fall in large countries but to rise in small countries; secondly, within the range of manufactured imports, intermediate goods – metals, chemicals, textiles – tend to become relatively less important than finished goods, particularly in small countries; thirdly, within the range of finished goods, the share of capital equipment in imports tends to be higher in small countries than in large at all stages of development. The behaviour of exports mirrors these import changes, particularly with respect to the growth of finished manufactures in world trade; Maizels noted in a 1955 cross-section a tendency for the share of finished goods in total exports to remain stable below 10–15 per cent until economies progressed to a 'European' level of development, after which it rose rapidly to 60–70 per cent. Taken together with the requirement that global trade must be in balance, these observations have two important corollaries; the first is explicitly mentioned by Maizels, the second not. They are that smaller countries must come to be net exporters of intermediate goods and net importers of finished goods, and that a major portion of trade in manufactures at a late stage of development must be the exchange among large industrial countries of a limited variety of finished consumer goods.

Our results justify Maizels' reservations over the existence of patterns in external trade, in the sense that the levels of explanation provided by such models as we tested were lower than those obtained in chapter 5 for corresponding features of the structure of domestic production. We have, however, found stable general relationships explaining total participation in trade in terms of size of country and colonial status and, although equations covering structural aspects of this trade had low explanatory power, some strong partial relationships emerged. These were sufficient, on the import side, to confirm Maizels' first proposition – that the response of the share of manufactures to increasing industrialisation is positive in small countries but negative in large – in the weaker form that the response is always negative, but less so in small countries. His other propositions – that in small countries finished goods come to take a larger share of imports, most of these being capital goods – could not be confirmed. On the export side, non-linearities were found not only in the evolution of the share of finished goods, but also in the share of manufactures as a whole; these non-linearities were especially marked in large developing countries and their co-existence with relatively smooth trends in the composition of imports implies – at least for large economies – a sharp movement from deficit to surplus in manufacturing trade when the share of manufactures is around 25–30 per cent of GDP.

During industrialisation countries accumulate physical and human capital, and their observed patterns of trade are reflections of how such changes in factor-endowments and technical knowledge increase the competitiveness of their exportable goods. Whether total trade increases or decreases as a result of industrialisation depends on whether the main basis for international commerce is relative capital endowments or differential rates of technical advance; in the former case the convergence in economic structure implicit in the growth patterns of chapter 5 is inimical to trade, while in the latter it serves to create new demands for the products of advanced technologies.

It proves difficult to deduce from aggregate trends whether the ratio of foreign trade to domestic production is in a secular decline in which the 1960s figure as a period of temporary respite, or whether the buoyant growth experienced then can be expected to continue. However, a comparison of the responses of exports of individual commodities to industrialisation with those responses expected under capital-based and technology-based theories of trade leads to the conclusion that, while at low levels of development the volume and commodity-mix of trade is dependent on capital per head, at higher levels it is based on technological factors. The volume of such trade is largely independent of economic structure. We conclude that the stimulus to trade is not lost as more and more countries attain high levels of industrialisation and that it works not through the capital intensity and large scale of production permitted by domestic growth, but through an increased capacity for technological advance and product differentiation – that is, through a shift in the basis for trade.

THE BASIS FOR BILATERAL TRADE

The development of trade theory

In classical economic theory commerce between nations was viewed as the outcome of different costs of producing sets of commodities in different locations, the differentials depending on the impact of non-transferable natural resources on the productivity of the labour engaged in manufacturing in each place. This simple Ricardian scheme provoked two schools of dissent. The first and longer established focused on the logical structure of the theory, its implicit assumptions and the consequences of their relaxation; the second and more recent relates to the empirical relevance of the theory – even when generalised – to trade in the postwar political and technological environment.

The Ricardian theory rests on three premises: that there is a single scarce factor (labour), that this factor co-operates with natural resource inputs of varying qualities in a single internationally viable technology and that conditions of demand for its products are identical at home and abroad. The Heckscher–Ohlin theory extends this to cases where there are two or more scarce factors and in making the generalisation shifts the rationale for international trade flows away from their proximate cause – the comparative costs of traded goods – towards their ultimate cause – the relative availability of factors of production, including produced factors such as capital equipment and labour skills.

The main predictions of the theory are that the exchange of goods between two countries will involve the export of those commodities which use intensively the factors with which each country is relatively well endowed and that, under ideal market conditions, this traffic will cause the price of each factor of production to be equalised between the two countries. Relaxation of the second and third assumptions of the Ricardian model – of common technologies and common demand patterns – destroys the Heckscher–Ohlin propositions, since the nexus between prices at which goods are offered for trade and the real structure of the trading economies is obscured. With a variable technology it may be impossible to classify commodities unambiguously as labour-intensive or capital-intensive, since a good which is labour-intensive in a labour-rich country might prove capital-intensive in a capital-rich trading partner. With variable tastes a similar ambiguity can occur, since preferences for the capital-intensive good in the capital-rich country might be so strong as to switch the price ratio between the two types of good in favour of the capital-intensive good in the labour-rich country and in favour of the labour-intensive good in the capital-rich country.

More fundamental to classical trade theory than its adoption of restrictive demand and supply constraints is its adherence to a static view of the trading environment and to the principle of individual rationality in international markets. The Heckscher–Ohlin theory has been formally applied to an economy with a growing labour force and capital stock by Oniki and Uzawa.[1] They show that, while the initial impact of opening a growing economy to trade is to encourage specialisation in the export of goods using its relatively abundant factor, the ultimate pattern of trade may be entirely contrary to this if industries producing capital goods use relatively capital-intensive technologies. At the same time a transition to less formal dynamic theories of trade has been initiated by Posner, Vernon and Linder.[2] Their contributions can be regarded as matching the static extensions of the Ricardian model with the empirical insights of growth-pattern studies, the former being concerned with the implications of greater

[1] H. Oniki and H. Uzawa, 'Patterns of trade and investment in a dynamic model of international trade', *Review of Economic Studies*, vol. 32, January 1965.

[2] M. V. Posner, 'International trade and technical change', *Oxford Economic Papers*, vol. 13 (new series), October 1961; R. Vernon, 'International investment and international trade in the product cycle', *Quarterly Journal of Economics*, vol. 80, May 1966; S. B. Linder, *An Essay on Trade and Transformation*, Stockholm, Almqvist & Wiksell, 1961.

international *varieties* of factor-endowments, production technologies and demand patterns and the latter with the *variations* which occur over time in these structural data as economies grow richer and industrialise.

Just as the Heckscher–Ohlin theory pushed the level of explanation of trading patterns past comparative costs and on to comparative factor-endowments, technologies and demand patterns, so the new theories of trade push past even these features to more primitive economic attributes such as income per head, population size and the stage of industrialisation. The main predictions of such theories are threefold. First, during industrialisation the content of a country's exports will shift from intensity in raw labour and natural resources towards factors which are produced in ever-increasing quantities (capital goods) or which accumulate as certain processes of production become familiar (labour skills). Secondly, the range of technologies developed in advanced countries will continuously overlap those used in less advanced countries, as countries at high levels of industrialisation encounter more and more new demands on their resources and devote large sums to research and development in an attempt to meet those demands. For the products affected, these technological gaps will lead to trade flows from highly industrialised countries to semi-industrial countries when the latter first encounter the new demands, but the flows will be reduced and even reversed when production starts up in the semi-industrial countries, since wage costs there will be lower and less initial outlay on research will be required. This sequence of events constitutes a 'product cycle'. Thirdly, to the extent that the relative price structure of an economy is dictated by internal demand conditions, it should find the most receptive export markets in countries at similar stages of development. Intensive trade between similar economies is, however, likely to be confined to the exchange of manufactures between advanced economies. This is because the prices of all goods produced in underdeveloped countries, and the prices of non-manufactures at all levels of development, owe more to supply conditions than to home demand and, although the relative price structures of countries at intermediate levels of development may match the structure of demand in similar economies, such countries may be frustrated in their bilateral exporting efforts by the absolute price advantages of the set of more advanced countries across the whole range of potential exports.

These models of trade under dynamic demand and supply conditions retain the classical assumption that observed flows represent genuine market transactions, in which the potential exporter offers his wares at cost and the importer chooses among alternative sources for each good the supplier whose goods prove least expensive once transport and transaction costs have been added to production costs. In practice international markets are less than ideal. The costs incurred by the exporter may be unrelated to factor-scarcities if the economy is centrally planned, or they may be artificially deflated by government subsidies if the economy is mixed. Conversely, the prices confronting the importer may be inflated by tariffs or other protective barriers against imports into his country. Moreover, the importer's choice may be independent of considerations of price, either because production techniques are so similar and transport costs so low as to make non-price attributes – design, speed of delivery – critical, or because seller and buyer are tied by international agreement or by their allegiance to the same multinational corporation.

Evidence on the importance of protectionist policies among industrialised countries has been presented in chapter 4, and their impact on the level of world trade as a whole during the interwar years will be assessed later in this chapter. In the postwar trading environment very high tariff barriers were encountered among semi-industrial countries aiming at import substitution. Little, Scitovsky and Scott found effective tariffs in excess of 100 per cent in large developing countries (Brazil, Argentina, India, Pakistan) in the mid-1960s, compared with 20–30 per cent in industrial countries.[1] Evidence of the importance of tariffs and non-price competition among industrial nations is supported by the demonstration due to Travis that in principle tariff levels need not be high to prohibit trade completely;[2] also by the evidence of Hufbauer and Chilas that in practice the degree of specialisation in international trade, even among such closely knit nations as those of the EEC, does not approach that found in the interregional trade of the United States.[3] Indirect support for the view that market imperfections dominate resource-endowments is also given by the results of Finger,[4] who shows that in several developed countries the factor content of imports and exports is very similar and that, if industries within each country are ordered by their capital–labour ratios, owing to technological convergence the rankings are indistinguishable.

Evidence on the importance of institutional factors in international commerce can be found in the high proportion of aid passing from

[1] I. M. D. Little, T. Scitovsky and M. FG. Scott, *Industry and Trade in Some Developing Countries*, London, Oxford University Press, 1970, pp. 174 and 274.

[2] W. P. Travis, 'Production, trade and protection when there are many commodities and two factors', *American Economic Review*, vol. 62, March 1972.

[3] G. C. Hufbauer and J. G. Chilas, 'Specialization by industrial countries: extent and consequences' in H. Giersch (ed.), *The International Division of Labour: problems and perspectives*, Tübingen, Mohr, 1974.

[4] J. M. Finger, 'Factor intensity and "Leontief type" tests of the factor proportions theory', *Economia Internazionale*, vol. 22, August 1969.

advanced to less developed countries which is tied to trade agreements or takes the form of credit facilities, and in the high and rising proportion of trade which is attributable to inter-branch transfers of goods within multinational corporations. For the United States this has been estimated as 21 per cent of total exports of manufactures in 1970 and for the United Kingdom as 24 per cent in the same year; in total world trade in manufactures such trade probably accounts for around 15–20 per cent.[1]

The principal effect of all these non-market influences on the pattern of trade is to increase greatly the element of reciprocity, both at a national level through the translation of aid links and political partnership into trade contracts, and at industry level through the practice of swapping tariff concessions product by product in the GATT negotiations. This movement towards trade in close substitutes among small groups of nations may be reinforced by the elevation of non-price factors such as product quality to an equal status with price differentials. Trade between similar countries will then be encouraged not only because industries adapt their price structures to each other's demand patterns, but also because the types of goods produced are mutually acceptable.[2]

The empirical testing of trade theories

Numerous empirical tests of the predictions of the trade theories outlined above, new and old, have been carried out in the past 25 years. Useful summaries of their methods and findings are provided by Hufbauer and Stern.[3]

All the tests have confronted two general problems – how to deal with the intrusion of institutional factors in the theoretical framework and how to interpret data which correspond only very crudely with the sophisticated models. Tariffs, for example, have been discounted in all but a few recent studies,[4] whereas their systematic bias against the

---

[1] For the derivation of these estimates see chapter 4, pp. 88–91 above, and appendix E, particularly tables E.2 and E.3.

[2] This position is most strongly associated with Linder, but earlier Frankel wrote: 'a country with a large internal market for low quality goods is more likely to compete successfully in countries with a demand for similar goods, than one whose internal markets are mainly in goods of a higher quality, because less adaptation of production processes to export requirements will be needed in the former case' (see H. Frankel, 'Industrialisation of agricultural countries and the possibilities of a new international division of labour', *Economic Journal*, vol. 53, June/September 1943).

[3] G. C. Hufbauer, 'The impact of national characteristics and technology on the commodity composition of trade in manufactured goods' in R. Vernon (ed.), *The Technology Factor in International Trade*, New York, National Bureau of Economic Research, 1970; R. M. Stern, 'Testing trade theories' in Kenen (ed.), 1975.

[4] An exception is the comprehensive model of E. E. Leamer, 'The commodity composition of international trade in manufactures: an empirical analysis', *Oxford Economic Papers*, vol. 26, November 1974.

comparative cost differentials which form the basis for trade in Ricardian and Heckscher–Ohlin theories has long been recognised. MacDougall has illustrated graphically how Anglo-American trade in the interwar period was hampered by high United States import levies on textiles and similar products in which the United Kingdom was relatively efficient and by high United Kingdom import levies on machinery and transport equipment in which the United States was relatively efficient.[1]

In the postwar period this bias in tariff structures has persisted among advanced countries, though at less prohibitive levels, and among developing countries tariffs are regularly raised against foreign competition with inefficient domestic industries in the hope that growth and experience will eventually iron out the underlying comparative cost differentials and render protection redundant. Direct private investment in foreign production, on the other hand, might be expected to be substituted for exports of products facing tariff discrimination, hence Diab's suggestion that the foreign sales of overseas branches of multinational United States companies should be counted as exports and their sales to the United States subtracted from American imports.[2] In fact there is little evidence that tariffs attract direct investment flows among advanced countries,[3] and even less that they employ factor-mixes appropriate to the investing rather than the receiving country. Helleiner has presented a well-documented thesis that the vertical division of production processes among Pacific countries promotes specialisation along Heckscher–Ohlin lines, with the United States and Japan sending high-technology products for labour-intensive assembly and packaging operations to labour-abundant centres like Hong Kong, Singapore, South Korea and Taiwan.[4]

The principal problem encountered in testing traditional trade theories is the existence of two-way trade in the same product between pairs of countries. For a single country with multilateral trading links the simultaneous import and export of one good is unsurprising, since its comparative advantage in the production of that good may vary across its trading partners; for such flows to occur with only one trading partner is, according to comparative cost theory, impossible.

This phenomenon of 'intra-industry trade' is important; Grubel and

---

[1] G. D. A. MacDougall, 'British and American exports: a study suggested by the theory of comparative costs – Part I', *Economic Journal*, vol. 61, December 1951, p. 699.

[2] M. A. Diab, *The United States Capital Position and the Structure of its Foreign Trade*, Amsterdam, North-Holland, 1956.

[3] See, for example, A. E. Scaperlanda and L. J. Mauer, 'The determinants of U.S. direct investment in the E.E.C.', *American Economic Review*, vol. 59, September 1969.

[4] G. K. Helleiner, 'Manufactured exports from less-developed countries and multinational firms', *Economic Journal*, vol. 83, March 1973.

Lloyd show that at the three-digit level bilateral exchanges within the same product groups accounted for 63 per cent of total trade among OECD countries in 1967.[1] They also found it to be especially common in trade in manufactures, particularly chemicals, and important in the total trade of the United Kingdom (almost 70 per cent) and France, but relatively unimportant in Germany, Japan and Australia. Moreover, for the OECD bloc as a whole, the proportion of intra-industry trade clearly increased in the 1960s, most noticeably in the fast-growing machinery sector; among individual countries an appreciable acceleration in the share of intra-industry trade occurred in the United Kingdom, Canada and most EEC countries.

Faced with these facts, some economists have attempted to minimise their significance for received theory by arguing that the problem is one of aggregation, so that the phenomenon evaporates when commodities are properly distinguished. This position is untenable because even at the most detailed level of published statistics the number of industries with high levels of intra-industry trade is still large. In Grubel and Lloyd's calculations for Australia – one of the least affected countries in their sample – the intra-industry trade ratio was only 6.2 per cent, but at the seven-digit level some 7 per cent of industries still exhibited ratios in excess of 75 per cent.[2] Taking the disaggregation further in an attempt to find data compatible with the theory of comparative costs is *reductio ad absurdum*. If the traded goods within these fine groups are not homogeneous they must be distinguished not by their nature but by their countries of origin, and when the same goods produced in different countries cannot be regarded as substitutes comparative costs will not determine which are exported and which imported.

A second reaction to the existence of intra-industry trade is to minimise its practical significance in tests of traditional theories by concentrating attention on net trade within product groups. Panić and Rajan, for example, have adopted Balassa's suggestion that a country's export–import ratios in various commodities should be used as indicators of where its comparative advantage lies;[3] Baldwin, also Branson and Junz, have attempted to uncover the sources of United States comparative advantage by regressing such net trade measures by industry on factor utilisation by industry.[4] This does great violence to

[1] H. G. Grubel and P. J. Lloyd, *Intra-Industry Trade*, London, Macmillan, 1975, chap. 3.
[2] Ibid, chap. 4.
[3] B. Balassa, 'Trade liberalisation and "revealed" comparative advantage', *Manchester School of Economic and Social Studies*, vol. 33, May 1965; National Economic Development Office, *Product Changes in Industrial Countries' Trade* by M. Panić and A. H. Rajan, London, 1971.
[4] R. E. Baldwin, 'Determinants of the commodity structure of US trade', *American Economic Review*, vol. 61, March 1971; W. H. Branson and H. B. Junz, 'Trends in US trade and comparative advantage', *Brookings Papers in Economic Activity*, no. 2, 1971.

the underlying theory however; Heckscher and Ohlin merely showed that in bilateral trade countries will tend to export goods using their relatively abundant factor, not that they will, within the range of exportable goods, export more of those goods production of which uses most intensively the relatively abundant factor; the volumes of goods passing between the countries are in fact determined by demand not supply conditions.[1] The method also ignores the possibility that intra-industry trade itself may vary systematically across products, so that in some commodities a low ratio of net trade to total bilateral trade may be less indicative of cost disadvantages than of the considerable scope for product differentiation in that type of commodity, or of a considerable degree of reciprocity between the countries involved.

For non-traditional theories the existence of two-way trade has no problems – it is even axiomatic in the case of theories based on similarities in demand patterns. The principal problem encountered in testing these theories is that of finding suitable measures of the differences between the demand and technological structures of trading partners; the most basic variables used have been income per head and geographical distance. The former relates to demand and product characteristics through the growth patterns discussed in chapter 5 and, to the extent that other factors – size, population density, openness, growth rates – were there found to modify the link between development paths and income levels, the measure is obviously incomplete. The importance of size in determining the nature of international specialisation has been stressed by Drèze, who points out that the product differentiation necessary to support the bilateral trade of similar economies is most easily achieved within large and wealthy countries which can support the large-scale production of a range of closely substitutable goods.[2] In a small economy where only a few large production lines can be manned, a more secure marketing strategy is to concentrate on manufacturing standardised products with a guaranteed outlet in structurally dissimilar countries.

Geographical distance has been interpreted not merely as an index of transport costs, but as an index of cultural affinity; dummy variables indicating contiguity have also been used in this context. Though such variables are always significant in the analysis of the structure of trade networks, their cultural interpretation seems dubious. The colonial system has left a legacy of culturally derived trading links, between the United Kingdom and Australasia, for example, more intensive than the

[1] This point is made explicit in R. F. Jones, 'Factor proportions and the Heckscher–Ohlin theorem', *Review of Economic Studies*, vol. 24, no. 1, 1956–7.

[2] J. H. Drèze, 'Quelques réflexions sereines sur l'adaptation de l'industrie belge au Marché Commun', *Comptes rendus des Travaux de la Société Royale d'Économie Politique de Belgique*, no. 275, December 1960.

distances involved would ever suggest; again, Drèze has made the acute observation that cultural cohesion *within* a country is often more conducive to exports based on product differentiation than is any cultural affinity with the foreign importer, since characteristic product designs often reflect the national tastes of the exporting country.[1]

General measures of economic distance other than income and location have also been investigated. Yamazawa uses dummies for free-trade blocs, colonial systems and non-market economies (the last to account for levels of East–West trade), also a measure of aid from developed to developing countries, all of which have obvious relevance in terms of our earlier discussion of reciprocity.[2]

In addition, several variables more directly tied to economic structure have been used to explain trade flows. The proportion of consumers' or producers' goods in total output, the concentration of firms within industries and their average size have been taken as proxies for similarities in productive structure; general similarities in the export vectors of trading countries have themselves been used in the analysis of bilateral flows. While these variables are statistically useful in explanation and prediction, they fail to penetrate to the heart of the new trade theories – the stage of development – in much the same way that correlations of trade performance with labour productivity, wage costs or relative prices fail to capture the factor-endowment basis for trade.

In addition to all these general problems in the empirical testing of trade theories, there are various problems in relation to individual theories. The pioneering study of the Ricardian model by MacDougall retained the expository device of a single variable factor, with the result that, although comparative United States and United Kingdom export performances by industry in third markets was found to be correlated with relative industry productivity levels, the mechanism by which this operated was obscure, as no correlation could be found between export unit values and labour costs.[3] Moreover, the origin of the productivity differences themselves is obscure; in subsequent multi-factor studies by Clague, Nelson, and Gehrels they were ascribed to technological and managerial factors rather than to differences in natural resource-endowments.[4] The pioneering study of the Heckscher–Ohlin model by

[1] J. H. Drèze, 'Les exportations entre CEE en 1958 et la position belge', *Recherches Économiques de Louvain*, vol. 27, December 1961.

[2] I. Yamazawa, 'Structural changes in world trade flows', *Hitotsubashi Journal of Economics*, vol. 11, February 1971.

[3] MacDougall, 'British and American exports – Part I'; J. Bhagwati, 'The pure theory of international trade: a survey', *Economic Journal*, vol. 74, March 1964.

[4] C. Clague, 'An international comparison of industrial efficiency: Peru and the United States', *Review of Economics and Statistics*, vol. 49, November 1967; Nelson, 'A "diffusion" model of international productivity differences in manufacturing industry'; F. Gehrels, 'Factor efficiency, substitution and the basis for trade: some empirical evidence', *Kyklos*, vol. 23, no. 2, 1970.

Leontief was also confined to a measurement of the intensity of employment in United States exports and imports of the two factors – labour and capital – commonly used in its textbook exposition;[1] although the resulting paradox of the relative capital intensity of United States imports has been satisfactorily explained by 'neo-factor-proportions' versions, it has proved difficult statistically to discriminate between the effects of raw labour and equipment and of such additional dimensions as human capital and plant size.

Tests of new theories of trade have either been piecemeal – as in testing product-cycle theories through case studies of synthetic fibres, electronics equipment, consumer durables and petrochemicals – or, where more generally applied, somewhat inconclusive.[2] In the case of supply-based theories this confusion over the determinants of aggregate trade has occurred because of collinearity between indices of research and development expenditures and neo-factors such as labour skills. In the case of demand-based theories it is due to the fact that tendencies towards intensive trade among similar countries in some commodities are offset by tendencies to specialisation on the basis of structural differences in others.

PATTERNS OF TRADE

Given these ambiguities in detailed empirical studies of the basis for trade, it is clear that our more aggregative growth-pattern methodology will not enable us to discriminate among alternative versions of the new theories. What it can perhaps do is to decide whether structural convergence during industrialisation implies a reduction in the share of traded goods in total production, or whether convergence and its dynamics set up forces of demand and supply which encourage an expansion in traded goods.

The relationships between trading patterns and economic structure are discussed here at two levels: we look first at factors determining total participation in trade and then move to models of the manufacturing content of export and import flows within this total. At each stage summary statistics of our cross-sectional data for 1963 and 1971 are presented, the type of relations expected to emerge explained and estimated, and the links between our results and their historical or institutional background critically examined.

---

[1] W. W. Leontief, 'Domestic production and foreign trade: the American capital position re-examined', *Economia Internazionale*, vol. 7, February 1954.

[2] Key references in this area are: G. C. Hufbauer, *Synthetic Materials and the Theory of International Trade*, London, Duckworth, 1966, and the essays reprinted in L. T. Wells (ed.), *The Product Life Cycle and International Trade*, Boston (Mass.), Harvard Business School, 1972.

The trade ratio

While the obvious starting point for our analysis of how participation in trade varies across countries is a consideration of the influence of size, some minor issues with respect to the definition and measurement of 'participation' and some major conceptual issues over the meaning of 'size' have to be resolved.

Our measure of participation (the index of openness) is the ratio of exports and imports of goods and services to GDP; that is, $t = (E+M)/Y$ as used earlier in the cluster analysis and equations of chapter 5. The principal problem with such a measure is the fact that trade – a pure demand concept – is a measure of activity more gross than GDP. In appendix C we show that there is a weak negative relationship between gross–net output ratios and the level of industrialisation, and a stronger positive relationship with the share of investment in national income. The index t may therefore be expected generally to overstate the dependence of economies on trade, but by a greater amount in fast-growing underdeveloped economies. A secondary problem with the trade ratio is that it says nothing about whether trade is balanced; if there is any imbalance, the country's participation in the international economy is greater than might be thought, since it must enter international capital markets as a borrower or a lender.

Although most commentators would agree with Maizels that size is the chief determinant of inter-country differences in the trade ratio,[1] there is less agreement over how it should be measured. In some senses the relevant concept is physical size or surface area, because small countries have lower transport costs to their frontiers than large and within a small tract of land there is unlikely to be either the level or the spread of natural resources to meet all the various demands; indeed, resource-endowments are often so specific as to make almost complete specialisation in one or two resource-based industries the most profitable pattern of development for small countries.

There are many qualifications to this argument. In most goods nowadays the main basis for competition is not transport costs however important these may have been historically; this would presuppose that neighbouring markets are large (valid for small European countries, but clearly inapplicable to small landlocked African ones where distance from ports is the prime determinant of openness) and contiguous, thus

---

[1] See K. W. Deutsch, C. J. Bliss and A. Eckstein, 'Population, sovereignty, and the share of foreign trade', *Economic Development and Cultural Change*, vol. 10, October 1961; S. Kuznets, 'Level and structure of foreign trade: comparisons for recent years', *Economic Development and Cultural Change*, vol. 13, part 2, October 1964, and 'Level and structure of foreign trade: long-term trends', *Economic Development and Cultural Change*, vol. 15, part 2, January 1967.

failing to account for the high trading levels found in island economies. [1] Paucity and skewness of indigenous natural resources contribute to the understanding of this last phenomenon, but automatically to associate balance of resources with size is misleading; a country such as Chile with a North–South orientation normally embraces a wider variety of geological and climatic conditions than a country like, say, Turkey, which is of equal size but confined to a limited latitude. Even among large countries skewness of resources can provide a basis for trade, since their settled area may be quite a small part of the total; conversely, in small countries resources have to be discovered and exploited, which may exceed the abilities of their inhabitants.

Table 6.1. *Trade ratios in relation to surface area*

Area	Number of countries	Trade ratio[a] 1963	1971
(Mha)		(percentages)	
0–10	36	78 ($\pm$46)	81 ($\pm$40)
10–25	21	52 ($\pm$26)	52 ($\pm$24)
25–50	18	50 ($\pm$27)	48 ($\pm$16)
50–250	34	43 ($\pm$24)	44 ($\pm$24)
250–1000	7	25 ($\pm$12)	24 ($\pm$13)

[a] Standard deviations given in brackets.
SOURCES: United Nations: Food and Agriculture Organization, *Production Yearbook 1972*; Statistical Office, *Yearbook of National Accounts Statistics 1972*.

There is nonetheless some tendency for trade ratios to decline with increasing area, as shown by table 6.1. For most middle-sized countries the ratio is around 40–50 per cent, for the handful of extremely large countries it is reduced to 25 per cent and for the numerous very small countries with surface areas below ten million hectares it rises to 80 per cent. There is considerable variation at the small end of the spectrum, with landlocked countries like Rwanda and Burundi trading only some 25 per cent of their total product, while populous coastal enclaves like Hong Kong and Singapore export and import goods to a value over twice that of their GDP. Amongst very large countries the mean trade ratio is rather artificially reduced, and its variance increased, by the inclusion in the sample of the United States ($t = 9$); if it is excluded the average trade ratio rises to 27.5.

[1] In the island economy cluster identified in chapter 5, the ratio of trade to GDP averaged 1.4, compared to 0.4 for underdeveloped countries, 0.3 for large developing countries, 0.7 for small developing countries and 0.5 for the industrialised countries (see table 5.7, p. 113 above).

Table 6.2. *Trade ratios in relation to population*

Population, 1963	Number of countries	Trade ratio[a]	
		1963	1971
		(percentages)	
Under 2 million	28	84 ($\pm$38)	91 ($\pm$36)
2–5 million	34	55 ($\pm$35)	56 ($\pm$26)
5–20 million	32	48 ($\pm$20)	47 ($\pm$20)
20–75 million	16	28 ($\pm$8)	32 ($\pm$10)
Over 75 million	6	16 ($\pm$4)	17 ($\pm$7)

[a] Standard deviations given in brackets.
SOURCES: as table 6.1.

The second sense in which size is commonly invoked as an explanation of cross-sectional differences in trade ratios is that of total population. The argument is that scale-economies can be achieved with a limited workforce only in a limited number of products, thus less populous countries are obliged to specialise in a narrow range of goods and swap these goods in international markets for the wider range entering final demand. This is the context in which size entered the analysis of industrial growth patterns and, in his seminal paper in this field, Chenery attempted to relate imports to GDP per head and population.[1] He derived a coefficient of almost unity on the former term, so – since the equation was linear on logarithms – the regression was tantamount to a log–linear regression of the import ratio, $m = M/Y$, on population size; Deutsch, Bliss and Eckstein later proposed a non-linear alternative for the total trade ratio, which fitted the cross-sectional scatter rather better.[2] Our data seem to indicate a consistent decrease in the ratio as population increases (table 6.2), but the groupings conceal a lot of individual variation and the correlation of population with area makes it difficult to interpret such tables.

A third interpretation of size is internal purchasing power or 'economic' size. One argument in favour of some connection with trade ratios is that, just as an insufficient labour force may impose supply limits on the volume of goods which can be produced at internationally competitive prices and create an import gap, so may an insufficient demand for goods in which the country has a competitive advantage give rise to an exportable surplus. Quite distinct is the argument that, if the intensity of bilateral trade flows depends on the mean economic bases of the trading partners, the overall trade ratio – the average for

[1] If trade is balanced, then the import ratio is simply half the total trade ratio (see Chenery, 'Patterns of industrial growth', p. 624).
[2] Deutsch, Bliss and Eckstein, 'Population, sovereignty, and the share of foreign trade', pp. 356–7.

Table 6.3. *Trade ratios in relation to GDP*

GDP, 1963	Number of countries	Trade ratio[a]	
		1963	1971
($ million)		(percentages)	
0–250	22	69 ($\pm$33)	72 ($\pm$32)
250–1,000	33	66 ($\pm$42)	65 ($\pm$40)
1,000–10,000	43	49 ($\pm$33)	49 ($\pm$27)
10,000–25,000	9	45 ($\pm$24)	49 ($\pm$27)
25,000–100,000	9	25 ($\pm$10)	29 ($\pm$14)

[a] Standard deviations given in brackets.
SOURCE: United Nations Statistical Office, *Yearbook of National Accounts Statistics 1972*.

each country of its transactions with a number of partners – will be larger the more numerous are transactions with economically more powerful countries. In a random distribution of trading links, economies with low GDP are more likely to find themselves in business with countries with a higher than a lower GDP; and vice versa. So there is a statistical as well as an economic reason for expecting a negative relationship between economic size and openness, and Kuznets has shown that the strength of this relationship is greater if bilateral trade flows depend on the arithmetic rather than the geometric means of the GDP of pairs of countries.[1]

A comparison of mean trade ratios in various ranges of economic size is given in table 6.3; the expected negative relationship is apparent, though differences between extreme sizes are less marked than when the data were classified by area or population. A similar relationship was uncovered in the connected time-series data for New Zealand, Australia, Argentina, Canada and the United States for years between 1884 and 1952 plotted by Clark.[2]

This evidence on size as a determinant of participation in trade is rather unsatisfactory because the ranges in the table conceal so much individual variation; also, since size definitions are treated seriatim the data at each stage have not been purged of alternative size effects. A more satisfactory way of isolating systematic from random elements is by conducting a multiple regression and the form chosen is

$$\log t = \alpha_0 + \alpha_1 \log Y + \alpha_2 \log N + \alpha_3 \log A \qquad (6.1)$$

[1] Kuznets, 'Level and structure of foreign trade: comparisons for recent years', pp. 15–25.
[2] C. Clark, 'Is international commerce necessary?', *Bulletin d'Information et de Documentation*, vol. 32, July 1953.

where Y, N and A are GDP, population size and land area respectively. The results obtained from 116 countries in a 1963 cross-section are shown in table 6.4 broken down by cluster.

We expect the coefficients α_1, α_2 and α_3 to be negative, expectations which are confirmed by the estimated t-statistics with respect to the GDP coefficient α_1 only for the small developing and island economies in Clusters IV and V, with respect to the population coefficient α_2 only for the least and most developed Clusters I and VI, and with respect to area (coefficient α_3) only for the advanced economies of Cluster VI. Our reservations about the usefulness of area as a variable in economies without rich neighbours or contiguous markets are amply justified by the results, which show that physical size is significant only in medium to large developed economies; indeed, for island economies and the smallest European economies in Cluster V, α_3 is paradoxically significant and *positive*; also paradoxical are the positive values for α_1 found for Clusters I and VI.

The resolution of both paradoxes lies in the fact that it is impossible to deduce from an equation such as 6.1 how much variation is attributable to functions of the size variables such as population density (N/A) and GDP per head (Y/N) – both of which have distinctive roles in the growth process – and how much to the size variables themselves. Population density has, for example, been suggested as an indicator of resource-endowment. For an island economy, a high ratio of land to labour greatly increases the likelihood of its specialising narrowly in

Table 6.4. *Trade ratios: growth patterns, 1963 cross-section*[a]

		Coefficient			$\overline{R}^2$
	α_0	α_1	α_2	α_3	
Cluster I	3.12	0.16	−0.36	0.02	0.26
		(2.02)	(3.74)	(0.47)	
Cluster II	4.96	−0.16	−0.06	—	0.22
		(0.86)	(0.60)	(0.03)	
Cluster III	7.65	−0.52	0.47	−0.10	0.34
		(1.41)	(1.00)	(0.37)	
Cluster IV	6.18	−0.33	0.13	0.01	0.37
		(2.55)	(0.66)	(0.17)	
Cluster V	7.42	−0.34	−0.04	0.31	0.77
		(2.39)	(0.24)	(4.53)	
Cluster VI	2.42	0.30	−0.48	−0.13	0.79
		(2.00)	(3.26)	(3.22)	

[a] Equation 6.1. estimated on subsamples from the sample of 116 countries; t-statistics given in brackets.

resource-based exportable products; since transport costs to ports are trivial in comparison with subsequent shipping costs, it is not surprising that a net positive coefficient on area was found for Cluster V. Historically, population density also provides a powerful descriptive index for charting the rise and fall of trade, not only in small satellite economies but in the large former colonies of North and South America and Australasia. In the nineteenth century, trade between Europe and its foreign settlements was of a vertical character, consisting of the exchange of transport services and outflows of capital and labour for food, raw materials and minerals; as the capital and labour accumulation overtook the rate of exploitation of farmlands and mineral resources in the colonies, so the character of the trade changed and its volume diminished.

The second implicit variable in equation 6.1, GDP per head, has been mooted as a determinant of cross-sectional differences in trading propensities and of historical trends, but with contradictory results. Both Chenery[1] and Tinbergen, who used a multiplicative formula for trade intensity to distinguish the effects of economic size from those of income,[2] found little correlation with the level of trade. Kuznets, using a compromise between multiplicative and additive intensity formulae, found a significant positive correlation;[3] Glejser, in a regression of import and export shares in GDP on population, distance from markets and preferential trading factors, as well as GDP per head, found a negative relationship for imports but a weak positive relationship for exports.[4] These cross-sectional studies contrast with the time-series evidence of Deutsch and Eckstein that trade has lagged behind total product in most developed countries since the end of the nineteenth century.[5] The meaning of such data is crucial to the interpretation of our cross-sectional regressions, since these show not a declining trend but rather two phases of fast-increasing participation in trade, separated by a stagnant transitional period when industrialisation is under way but incomplete (chart 6.1).

Deutsch and Eckstein base their deductions on two sets of data: long time-series for five developed economies (the United Kingdom, the United States, Germany, Denmark and Norway) starting in the early or mid-1800s and shorter series for these and six similar economies starting around 1900. The long series show steep rises in the trade ratios of the

---

[1] Chenery, 'Patterns of industrial growth'.

[2] J. Tinbergen, *Shaping the World Economy*, New York, Twentieth Century Fund, 1962.

[3] Kuznets, 'Level and structure of foreign trade: long-term trends'.

[4] H. Glejser, 'An explanation of differences in trade–product ratios among countries', *Cahiers Économiques de Bruxelles*, no. 37, February 1968.

[5] K. W. Deutsch and A. Eckstein, 'National industrialization and the declining share of the international economic sector 1890–1959', *World Politics*, vol. 13, January 1961.

Chart 6.1. *The trade ratio :*[a] *growth patterns by cluster*

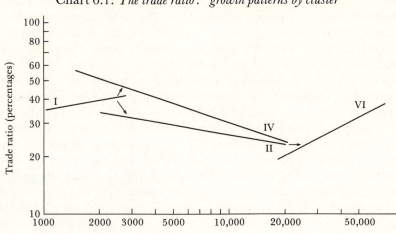

GDP ($ million, 1963)

[a] Ratio of total trade to GDP.
SOURCE: calculated from table 6.4.

United Kingdom, Germany and Denmark early in their industrialisation tailing off in the 1930s; the United States data are more stable
with a slight downward trend, the Norwegian volatile with no
discernible trend. Over the period 1900–54 average growth rates of
income are found to exceed average growth rates of trade in ten of the
countries but not Canada, with the implied decline in the trade ratio
most pronounced in the Netherlands, Germany and Switzerland. The
analysis may be questioned for estimating trends from series ending
either in the major depression of the 1930s or in the minor depression
accompanying the Korean war in the early 1950s, and including in their
later stages the extraordinary stimuli to self-sufficiency of two world
wars. This is the line taken by Kuznets,[1] who rests his argument against
the thesis on pre-1913 trends. These were generally upward, except for
young developing countries like Australia and the United States where
the destruction of vertical specialisation was occurring along the lines
explained above.

How legitimate it is to discount most of the twentieth century data as
subject to extraneous disruption depends on the level at which the
theory of declining trade ratios is pitched. On the one hand it is possible
to identify the origins of the decline in economic processes intrinsic to
growth and industrialisation which militate against trade – the
increased share of services in developed countries, the convergence of

[1] Kuznets, 'Level and structure of foreign trade: long-term trends'.

industry-mixes in developing countries, the depletion of natural resources and diminishing returns from the land in underdeveloped countries – and one can point to a number of catalytic factors in recent economic history which might accelerate these processes – the exploitation of new energy sources, the dissemination of technical expertise and the substitution of synthetic for natural materials. Such arguments summarise the concerns first expressed by Torrens and echoed over a century later by Keynes, Lewis and Robertson;[1] the truth of the arguments is also a necessary condition for the patterns of import substitution sought by Chenery. Though dependent on an anti-trade bias in technical progress,[2] they are essentially independent of extra-economic forces. On the other hand, it is arguable that the political decisions favouring restrictive commercial policies in the 1930s and the 1950s are part of a larger socio-economic process by which national economic interests inevitably come to dominate international interests. Again, in the writings of this argument's main proponents – Sombart, Robinson and Johnson[3] – a fundamental process is hypothesised and this is hastened by, rather than originating in, specific recent events.

The common denominator in all these analyses of the 'new mercantilism' is the increasing interest of governments in controlling production to the benefit of the lower middle classes, who are at a disadvantage in the initial phases of industrial growth. For Sombart, who believed implicitly in Say's Law, the increased domestic activity and reduced motivation among the wealthy capitalist classes to exploit overseas markets sufficed to refute the classical (Marxian) thesis that international commitments of socio-economic systems would tend to dominate their national commitments. For post-Keynesian writers, and for precursors such as Hegel and Hobson,[4] the significance of government encroachment lay not in its power to redistribute the benefits of a fixed volume of production between foreign and home markets, or between rich and poor classes, but rather in its power to create demand for an invariably excessive full-employment volume of

[1] R. Torrens, *Essay on the Production of Wealth*, London, 1821; J. M. Keynes, 'National self-sufficiency', *Yale Review*, vol. 23, June 1933; W. A. Lewis, 'World production, prices and trade 1870–1960', *Manchester School of Economic and Social Studies*, vol. 20, May 1952; D. H. Robertson, 'The future of international trade', *Economic Journal*, vol. 48, March 1938.
[2] At least in the analysis in J. R. Hicks, 'An inaugural lecture: II, the long-run dollar problem', *Oxford Economic Papers*, vol. 5, June 1953.
[3] W. Sombart, *Die deutsche Volkswirtschaft im neunzehnten Jahrhundert* (3rd edn), Berlin, G. Bondi, 1913; J. Robinson, *The New Mercantilism*, Cambridge University Press, 1966; H. G. Johnson, 'Mercantilism: past, present and future', *Manchester School of Economic and Social Studies*, vol. 42, March 1974.
[4] G. W. F. Hegel, *Philosophy of Right* (tr. W. T. M. Knox), London, Oxford University Press, 1942, p. 150; J. A. Hobson, *Imperialism: a study*, London, Nisbet, 1902.

production by restricting imports and diverting income towards classes with low savings propensities.

The eventual need for the exercise of such powers of protection was indicated by the increasing impossibility of a 'colonial solution' to the problem of under-consumption in advanced capitalist economies, as the comparative advantage of colonial economies altered with the accumulation of human and physical capital and as the class of foreign capitalists in the colonies was displaced as the main political pressure group by indigenous interests in a manner parallel to the displacement of the entrepreneurial class in the parent countries. The actual exercise of powers of protection in the twentieth century was hastened in the 1930s, when countries competed for shares of limited international purchasing power by means of aggressive devaluations and the erection of tariff barriers, the 1914–18 war having demonstrated to most of the protagonists how far defensive import substitution could proceed and to most of the peripheral nations the attractions of self-reliance.

In the first, purely economic view of trading propensities, political events are completely exogenous and periods in which their influence was pronounced should indeed be disregarded in attempting to identify underlying relationships. In the second, socio-economic view of trading propensities, political events are endogenous expressions of inexorable forces in the world economy and the declining trade ratios observed in the 1930s and 1950s are genuine outcomes of the system. More recent data on trade shares and more recent developments in the trading environment do not appear to confirm this second view. A comparison of the position in 1971 with average late nineteenth century values of the ratio of commodity trade to national income (the definition used by Deutsch and Eckstein) shows an increase for six out of the eleven countries on which we have reliable data (table 6.5); in the shorter postwar period the declining ratios experienced by the majority of these economies between 1955 and 1963 were promptly reversed between 1963 and 1971.

The last period covers three important rounds of general trade liberalisation by developed countries under the auspices of GATT; it also marks the formation of several large free-trade blocs among developed countries (EEC and EFTA) and among developing countries (the Latin American Free Trade Association, the Central American Common Market and the Association of Southeast Asian Nations). But, even among newly independent underdeveloped countries, while trading links with parent economies clearly weakened – out of the 40 nations achieving independence between 1958 and 1965, in 22 the share of exports going to their former parent countries fell noticeably between 1963 and 1971 and the parent countries' share in

Table 6.5. *Share of commodity trade in national income :[a] historical comparisons, 1800–1971*

Percentages

	19th century		Interwar period		Postwar period		
	Early	Late	1920s	1930s	1955	1963	1971
United States	15	14	11	8	8	7	9
United Kingdom	20	56	42	34	44	33	37
Japan	..	16	37	36	25	20	22
France	16	33	51	24	24	22	28
Germany	28	35	34	20	37	32	38
Italy	..	22	26	28	26	28	33
Denmark	..	55	57	49	60	55	52
Norway	..	44	43	36	63	58	59
Sweden	..	35	32	25	46	41	44
Argentina	..	..	..	36	30	18	14
Australia	..	40	35	..	38	29	26
Canada	..	28	36	26	28	34	41

[a] Figures differ from our trade ratios in that services are excluded from the numerator and net income from abroad is included in the denominator. The second difference is trivial, but the first may be important when (as in Norway) income from shipping or other services is large in relation to trade in goods and also makes a large contribution to total national income. Also, the data are in current prices and Lipsey has shown that the gentle downward movement in the United States series is completely explained by a relative decrease in the prices of traded *vis-à-vis* non-traded goods which resulted from the growth of service industries and of protective duties on competitive imports in the interwar years (R. E. Lipsey, *Price and Quantity Trends in the Foreign Trade of the United States*, Princeton (NJ), National Bureau of Economic Research, 1963).

SOURCES: Deutsch and Eckstein, 'National industrialization'; Kuznets, 'Level and structure of foreign trade: long-term trends', table 4; United Nations Statistical Office, *Statistical Yearbook* (various issues).

their imports rose in only four cases – the foreign sector as a whole did not contract, nor did the commodity concentration of exports decrease more rapidly than in sovereign states at similar levels of development.

To quantify the long-term effects of colonial status and the short-term effects of independence, the following regression was run on pooled data from 1963 and 1971 cross-sections of the countries in Clusters I and IV:

$$\log t = \beta_0 + \beta_1 \log y + \beta_2 \log \mathcal{N} + \beta_3 \log A + (\beta_4 + \beta_5 D)C \qquad (6.2)$$

where D is a dummy taking the value 1 with data from 1971 and C another dummy taking the value 1 for the 40 former colonies which had achieved some measure of independence by the early 1960s. The results shown in table 6.6 suggest that the basic effect of colonial status is to raise the trade ratio by about 20–30 per cent (exp β_4 is 1.35 for Cluster I, but 1.17 for Cluster IV) and that this was not significantly reduced

Table 6.6. *Effects of colonial status and independence on the trade ratio,*
1963–71[a]

	Coefficient						$\bar{R}^2$
	β_0	β_1	β_2	β_3	β_4	β_5	
Cluster I	2.51	0.25 (4.64)	−0.45 (7.51)	0.01 (0.32)	0.30 (2.87)	0.07 (0.69)	0.48
Cluster IV	5.26	−0.18 (1.84)	−0.11 (0.94)	0.07 (1.65)	0.16 (0.82)	0.22 (0.89)	0.47
Whole sample	3.59	0.13 (4.89)	−0.36 (10.39)	−0.04 (2.22)	0.01 (0.05)	0.10 (0.99)	0.55

[a] Equation 6.2 estimated on a sample of 116 countries, or subsamples from it; t-statistics given in brackets.

ten years after independence (β_5 is not significant at 5 per cent in either regression).[1]

Neither the general mood of trade liberalisation nor this evidence of the continuing participation of ex-colonies in foreign trade constitutes incontrovertible proof that the trend of world trade was exemplified in the 1960s rather than the 1950s. Advocates of the new mercantilist view can point out, first, that few of the newly independent countries before they embarked on autarkic trade policies approached the level of development attained by, say, Australia or Argentina; secondly, that customs unions represent for advanced countries a new sort of secured market which is a substitute for colonial markets and, in the case of the European organisations, serves as a buttress against the economic power of the United States; thirdly, that most tariff concessions are granted only because a number of alternative devices – subsidies, preferential procurement policies, peculiar quality standards – are now common-place and have proved more effective than tariffs.[2] Looking at table 6.7, which shows how openness changed in the 1960s, it is indeed plausible that the increased trade of European countries is due to the higher intra-trade within the EEC and EFTA; it is plausible also that the decreased

[1] Our estimate of the basic effect is in close agreement with that obtained by Deutsch, Bliss and Eckstein, but their inference that this effect would be reversed upon independence is not supported by our data for 1971.

[2] Subsidies are also relatively more efficient than tariffs in a welfare sense, since they involve distortions in the distribution of production between domestic and foreign plants, but no distortions in the consumer's allocation of his expenditures across goods. On the meaning of non-tariff barriers and their techniques of operation, see G. Ohlin, 'Trade in a non-*laissez-faire* world' in P. A. Samuelson (ed.), *International Economic Relations*, London, Macmillan, 1969, and R. E. Baldwin, *Nontariff Distortions of International Trade*, Washington (DC), Brookings Institution, 1970.

Table 6.7. *Movements in the trade ratio around the cross-sectional pattern, 1963–71*

Percentages

	Trade ratio 1963		Movement, 1963–71	
	Actual	Estimated[a]	Actual	Necessary for convergence[b]
United States[c]	9	23	+3	+14
United Kingdom	39	43	+5	+4
Japan	19	21	+2	+2
France	26	30	+7	+4
Germany	36	33	+6	−3
Italy	31	27	+7	−4
Denmark	63	64	−3	+1
Norway[d]	80	49	+1	−31
Sweden	44	47	+5	+3
Australia	34	28	−3	−6
Canada[c]	37	32	+7	−5
India[c]	12	18	−3	+6
Indonesia	18	27	+12	+9
Israel	66	71	+18	+5
Pakistan	18	25	−5	+7
Philippines	32	26	+4	−6
Argentina[e]	20	29	−4	+9
Brazil[e]	20	21	−4	+1
Chile[e]	29	31	−5	+2
Colombia	25	37	+5	+12
Mexico[e]	21	24	−4	+3
Puerto Rico[e]	111	108	−9	−3

[a] Based on regressions in table 6.4.
[b] Difference between 1963 actual and 1963 estimated.
[c] These countries were not included in the samples on which the regressions were based owing to their extreme position on the size scale.
[d] The Norwegian trade ratio is strongly influenced by payments and receipts for shipping services which have little to do with Norway's size or structure; the model inevitably underpredicts total participation in trade – in commodity trade alone the ratio in 1963 was 51.
[e] The trading behaviour of these countries was heavily dependent on protective commercial policies over this period.

trade of Latin American countries can be traced to inward-looking commercial attitudes.

Whether the trends in world trade in the 1960s are permanent or a transient phenomenon is to some extent unclear. But we should note that the new devices of protection which are presumed to occupy the role formerly assigned to tariff barriers depend for their effectiveness on the changed character of goods traded among industrialised countries – the greater share of technology-intensive quality-differentiated finished products. This was a structural trend predictable from Maizels' study; what was not then perceived was that the existence of such products greatly expands the basis for trade between countries with apparently similar factor-endowments and with avowedly similar growth and employment objectives. The immediate prospects for world trade in manufactures can thus be regarded as the outcome of two opposing forces inherent in its changed structure – trade creation arising from these increased opportunities for specialisation and trade inhibition arising from the growth of new protective devices.

The commodity composition of trade

From the consideration of the behaviour of the aggregate volume of trade during industrialisation, we now consider what systematic changes may be expected in the share of traded commodities within the total.

The nature of the changes in the commodity composition of manufactured goods trade in the 1950s and 1960s and their relationships to earlier trends can be seen in tables 6.8 and 6.9. The former shows relative growth in value and the latter relative growth in volume of seven broad classes of manufactures. There is one striking similarity between the two in the long-run decline of textiles *vis-à-vis* engineering products; the significant differences are the flat value share of chemicals in contrast with its relatively steep rise in volume and the declining

Table 6.8. *Commodity pattern of world trade in manufactures,*[a] *1899–1971 (values at current prices)*

	1899[b]	1913[b]	1929	1937	1955	1963	1971
			(percentages)				
'Expanding'[c]							
Machinery	8.3	10.9	14.4	16.4	22.6	27.8	27.2
Transport equipment	3.8	5.5	10.1	10.7	15.5	17.4	22.2
'Stable'[c]							
Basic metals	11.6	13.8	12.0	15.6	15.2	11.8	10.7
Chemicals	8.3	9.5	8.7	10.8	11.5	11.8	11.5
'Declining'[c]							
Other metal goods	7.2	6.6	6.0	6.6	4.8	3.6	3.4
Textiles	40.0	32.9	27.5	20.4	12.3	9.7	8.0
Other manufactures	20.8	20.8	21.3	19.5	18.1	17.9	17.0
				($ billion)			
Total value	*3.12*	*6.51*	*11.92*	*9.07*	*33.90*	*64.82*	*174.15*

[a] Exports of eleven main exporting countries.
[b] Derived from Maizels' data, which excluded exports from the Netherlands, by grossing up his figures in the ratio of exports in 1929 inclusive of the Netherlands to those exclusive.
[c] As classified by Maizels.
SOURCES: calculated from Maizels, *Industrial Growth and World Trade*, table A.5; appendix table A.5.

trend in the value of 'other manufactures' masking a more stable volume performance. In both sectors the realisation of scale-economies and technological advances – in polymer production, glass-making and paper-making for example – have kept inflation in their unit costs below that for manufacturing as a whole. The trends within the series in both tables are not always consistent; trade in basic metals and chemicals, for example, expanded relatively fast in prewar periods, but fell off in postwar periods such as the 1920s and the early 1950s.

In spite of these short-run fluctuations, Maizels found it convenient to summarise long-term growth differentials by classifying each commodity as 'expanding', 'stable' or 'declining', as also shown in tables 6.8 and 6.9. In general more recent data confirm his classification, but some questions arise. In volume and value terms there was a relative decline over the period 1963–71 in exports of machinery because of the sharp increase in trade in transport equipment and the revival of trade in chemicals from its postwar deceleration. Likewise, exports of basic metals fared worse on all counts than miscellaneous metal goods in the period 1963–71, but are classified as 'stable', while the latter are classified as 'declining'.

Instead of considering the separate regressions of value and volume on time, as Maizels did in framing his classifications, it is possible to take a more integrated view of such trends in aggregate product groups. This

Table 6.9. *Commodity pattern of world trade in manufactures, 1899–1971 (relative volumes)*[a]

Indices, 1929 = 100

	1899	1913	1937	1955	1963	1971
'Expanding'[b]						
Machinery	62	85	94	130	138	127
Transport equipment	17	31	105	147	158	193
Chemicals	83	108	112	168	214	255
'Stable'[b]						
Basic metals	81	105	106	95	82	67
Other manufactures	100	103	100	94	92	86
'Declining'[b]						
Other metal goods	107	108	87	65	42	36
Textiles	183	135	99	54	48	46

[a] Actual volume indices as percentages of index for total manufactures.
[b] As classified by Maizels.
SOURCES: Maizels, *Industrial Growth and World Trade*; United Nations Statistical Office, *Monthly Bulletin of Statistics*; NIESR estimates.

Chart 6.2. *Relationships between movements in relative volumes and relative unit values in world trade in manufactures, 1899–1971*

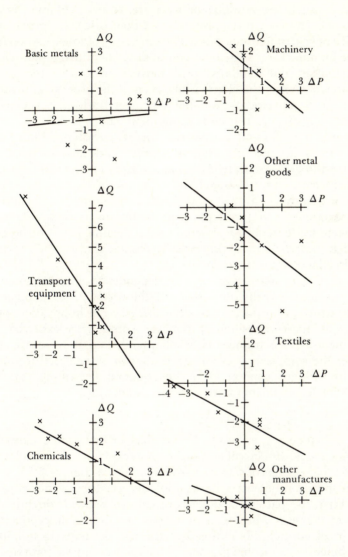

Notes: (i) ΔQ is change in relative volume index and ΔP change in relative unit value index, both in percentages per annum.

   (ii) Regressions (drawn as sloping lines) were run on the changes (shown as X) in the periods 1899–1913, 1913–29, 1929–37, 1937–55, 1955–63 and 1963–71.

SOURCES: calculated from tables 6.8 and 6.9.

depends on the fact that value and volume trends are not independent; their divergences represent movements in prices, which in turn determine in part how relative volumes move. Chart 6.2 shows the generally inverse relationships between the relative volume changes of exports of each of our seven products and their price changes relative to the price of traded manufactures. The long-run volume trend relative to that for manufactures in general can then be identified separately from the fluctuations due to relative price movements as the intercept of the regressions shown in the chart. Thus, even in the absence of favourable relative price movements, we should expect trade in the expanding groups – machinery, transport equipment and chemicals – to grow respectively 1.4, 2.0 and 1.2 per cent per annum faster than trade in manufactures in general, whereas textiles and miscellaneous metal goods tend to grow respectively 2.0 and 1.2 per cent per annum slower. The coefficients on the change in relative unit values show also that one of the expanding groups – transport equipment – would gain disproportionately from a 1 per cent decline in its costs, whereas the stimulus to trade in chemicals from such a decline would be no greater than that experienced by otherwise declining sectors, such as textiles and miscellaneous metal goods.

The trends in and relative price dependence of these commodity shares in trade are really the outcome of the systematic demand and cost changes which occur during economic growth. The implications of these changes for the composition of domestic output were explored within the growth-pattern framework of chapter 5 and it is natural to ask whether the composition of foreign trade can be analysed in the same way. In its most general form the equation describing contrasting patterns of development in two sectors X_1 and X_2 is

$$X_1/X_2 = \phi(y, \mathbf{U}, \mathbf{V}) \tag{6.3}$$

where y is income per head, $\mathbf{U}$ the class of orthogonal explanatory variables and $\mathbf{V}$ the class of non-orthogonal explanatory variables which cause the parameters of ϕ to vary from country to country.

Two special problems arise in applying this sort of model to trade flows. First, the pattern of imports or exports depends directly on the vector of domestic outputs of industries consuming or producing the goods involved and only indirectly – through the patterns in industrial development – on income per head. Deviations from the path described by equation 6.3 will tend to be correlated with corresponding deviations of industries from typical growth patterns, thus a higher level of statistical explanation may be achieved by replacing income per head by the actual relative sizes of industries. A similar effect can be obtained by transforming the dependent variables into measures of import substitution by expressing them as deviations from some 'normal' relationship with industrial output; this is the method used by Chenery. The second general difficulty in translating trade patterns into an equation such as 6.3 is that it offers a supply-biased explanation for exports and a demand-biased explanation for imports. While the pure theory of international trade has tended to emphasise supply factors and the empirical investigation of single-country trade relations has typically tended to start from demand factors, these more general shortcomings are no apology for the self-contradictory and incomplete treatment of exports and imports by the growth-pattern equation. We should note in particular that the omission of one side of the market makes it unlikely that high levels of explanation can be achieved with equations such as 6.3.

In addition to these trade-specific problems, two more familiar decisions must be made: the level of disaggregation must be fixed and the additional explanatory variables specified. In both cases care has been taken to see that the propositions advanced by Maizels – and discussed in the introduction to this chapter – can be tested by the equations. Thus we look at the share of manufactures in total export and import trade (shown in tables 6.10 and 6.11 respectively), the share of capital goods in total imports and the shares of individual industries with primarily intermediate or primarily finished products in total manufactured exports and imports; the additive effects **U** are attributed to population size, the investment ratio and the colonial dummy C; the variables in **V** inducing changes in the reactions of trade structure to

Table 6.10. *Share of manufactures in the exports of industrialised countries,[a] 1899–1971*

Percentages

	1899	1913	1929	1955	1971
United States	30	34	48	62	70
United Kingdom	64	77	67	79	83
Japan	42	49	48	87	91
France	55	58	68	64	72
Germany	70	72	78	86[b]	88[b]
Italy	41	45	58	62	76
Belgium-Luxembourg	46	45	73	80	79
Netherlands	..	..	38	48	55
Canada	7	10	37	47	59
Sweden	30	41	43	53	69
Switzerland	75	77	84	92	96

[a] Based on values at current prices.
[b] West Germany only.
SOURCES: as table 6.9.

Table 6.11. *Share of manufactures in the imports of industrialised countries,[a]*
19th century to 1963

Percentages

	Late 19th century[b]	Interwar period[c]	1963
United States	42[d]	40	46
United Kingdom	20[d]	20	33
Japan			
Manufactures	50	35	24
Capital goods	18	14	25
France	16	16	47
Germany	25[d]	27	43
Italy	38	..	48
Denmark			
Manufactures	30	34	63
Capital goods	11	14	25
Sweden			
Manufactures	45	50	66
Capital goods	12	25	31
Canada			
Manufactures	63	60	68
Capital goods	24	22	40

[a] Based on values at current prices.
[b] Average for years 1880–1900, except Italy and Canada, for which only 1913 figures are available.
[c] Average for years 1925–35.
[d] Early 19th century figures also available: United States, 64 per cent; United Kingdom 6 per cent; Germany, 34 per cent.
SOURCES: Kuznets, 'Level and structure of foreign trade: long-term trends'; N. A. Adams, 'Import structure and economic growth', *Economic Development and Cultural Change*, vol. 15, January 1967; United Nations Statistical Office, *Yearbook of International Trade Statistics* (various issues).

income and size are treated mainly by partitioning the sample into our clusters, within which relations may be presumed stable, but also by introducing population size as a continuous modifier of the income elasticity of product shares in trade and incorporating second-order terms in Y_m to account for other non-linearities. The two alternative regressions are then:

$$\log X = \gamma_0 + (\gamma_1 + \gamma_2 \log Y_m) \log Y_m + \gamma_3 \log N \\ + \gamma_4 \log i + (\gamma_5 + \gamma_6 D) C \tag{6.4}$$

and

$$\log X = \gamma_0 + (\gamma_1 + \gamma_2 \log N) \log Y_m + \gamma_3 \log N \\ + \gamma_4 \log i + (\gamma_5 + \gamma_6 D) C \tag{6.5}$$

where X is one of the trade shares which we have chosen to investigate.

Very few hypotheses other than those embodied in these two

equations have been tested in this sort of framework. In studying the share of manufactures in the total exports of a large number of countries, Banerji introduces non-linearity in a slightly different manner, by examining the merits of semi-logarithmic specifications over simple linear alternatives.[1] He also introduces another plausible explanatory variable, population density, with rather mixed results; low density does not seem to be conducive to exports of semi-processed manufactures (metals, textiles) as might have been expected from its known influence on productivity in these sectors,[2] but instead high density biases exports towards machinery and other finished goods in countries with established records in exporting manufactures. In spite of the importance of population density in explaining inter-country labour productivity differences in individual sectors, it seems that the effects are not sufficiently variable across sectors to affect the structure of manufactured exports.[3] Preliminary screening of our data on 116 countries with a variety of demographic variables showed that neither density of settlement nor the sectoral distribution of the labour force contributed much to the understanding of inter-country differences in trade structure. A significant exception occurred within Cluster VI, the developed economies, where two thirds of the difference between the share of manufactures in the exports of a densely populated country like Belgium (83 per cent) and that of a more sparsely populated country at a comparable level of industrialisation like Denmark (55 per cent) could be so explained.[4]

Parallel methods to those of Banerji have been applied to imports. In analysing the share of manufactures Bhagwati and Cheh used semi-logarithmic regressions to test for non-linearity;[5] they looked separately at the effects of GDP per head and the share of manufacturing industry in GDP, but did not consider population size as a potential determinant

---

[1] R. Banerji, 'Major determinants of the share of manufactures in exports: a cross-section analysis and case study on India', *Weltwirtschaftliches Archiv*, vol. 108, no. 3, 1972.
[2] See tables 5.17 and 5.18 above.
[3] This contradicts the evidence of Keesing and Sherk that the share of manufactures in exports is significantly positively related to population density, but that, within the range of manufactured exports and imports, net exports of machinery increase at the expense of more resource-based goods only in developing countries (see Keesing and Sherk, 'Population density in patterns of trade and development').
[4] The estimated equation was:

$$\log E_m = 1.18 + 0.23 \log Y_m + 0.14 \log N_a + 0.28 \log (N/A) \quad (\overline{R}^2 = 0.54)$$
$$\quad\quad\quad\quad\quad (0.35) \quad\quad (0.55) \quad\quad (3.15)$$

where E_m = share of manufactures in exports, Y_m = share of manufactures in GDP, N_a = share of working population engaged in agriculture, N/A = population density. Figures in brackets are t-statistics.
[5] J. Bhagwati and J. Cheh, 'LDC exports: a cross-sectional analysis' in L. E. di Marco (ed.), *International Economics and Development*, New York, Academic Press, 1973.

Table 6.12. *The share of manufactures in total exports : growth patterns 1963–71[a]*

				Coefficient				$\bar{R}^2$
	γ_0	γ_1	γ_2	γ_3	γ_4	γ_5	γ_6	
Cluster I	1.51	−0.74	0.33	0.16	−0.20	−0.48	0.68	0.16
		(0.40)	(0.79)	(1.21)	(0.46)	(1.23)	(1.67)	
Cluster II	22.67	−3.70	1.81	−6.14	−2.06	−4.53	1.36	0.52
		(0.80)	(1.11)	(1.25)	(1.77)	(0.98)	(0.96)	
Cluster IV	−2.59	3.48	−0.43	0.39	−0.76	1.18	−0.01	0.41
		(1.58)	(0.90)	(1.87)	(0.74)	(1.36)	(0.01)	
Cluster VI	−3.13	2.47	−0.20	0.10	0.32			0.11
		(1.22)	(0.80)	(0.71)	(0.42)			
Total	−2.00	0.01	0.23	0.23	0.79	−0.12	0.22	0.36
		(0.01)	(1.15)	(3.47)	(2.86)	(0.39)	(0.62)	

[a] Equation 6.4 (or 6.5 in the case of Cluster II) estimated on a sample of 99 countries, or subsamples from it; t-statistics given in brackets.

of the structure – as opposed to the level – of trade; as a result the fit of the estimated equations is poor, but the variable for industrialisation performs better than that for income, confirming our earlier suspicions.

In studying the share of capital goods in total imports, Adams eschews regressions altogether, but finds an interesting tendency for the share to be lower in small underdeveloped countries than in large, but higher in small developed countries than in large.[1] The latter part of this proposition – the greater dependence of small industrialised countries on imported capital – is Maizels' argument; the former is its mirror image. The latter part has significant implications for the pattern of specialisation – for large advanced countries the shift to heavy manufacturing represents a balanced response to the changing state of demand and technical knowledge, and involves import substitution across the board; for small countries a balanced response is impossible because of scale barriers to entry in international markets, so specialisation within branches of industry increases and import dependence grows rather than falls. The former part of Adams' proposition seems to have a purely algebraic interpretation: given the same rates of investment in a large and a small developing economy each heavily dependent on foreign capital, imports of capital goods into each will be the same fraction of GDP, but other manufactured imports – and hence total imports – will be much larger in the small country.

[1] Adams, 'Import structure and economic growth: a comparison of cross-section and time-series data'.

When equations 6.4 and 6.5 are applied to the shares of manufactures in total exports and imports, and to the share of capital goods in total imports, the results shown in tables 6.12–14 are obtained. In the case of manufactured exports the estimation has been performed on pooled data from 1963 and 1971 in an attempt to identify the effects of independence from colonial rule; otherwise 1963 data are used. Equation 6.4 proved superior in describing exports and equation 6.5 in describing imports.

The levels of explanation achieved are not high. In particular, very little of the variation in manufactured exports and imports among the least developed countries in Cluster I could be accounted for and the most significant findings for these countries concern the impact of the colonial dummies, which are found to depress the share of manufactures in exports and of capital goods in imports by about a third and a tenth respectively; however, the effect on exports is more than reversed soon after independence.[1] Although the fit of the equations is usually higher for other clusters, the estimated coefficients are all poorly defined; the most significant findings concern the positive effect of population (coefficient γ_3) on manufactured exports and imports of capital goods among the small semi-industrial countries of Cluster IV and its negative effect on manufactured imports among the advanced economies of Cluster VI. The coefficients estimated from the total data are rather better defined and show clearly that population size is an important determinant of inter-country differences in trade structure, all the ratios investigated increasing by about a quarter of their initial values with a doubling in population.

The interactions of population size, domestic industrialisation and trade structure are shown clearly in chart 6.3, where the shares of manufactures in exports and imports calculated from the general equations at various levels of the share of manufacturing in GDP are plotted for a typical small country with a population of ten million and a large country with one of fifty million. For the small country trade in manufactures is in balance – assuming total trade to be in balance – at point A, corresponding to a domestic manufacturing share in GDP of 40–45 per cent; among small countries this sort of level of domestic industrialisation had been attained only by Switzerland in 1963 and only by Switzerland and the Netherlands in 1971. On the other hand, trade in manufactures ceases to be in deficit for the large country much

---

[1] An attempt to gauge the effect of the removal of colonial status on the overall level and direction of trade is made in E. Kleiman, 'Trade and the decline of colonialism', *Economic Journal*, vol. 86, September 1976; Kleiman concludes that the progressive reduction in the share of trade with the parent country after independence produced some reduction in the relative rise of the traded goods sector in a sample of 44 United Kingdom and French dependencies in the period 1960-2 to 1968-70.

Chart 6.3. *Shares of manufactures in total trade: growth patterns for large and small countries*

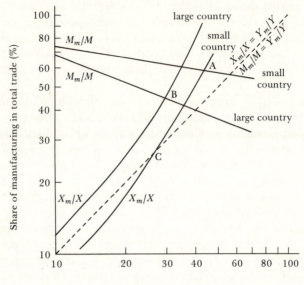

Share of manufacturing in GDP (%)

Note: Large country has population 50 million; small country has population 10 million.
SOURCES: calculated from tables 6.12 and 6.13.

earlier in its development, when the share of manufactures in GDP is only 30 per cent (point B). Both equilibria are attained with shares of manufactures in trade greatly in excess of their share in domestic production – 50 per cent higher for the large country, 30 per cent higher for the small country.

In practice net trade in manufactures is positive for many small industrial countries with domestic manufacturing shares in GDP rather lower than the 40–45 per cent suggested by the general growth pattern, the reason being that the general pattern understates the rapidity of the increase in export industrialisation in the later stages of domestic industrialisation. This sharp growth, noted by Maizels, is apparent if the pattern of exports is plotted by cluster, as in chart 6.4; here, an increase in the share of domestic manufacturing from 25 to 35 per cent, which carries countries from Clusters II and IV into Cluster VI, is associated with increases in the share of manufactures in exports from 40 per cent to almost 90 per cent in the case of a large country of fifty million inhabitants and from 20 to 80 per cent in the case of a country with a population of ten million. On the other hand, the share of manufactures in imports is, according to the regressions of table 6.13, quite insensitive

Chart 6.4. *Shares of manufactures in exports : growth patterns by cluster*

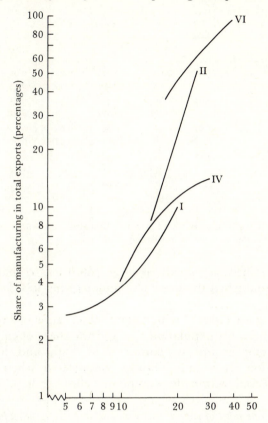

Share of manufacturing in GDP (percentages)

SOURCE: calculated from table 6.12.

to industrialisation levels except in the large developing countries, where the share falls 10–15 per cent for every 5 per cent increase in the share of manufacturing in GDP. Consequently, net trade in manufactures follows a sigmoid shape, with the transition from deficit to surplus particularly marked among large countries at intermediate stages of development.

The general patterns followed by the share of capital goods in exports show a continuous process of import substitution for foreign sources of capital goods, their share in total imports falling from around 30–40 per cent in the earliest stages of industrialisation to 20–25 per cent in later stages. The process is clearly more difficult for the smaller countries, which start with lower initial shares of capital goods in imports but

Table 6.13. *The share of manufactures in total imports: growth patterns, 1963*[a]

	Coefficient						$\bar{R}^2$
	γ_0	γ_1	γ_2	γ_3	γ_4	γ_5	
Cluster I	4.06	0.02 (0.23)	−0.01 (0.26)	0.04 (0.39)	0.06 (0.55)	−0.04 (0.69)	0.07
Cluster II	−1.17	0.89 (0.46)	−0.47 (0.67)	1.45 (0.69)	0.85 (0.91)	1.29 (0.65)	0.49
Cluster IV	3.50	0.03 (0.38)	0.04 (0.69)	−0.05 (0.33)	0.19 (0.88)	0.01 (0.06)	0.36
Cluster VI	−0.37	3.45 (0.47)	−0.48 (0.43)	−0.18 (4.17)	−0.43 (1.24)		0.63
Total	4.18	0.05 (0.96)	−0.09 (4.29)	0.22 (3.82)	−0.01 (0.16)	−0.08 (1.39)	0.30

[a] Equation 6.5 (or 6.4 in the case of Cluster VI) estimated on a sample of 99 countries, or subsamples from it; t-statistics given in brackets.

fail to reduce these as quickly as large countries, so that the relative shares are equal when the share of manufacturing in GDP is about 30 per cent.

This finding is consistent with Adams' observation of a reversal in the relationship between population size and the share of capital goods in imports among groups of countries at high and low levels of industrialisation. It is only slightly complicated when we consider patterns observed within developmental clusters; here we find from

Table 6.14. *The share of capital goods in total imports: growth patterns, 1963*[a]

	Coefficient						$\bar{R}^2$
	γ_0	γ_1	γ_2	γ_3	γ_4	γ_5	
Cluster I	3.08	−0.25 (1.52)	0.08 (1.06)	−0.13 (0.72)	0.29 (1.55)	−0.20 (1.85)	0.31
Cluster II	0.03	0.34 (0.11)	−0.12 (0.10)	0.45 (0.13)	0.70 (0.45)	0.76 (0.24)	0.21
Cluster IV	3.60	−1.12 (1.39)	0.25 (1.41)	0.16 (3.37)	0.25 (0.84)	0.06 (0.35)	0.68
Cluster VI	2.95	−0.98 (0.42)	0.12 (0.13)	−0.41 (0.14)	1.07 (0.69)		0.09
Total	2.66	−0.11 (0.87)	−0.07 (1.20)	0.24 (1.62)	0.28 (1.48)	−0.12 (0.75)	0.10

[a] Equation 6.5 (or 6.4 in the case of Cluster VI) estimated on a sample of 99 countries, or subsamples from it; t-statistics given in brackets.

Table 6.15. *Shares of commodity groups in manufactured exports: general growth patterns, 1963 cross-section[a]*

	Coefficient						$\overline{R}^2$
	γ_0	γ_1	γ_2	γ_3	γ_4	γ_5	
Basic metals	−3.35	1.09 (0.23)	−0.30 (0.36)	0.34 (1.96)	1.44 (1.49)	0.72 (1.04)	0.13
Machinery	9.15	−9.89 (1.98)	2.02 (2.25)	−0.03 (0.18)	1.23 (1.19)	0.27 (0.36)	0.39
Transport equipment[b]	−3.69	−0.99 (0.19)	0.35 (0.37)	0.18 (0.92)	1.37 (1.26)	1.07 (1.38)	0.22
Other metal goods	−2.96	2.71 (0.62)	−0.56 (0.70)	0.17 (1.02)	0.33 (0.36)	−0.14 (0.22)	0.05
Chemicals	−2.17	4.00 (0.94)	−0.65 (0.85)	−0.12 (0.74)	−0.35 (0.40)	−0.88 (1.40)	0.18
Textiles	2.91	2.53 (0.65)	−0.50 (0.71)	0.10 (0.67)	−1.11 (1.38)	−0.68 (1.18)	0.15

[a] Equation 6.4 estimated on subsamples from the sample of 116 countries; t-statistics given in brackets.
[b] SITC 73 only; aero engines and ships' engines included under machinery.

table 6.14 that within the least developed clusters a large population indicates high shares of capital goods in imports, whereas within the most developed cluster the opposite is true above the transitional level of industrialisation found from the general patterns.[1] However, among the semi-industrial countries of Clusters II and IV a similar reversal occurs, but at a much lower level of industrialisation when the share of manufactures is only 15 per cent of GDP. This cannot be accounted for by differences in investment rates between the two clusters. It may, however, have a purely statistical explanation in the influence of the exceptionally high ratio (42 per cent) experienced by one of the most industrialised members of Cluster IV – South Africa.

Pursuing the general patterns to a more disaggregated level produces the results shown in tables 6.15 and 6.16. These equations for the shares in manufacturing exports and imports of six sectors fit the data no better than their aggregate counterparts and the directions in which size and growth shift the structure of trade are equally uncertain. One major feature does stand out – the fact that export structure is much more sensitive than import structure to the advance of industrialisation; also a few minor features are of some significance – the increased trade in basic metals due to high rates of investment, the retardation due to colonial

[1] Recalling that the total effect of population size in an equation of the form 6.5 is not simply γ_3, but $(\gamma_2 \log Y_m + \gamma_3)$.

Table 6.16. *Shares of commodity groups in manufactured imports: general growth patterns, 1963 cross-section[a]*

	Coefficient						$\bar{R}^2$
	γ_0	γ_1	γ_2	γ_3	γ_4	γ_5	
Basic metals	0.87	−0.24 (1.00)	0.12 (1.58)	−0.14 (0.63)	0.60 (2.68)	−0.15 (1.00)	0.64
Machinery	2.30	0.12 (0.77)	−0.04 (0.75)	0.18 (1.33)	0.18 (1.29)	−0.17 (1.82)	0.50
Transport equipment[b]	2.08	−0.02 (0.08)	−0.08 (0.83)	0.20 (0.70)	0.24 (0.83)	−0.14 (0.73)	0.08
Other metal goods	2.14	−0.32 (1.18)	0.04 (0.48)	−0.13 (0.50)	0.07 (0.27)	0.19 (1.08)	0.21
Chemicals	3.62	0.13 (0.49)	−0.03 (0.37)	0.06 (0.25)	−0.44 (1.77)	−0.26 (1.50)	0.12
Textiles	3.93	−0.16 (0.27)	0.02 (0.09)	−0.31 (0.58)	−0.24 (0.45)	0.36 (0.97)	0.31

[a] Equation 6.5 estimated on subsamples from the sample of 116 countries; t-statistics given in brackets.
[b] SITC 73 only; aero engines and ships' engines included under machinery.

rule in imports of chemicals and capital goods (machinery, transport equipment) and the very diverse shares of chemicals and miscellaneous metal goods in trade found at all levels of development as a result of the wide range of activities subsumed under these headings.

The values calculated from these equations for the shares of each sector in manufactured exports and imports show two interesting features. It is clear that export structure is more *dynamic* than import structure, the main form of this being the replacement of textile exports by machinery. In the earliest phases of industrialisation textiles contribute about 35 per cent of manufactured exports and machinery nothing, whereas in its most advanced phases the share for machinery rises to 35 per cent and for textiles it dwindles to 15 per cent. What is less apparent is that exports are uniformly more *concentrated* than imports throughout development, the normalised Hirschman indexes for the shares considered being around 0.14 for exports and 0.02 for imports.[1]

Net trade balances by sector can be computed from the coefficients in tables 6.15 and 6.16 in conjunction with the manufacturing shares estimated above. These show deficits persisting up to quite high levels of industrialisation in all branches of manufacturing except textiles and

[1] A. O. Hirschman, *National Power and the Structure of Foreign Trade*, Berkeley, University of California Press, 1945, gives as a measure of the structure of foreign trade $(\Sigma y_i^2)^{\frac{1}{2}}$, where y_i denotes the proportion of a country's trade that is with another country i.

Table 6.17. *The share of an 'expanding' commodity in trade in manufactures: the case of machinery, 1963*

	Coefficient						$\bar{R}^2$
	γ_0	γ_1	γ_2	γ_3	γ_4	γ_5	
Exports[a]							
Cluster I	14.24	−16.34 (1.65)	3.31 (1.75)	−1.32 (3.20)	2.92 (1.46)	1.64 (1.46)	0.69
Cluster II	−28.71	12.12 (0.29)	−1.66 (0.23)	0.49 (0.52)	2.81 (0.44)		0.47
Cluster IV	36.38	−29.86 (4.06)	5.81 (4.11)	−0.18 (0.71)	0.71 (0.48)	−0.38 (0.65)	0.88
Cluster VI	−38.76	26.94 (1.13)	−3.66 (1.03)	0.16 (0.90)	−2.43 (1.91)		0.67
Imports[b]							
Cluster I	2.09	−0.32 (0.73)	0.15 (1.13)	−0.29 (0.91)	0.69 (2.44)	−0.18 (1.18)	0.83
Cluster II	−1.27	0.74 (0.62)	−0.09 (0.26)	0.41 (0.42)	0.75 (0.74)		0.59
Cluster IV	1.18	0.28 (2.09)	−0.08 (0.88)	0.30 (1.27)	0.38 (1.82)	−0.02 (0.22)	0.87
Cluster VI	2.93	−0.35 (0.59)	0.06 (0.27)	−0.14 (0.19)	0.44 (1.01)		0.23

[a] Equation 6.4 estimated on subsamples from 99 countries.
[b] Equation 6.5 estimated on subsamples from 99 countries.

clothing. As with the estimates of net trade in manufacturing as a whole, the general patterns conceal considerable variations between large and small industrialising countries and give an unduly adverse impression of the trade balances experienced by mature economies.

Net trade by clusters can be estimated for the two most distinctive product groups – textiles and machinery – using the equations for which the coefficients are set out in tables 6.17 and 6.18. In textiles, the high average trade balances at intermediate levels of development are shown to be inflated by the virtual self-sufficiency of the largest semi-industrialised countries in Cluster II, which disguises continuing deficits among their smaller peers. In machinery this disparity is less marked, although large countries start to move towards balance earlier than small countries. More significant is the fact that mature economies achieve a trade surplus sooner than is predicted by the general pattern and that the surplus grows to a much higher percentage of total trade (40 per cent against 25 per cent).

Table 6.18. *The share of a 'declining' commodity in trade in manufactures: the case of textiles, 1963*

	Coefficient						$\overline{R}^2$
	γ_0	γ_1	γ_2	γ_3	γ_4	γ_5	
Exports[a]							
Cluster I	−3.62	5.59	−1.06	0.06	−0.14	−0.45	0.17
		(0.52)	(0.52)	(0.13)	(0.07)	(0.37)	
Cluster II	34.92	−23.75	4.23	0.16	0.37		0.39
		(1.00)	(1.02)	(0.29)	(0.10)		
Cluster IV	6.51	−4.76	0.91	−0.59	0.97	−0.68	0.19
		(0.22)	(0.22)	(0.82)	(0.22)	(0.41)	
Cluster VI	32.41	−16.21	2.62	−0.19	−1.51		0.24
		(0.65)	(0.70)	(0.97)	(1.13)		
Imports[b]							
Cluster I	8.23	−1.36	0.20	−0.64	−0.80	0.25	0.58
		(0.69)	(0.33)	(0.45)	(0.63)	(0.36)	
Cluster II	4.94	0.68	−0.67	0.79	−0.64		0.52
		(0.10)	(0.35)	(0.14)	(0.11)		
Cluster IV	10.56	−0.88	0.55	−1.53	−1.85	−0.21	0.71
		(1.70)	(1.61)	(1.67)	(2.34)	(0.64)	
Cluster VI	5.09	1.48	−0.19	0.36	−2.22		0.50
		(1.00)	(0.34)	(0.20)	(2.04)		

Notes: see notes to table 6.17.

DEVELOPMENT PATTERNS AND THE BASIS FOR TRADE: A SYNTHESIS

From our growth-pattern analysis we have extracted a series of 'stylised facts' about the level and structure of foreign trade in countries of various kinds and at various stages of development. In conclusion it is worth asking what inferences, if any, can be drawn about the value of the competing theories of the basis for trade described earlier in the chapter.

In surveying the theoretical and empirical work on international trade flows, we placed emphasis on the disunity of the former and the merely partial success of the latter. This is not an unsatisfactory state of affairs, since it has bred a consensus that no single theory is capable of explaining the country-to-country linkages observed for all types of commodity, but rather that each theory is peculiarly suited to the analysis of trade in certain limited sets of commodities and of countries. The sets involved can be deduced from the areas in which empirical tests of particular theories have proved especially robust; attempts to classify commodities into such sets have been made on this basis by Hirsch and by Gray.[1]

Hirsch distinguishes Ricardian from non-Ricardian goods by the importance of specific resource-endowments in their production; within non-Ricardian goods he distinguishes Heckscher–Ohlin goods from product-cycle goods by the importance of labour skills in their production; within both Ricardian and non-Ricardian he distinguishes mature goods from immature goods on the basis of their physical capital intensity. Gray considers both supply and demand conditions and as a result his groupings cut across those of Hirsch. Within Ricardian goods, for example, he separates those which are in inelastic supply because of an irremediable constraint on natural resources from those which are constrained by lack of local expertise in exploiting resources – a condition which can be remedied. Similarly, within non-Ricardian goods he separates those which are in demand because of their countries of origin from those which are in demand because of quality factors which can be replicated in any country.

From such classifications it is a short step to classifying countries by their main basis for trade. Countries with high proportions of agricultural or mineral products in their exports – our Clusters I and III respectively – can be expected to follow the dictates of Ricardian theory in their choice of trading partners. Countries with significant proportions of manufactured products in their exports might, on the other hand, engage in trade along Heckscher–Ohlin or technological-gap lines. Evidence on this is mixed. Kojima doubts whether the Heckscher–Ohlin theory is a likely explanatory hypothesis because net exchanges among most industrial countries in each commodity class are so small; exceptions are Australia and New Zealand, which indulge in extensive vertical trade with Western Europe, North America and Japan. Hirsch, on the other hand, found that in pairs of countries at slightly different levels of industrialisation there were high surpluses in skill-intensive 'mature' goods (clothing) in the less industrialised and high surpluses in 'immature' goods (chemicals, some engineering) in the more industrialised. These findings can be reconciled if countries in the process of industrialisation are regarded as undergoing transition from a state in which their manufactured exports are determined along Heckscher–Ohlin lines to a state in which their exports are primarily determined by technological and marketing factors. This transition is discernible to some extent in the patterns of export trade estimated above and presented in table 6.15.

[1] S. Hirsch, 'Hypotheses regarding trade between developing and industrial countries' in Giersch (ed.), *The International Division of Labour*; H. P. Gray, 'A tripartite model of international trade', *Economia Internazionale*, vol. 27, May 1974.

Chart 6.5. *Indicators of physical and human capital, 1963*

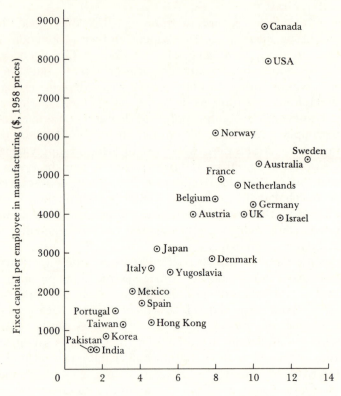

Skilled/total employees in manufacturing (percentages)

Notes: (i) See notes *a* and *b* to the source table for details of the basis of calculation.

(ii) The following values represent arbitrary extrapolation from 'similar' countries: fixed capital per employee for Hong Kong, India and Pakistan, proportion of skilled employees for France, Germany, United Kingdom and Australia.

SOURCE: Hufbauer, 'The impact of national characteristics and technology', table 4.

Considering first the transition from trade based on raw factor-endowments to trade based on technological achievements, in the course of industrialisation both physical and human capital are accumulated. Chart 6.5 illustrates their correlation with industrialisation in a cross-section of economies at the levels of industrialisation in about 1963, physical capital being measured by cumulated investment expenditure in manufacturing over the decade 1953–64 and human capital by the proportion of professional, scientific and technical personnel in total employment. The correlation of these two measures has been cited as a difficulty in the investigation of sources of comparative advantage when skills are treated as factors of production, but in a straight confrontation of the Heckscher–Ohlin and product-cycle theories the predictions of each prove distinctive. The Heckscher–Ohlin theory asserts that in trade between a fully industrialised country and a less industrialised country relative factor-endowments will lead the former to specialise in the export of capital-intensive goods. In similar circumstances the product-cycle theory asserts that the more industrialised country will tend to specialise in the export of goods which are most amenable to technical advances and in which the skilled labour necessary to bring about these advances is most intensively employed. Thus the two theories can be tested by observing how goods produced by capital-intensive but unskilled operations fare in total exports as compared with goods produced by skill-intensive but low-capital techniques. As industrialisation progresses the former should grow faster than the latter under the Heckscher–Ohlin theory, but the opposite should happen under the product-cycle theory.

Table 6.19. *Factor utilisation in United States production of traded goods, 1963*

	Capital per man		Skill ratio[a]	
	Value	Rank	Value	Rank
	($ 000)		(%)	
Basic metals	21.7	*6*	6.2	*2*
Machinery	6.6	*2* ⎫		
Transport equipment	9.3	*4* ⎬	12.2	*4–5*
Other metal goods	7.0	*3*	9.7	*3*
Chemicals	19.6	*5*	15.5	*6*
Textiles	3.9	*1*	1.6	*1*

[a] Proportion of labour force accounted for by professional, technical and scientific personnel.

SOURCE: Hufbauer, 'The impact of national characteristics'.

The elasticities of six types of traded product with respect to the share of manufactures in GDP were given in table 6.15, and in table 6.19 some indication – admittedly crude – of the capital and skill intensities used to produce each type of good is given. Like the data of chart 6.5, these figures are taken from Hufbauer's paper. They relate to the United States and to very broad commodity groups, so that the differences in factor-endowments are smaller than would be obtainable with more disaggregated data. Although factor reversals have been found to be uncommon, some caution should be exercised in generalising from such figures about the basis for trade in less developed countries.

It is clear from table 6.19 that the comparative behaviour during industrialisation of trade in basic metals and in machinery is critical in discriminating between the alternative theories. The former product group is highly capital-intensive but does not employ much skilled labour; the latter is not particularly capital-intensive but does engage large numbers of skilled technicians. In contrast, textiles are at the bottom of both scales, whereas chemicals and transport equipment are high. Table 6.20 therefore shows for basic metals and for machinery the expected direction of the effect of industrialisation on their shares in manufacturing exports, the actual effects found from the general patterns of table 6.15 above evaluated at low and high levels of industrialisation, and the actual effects found within clusters of countries at different stages of development.

Table 6.20. *Shares in exports of basic metals and*
machinery: elasticities with respect to
industrialisation

	Basic metals	Machinery
Elasticities:		
With low Y_m	$+0.1^a$	-3.4
With high Y_m	-1.0	$+4.0$
In Cluster I	-3.6^a	-5.7
In Cluster II	-2.2	$+2.2^a$
In Cluster IV	-1.0^a	$+4.9$
In Cluster VI	-3.4	$+0.9$
Signs expected under:		
Heckscher–Ohlin theory	$+$	$-$
Product-cycle theory	$-$	$+$

[a] Not significantly different from zero in statistical terms.
SOURCES: tables 6.15 and 6.17; NIESR estimates.

The general patterns show a transition from the trends expected under Heckscher–Ohlin conditions to those expected under product-cycle conditions as the level of industrialisation is raised; the share for basic metals rises slightly when manufacturing grows to 10 per cent of GDP, but falls at an increasing rate thereafter, while the machinery share switches from a falling trend to a rising trend when this index is about 12 per cent. The patterns by cluster show both shares falling during industrialisation in the least developed countries, but the share for basic metals falls less than that for machinery. At intermediate levels of development the basic metals share continues to fall, but the machinery share turns round very rapidly. Finally, among the most developed countries of Cluster VI there is a steady but significant upward trend in the share achieved by machinery exports, while the share of basic metals falls sharply. The samples involved in our regressions are, of course, small and the level of commodity aggregation is very high. Nonetheless, the equations – especially those describing the growth of machinery exports – are not inconsistent with our speculation that during industrialisation a transition occurs from a trading pattern based mainly on relative factor-endowments along the lines suggested by the Heckscher–Ohlin theory towards a pattern based mainly on technological leads and lags along the lines suggested by the product-cycle theory.

7

THE EFFECTS OF TRADE ON GROWTH
by *R. A. Batchelor*

INTRODUCTION

This chapter complements the last: there we examined the patterns of change in the level and structure of trade which occur during industrialisation and growth; here we examine how income grows as a result of these structural changes in trade. This sort of interaction was discussed earlier in relation to domestic industrialisation and productivity (chapter 5) and was summarised in the two equations

$$X_1/X_2 = \phi(y) \tag{7.1}$$

$$g(y) = \psi(X_1/X_2) \tag{7.2}$$

where X_1/X_2 is the ratio of contrasting economic variables, y income per head and $g(y)$ its rate of growth. The contrasts considered in chapter 6 using equation 7.1 included the ratio of trade as a whole to domestic activity and the shares of manufactures, capital goods and other commodity groups in exports and imports. However, when considering equation 7.2 we shall be concerned mainly with the effects of export structure and openness in general, since these variables can be changed by external forces, whereas import structure and import levels, being conditioned by domestic requirements, tend to follow rather than lead domestic growth.

The structure of exports can actively affect income by several routes. If the composition of exports is biased towards products with fast-growing markets, the response of exports to any general increase in overseas demand will be that much greater and, in an economy working below full employment, so too will be the effect on total income; furthermore, any preferential response of investment to growth in exports as against growth in other sources of demand will mean that the higher the share of exports in any increase in demand the greater, other things being equal, will be the effect on total expenditure. These impact effects are simply due to the fact that exports and investment are components of total expenditure and that interrelations exist between them. Growth of exports has exactly the same effect on income as an equivalent growth in consumption, but consumption is not likely to increase autonomously any more than imports. If in fact both move in response to total income, the impact effects of other components such as exports and investment are 'multiplied' and their eventual effects cease to be proportionate to their shares in total expenditure. Further, growth of exports acts as a stimulus to investment in the same way as it was supposed that total output did in 'accelerator' theories of investment; again the total effect on growth will be increased by the multiplier effect of the induced investment. In a fully employed economy such multipliers cannot operate, as growth in one element of total output will necessarily be offset by a decline in another; growth can then be achieved only by increasing labour productivity. Growth in exports or a change in their composition will increase total product only if it diverts resources from one sector to another with a faster rate of productivity growth, or if diverting resources from home to export production accelerates growth of productivity within a given sector. This latter effect can arise directly, or indirectly if exporting firms require inputs from other firms with faster productivity growth.

Exports may also affect output growth passively – adversely if they subtract from the resources available for domestic investment, or beneficially if they add to the foreign exchange available to finance imported inputs. In practice these imported inputs may be investment goods too sophisticated to be produced domestically, or raw materials of which the domestic supply is inadequate.

Maizels summarised the implications for development patterns of such export-propelled growth:

> In general, small countries, or countries with limited natural resources, are more likely to find that economic growth can be accelerated by export specialization than are large countries or countries with a variety of natural resources. The extent to which resources in a developing economy can profitably be invested in export industries depends on the relative elasticities of supply and demand for imports and exports.[1]

His major contribution in this context came, however, in his later book, in which the 'passive' role of exports in closing balance of payments gaps was investigated in the framework of Chenery and Strout's two-gap model of a developing economy.[2] The active and passive links between exports and growth are discussed below on the basis of a Keynesian open-economy model of income determination, which in its most complicated version converges on this two-gap model; the form of our discussion is to relate Maizels' findings, and those of other, more recent

---

[1] Maizels, *Industrial Growth and World Trade*, pp. 111–12.
[2] A. Maizels, *Exports and Economic Growth of Developing Countries*, Cambridge University Press, 1968; H. B. Chenery and A. M. Strout, 'Foreign assistance and economic development', *American Economic Review*, vol. 56, September 1966.

studies, to the predictions of successively more complex versions of this model and to re-estimate some of the basic linkages between trade structure and growth by using our data on a cross-section of economies over the period 1960–70.

MEASURING THE CONTRIBUTION OF EXPORTS

Growth in total output can be divided into two additive components – one due to the share of exports in economic activity, the other to all other sources of growth. This we do by writing equation 7.2 in terms of total income rather than income per head, in the form:

$$g(\varUpsilon) = \alpha + \beta e \qquad (7.3)$$

where $\varUpsilon$ is total expenditure and e is the ratio of exports to total expenditure. The parameter β, along with e, determines the export contribution; the parameter α measures all residual contributions to growth. The values taken by these parameters depend on the assumptions that are made about the effects of exports on other components of GDP and about the productive potential of the economy. In this section we look first at the theoretical estimates of α and β generated by simple macroeconomic models and then at how well each model performs in accounting for actual rates of growth in major world regions in the 1960s.

Alternative accounting frameworks

In an economy with a private sector, a public sector and a foreign sector, total expenditure is the sum of private consumption (C), investment (I), public current expenditure *net* of indirect taxation (B) and exports *less* imports of goods and services $(E\text{-}M)$. This identity in itself gives some indication of the determinants of α and β, as

$$\varUpsilon = C + I + B + (E\text{-}M)$$
$$\Rightarrow \alpha = cg(C) + ig(I) + bg(B) - mg(M)$$

and $$\beta = g(E) \qquad (7.4)$$

where lower case c, i, b and m represent shares in total expenditure. On the face of it, the effect of openness is felt only if exports are themselves growing, and even then output grows only by the amount of growth in exports. There are in practice, however, relationships among the components of total expenditure which modify the values taken by α and β. In particular, consumption, taxation and imports are determined by behavioural or mechanical relationships with total expenditure and, for equilibrium to obtain, two important conditions must hold. First, the sum of injections into the system (investment, exports, government current expenditure) must exactly balance *ex post* any leakages from it (savings, imports and tax revenues). Secondly, total expenditure cannot exceed *ex post* the maximum output attainable with existing supplies of productive factors (labour, capital and raw materials).

Supposing that there are ample supplies of labour and that this factor can be freely substituted for capital and raw materials, then the economy can operate at a variety of capital–output ratios. Supposing also that the government budget, which we write as the difference between taxes (Q) and expenditure (R), is compensatory in the sense that it makes good any mismatch between *ex ante* investment and exports on the one hand and *ex ante* savings and imports on the other, we can then isolate the effects of interrelationships among the constituents of total expenditure in equation 7.3 by eliminating any complications in reaching equilibrium. Without loss of generality we can assume that consumption, taxation and imports grow in strict proportion to total expenditure; then,

$$C = (1-s)Y, \; Q = qY, \; M = mY$$

$$\Rightarrow \alpha = (s+m+q)^{-1} \left[ig(I) + rg(R) \right]$$

and

$$\beta = (s+m+q)^{-1} g(E) \tag{7.5}$$

where s is the marginal (average) propensity to save, q the marginal (average) rate of tax on expenditure and m the marginal (average) propensity to import. Export growth is still necessary for openness to have any impact on growth, but output grows by more than the increase in exports. Exactly how much more is determined by $(s+m+q)^{-1}$, the open-economy multiplier. It will be observed that in this model the effects of increased exports are identical to those of increased investment or government expenditure, since this multiplier applies to all such injections. If, however, investment growth is endogenously determined by, say, the rate of growth of total output, or even the rate of growth of exports, then exports become the only independent source of growth and the value of the multiplier alters; for example:

$$I = iY$$

$$\Rightarrow \alpha = (s+m+q-i)^{-1} rg(R)$$

and

$$\beta = (s+m+q-i)^{-1} g(E) \tag{7.6}$$

or

$$I = jE$$

$$\Rightarrow \alpha = (s+m+q)^{-1} rg(R)$$

and

$$\beta = (s+m+q)^{-1} (1+j)g(E) \tag{7.7}$$

In both cases the multiplier is increased by the product of the investment coefficient i or j and the simple open-economy multiplier.

Now, relaxing the assumption that government expenditure is used to equilibrate total inflow and outflow and supposing it is instead directed at the more conservative objective of balancing the public sector budget, $R = qY$ at all times. This yields an implicit *ex post* investment function, since for equilibrium we must now have the savings–investment gap equal to the foreign trade gap. That is:

$$I - sY = mY - E$$

$$\Rightarrow I = (s+m)Y - E \tag{7.8}$$

$$\Rightarrow \alpha = g(I)$$

and $$\beta = (s+m)^{-1}[g(E) - g(I)] \tag{7.9}$$

The investment function 7.8 can be regarded as a sum of functions like those producing 7.6 and 7.7, but with the property that increasing exports necessitates a *reduction* in investment $(i = s+m, j = -1)$. The resulting parameters α and β show that expenditure will grow at the rate of growth of investment unless exports grow faster or more slowly. If exports grow faster they contribute positively to growth by an amount determined by the multiplier $(s+m)^{-1}$ in conjunction with the trade share. Conversely, if exports fail to keep pace with investment, a high trade share will have a negative effect on growth since β will turn negative.

Finally, relaxing the assumption that capital, raw materials and labour are all freely substitutable, there is the possibility that actual output may fall short of *ex ante* expenditure plans. First, if output is related to capital stock by a fixed capital–output ratio $(1/k)$, then any growth in output is limited by the level of new investment, so

$$g(Y) = ki, k > 0 \Rightarrow I = k^{-1} Y g(Y) \tag{7.10}$$

If this necessary technical relationship is compared with the *ex post* investment function 7.8, we find

$$g(Y) = ki$$

$$\Rightarrow \alpha = (s+m)k$$

and $$\beta = -k \tag{7.11}$$

Hence, if output is limited by the rate of domestic capital formation via the incremental capital–output ratio $1/k$, a large trade share *reduces* the rate of growth in proportion to this ratio irrespective of the rate of growth of exports.

A second possibility is that output is limited by raw materials, extra supplies of which have to be imported; alternatively it could be assumed with the same outcome that output was constrained by particular capital goods which were necessarily imported. In these cases,

$$g(Y) = lm, \, l > 0 \Rightarrow M = l^{-1}Yg(Y) \qquad (7.12)$$

Now the injections–leakages identity which produced 7.8 can be turned round to generate an expression for *ex post* imports rather than investment, namely

$$I - sY = mY - E \Rightarrow M = I - sY + E \qquad (7.13)$$

Together with 7.12 this implies that in equilibrium

$$g(Y) = lm$$

$$\Rightarrow \alpha = (i - s)l$$

and

$$\beta = l \qquad (7.14)$$

where, since i is the domestic investment ratio I/Y, $i - s$ is the inflow of capital necessary to cover the investment–savings gap expressed as a fraction of total expenditure. Hence if output growth is limited not by domestic capital formation but by the inflow of imported inputs, a large trade share will *increase* the rate of growth in proportion to l, the incremental output–import ratio.

Thirdly, we must consider the possibility that output is limited by a factor which does not, like capital, increase with output growth and is not, like raw materials or advanced technology, available through trade; the factor is the supply of effective labour. In principle, no economy can in the long run grow faster than its natural growth rate and all the results enunciated above hold only in the medium term in a situation of underemployment; increases in openness in a fully employed economy will give rise to a once-off gain from trade, but will have no effect on the maximum growth rate of output. In practice the labour supply is not immune from accelerator relationships which increase participation rates and the rate of increase of population through births or immigration, nor from productivity changes induced by trade.

A variety of expressions for the parameters α and β have been generated by our simple model of expenditure and output determination. To summarise their implications we can say, first, that in situations where public expenditure is geared to filling any gaps between investment and export demands and the supply of savings and imports, the effects of openness are dependent on the rate of growth of exports, and vice versa; but, secondly, that in situations of imperfect factor substitution, the effects of openness on growth are independent of the rate of growth of exports: if output is effectively constrained by domestic capital formation output growth is inversely related to the export share, while if output is effectively constrained by the amount of imported factors which can be afforded its growth depends directly on the export share.

The experience of the 1960s

Data collected by the United Nations allow us to measure the direct contribution of exports and other components of total expenditure to overall growth in the period 1960–70. The results for main economic regions are shown in table 7.1. Relative to growth of output, exports make major contributions only in Western Europe, Oceania and Africa, though in no case does trade growth account for more than about a third of output growth and the comparatively high trade contributions stem from differing circumstances. In Europe and Oceania they arise from the combination of moderately high export growth rates and moderately high trade shares, in Africa from exceptionally low export growth rates in conjunction with exceptionally high trade ratios. A similar variety of explanations can be found for low export contributions

Table 7.1. *Direct contributions of exports and other factors to economic growth,*[a] *1960–70*

Percentages p.a.

	Growth in output (actual, 1955–69)	Exports			Contributions of:	
		Share in output	Growth	Contribution	Investment	Government
Developed market economies	5.1	11.4	8.4	0.96	1.24	0.77
North America	4.6	5.7	7.3	0.42	0.80	0.93
Western Europe	4.7	19.6	8.3	1.63	1.32	0.54
Oceania	5.1	18.2	6.6	1.20	1.46	0.71
Japan	10.8	11.0	15.8	1.74	4.17	0.59
Developing economies	5.2	16.4	6.3	1.03	1.05	0.74
Africa	5.0	26.0	3.9	1.01	1.82	1.19
Asia[b]	4.6	12.0	7.1	0.85	1.10	0.58
Latin America	5.5	15.9	5.5	0.87	1.05	0.52

[a] Contributions calculated from coefficients in equation 7.4.
[b] Excludes Middle East and Japan.
SOURCES: United Nations Statistical Office, *Yearbook of National Accounts Statistics 1972*, vol. III, tables 4A and 5; United Nations Economic Commission for Africa, *A Survey of Economic Conditions in Africa 1972*, New York, 1973, chap. 3; United Nations Economic Commission for Europe, *Economic Survey of Europe in 1971*, Part 1: *The European Economy from the 1950s to the 1970s*, New York, 1972.

– in developing Asia both the growth rate and the share in total expenditure are fairly small, in North America export growth is not particularly low but economies are rather closed to trade. While the export contribution never accounts for much of the growth of GDP, it is frequently a more powerful force for growth than investment – as in Western Europe – or government expenditure – as everywhere except North America and Africa.

Aggregation of the data into large regions does of course conceal much useful information about the interrelations of trade, investment and growth in individual economies. Two particular features of the disaggregated data should be noted. The first is that the role of exports in economic growth in Western Europe is confirmed for national economies; both Italy and the United Kingdom, for example, lagged behind the rest of Europe in the rate of capital formation in the 1960s (3.9 and 4.9 per cent per annum as against a European average of 5.9), but an exceptionally high export growth rate (12.1 per cent per annum) allowed Italy to grow 0.6 per cent faster than average, while the low United Kingdom export growth rate condemned it to overall growth at least 1 per cent slower than average (in fact owing to other factors the United Kingdom growth rate was almost 2 per cent slower). The second significant feature is the way in which results for Asia and Latin America as a whole are dominated by a few large or fast-growing countries. In the case of Asia we have separated out the most dominant economy, Japan, but even in the remainder the exceptional export performances of Korea, Taiwan and Singapore tend to mask the slow pace of trade expansion in, say, Indonesia and Sri Lanka, where exports grew at only 3.7 and 0.5 per cent per annum throughout the decade, as against 7.1 per cent per annum for Asia as a whole. In the case of Latin America the bias operates in the other direction, with slow growth in the large closed economies of Argentina, Brazil and Mexico masking the significant effects of trade on very small Caribbean countries, such as Costa Rica, Honduras and Jamaica; all of these have export ratios in excess of 20 per cent and in the first two exports grew at more than 10 per cent per annum in the 1960s.

It is important to discover how well the data conform with our simple aggregate growth model and whether we can determine which version is most realistic. The model splits total GDP growth into an export contribution βe and a residual contribution α from investment and other sources, but equations 7.4, 7.5, 7.9, 7.11 and 7.14 give quite different accounts of the sizes and signs of these contributions.

In table 7.2 an attempt is made to compute what the contributions of exports and other sources of growth would be if open-economy multipliers were fully operative in each region. The multipliers are

Table 7.2. *Indirect contributions of exports and other factors to economic growth, 1960–70 : open economies*

	Multiplier[a]	Growth contributions[b]			Actual growth rate
		Exports	Other	Total	
		(percentages p.a.)			
Developed market economies	2.1	2.0	4.2	6.2	5.1
North America	2.4	1.0	4.2	5.2	4.6
Western Europe	1.7	2.8	3.2	6.0	4.7
Oceania	1.8	2.2	3.9	6.1	5.1
Japan	1.9	3.3	9.0	12.3	10.8
Developing economies	2.2	2.3	3.9	6.2	5.2
Africa	1.9	1.9	5.7	7.6	5.0
Asia[c]	2.6	2.2	4.4	6.6	4.6
Latin America	2.2	1.9	3.5	5.4	5.5

[a] Calculated as the inverse of the sum of the ratios of savings, imports and taxation to national income as in equation 7.5.
[b] Calculated by applying the multiplier to the direct contributions shown in table 7.1.
[c] Excludes Middle East and Japan.

defined as the inverse of the ratio of savings, imports and taxation to national income, as in equation 7.5 above. While we should again stress that the experiences of individual economies may deviate markedly from regional averages, the table does suggest that the multiplier takes values around two irrespective of the level of development. Comparing the last two columns of table 7.2, it is clear that in all regions except Latin America actual growth fell short of that indicated. The shortfall is most marked in other developing countries, where the full operation of the multiplier should have resulted in growth rates about $1\frac{1}{2}$ times those actually achieved; among developed countries the proportionate shortfall is greatest in Western Europe and least in North America and Japan, though in the latter case the absolute discrepancy is quite large.

The first of three possible reasons for the failure of the multiplier to work itself out is that we have, in using proportional savings and import ratios, simply overestimated its value. However, while cross-sectional studies of the consumption function have generally found that savings grow more than proportionately with income, time-series tend to support our assumption;[1] similarly, while very high import propensities are found in a few countries, econometric work on import demand functions suggests that proportionality is the general rule and ascribes

[1] An early investigation of United States time-series is in S. Kuznets, *Uses of National Income in Peace and War*, New York, National Bureau of Economic Research, 1942; the disparity with cross-sectional data was noted in I. Friend and S. Schor, 'Who saves?', *Review of Economics and Statistics*, vol. 41, May 1959.

Table 7.3. *Indirect contributions of exports and investment to economic growth,[a] 1960–70: balanced budget constraint*

	Private sector multi- plier	Growth in exports *less* investment	Export contribu- tion	Invest- ment growth rate	Total growth rate	Actual growth rate
			(percentages p.a.)			
Developed market economies	*3.1*	2.2	0.8	6.2	7.0	5.1
North America	*4.3*	2.6	0.6	4.7	5.3	4.6
Western Europe	*2.3*	2.4	1.1	5.9	7.0	4.7
Oceania	*2.3*	0.6	0.3	6.0	6.3	5.1
Japan	*2.3*	1.9	0.5	13.9	14.4	10.8
Developing economies	*2.9*	−0.4	−0.2	6.7	6.5	5.2
Africa	*2.6*	−7.0	−4.7	10.5	5.8	5.0
Asia[b]	*3.4*	−0.3	−0.1	7.4	7.3	4.6
Latin America	*2.9*	−0.7	−0.3	6.2	5.9	5.5

[a] Contributions calculated from coefficients in equation 7.9, with export contribution as multiplier × growth in exports *less* investment × export share in output (table 7.1).
[b] Excludes Middle East and Japan.

the excess in the growth of trade over production in the 1960s to improvements in the quality and price competitiveness of traded goods over non-traded goods.[1]

The second circumstance in which the multiplier would be modified is when there are interrelations among its components. As we have seen in equations 7.6 and 7.7, any positive relationship between investment and growth tends to increase its value. More interesting is equation 7.9, which shows that the export growth contribution is altered completely if the public sector current account is always in balance, the multiplier then increasing to that of the private sector alone, a parameter which according to table 7.3 takes values between 2.3 and 4.3. On the other hand, exports contribute positively to growth only if they grow faster than investment. The net effect of these forces would be to raise the theoretically predicted rates of growth for all developed market economies outside North America even further above their actual performances, but to lower the predicted rates of growth in Africa and Latin America, where fiscal orthodoxy would mean that their relatively sluggish exports became a real drag on the rate of investment.

The third possible explanation for incomplete multiplier effects is that

[1] A comprehensive list of estimates of income elasticities of imports is given in H. S. Houthakker and S. P. Magee, 'Income and price elasticities in world trade', *Review of Economics and Statistics*, vol. 51, May 1969.

shortages of productive factors limited the sustainable growth rate. The growth implied in situations when the factor shortage occurs in investment or in imports is given by equations 7.11 and 7.14 respectively; openness is detrimental to growth in the former case but beneficial in the latter. The growth rates possible under each constraint cannot, however, be computed unless we know the technical coefficients k and l connecting capital and imported inputs to increases in output. Except in the 'corner solution' when both constraints hold simultaneously, it is impossible to deduce both coefficients from actual data since there must be excess unproductive supplies of one factor.

Further discussion of this model appears on page 224 below. Meanwhile, three observations on equations 7.11 and 7.14 may give some clue as to whether the model is applicable to growth in the West European and Asian economies which were so poorly described by multiplier relationships. First, among a group of countries with similar internal growth factors – similar α contributions – an inverse relationship between growth and the export share ought to be observed if the investment constraint is binding and a direct relationship if the import constraint is binding. Secondly, looking at movements in

Chart 7.1. *Growth rates and export shares for European countries, 1960–70*

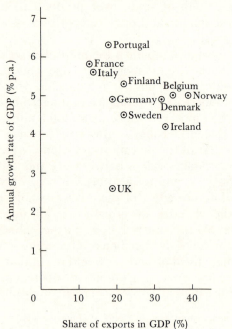

Share of exports in GDP (%)

SOURCE: NIESR estimates.

individual countries over time, it is possible to infer what *changes* in growth ought to follow from changes in savings and import shares under each constraint and compare these with what actually happened. Thirdly, the means of relaxing both constraints lies in a country's ability to attract capital inflows, since, so long as they are not used for current consumption, these augment the stock of investible funds and add to the stock of foreign exchange available to purchase imports.

Chart 7.2. *Growth rates and export shares for Asian countries, 1960–70*

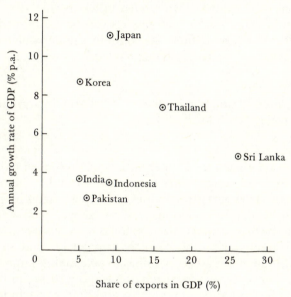

SOURCE: as chart 7.1.

In charts 7.1 and 7.2 we have plotted growth rates against export shares for both European and Asian economies in the 1960s. In the first, all countries except the United Kingdom cluster around a negatively sloped line, suggesting that in Western Europe as a whole growth was conditional on the rate of investment, so that exports 'competed' with investment for available resources; hence growth was rather higher in the relatively closed economies of Portugal and France than in the more open economies such as Belgium, Denmark and Ireland. In the second chart the economies of Asia fall into two groups; in the fast-growing one there is some suggestion of a negatively sloping investment constraint and in the slow-growing one a hint of a positively sloping import constraint, but both inferences are very weak and rely on the positions of the two outlying countries (Thailand and Sri Lanka).

TRADE GROWTH AND THE RATE OF ECONOMIC DEVELOPMENT

The implication of our accounting exercises is that for equilibrium growth it is the share of trade rather than its rate of growth which is important, since in the majority of countries actual growth conforms most closely with the supply-constrained version of our model. Most studies of the effects of trade on growth have, however, focused on the relation between output growth and export growth. In this section we look first at the simplest version of this relationship and build up from it an aggregate model which can test the main generalisations that have emerged from these studies. Two related issues are then discussed: how the direction of causation in such models can be established and how economic historians have defined the conditions under which export-led growth can occur at a more disaggregated level.

Aggregate relationships

Emery attempted to summarise all export-led growth arguments into a single empirical generalisation of the form

$$g(y) = \alpha + \beta g(E) \qquad (7.15)$$

which is an exact analogue of our equation 7.2, in the sense that growth of income per head is again the dependent variable.[1] Because of the symmetry between export growth rates and export shares in the reduced forms of our model in equations 7.5–7.9 above, such a relation is possible, but theory suggests that β should vary systematically across countries – directly with the share of exports in total expenditure, inversely with the marginal propensities to save and to import and with the tax rate. However, the fixed relation is quite strong in practice, as shown by the first equation in table 7.4, and Emery concluded that a 1 per cent increase in GDP could usually be achieved by an expansion of 2.4 per cent in exports. A re-estimation of this equation with our data casts doubt on the stability of his result; in the last equation in table 7.4 the estimated coefficient on export growth (β) is only 0.13, so that the rate of expansion in exports necessary to support an increase of 1 per cent in GDP rises to $1/0.13 = 7.7$ per cent.

There are four possible reasons for this discrepancy. The first is Emery's method of estimation. Recognising that the growth of exports and total output are interdependent, he adopts a diagonal regression rather than the more normal procedure of minimising the sum of squared residuals on the dependent variable. He does, however, quote results for this normal case which are shown in footnote *a* to table 7.4; β falls from 0.41 to 0.33 but is still significantly higher than our estimate.

---

[1] R. F. Emery, 'The relation of exports and economic growth', *Kyklos*, vol. 20, no. 2, 1967.

Table 7.4. *Regressions of growth in output on growth in exports: a comparison of published studies*

Author(s)	Type	Sample		Coefficients		$\bar{R}^2$
		Size	Period	α	β	
Emery[a]	General	50	1953–63	0.20	0.41	n.a.
Syron,	Developing	..	1953–63	0.81 (2.61)	0.33 (7.33)	0.62
Walsh	Advanced	..	1953–63	−0.16 (0.43)	0.37 (8.22)	0.86
Maizels	Mainly developing	16	1953–62	..	0.55 (3.67)	0.47
Batchelor, Major, Morgan[b]	General	86	1960–70	1.92 (9.03)	0.13 (10.72)	0.57

[a] From a diagonal regression; normal error assumptions produce the equation:
$$g(y) = 0.66 + 0.33g(E), \bar{R}^2 = 0.57 \text{ (t-statistics in brackets).}$$
$$(0.57)\ (9.94)$$
[b] Equation 7.15 is estimated on a sample of 116 countries.

SOURCES: Emery, 'The relation of exports and economic growth'; Syron and Walsh, 'The relation of exports and economic growth: a note'; Maizels, *Exports and Economic Growth of Developing Countries*; NIESR calculations.

A second possible explanation lies in Emery's construction of the export volume series, which is defined for each country as its dollar exports deflated by the United States wholesale price index. Our series is taken directly from each country's own-currency values series deflated by its own official export price index. The two procedures are equivalent only if exchange rates move continuously to maintain internal purchasing power parity between the dollar and all other currencies and this situation was not approached in the 1950s and 1960s, when rates were fixed or changed discretely and were palpably affected by extraneous factors such as interest-rate differentials and trade balances.

The two other rationalisations of the different coefficients in Emery's equation and ours in table 7.4 are potentially more serious since they undermine the basis for any generalisation. They are that the observed relationships are unstable both across countries and through time.

Our data include more countries, with a wider coverage of less developed countries than Emery could collect. Syron and Walsh reworked equation 7.15 using Emery's data, but splitting the sample into high-income and low-income groups, with the results also shown in table 7.4.[1] These showed no significant difference in the growth coefficient β (0.33 for poorer countries, 0.37 for richer), but it appeared

[1] R. F. Syron and B. M. Walsh, 'The relation of exports and economic growth: a note', *Kyklos*, vol. 21, no. 3, 1968.

that for less developed countries the autonomous rate of growth – the constant term α – was greater. In the absence of any stimulus from exports, on their reckoning growth in poor countries would be around 1 per cent per annum faster than in rich countries. This picture is complicated, however, by Maizels' finding in a small sample, consisting mainly of less developed countries but also including Ireland and New Zealand, of a growth coefficient of 0.55 over virtually the same period.[1] Clearly these countries, all in the Sterling Area, exhibit quite different characteristics from those of most developing economies, which implies that factors other than the level of development modify the autonomous and induced components of the simple equation 7.15.

In our usual notation a more general formulation is

$$g(y) = \psi[g(E), \mathbf{U}, \mathbf{V}] \qquad (7.16)$$

where $\mathbf{U}$ is a set of variables additional to export growth which might explain variations in output growth – for example, investment in our open-economy model – and $\mathbf{V}$ is a set of variables determining β, the impact of export growth on income growth. So we can write

$$g(y) = \alpha(\mathbf{U}) + \beta(\mathbf{V})g(E) \qquad (7.17)$$

The functions $\alpha(\mathbf{U})$ and $\beta(\mathbf{V})$ may be discrete, in which case it is necessary to split the sample into groups of countries with shared $(\mathbf{U}, \mathbf{V})$ characteristics before stable relationships can be estimated, or they may be continuous, in which case the data can be pooled and the parameters of $\alpha(\mathbf{U})$ and $\beta(\mathbf{V})$ estimated if they are given a suitable functional form.

Syron and Walsh effectively followed the first procedure, when they split Emery's sample into low-income and high-income groups, and again when they split it into groups with high, moderate, or low shares of foodstuffs in exports. Their argument in the latter case was that linkages from exports to investment would be weakest among food exporters. This point is examined in more detail below, but their results bear out the expectation of a low correlation between output and export growth among the food exporters, where R^2 falls to zero and α is found to be negative. In contrast, R^2 rose to 0.72 and α to 0.41 for the countries where food accounted for under one third of total exports.

As another example of the sample-splitting procedure, we have set out in table 7.5 results of regressions using our data split into clusters, a partitioning which relies on a greater number of indices of structural similarity. The regressions show strong linkages between export growth and income growth in all clusters, with the highest growth coefficients

---

[1] Maizels, *Exports and Economic Growth*, pp. 44–5.

Table 7.5. *Regressions of growth in output on growth in exports by cluster (Emery's model)[a]*

	Constant (α)	Coefficient (β) on export growth	$\overline{R}^2$
Cluster I	0.55 (1.58)	0.27 (4.79)	0.37
Cluster II	2.73 (3.66)	0.16 (2.81)	0.46
Cluster IV	1.55 (5.58)	0.12 (14.94)	0.93
Cluster VI	−0.46 (0.70)	0.57 (7.61)	0.80

[a] Equation 7.15 estimated on subsamples from 116 countries; t-statistics given in brackets.

found in the most advanced countries (Cluster VI). Autonomous sources of growth are most evident in countries at intermediate levels of development, particularly in the large semi-industrial countries of Cluster II, and the non-significant constant for Cluster VI confirms Syron and Walsh's picture of high-income countries. Overall, this simple linear relationship explains 80 per cent of observed differences among the growth rates of the most industrialised countries, and over 90 per cent of such differences among small semi-industrial countries – a remarkable result.

Three examples are extant of an alternative method of seeking stable relationships between income and export growth by substituting continuous expressions for $\alpha(\mathbf{U})$ and $\beta(\mathbf{V})$. One is due to Massell, Pearson and Fitch, who add variables for capital flows to the right-hand side of a linear regression between income growth and export growth; another is due to Lubitz, who adds the investment ratio.[1] Only Severn modified β, pointing out that this growth coefficient should depend on the share of exports in total income.[2] His rationale is not, however, a model of income determination such as we have developed; he merely substitutes for Emery's equation 7.15 the alternative form

$$D(y) = \alpha + \beta D(e) \qquad (7.18)$$

where $D(y)$ and $D(e)$ are changes rather than rates of growth – an equation with no more *a priori* validity than its predecessor.

All of these hypotheses, along with Syron and Walsh's contention that

[1] B. F. Massell, S. R. Pearson and J. B. Fitch, 'Foreign exchange and economic development: an empirical study of selected Latin American countries', *Review of Economics and Statistics*, vol. 54, May 1972; R. Lubitz, 'Export-led growth in industrial economies', *Kyklos*, vol. 26, no. 2, 1973.
[2] A. K. Severn, 'Exports and economic growth: comment', *Kyklos*, vol. 21, no. 3, 1968.

non-agricultural exports show stronger linkages to growth than exports of foodstuffs, can be tested in the following framework:

$$g(y) = \alpha(f, i) + \beta(e, e_m)g(E)$$

where
$$\alpha = \alpha_0 + \alpha_1 f + \alpha_2 i$$

$$\beta = \beta_0 + [\beta_1 + \beta_2(e_m/e)]e \qquad (7.19)$$

and where $f = m - e$ is the capital inflow as a proportion of GDP and e_m the share of manufactured exports in total expenditure. Suppressing the coefficients α_1, α_2, β_1 and β_2 gives Emery's equation, suppressing α_1, α_2, β_0 and β_2 Severn's version, suppressing α_2, β_1 and β_2 the equation including net capital inflows used by Massell *et al.* and suppressing α_1 and β_1 an approximation to the equation investigated by Lubitz, though he looked explicitly at the rate of growth of manufactured exports and not at the way the share of manufactures affects the growth coefficient. All of these options have been estimated and the results are shown in table 7.6.

The full model explains about two thirds of the observed variations in growth rates across countries in the 1960s and very little autonomous growth – as measured by α_0 – is left over from that attributed to capital inflows, investment and export structure. A 10 per cent difference in the share of investment in GDP was generally associated with a 1 per cent per annum difference in the rate of growth of income per head; capital inflows, so far as they can be measured by the trade deficit, appear to reduce the growth rate, a difference of 10 per cent in the share of any

Table 7.6. *Regressions of growth in output on growth in exports (alternative models)[a]*

| Eqn. no. | Independent factors | | | Linkage modifiers | | | $\overline{R}^2$ |
	α_0	α_1	α_2	β_0	β_1	β_2	
(1)	0.10	−0.05	0.10	0.23	−0.23[b]	0.20[b]	0.64
	(0.21)	(2.48)	(3.55)	(4.96)	(2.48)	(0.59)	
(2)	2.08			0.13			0.54
	(10.07)			(10.18)			
(3)	2.53				0.23[b]		0.44
	(11.89)				(8.37)		
(4)	2.10	−0.01		0.13			0.53
	(9.83)	(0.44)		(10.13)			
(5)	0.88		0.06	0.12		0.68[b]	0.61
	(2.05)		(2.27)	(10.11)		(2.22)	

[a] Equation 7.9 estimated on the sample of 116 countries, both with the full model (equation (1)) and with alternative zero constraints on certain coefficients; t-statistics given in brackets.
[b] Actual coefficients multiplied by 10^2.

trade deficit in GDP being associated with a $\frac{1}{2}$ per cent per annum reduction; the modifiers to the export growth rate – the export share in GDP and the manufactured export share in GDP – both perform poorly, the former having a small coefficient (β_1) of the wrong sign (negative) and the latter an insignificantly small positive coefficient (β_2). The net effect of export growth is therefore shown by the constant β_0; a 1 per cent per annum increase in GDP per head requires on average a growth of $1/\beta_0 = 4.3$ per cent in exports, a lower figure than that obtained from an equation which omitted capital flows and investment, but still higher than that found by Emery.

The other equations in table 7.6 show there is considerable collinearity between the variables for capital inflows and export shares. When the variables for the trade balance and manufactured export shares are dropped to produce Severn's equation (3), the modifier to the total export share (β_1) proves very significant; on the other hand, when the trade share modifiers are dropped to obtain equation (4) used by Massell *et al.*, the apparent effect of capital inflows (α_1) becomes insignificant. Perhaps the most stable alternative to the full model is Lubitz's type of equation (5), from which variables for both capital flows and total export shares are omitted; although all coefficients are definitely non-zero and of the correct sign, and although the overall level of explanation is almost as high as that of the full model, the unexplained constant α_0 increases significantly.

Reworking the full model on each cluster separately produces a richer and more stable set of results. Capital inflows, for example appear from the values of α_1 in table 7.7 to be definitely beneficial to growth in the least developed countries and the most advanced countries; differences in the investment ratio among members of these homogeneous groups (shown by α_2) do not provide a particularly strong explanation of differences in growth performance, and openness significantly modifies the impact of export growth on output growth in less developed countries but not in advanced economies. Attempts to rid these equations of collinearity, which is especially severe with such small samples, yielded the set of equations of Lubitz's type in table 7.7. In some respects the patterns become clearer. For the least developed countries investment and export growth are equally significant, though development of *industrial* exports is not obviously correlated with income growth. For developing countries, growth in domestic investment is the mainspring of output growth in large countries, whereas exports – particularly manufactured exports – take on this role in the smaller countries. For advanced countries both sources of growth are again equally significant, with the effects of exports more or less independent of their share in GDP.

Table 7.7. *Regressions of growth in output on growth in exports 1960–70, by cluster*[a]

	Independent factors			Linkage modifiers			$\overline{R}^2$
	α_0	α_1	α_2	β_0	β_1	β_2	
Cluster I	0.40	0.06	0.16	−0.23	0.62[b]	−0.21[b]	0.94
	(0.21)	(2.31)	(1.43)	(1.43)	(2.93)	(0.19)	
	−0.50		0.16	0.10		−0.37[b]	0.90
	(0.21)		(1.15)	(6.54)		(0.27)	
Cluster II	−0.94	−0.06	0.27	0.12	−1.01[b]	1.86[b]	0.31
	(0.37)	(0.24)	(1.44)	(0.98)	(0.29)	(0.38)	
	−0.56		0.22	0.11		0.51[b]	0.53
	(0.29)		(2.01)	(1.35)		(0.38)	
Cluster IV	0.65	−0.10	0.03	0.10	0.53[b]	2.76[b]	0.48
	(0.67)	(2.22)	(0.42)	(0.84)	(0.96)	(0.63)	
	−0.08		0.07	0.15		8.20[b]	0.34
	(0.08)		(0.88)	(1.91)		(1.80)	
Cluster VI	−0.66	0.14	0.11	0.40	−0.63[b]	0.02[b]	0.65
	(0.44)	(2.04)	(1.62)	(4.10)	(1.22)	(0.04)	
	−1.32		0.17	0.31		−0.63[b]	0.48
	(0.74)		(2.22)	(2.86)		(1.23)	

[a] Equation 7.19 estimated on subsamples from 116 countries, both with the full model and with α_1 and β_1 constrained to zero; t-statistics given in brackets.
[b] Actual coefficients multiplied by 10^2.

Statistical significance tells us nothing about the relative feasibility of increasing growth rates by higher investment and higher exports. A better measure of this can be gained from the figures in table 7.8, which show the changes in investment and exports that we estimate necessary to induce increases of 1 per cent per annum in the growth of GDP. For Clusters I, II and VI the required increases in exports would take total

Table 7.8. *Estimated increases in investment and exports needed for GDP to grow 1 per cent per annum faster*

	Actual values[a]			Change needed[b]	
	GDP growth	Investment ratio	Export growth	Investment ratio	Export growth
	(% p.a.)	(%)	(% p.a.)	(%)	(% p.a.)
Cluster I	1.8	12	4.6	+6.3	+10.4
Cluster II	3.8	17	6.7	+4.6	+7.1
Cluster IV	2.3	19	6.3	+14.3	+2.2
Cluster VI	3.9	25	7.7	+5.9	+4.8

[a] Averages for the 1960s in each cluster.
[b] Calculated from table 7.7.

export growth to unreasonable levels; on the other hand, the required changes in investment are quite feasible – an average increase of 50 per cent over existing low levels in the least developed countries and an increase of about 25 per cent in large semi-industrial countries and advanced countries. In the case of the smaller semi-industrial countries of Cluster IV the opposite conclusions can be drawn; while growth through investment is extremely hard-won – doubling it produces an increase of just over 1 per cent per annum in GDP growth – exports need only increase by just over 2 per cent per annum to achieve the desired result.

The conditions for export-led growth

The statistical significance of our estimated relationships between output growth and export growth also tells us little about whether the assumed direction of causation, from the latter to the former, is correct. If we believe in the co-existence of a 'patterns' equation with a feedback (equations 7.1 and 7.2), the relationship is in general a reciprocal one and the question of causation turns on whether in practice cycles of income growth and changes in the level and structure of trade are more often initiated by external than by internal forces. Two types of test have been applied to answering this question.

One method is to look at the relative *sizes* of external and internal shocks. Nurkse, for example, believed that the growth of import demand in European economies in the nineteenth century was the largest source of change in the economies of their less developed settlements in the Americas and Australasia, but that in the twentieth century the 'engine of growth' was seriously threatened by reductions in the European countries' income elasticities of demand for imports because of their development of synthetics and high-productivity agriculture.[1] Lewis also believed that exports were in practice a major growth area for peripheral countries, not because of any accident of income growth abroad but because exporters faced a more price-elastic demand than home producers, so that small productivity improvements brought large increases in activity in export industries.[2] For the centre as well as the periphery exports turned out to be a very significant performance indicator; Meyer, for example, has shown that the deceleration of United Kingdom exports in the late nineteenth century – a result of the industrialisation of Germany and the United States and of the encroachment of Asian producers on textile markets – was sufficient to explain the whole deceleration in United Kingdom income growth from 4.1 per cent per annum in 1854–72 to 1.75 per cent per annum in

[1] R. Nurkse, *Patterns of Trade and Development*, New York, Oxford University Press, 1961.
[2] W. A. Lewis, *The Theory of Economic Growth*, London, Allen & Unwin, 1955.

1873–1907.[1] The contrary view to all this has been summarised by Kravis, who maintains that participation in trade is not a good indicator of the success or failure of peripheral countries to industrialise in the nineteenth century. The United States, for example, received little impetus from its small foreign sector and even in Australia internal sources of growth may have been as important as external sources; meanwhile many countries such as Egypt, India and the East Indies, which all participated heavily in trade with Western Europe, failed completely to absorb the factory system into their way of life and remained materially poor.[2]

The second method of fixing internal or external disturbances as prime causes of self-sustained growth is to look at the *timing* of such shocks. Again, the early interpretation of the historical experience of developing countries in terms of export-led growth has been questioned by, for example, Kindleberger, whose researches into British and French development turned up certain periods when exports happened to lead and others when they clearly lagged.[3] Moreover, it was clear that superficial uniformities in the development of both countries, such as the continuous increase in the trade ratio, stemmed from quite different internal developments – technical innovation in the British steel industry, social reorganisation and urbanisation in France. A series of case studies of peripheral economies has also found little consistency in the timing of export growth and domestic growth.[4]

The constructive outcome of this debate has been the recognition that growth of external trade can be sometimes the cause and sometimes the consequence of internal growth, and attention has moved to the problem of defining carefully the circumstances under which each relationship would hold. In particular, economic historians have been drawn to the detailed study of two quite different instances of export-led growth – when the leading sector is a primary producer, or when it is a high-productivity capital-intensive producer of manufactures. The first instance can be illustrated by the development of Australia and North America in the nineteenth century, the second by the development of Japan and some Western European countries, especially Italy, in the

[1] J. R. Meyer, 'An input–output approach to evaluating the influence of exports on British industrial production in the late 19th century', *Explorations in Entrepreneurial History*, no. 8, October 1955.

[2] I. B. Kravis, 'Trade as a handmaiden of growth: similarities between the nineteenth and twentieth centuries', *Economic Journal*, vol. 80, December 1970.

[3] See, for example, C. P. Kindleberger, 'Foreign trade and economic growth: lessons from Britain and France 1850 to 1913', *Economic History Review*, vol. 14 (second series), December 1961.

[4] J. V. Levin, *The Export Economies: their pattern of development in historical perspective*, Cambridge (Mass.), Harvard University Press, 1960; C. Issawi, 'Egypt since 1800: a study in lop-sided development', *Journal of Economic History*, vol. 21, March 1961; M. Mamalakis and C. W. Reynolds (eds.), *Essays on the Chilean Economy*, Irwin, Homewood (Ill.), 1965.

twentieth century. In both cases there is some suggestion that aggregate estimates of growth linkages such as we have tried in tables 7.5–7.7 are misleading, since the linkages are not universal and depend not simply on the overall structure of the economy but rather on the characteristics of the precise exporting industry in each country. To estimate the impact of exports on growth it is not sufficient to know the proportions of primary products and manufactures in total trade and production; we also need to know the physical attributes of the dominant export and the market structure and technology within which it is produced.

The first theory of export-led growth, the 'staple theory', is concerned with the value to less developed countries of an expansion of resource-based industries which can produce a surplus well above local requirements. The contribution to industrialisation of such a leading sector can be measured by the increase in the quantity and quality of productive factors which it generates and by the encouragement it gives through external effects to the parallel development of more capital-intensive industries.

Generally, the intrinsic nature of the staple good and the competitiveness of its market are less important than its production function in determining the size of its contribution to long-term growth. Bulky commodities did, however, have a reputation for attracting cheap capital imports because of the spare capacity they left on shipping backhauls – a reputation less justified today when transport costs are lower and bulk carriers highly specialised; likewise, perishable commodities had a reputation for encouraging local processing and packaging which may have lost its validity when fast, refrigerated transport became available. As to the impact of competitive conditions on factor efficiency, it is interesting to contrast the success in promoting domestic growth of Australian wool and North American wheat, which both had to displace indigenous production in Western Europe, with the failure of tea and coffee exports from the equally open economies of India and South America, which both enjoyed natural monopolies. More recently, the adverse effects of monopoly, albeit contrived by multinational companies rather than the accident of resource-endowments, can be seen in the failure of Jamaican bauxite exports to provide any secondary benefits by way of local processing.

Production conditions in the staple industry can increase supplies of labour and capital if they require skills not locally available or if the revenues are so distributed as to yield a high rate of saving. Baldwin has offered in explanation of the greater success in Africa of mineral exporting rather than plantation economies the suggestions that the former attracts skilled immigrant labour while the latter can be worked by indigenous labour, and that the more advanced capital-based technology of the mines offers more scope for general productivity advances than does the simpler organisational routine of the plantation.[1] The effects on capital formation of Canadian wheat exports have been studied by Chambers and Gordon,[2] and later by Caves,[3] on the argument that the wheat boom of 1900–11 involved a significant redirection of income towards a rentier class with a high savings propensity.

Labour and capital growth and improvement can indeed go hand in hand in some circumstances; if the immigrant labour is attracted by high wages and its expenditure pattern takes some time to adapt, a large reservoir of savings can be formed and investment per worker raised accordingly. In other circumstances, however, staple production sets up irreconcilable tensions between labour and capital, between classes of labour, or between the entire primary and secondary sectors. The interaction of capital with labour skills is generally built up through the introduction of local workers to successively more complex tasks – from initial repair and maintenance work on mining equipment to the engineering of spare parts and then whole machines. If the technology is too far beyond local experience such a transition is impossible and this undoubtedly explains why the most advanced mining operations – extraction and refining of petroleum – have not benefited the local economy as much as might be expected.

The existence of an immigrant class, if skilled, need not lead to the dissemination of skills throughout the local workforce if the necessary background educational facilities are not available or if the immigrants adopt restrictive practices, as in Baldwin's study of the behaviour of white engineers in Rhodesia.[4] If they are unskilled the immigrants may fail to adapt as the staple product is overtaken by industrial development. The existence of a rentier class need not lead to higher savings, as Brazilian experience shows,[5] and the problems of channelling savings into investment can be very acute in large-scale projects in less developed countries when the rentier class is foreign and profits accrue abroad.

Finally, the secondary effects of the expansion of the staple sector need not be beneficial to the industrial sector. As with labour skills,

[1] R. E. Baldwin, 'Export technology and development from a subsistence level', *Economic Journal*, vol. 73, March 1963.
[2] E. J. Chambers and D. F. Gordon, 'Primary products and economic growth: an empirical measurement', *Journal of Political Economy*, vol. 74, August 1966.
[3] R. E. Caves, 'Export-led growth and the new economic history' in J. Bhagwati, R. W. Jones, R. A. Mundell and J. Vanek (eds.), *Trade, Balance of Payments and Growth*, Amsterdam, North-Holland, 1971.
[4] R. E. Baldwin, *Economic Development and Export Growth: a study of Northern Rhodesia 1920–1960*, Berkeley, University of California Press, 1966.
[5] J. Bergsman, *Brazil: industrialization and trade policies*, London, Oxford University Press, 1970.

capital inputs to the staple sector may be too sophisticated; leading sectors making heavy demands on construction, for example, are more likely to generate local employment than sectors requiring complex machinery. Some staples, especially mineral extraction, mainly demand power and it is a matter of luck whether coal or oil can be obtained locally, or whether they must be imported and this particular linkage lost; also the need to construct transport facilities often diminishes the profitability of local processing, so that this discouragement to industrialisation has to be set against the opportunities which the transport facilities provide for other activities.

The second theory of export-led growth is, unlike the first, tailored to the description of interactions between exports and the natural growth rate of fully employed mature economies. There have been two formal expositions of this process, by Lamfalussy and by Beckerman;[1] in both there is a reciprocal relationship between the rate of growth of exports and the rate of growth of labour productivity which ensures that any exogenous disturbance in the foreign sector tends to be magnified by induced changes in labour efficiency and the resulting increase in export price competitiveness. There are differences of detail over the precise form of this export–productivity nexus, differences which derive in part from the different viewpoints of the two authors – one impressed by the success in the 1950s of the economies which formed the EEC at the end of the decade in overtaking product per head in the United Kingdom, the other by the frustrations encountered by the United Kingdom in trying to close this gap and the general hardening of divisions in the rest of Western Europe between fast-growing and slow-growing countries.

The alternative forms of export function are, in our notation,

Lamfalussy: $$f = \alpha[g(y) - g(P'/W)] \qquad (7.20)$$

Beckerman: $$g(E) = \alpha_0 + \alpha_1[g(y/y') - g(W/W')] \qquad (7.21)$$

where f is again the ratio of foreign capital inflow to GDP, P and W are prices and wages, and a prime indicates the 'rest of the world' value of the variable. Both equations have in effect the change in relative price competitiveness as their determining variable. Lamfalussy has as his determinant the balance of trade, Beckerman the growth of exports; Beckerman also has a constant term corresponding to what we have labelled 'market growth' effects in chapter 4.

---

[1] A. Lamfalussy, 'Contribution à un théorie de la croissance en économie ouverte', *Recherches Économiques de Louvain*, vol. 29, December 1963; W. Beckerman, 'Projecting Europe's growth', *Economic Journal*, vol. 72, December 1962.

The alternative forms of productivity function are:

Lamfalussy: $i = \beta_0 + \beta_1 g(Y)$

$$g(y) = \beta_2 + \beta_3 i \tag{7.22}$$

Beckerman: $g(y) = \beta_0 + \beta_1 g(E) \tag{7.23}$

The Lamfalussy argument in equation 7.22 is that a general accelerator relationship determines investment as a function of the growth of output, irrespective of its composition,[1] and that labour productivity is raised by the technology embodied in new machines. In contrast, Beckerman's equation 7.23 asserts that increases in export growth are the only endogenous sources of productivity growth. One argument used to support this hypothesis was that new investment bred productivity growth as in the Lamfalussy model, but that such investment depended on confidence about future output; in an economy where demand was managed ineptly by stop–go fiscal policies, entrepreneurs could not count on the stability of home sales and therefore invested only when export sales were healthy. An additional argument, echoed by Kaldor,[2] was that exports were concentrated on sectors with high productivity growth rates such as manufacturing, whereas domestic output contained less dynamic sectors such as services and public utilities. In Lamfalussy's framework, then, export growth is sufficient to induce a sustained growth of product per head, but it is not necessary – he simply believed that in practice the high price-sensitivity of foreign trade explained the extraordinary growth of the Six during the phase of trade liberalisation; in Beckerman's framework export growth is absolutely necessary – in practice United Kingdom domestic growth seemed too uncertain to initiate a 'virtuous circle' of improvements in productivity and competitiveness.

The influence of the historical context shows clearly also which parts of the background to these relationships Lamfalussy and Beckerman chose to sketch in detail and which were left impressionistic. Recalling that *ex post* the sum of exports and investment cannot exceed the sum of savings and imports, if an export-led boom is to succeed in raising investment without drawing in imports domestic savings must be increased. Lamfalussy took some trouble to show how balance of payments crises might be avoided, by linking savings as well as investment to the rate of growth of output. This unusual relationship was justified by a version of the permanent income hypothesis in which

---

[1] He asserted elsewhere that investment would be more stimulated by exports because for most European producers they were more profitable than home sales (A. Lamfalussy, *The United Kingdom and the Six: an essay on economic growth in Western Europe*, London, Macmillan, 1963).

[2] Kaldor, *Causes of the Slow Rate of Economic Growth of the United Kingdom*.

consumption depends on lagged income, so that the savings ratio is higher in a growing economy than in a stationary economy at the same income level. He also pointed out that a rising investment ratio would be accompanied by a rising share of profits and that the propensity to save out of profits was very high. Beckerman, on the other hand, was faced with the facts of high import propensities and recurrent foreign exchange crises in the United Kingdom; he therefore went to some trouble to emphasise that increases in export competitiveness would rapidly become self-sustaining as wage increases should not absorb all of the productivity increases from equation 7.23.

Both models were originally presented as thought-schemes rather than operational econometric models of postwar growth in Western Europe. Three attempts have, however, been made to establish their empirical validity.

First, Stern estimated the export and investment productivity sectors of the Lamfalussy and Beckerman models using aggregate time-series data for the Italian economy in the period 1951–63.[1] His results showed that, while the latter model performed reasonably well, the former was of little help in tracking Italian growth, the reaction of investment to income changes varying with the state of capital utilisation, productivity growth accelerating only if investment was concentrated on manufacturing, and the function 7.20 explaining only 14 per cent of observed variations in the balance of trade. In a more disaggregated setting, Stern found that accelerator relationships were strongest in industries which contributed most heavily to the expansion of exports; also that these same industries probably benefited from productivity-based price advantages, although the connection between investment and productivity growth could not be conclusively established.

The second study is that by Batchelor and Bowe on United Kingdom exports by industry in the 1960s.[2] Productivity is treated as dependent in the long run on technical advance, either embodied in new investment or occurring autonomously, and in the short run on the level of output via possible scale-economies. Investment is also described in terms of a combination of induced elements governed by a flexible accelerator process and residual time-related factors. In analysing output effects on both productivity and investment, exports and domestic sales are considered separately. The results agree well with Stern's findings, significant investment accelerators being observed only in manufacturing and productivity growth owing more to autonomous factors and the degree of capacity utilisation than to new investment.

[1] R. M. Stern, *Foreign Trade and Economic Growth in Italy*, New York, Praeger, 1967.
[2] R. A. Batchelor and C. Bowe, 'Forecasting UK international trade: a general equilibrium approach', *Applied Economics*, vol. 6, June 1974.

The net effect on export growth of these simultaneous changes in investment, productivity and prices is not explosive; overall an increase of 1 per cent in exports due to market growth will generate only a further 0.6 per cent growth before the stimulus peters out.[1]

The third test of export-led growth theories in advanced economies is that carried out by Lubitz, who regressed the average rate of growth of GDP in eleven developed countries in the period 1950–69 on export growth and the investment ratio, arguing that if the primary effect of exports is via induced investment its own coefficient ought to be insignificant.[2] His conclusion, like ours in table 7.7 above, is that exports exercise a significant independent effect; whether this refutes the export-led hypothesis seems doubtful, however, since exports are part of the GDP identity and this would tend to produce positive correlations even if no feedback relationship existed.

TRADE STRUCTURE AND THE RATE OF ECONOMIC
DEVELOPMENT

So far we have considered mainly the effects of trade growth on output growth and trade structure has been discussed only in so far as it modifies these effects. We turn now to the direct effects of trade structure on economic growth – the pure version of the feedback equation 7.2 with which the chapter began. The distinction between active and passive roles for trade structure developed in the introduction is retained in this section. Active structural effects can arise if they affect rates of investment or of productivity growth; passive effects arise if exports compete with scarce investment resources or augment the supply of scarce imported resources.

Active effects on investment and productivity

The active effects of trade structure can be broken into two distinct types which, though not unrelated, have formed separate branches of the literature on growth economics. The first can be explained within a simple open-economy model with only two goods, since it is the contrast between productivity growth in traded and non-traded goods which is critical in stimulating or retarding development. The second argument requires a multi-product framework, since it is the balance or concentration of exports which may affect output growth.

One illustration of the first type of argument was given in chapter 5, where valued added per head in the principal export sectors of less developed countries – food processing, light consumer goods – was

---

[1] Ibid, table 3.
[2] Lubitz, 'Export-led growth in industrial economies'.

found to be highest in economies with high trade ratios.[1] The rationale was that any production of traded goods, so long as it was not protected by tariff barriers, represented an efficient use of labour and scarce capital, since the industries were subject to the discipline of international competition. An illustration of the second argument lies in the plight of less developed countries exporting only one or two primary products, where small fluctuations in world demand and world prices can have devastating effects on trading profits. If risk as well as expected average returns enters into investors' calculations, the rate of capital formation – and hence the rate of output growth – will be lower than in similar economies with less potentially volatile export-mixes.

To test whether the first type of effect shows up in our cross-sectional data, a linear regression was conducted of growth in income per head over the period 1960–70 on the ratio of traded to non-traded goods (represented by the trade ratio $t = (X+M)/Y$), the share of manufactures in exports and the share of capital goods in imports. That is

$$g(y) = \gamma_0 - \gamma_1 t + \gamma_2(e_m/e) + \gamma_3(m_k/m) \tag{7.24}$$

Positive coefficients should be observed on all three explanatory variables, for reasons explained above in the cases of t and e_m/e, and because the more imports consist of factors of production rather than consumption goods the higher is labour productivity.

The results shown in table 7.9 do not give unqualified support to any of our hypotheses. The trade ratio, which at the industry level provided a good indicator of cross-country productivity differentials, has a generally perverse effect on aggregate productivity movements through time as shown by γ_1. While productivity growth in the sample as a whole is certainly higher in countries with high shares of manufactures in exports and high shares of investment goods in imports, within clusters of countries at equivalent stages of development no such certainty is possible. Exports of manufactures benefit only the large semi-industrial countries in Cluster II and appear to be associated with low growth rates in the smaller countries of Cluster IV. Imports of capital goods, on the other hand, do benefit these small semi-industrial countries rather more obviously than their larger counterparts; in advanced countries their effect is zero, possibly because the factor which advanced countries look for in imports is raw materials rather than capital equipment, the differences in quality and variety being smaller than in the semi-industrial countries.

Our test of the predictions of the second theory, postulating a connection between export concentration and economic growth, was conducted in two stages. First, we sought a correlation between the

[1] p. 43 above.

Table 7.9. *The impact of trade structure on growth in income per head, 1960–70[a]*

	Coefficient				$\bar{R}^2$
	γ_0	γ_1	γ_2	γ_3	
Cluster I	0.70	0.02	0.08	−0.04	0.07
	(0.80)	(0.75)	(1.26)	(0.19)	
Cluster II	2.26	−0.11	0.04	0.73	0.54
	(1.30)	(1.53)	(1.91)	(1.32)	
Cluster IV	−1.01	−0.03	−0.10	0.93	0.75
	(0.59)	(0.88)	(2.39)	(4.60)	
Cluster VI	3.27	−0.02	0.02	0.03	0.19
	(1.55)	(0.62)	(1.28)	(0.16)	
Whole sample	1.61	−0.01	0.03	0.16	0.18
	(2.64)	(0.55)	(3.20)	(2.00)	

[a] Equation 7.24 estimated on the sample of 116 countries and subsamples from it; t-statistics given in brackets.

instability of export receipts and an index of product concentration; second, we sought correlations between the instability index and growth factors such as the level of investment in domestic and imported capital and the rates of growth of exports and labour productivity. In this second set of equations the effect of export instability was allowed to vary positively with the share of exports in G D P. The two stages involved the following regressions:

$$V(E) = \delta_0 + \delta_1 H(E) \qquad (7.25)$$

and

$$i, m_k, g(E), g(y) = \epsilon_0 + (\epsilon_1 + \epsilon_2 e) V(E) \qquad (7.26)$$

where V is the instability index – the average percentage deviation of exports from trend – and H the Hirschman index of product concentration defined on page 184 above.[1]

Previous studies along these lines, generally using idiosyncratic instability measures, have failed to achieve unanimity on the strength of either of the two relationships. MacBean, for example, found no significant differences among instability indexes between less developed and advanced countries, and no evidence of any association with commodity concentration in either group; in a subsequent study of South East Asian countries, Naya also found that geographical concentration and concentration on primary production had generally

[1] These indices are taken from U N C T A D, *Handbook of International Trade and Development Statistics 1972*, tables 4.10 and 4.11.

Table 7.10. *Product concentration and stability of earnings on exports, 1960–70[a]*

	Mean $- \overline{V(E)} -$ of dependent variable	Coefficient		$\overline{R}^2$
		δ_0	δ_1	
Cluster I	7.05	3.02 (1.88)	7.86 (2.62)	0.07
Cluster II	4.12	1.65 (1.87)	8.04 (3.02)	0.31
Cluster IV	5.04	1.86 (1.56)	6.74 (2.89)	0.23
Cluster VI	3.29	1.83 (3.00)	6.71 (3.14)	0.21

[a] Equation 7.25 estimated on subsamples from 116 countries; t-statistics given in brackets.

insignificant effects on instability, although one type of geographical concentration – similar neighbouring economies taking a high proportion of total exports – did significantly increase export instability.[1] Following on from MacBean's work, Coppock confirmed that any linkage between export instability and income growth was hard to find; subsequently Kenen and Voivodas obtained equally poor results when they regressed output growth and investment growth on product concentration indexes, inflation rates and the trend of export growth in a sample of less developed countries in the 1950s and 1960s.[2] On the other hand, Glezakos has argued that with a proper choice of index and real income per head rather than nominal total income as the dependent variable, very significant effects can be found in such a sample; his estimate is that export instability explains about a quarter of the observed variations in less developed countries' growth rates in the 1950s and 1960s.[3]

Using our sample of 116 countries broken into clusters, the results shown in table 7.10 are obtained. The destabilising influence of concentration on export receipts (shown by δ_1) is unequivocally confirmed throughout the sample. This is in itself remarkable, since all the countries of Cluster VI – except, perhaps, Chile and Iceland – have developed far beyond the stage of dependence on primary products used

[1] A. MacBean, *Export Instability and Economic Development*, London, Allen & Unwin, 1966; S. Naya, 'Fluctuations in export earnings and economic patterns of Asian countries', *Economic Development and Cultural Change*, vol. 21, July 1973.
[2] J. D. Coppock, *International Economic Instability: the experience after World War II*, New York, McGraw-Hill, 1962; P. B. Kenen and C. S. Voivodas, 'Export instability and economic growth', *Kyklos*, vol. 25, no. 4, 1972.
[3] C. Glezakos, 'Export instability and economic growth: a statistical verification', *Economic Development and Cultural Change*, vol. 21, July 1973.

Table 7.11. *Effects of export instability on growth factors, 1960–70*[a]

		Cluster			
		I	II	IV	VI
Investment ratio	ϵ_1	−0.92	−1.10	−0.93	−0.59
		(2.55)	(0.80)	(1.75)	(0.47)
	ϵ_2	0.06	0.07	−0.09	0.02
		(4.00)	(1.21)	(0.23)	(0.86)
	$\bar{R}^2$	0.30	−0.03	0.30	−0.04
Imported capital ratio	ϵ_1	−0.58	−1.42	−1.05	−1.80
		(4.93)	(4.29)	(2.50)	(2.77)
	ϵ_2	0.04	0.06	0.01	0.05
		(7.69)	(3.92)	(1.71)	(3.98)
	$\bar{R}^2$	0.61	0.63	0.27	0.48
Export growth	ϵ_1	−0.31	−1.23	−0.45	0.53
		(16.77)	(1.71)	(1.28)	(1.10)
	ϵ_2	—	0.04	—	−0.01
		(1.11)	(1.21)	(0.47)	(1.26)
	$\bar{R}^2$	0.22	0.09	—	−0.02
Productivity growth	ϵ_1	−0.28	−1.23	−0.21	0.53
		(3.29)	(1.53)	(0.93)	(1.17)
	ϵ_2	0.01	0.03	—	−0.01
		(1.75)	(0.88)	(0.20)	(1.10)
	$\bar{R}^2$	0.20	0.06	0.01	—

[a] Equation 7.26 estimated on subsamples from 116 countries with constant terms (ϵ_0) not shown; t-statistics given in brackets.

in rationalising the relationship; the mean Hirschman index of product concentration is only 0.22 in Cluster VI as against 0.51 in Cluster I. Moreover, while product concentration is hardly a complete explanation of export instability – witness the low $\bar{R}^2$ – it is a more complete explanation in semi-industrial and industrial countries than in the underdeveloped countries, where over 90 per cent of inter-country variations in instability remain unaccounted for.

None of the paradoxes unearthed by MacBean and Coppock appears in our second stage regressions either, as the results in table 7.11 show. The most striking results are the significantly depressing effects of export instability on all sources of growth in the least developed countries, and the large contribution which instability makes to the explanation of differences in investment ratios, productivity growth and export growth among members of the cluster. In more developed countries export instability has a less pervasive influence, although it invariably reduces the rate of investment of foreign capital and also has a statistically significant negative influence on the overall rate of investment in small developing countries. The existence of a large export base generally softens the impact of a given degree of instability, positive coefficients ϵ_2

Table 7.12. *Effects[a] on economic growth of a reduction of 0.25 in the export concentration index*

	Cluster			
	I	II	IV	VI
Mean values of:				
Concentration index	0.5	0.3	0.5	0.2
Instability index	7.1	4.1	5.0	3.3
Investment ratio (%)	14.2	16.9	17.6	24.1
Imported capital ratio (%)	6.3	4.4	4.9	7.2
Export growth rate (% p.a.)	4.5	5.9	5.1	5.3
Productivity growth rate (% p.a.)	1.8	3.9	3.0	4.1
Change in:				
Instability index	−1.96	−2.00	−1.64	−1.68
Investment ratio (%)	−0.79	+0.63	+1.63	+0.14
Imported capital ratio (%)	−0.39	+1.66	+1.14	+1.03
Export growth rate (% p.a.)	+0.44	+1.67	+0.61	−0.40
Productivity growth rate (% p.a.)	+0.30	+1.79	+0.38	−0.39

[a] Derived from the estimated coefficients in tables 7.10 and 7.11.

being found in all the Cluster I regressions.

The practical significance of all these statistically significant export concentration and instability effects can be assessed only if we put some value on the maximum feasible changes in the concentration index and translate this into changes in growth factors by multiplying by the expressions $\delta_1(\epsilon_1 + \epsilon_2 e)$ appropriate to each. Apart from the petroleum exporting economies and other monocultural territories such as Mauritius (sugar), the potential for reducing H is not great; table 7.12 shows the mean difference between the least developed and most developed clusters to be around 0.3.

Our working in the lower part of table 7.12 is based on a reduction of 0.25 in the export concentration index, which decreases the export instability of Cluster I countries to around the same levels (± 5 per cent) as semi-industrial countries and reduces the instability of Cluster II and IV countries to something like the ± 3 per cent found in industrialised countries. These changes have negligible effects on investment ratios and leave other growth factors only marginally different in the least developed and the most developed clusters. For semi-industrial countries, however, reduced export instability increases the capacity to import capital goods by 25 per cent and in the larger economies adds almost one third to export growth (over $1\frac{1}{2}$ per cent per annum) and one half to productivity growth (nearly 2 per cent per annum). Our arithmetic implies that reduced product concentration is unlikely to make much impact on growth in less developed countries as a whole, but could well double the rate of growth of certain semi-industrial economies such as Brazil, Chile, Egypt and the West Indies, which either have the scale to compete internationally in a wider range of goods or have extremely biased exports at present.

Passive effects of exports on growth

The strategic importance of exports and other sources of foreign exchange in stimulating savings and import propensities was first formalised as Chenery and Strout's two-gap model of economic growth. Their model corresponds with our fixed-proportions model (equations 7.10–7.14). It has found frequent application in the assessment of the foreign exchange needs of developing countries with ambitious growth targets and in decisions on whether these needs are better served by trade expansion or by inflows of foreign aid.[1] Relatively few attempts have been made to discover whether the model fits historical experience, or which of the two 'gaps' has imposed the more severe constraint on growth. Maizels, for example, takes it for granted that the shortage of imported inputs always dominates the shortage of domestic investment, but we have shown above that the model is redundant in accounting for growth in some major world regions, notably Latin America, and where it is clearly applicable – Asia, for example – the dominant constraint probably varies from country to country.

Two crucial assumptions of the model are that imports constitute a distinct factor of production and that very little substitution is possible between imported inputs, home investment and labour. Diwan tried to test the former using Indian data by means of a logarithmic regression of output on capital stock and imports; imports proved statistically significant and contributed somewhat to the overall fit.[2] Michalopoulos, using Argentine data, tested the second assumption by computing the elasticity of substitution between imports and capital goods in a production function with a constant elasticity of substitution; this proved extremely high, about 2.3, and he concluded that the two-gap model was inappropriate.[3] Both tests are suspect, however. Diwan's logarithmic regression implicitly assumes an underlying Cobb–Douglas technology in which there is a unit elasticity of substitution; Michalopoulos's chosen country does not provide a firm basis for

---

[1] Notably in H. B. Chenery and M. Bruno, 'Development alternatives in an open economy: the case of Israel', *Economic Journal*, vol. 72, March 1962; I. Adelman and H. B. Chenery, 'Foreign aid and economic development: the case of Greece', *Review of Economics and Statistics*, vol. 48, February 1966.

[2] R. K. Diwan, 'A test of the two gap theory of economic development', *Journal of Development Studies*, vol. 4, July 1968.

[3] C. Michalopoulos, 'Production and substitution in two-gap models', *Journal of Development Studies*, vol. 11, July 1975.

rejecting the two-gap model in general – as indicated above, Latin American growth is atypical – and his results reflect only the consequences of determined import substitution policies carried out by Argentina, Brazil and other large Latin American countries.

Direct testing of the technological conditions under which exports could exert a passive influence on output growth has not, then, yielded any results capable of generalisation. More successful have been indirect tests of such influences. The most satisfactory is that of Weisskopf, who makes savings a function of exports and other foreign exchange inflows as well as income and considers the alternative investment functions which can then arise.[1] There are three of these, depending on whether growth is jointly constrained by both imports and investment, or whether it is constrained by one of these factors in conjunction with the growth of effective labour. After running regressions of these alternative investment functions on time-series data from each of 38 developing countries with deficits, Weisskopf scores each function on its overall fit and conformity with *a priori* expectations about the signs and sizes of its coefficients; he then deduces the dominant constraint on the basis of these scores. His main conclusion is that trade-constrained growth is far less prevalent than is commonly supposed, eight of his sample definitely falling into this category, as against 24 definitely constrained by domestic savings and six where both constraints may have been operative.

In contrast to this case-by-case approach, Voivodas sought to establish by means of regressions of output growth on export shares what constraint dominates for less developed countries as a whole;[2] his rationale is precisely that which produced our equations 7.11 and 7.14. There are two difficulties with this technique – first, our accounting exercises showed there were regional disparities in the applicability of the model; second, our theoretical analysis showed that the residual growth contribution α in the relationship between growth and exports was not constant, but depended rather on savings, investment and import propensities.

To the extent that production functions and factor availabilities are associated with the fundamental structural features used in chapter 5 to partition our data into clusters, the first objection to Voivodas's method can be evaded by conducting his tests on each cluster separately. As to the second problem, we have to ask how the assumption of a constant α is likely to bias the results of these tests. Supposing that, with Weisskopf,

[1] T. E. Weisskopf, 'An econometric test of alternative constraints on the growth of underdeveloped countries', *Review of Economics and Statistics*, vol. 54, February 1972.
[2] C. S. Voivodas, 'Exports, foreign capital inflow and economic growth', *Journal of International Economics*, vol. 3, November 1973.

Table 7.13. *The role of exports in growth with constrained factor supplies : critical regressions on export ratio*

	Cluster				Whole sample
	I	II	IV	VI	
Output growth[a]					
Constant	3.34	7.75	1.87	6.98	4.26
	(4.45)	(6.98)	(0.67)	(5.69)	(7.36)
Coefficient	0.06	−0.10	0.14	−0.07	0.04
	(1.71)	(1.36)	(1.73)	(1.45)	(1.98)
$\bar{R}^2$	0.05	0.09	0.12	0.07	0.03
Domestic investment ratio[b]					
Constant	9.63	15.16	13.45	20.64	12.04
	(8.71)	(4.84)	(6.77)	(7.12)	(8.62)
Coefficient	−0.13	−0.26	−0.12	−0.11	−0.04
	(2.48)	(1.24)	(1.98)	(0.92)	(0.77)
$\bar{R}^2$	0.12	0.06	0.16	−0.01	−0.01
Imported capital ratio[c]					
Constant	1.47	2.32	3.95	1.89	2.37
	(2.38)	(2.77)	(1.68)	(0.97)	(2.70)
Coefficient	0.20	0.19	0.15	0.19	0.20
	(6.82)	(3.43)	(2.16)	(2.48)	(5.88)
$\bar{R}^2$	0.54	0.55	0.20	0.24	0.27

[a] Equations 7.27 or 7.28 estimated on data from the sample of 116 countries for the period 1960–70.
[b] Equation 7.8 estimated on the same data, assuming that equation 7.7 holds.
[c] Equation 7.13 estimated on the same data, assuming that equation 7.12 holds.

we write savings as an increasing function of exports as well as other income,[1] then under the domestic capital constraint equation 7.3 would be subject to parameter values similar to those in equation 7.11, so that

$$g(Y) = (s_0 + m)k - [1 - (s_1 - s_0)]ke \qquad (7.27)$$

and under the import constraint equation 7.3 would be subject to parameter values similar to those in equation 7.14, so that

$$g(Y) = (i - s_0)l + [1 - (s_1 - s_0)]le \qquad (7.28)$$

where

$$C = (1 - s_0)(Y - E) + (1 - s_1)E \qquad (7.29)$$

The factor $(s_1 - s_0)$ represents the difference between average propensities to save out of income derived from non-exports and exports respectively and, since both propensities are positive and less than unity,

[1] We could also tie investment to exports and even relate imports to exports (on the argument that exports were import-intensive) without disturbing the results.

the difference must also be less than unity. Hence the signs of the coefficients on the export share under the two regimes always differ and the introduction of plausible systematic variation in the intercepts should not create identification problems.

The results of running this critical regression cluster by cluster are shown in table 7.13, along with confirmatory estimates of the side relations showing exports competing with investment but attracting capital imports. In the least developed group, and in the group of small developing countries, marginally significant positive correlations of growth with export shares are found; the assumption that this represents the general operation of foreign exchange constraints is supported by very strong correlations of capital imports with export receipts, though competitive inverse movements of investment and exports are also present in the data. In contrast, in the larger developing countries and in mature economies a weak negative correlation between growth and export share is found; this may not be particularly significant for the latter, as investment rates are hardly affected by export movements; in such advanced economies there is even evidence that exports stimulate investment more than do other forms of sales (see page 216 above).

8

PROSPECTS

by *R. L. Major*

INTRODUCTION

As we have shown in earlier chapters, for 25 years or so before the recession of 1974–5 world output of manufactures had been increasing at a pace (just over 6 per cent a year) which previously in this century had been attained only in the periods immediately preceding and following the great depression of 1929–31. The growth of world trade in manufactures over the same 25 years had been even more exceptional (at an annual rate of around 9 per cent in volume terms over the whole period and as much as 11 per cent after 1967).

The recession was confined to the market economies and the fall in world manufacturing output even in 1975 was only marginal, as production continued to rise rapidly in the centrally planned countries. However, a marked recovery in 1976, when growth of manufacturing output was in the region of 8 per cent, was followed by rises which appear to have fallen rather short of 6 per cent in both 1977 and 1978. Moreover, world trade in manufactures has fallen more markedly below its recent trend, with a fall of 5 per cent in volume in 1975 followed in 1976 by a return to no more than the pre-recession rate of increase of 11 per cent and in 1977 and 1978 by rises of only about 5 per cent. Our remaining task is to consider the factors which may determine whether the rapid growth of the 1950s and 1960s will be regained or whether the reversion to something nearer to historical growth rates and relationships for output and trade will prove to be lasting.

IMPLICATIONS OF HIGHER OIL PRICES

A complete return to historical patterns of trade in particular clearly cannot be envisaged after the huge rises in the price of petroleum in the latter part of 1973. The most spectacular effect of these and subsequent price increases in 1974 was a major transfer of purchasing power from oil consumers to oil producers, which was quickly reflected in trade flows and the international balance of payments. There was also a severe initial impact on domestic demand in oil-importing countries, which, though general, was naturally most serious for producers of tankers and motor vehicles. In the rather longer run, however, a more important factor may prove to be the stimulus given in these countries to the development of alternative sources of energy.

The specialist oil exporters' share of world imports of manufactures (including those of the centrally planned countries) increased from little more than 4 per cent in 1972 to nearly 10 per cent in 1977. Manufactured goods account for about four fifths of their total imports (compared with rather less than three fifths for the rest of the world) and between these two years the total volume of oil exporters' imports appears to have risen at an overall *annual* rate approaching 30 per cent, which is the amount by which world trade grew over the whole five-year period. The oil exporters' share of the market economies' reserve assets in gold, foreign exchange and Special Drawing Rights (SDRs) on the International Monetary Fund (IMF) nevertheless increased from 7 per cent at the end of 1972 to nearly 25 per cent five years later.

In 1978 the position altered abruptly, the oil exporters' aggregate balance on current transactions with the rest of the world worsening so sharply that the level of their foreign reserves was substantially reduced. A rapid increase in production of oil from the North Sea and Alaska, at a time when the overall expansion of the industrial countries' economies was relatively slow, resulted in a marked weakening in demand for OPEC oil, which, however, is unlikely to continue as North Sea and Alaskan production first levels out and then declines in the late 1980s. Programmes in importing countries for the development of new indigenous sources of energy (natural gas and nuclear power as well as oil) have received fresh impetus in 1979 as a result of the renewed shortage of oil and the second round of steep price rises which followed the Iranian revolution, but they had fallen behind schedule in the intervening period when the price of oil was declining in real terms.

Expectations about the oil-importing countries' future dependence on supplies from OPEC have varied widely. OECD forecasts published in 1974 put the requirement for OPEC oil by non-OPEC market economies, then running at about 30 million barrels per day but about 5 per cent lower by 1978, at only about 24 million barrels per day in 1985.[1] This was based on a rate of growth in member countries' GDP which now implies an annual average of 6 per cent from 1975 to 1985, and on the assumption (then thought pessimistic) of a price in 1985 equivalent to $9 per barrel in 1972 dollars (about $15 in 1979 dollars if adjusted by the deflator for GNP in the United States national accounts, or $20 if adjusted by world export prices for manufactures). By 1977 the postulated rate of growth in GDP for 1975–85 had been lowered to $4\frac{3}{4}$ per cent, but the forecast of the daily oil requirement in

[1] OECD, *Energy Prospects to 1985*, Paris, 1974.

1985 had gone up, on a similar price assumption, to nearly 35 million barrels, though it was suggested that something very close to the original figure was still attainable given appropriately resolute policies to reduce consumption.[1] A study in 1977 by a group of experts sponsored by the Massachusetts Institute of Technology gave consumption figures only slightly above the revised OECD forecast, as did one which Petroleum Economics Limited conducted in the same year for the United States Department of Energy.[2] On the other hand, a survey by the Central Intelligence Agency in the United States was much more pessimistic, putting the daily requirement of OPEC oil as high as $41\frac{1}{2}$–48 million barrels in 1985.[3] This may have been an overestimate, but the related suggestion that demand would by then substantially exceed productive capacity, so that prices would rise sharply to ration available supplies, has gained in plausibility from developments in 1979.

A United Nations study prepared by Leontief and others and published in 1977 showed the oil exporters' trade surplus, which averaged about $60 billion a year from 1975 to 1977, as recovering from $15 billion in 1980 to over $100 billion in 1990 and 2000.[4] This was on the basis of a calculation that prices of petroleum, which in 1975 were $4\frac{3}{4}$ times as high in relation to the general price level as they had been in 1970, would in the year 2000 be $3\frac{1}{4}$ times as high. The wide range of uncertainty over price relationships as well as over the level of demand for oil must make any such forecast highly speculative. It is, however, clear in any case that the oil-producing countries will not be able to sustain import increases of the magnitude of the mid-1970s. Indeed the annual rise in the total volume of their imports came down from perhaps 35–40 per cent in both 1974 and 1975 to about 25 per cent in 1976 and 1977 and only 5–10 per cent in 1978.

The slower growth of oil producers' imports has been partly the result of infrastructural problems, particularly inadequate port facilities, which in some cases at least have been or are being overcome. The absorptive capacity and the purchasing power of the individual countries are, however, becoming increasingly ill-matched. The OPEC countries' aggregate current surplus has become heavily concentrated in Saudi Arabia, Libya, the United Arab Emirates, Kuwait and Qatar, and some of the other countries have been borrowing on a substantial scale both from international organisations and on the international capital

---

[1] OECD, *World Energy Outlook*, Paris, 1977.

[2] Massachusetts Institute of Technology, *Energy: global prospects 1985–2000*, New York, McGraw-Hill, 1977; United States Department of Energy, *A Technical Analysis of the International Oil Market*, Washington (DC), US Government Printing Office, 1978.

[3] United States Central Intelligence Agency, *The International Energy Situation: outlook to 1985*, Washington (DC), US Government Printing Office, 1978.

[4] W. Leontief et al., *The Future of the World Economy*, New York, Oxford University Press, 1977, p. 9.

markets. Of the four with the largest populations among the oil exporters (accounting between them for over four fifths of the total), Indonesia, Nigeria and Algeria were already back in deficit on current account in 1976 and 1977, Algeria very heavily, and Iran's annual surplus had fallen to less than $5 billion from $12 billion in 1974.

Saudi Arabia has highly ambitious development plans. The current one, which involves expenditure of $142 billion over five years, is intended to raise the output of the non-oil sectors of the economy at an annual rate of over 13 per cent between 1975 and 1980 – a target which in the second year was far exceeded. But the absorptive capacity of a country with about ten million inhabitants must clearly be fairly limited, even though Saudi Arabia and Iran (population about 35 million) were expected before the change of regime in Iran to be employing well over a million foreign workers between them by the end of the present decade.

The oil exporters' holdings of gold and SDRs have remained comparatively small (only about $2 billion at the end of 1978). Virtually all their surpluses on current account have been invested in either short-term or long-term assets in the importing countries and the surpluses have thus had little impact on the aggregate reserve holdings of oil-importing countries. In other words the effect has been the creation of additional reserves held by the oil exporters rather than a transfer to them of reserves previously held by the importing countries.

The knowledge that collectively their higher net payments to the oil exporters are broadly matched by higher net capital inflows from the latter may bring little comfort to the oil importers individually. The inflows have been heavily concentrated on the United States and the United Kingdom, which according to the Bank of England received between them some $75 billion, almost half the oil exporters' total surplus, over the four years 1974–7. As $10 billion went to international organisations, this left less than half the total for all other countries (although they received the whole of the $12 billion surplus in 1978). Moreover, while the oil exporters' funds have so far proved on the whole less volatile than was feared at first, their unreliability as a source of finance was demonstrated by the United Kingdom's experience in the first half of 1978, when over £2 billion of these funds were withdrawn. The restraining influence of such considerations on domestic economic policies is reinforced by pressure for the elimination of deficits from the IMF and from countries such as Germany which are already in surplus. Moreover, the severe worsening in the industrial countries' terms of trade which has resulted from the rises in the price of oil implies, of course, that domestic purchasing power is lower than it would otherwise have been at any given level of output and balance of payments.

Though some of the oil producers' current surpluses may be used directly or indirectly to generate additional investment in the physical sense, their net effect must continue to be to increase the world's propensity to save.

In terms of growth rates the impact of sudden big price rises is likely to be predominantly once-for-all. Estimates by Fried and Schultze implied that in 1974 their effect was to hold OECD countries' output down to about $2\frac{3}{4}$ per cent below the level it would otherwise have reached (with a smaller reduction in the United States but a much bigger one in Japan).[1] But on the assumption, which has now proved wide of the mark, that the real price of oil would be the same as in 1974, they suggested that living standards in 1980 might be adversely affected to the extent of only about $1\frac{1}{4}$ per cent in the United States, $2\frac{1}{2}$ per cent in Western Europe and $4\frac{1}{2}$ per cent in Japan. The process of adjustment would cost about $\frac{1}{2}$ per cent of GNP in each case as a result of economies in fuel consumption and switches to domestic from previously cheaper foreign sources of supply, the remaining loss representing the transfer of resources to foreign producers.[2]

Although the longer-run effects in oil-importing countries will probably be quite small, living standards will, nevertheless, tend to be lower because each unit of energy consumed will use more resources than when oil was relatively cheap. Moreover the productivity of capital may be reduced relatively to that of labour, to the detriment of countries where the latter is comparatively scarce and costly.

THE GROWTH OF OUTPUT IN DEVELOPED COUNTRIES

While OECD countries' aggregate GDP was increasing at 5 per cent a year in the ten years before the recession, the annual rate of rise in their manufacturing production was about 6 per cent. There are, however, a number of grounds for thinking it unlikely that either total output or the share of manufacturing industry within the total will again increase so rapidly, except perhaps for relatively short periods, during the remainder of the present century.

Of the total increase of 60–65 per cent in GDP between 1963 and 1973, rather less than 40 per cent, representing an annual rate of rise of about $3\frac{1}{2}$ per cent, was attributable purely to rising output per man–year within the three broad sectors distinguished in table 8.1 (agriculture, manufacturing industry and the rest). There was a rise of

---

[1] E. R. Fried and C. L. Schultze (eds.), *Higher Oil Prices and the World Economy*, Washington (DC), Brookings Institution, 1975.
[2] There would also be a further transfer due to higher prices, estimated to be very small in Japan but worth about 2 per cent of GNP in North America and Western Europe, from consumers to domestic oil producers.

Table 8.1. *Contributions to the growth of output in OECD countries,[a] 1963–73*

	Annual rates of increase			Contributions to growth/ 1963 GDP or GNP		
	Employ- ment	Output per employee	Output	Employ- ment[b]	Output per employee[c]	Output
	(percentages p.a.)			(percentages)		
Agriculture	−4.1	6.6	2.2	−1.9	4.9	1.3
Manufacturing	1.6	4.4	6.1	5.0	16.1	23.8
Other	2.1	2.5	4.6	14.8	17.9	36.8
GDP or GNP	1.1	3.7	4.9	12.2	44.3	61.9

[a] Based on data for Belgium, Canada, France, Germany, Italy, Japan, New Zealand, Norway, Spain, United Kingdom and United States, which (at the 1970 prices and exchange rates used for calculating output) accounted for 91.5 per cent of total OECD GDP. This total increased by 63.6 per cent in 1963–73.
[b] Percentage increase in GDP or GNP 1963–73 that would have resulted from the actual change in employment if output per employee had remained constant.
[c] Percentage increase in GDP or GNP 1963–73 that would have resulted from the actual change in output per employee if employment had remained constant.
SOURCES: NIESR calculations based on OECD, *National Accounts of OECD Countries* (various issues) and *Labour Force Statistics 1962–1973*, Paris, 1975.

about 12 per cent in employment and, of the remaining 11 per cent or so, about half each came from the unallocated residual due to the interaction of higher employment with higher output per head and from the effects of a redistribution of labour between the three sectors – principally transfers from agriculture to the other two sectors, where productivity was much higher.

The labour force

The scope for increasing output by changes of occupation within the labour force is now greatly reduced. Inter-sectoral differences in productivity tend to diminish, as we have shown in chapter 5, as levels of efficiency in each sector improve, and employment in agriculture in OECD countries had already fallen by 40 per cent between 1960 and 1976, so that the pool of surplus labour there has been rapidly depleted. It is believed, moreover, that potential employees have become increasingly 'choosy', in particular that there is now greater resistance to mobility both between occupations and geographically. Concrete evidence to this effect is lacking, but OECD estimates suggest that unemployment was higher in the early 1970s than in the mid-1960s at similar pressures of demand.[1]

It is estimated that in the 1960s net immigration added at least $\frac{1}{2}$ per cent a year to the growth of the labour force in Australia, Canada,

[1] OECD, *Economic Outlook*, no. 19, July 1976, p. 147.

France, Germany, Sweden and Switzerland,[1] and the reflux of foreign labour during the recession could clearly be reversed again as demand for labour recovers. Nevertheless, the possibilities of labour migration from southern to central and northern Europe have been shown to be limited by the social strains which result in the host countries, so that it will probably make a considerably smaller contribution in future. There should be scope, however, for making greater indirect use of foreign labour by the transfer of at least part of the process of production to less advanced countries where labour may be more plentiful.

The large pool of unemployed (about $5\frac{1}{2}$ per cent of the labour force in OECD countries from 1975 to 1978 compared with an average of about 3 per cent from 1962 to 1973) provides another potential source of additional workers for the time being. The ILO expects the average annual rise in the total labour force in industrial countries to be maintained from 1975 to 1980 at 1.1 per cent as in 1960–75. But the increase is expected to slow down markedly over the following fifteen years and to average about one third less, that is approximately $\frac{3}{4}$ per cent per annum, for the last twenty years of the century.[2]

Probably the main potential source of error in projections of the labour force is the variation in rates of participation, especially among women. The ILO indicates that the proportion of women aged between 20 and 65 who were members of the labour force increased in the developed countries from 45.5 per cent in 1950 to 56.1 per cent in 1975, but will reach only 60.9 per cent in 2000. The effects of this slowing down are, however, more than balanced by an expected deceleration of the rate of fall in participation rates for teenagers, adult men, and women of 65 and over. For the whole population in or beyond their teens the rate is shown as rising slightly to 55.2 per cent at the end of the century, after falling between 1950 and 1975 from 58.7 to 54.9 per cent.

In general it appears that for the developed countries to achieve past rates of growth is likely, after a few more years, to require faster rates of increase in output per man–year in individual economic sectors. On the whole it seems improbable that such rates will be achieved, especially as recent, clearly marked trends would have to be reversed. (The annual growth of output per employee among OECD countries is estimated to have fallen from $3\frac{3}{4}$ per cent in the mid- to late 1960s to $2\frac{3}{4}$ per cent in the early 1970s and in the seven major countries there was an average decline (unweighted) of $2\frac{3}{4}$ per cent in annual productivity growth in 1973–7 as compared with 1963–73, with only $\frac{1}{4}$ per cent attributable to structural changes.[3])

[1] OECD, *Towards Full Employment and Price Stability* by P. McCracken *et al.*, Paris, 1977.
[2] ILO, *Labour Force Estimates and Projections, 1950–2000*, Geneva, 1977.
[3] OECD, *Economic Outlook*, no. 16, July 1976, p. 139.

Table 8.2. *Changes in the size and composition of the labour force in developed countries, 1960–2000*

Percentages p.a.

	Annual rates of increase		
	1960–75	1975–80[a]	1980–2000[a]
Men			
Aged under 20	0.6	−0.1	−0.5
Aged 20–54	1.2	1.4	0.9
Aged over 54	−0.2	0.7	1.0
Total	*0.9*	*1.1*	*0.7*
Women			
Aged under 20	1.0	0.4	−0.2
Aged 20–54	1.9	1.5	1.2
Aged over 54	0.1	1.4	1.3
Total	*1.4*	*1.2*	*0.9*
Whole labour force			
Aged under 20	0.8	0.2	−0.3
Aged 20–54	1.5	1.5	1.0
Aged over 54	−0.1	0.9	1.0
Total	*1.1*	*1.1*	*0.8*

[a] ILO forecasts.

SOURCE: ILO, *Labour Force Estimates and Projections, 1950–2000*.

If labour does become less plentiful after the effects of the recession have worn off, the rate of reduction in annual hours worked will probably slow down. On the other hand, the change in the composition of the labour force is likely to be less favourable to improvements in productivity in the last quarter of the century than it was between 1960 and 1975. As shown in table 8.2, the ILO expects workers approaching retiring age to constitute a rising proportion of the labour force after 1980. Thus the tendency for the number of workers aged between 20 and 54 to rise faster than the labour force as a whole is likely to become less marked for both men and women. Moreover the main occupational change will probably be a net movement out of manufacturing industry into services, where, at least by conventional methods of measurement, productivity improves much more slowly. Thus the crucial question may be how far any constraints which may operate on the labour side can be overcome by more rapid injection of capital.

Gross fixed investment

OECD calculations based on data available from a limited number of countries suggest that the output obtainable from a given capital stock did not change much on the whole between the early 1960s and the early 1970s. While there appears to have been an upward trend in capital–output ratios in Germany and the United Kingdom in particular, and to a lesser extent in Canada and France, the opposite was true of Italy especially, and also of Belgium and Norway, with little change in Sweden and the United States.[1] The fall in Italy was, however, attributable to the declining share of output devoted to housing, where the ratio is of course exceptionally high. This decline continued in the mid-1970s, but can hardly go on much longer at the same kind of pace. (The share of residential building in Italian GDP had fallen to 3.1 per cent in 1975 from 7.0 per cent in 1963.)

More generally, the factors limiting the growth of the manufacturing labour force (demographic trends, depleted agricultural population and declining mobility) are likely also to mean that construction investment, particularly residential building, will not grow very fast in coming years. On the other hand, if we are right in suggesting that services will continue to increase their share of output, while the rate of rise in the relative contribution of manufacturing industry will begin to fall, this will tend, other things being equal, to raise the rate of investment needed for a given growth in aggregate production (since services generally have a substantially higher capital–output ratio than manufacturing).

Additional investment will also be needed at least for a time for pollution control and the transfer of resources to the energy sector. Additional pollution control could represent about 1 per cent of GDP, and more for Japan (where anti-pollution investment had risen by 1974–5 to 2 per cent of GDP from much less than 1 per cent a few years earlier) and the United States (where about 5 per cent of business expenditure on new plant and equipment from 1973 to 1978 was devoted to pollution abatement and total anti-pollution expenditure rose from 1.6 per cent of GDP in 1972 to 2.0 per cent from 1975 to 1977). These OECD estimates seem reasonably consistent with calculations that to achieve and maintain 1970 United States standards for pollution would absorb 1.4–1.9 per cent of GDP in North America, Japan, Oceania and the higher-income countries of Western Europe.[2] More tentative suggestions were that the additional new investment in energy consequent upon the upsurge in oil prices of 1973–4 could by 1985 represent an additional $1\frac{1}{2}$ per cent of GDP.[3]

If labour is in fact less plentiful, this should lead to greater emphasis on productivity, and the combination of price controls in some countries with rapid inflation almost everywhere seems already to have encouraged labour-saving investment in industry. For example, surveys

[1] Ibid.
[2] Leontief *et al.*, *The Future of the World Economy*, pp. 6–7.
[3] OECD, *Economic Outlook*, no. 25, July 1979, p. 139.

conducted by the IFO-Institut für Wirtschaftsforschung suggest that in Germany the proportion of industrial investment intended for rationalisation and replacement as opposed to expansion of capacity increased between 1962 and 1976 from 55 to 77 per cent. A tendency in most major countries to devote a rising proportion of capital expenditure to machinery and equipment and a falling proportion to plant points in the same direction. On the other hand, this kind of allocation of available capital resources increases the likelihood of a shortage of capacity becoming an obstacle to rapid recovery in the aftermath of the recession. As the Commission of the European Communities puts it:

A certain amount of capacity has been permanently lost as a result of the closing down of establishments or because it has been idle too long, while other capacity has become out of date as a result of change in relative prices and the structure of demand. This is a continual process, but there is some evidence that it has accelerated in some countries due to the recession. This implies that the trend of potential growth has been weakened . . . In a number of countries . . . the weakness of investment had become apparent well before the crisis.[1]

An important long-term cause of this weakness is probably the declining share of profits, especially post-tax, in the national income in most of the major countries. The share of the national income accruing to labour rose sharply between 1960 and 1974 in all the major countries (though it has since fallen in most of them) and, at least in the three biggest in economic terms – the United States, Japan and Germany – movements in this share have a close inverse relationship with changes in the rate of growth of fixed investment. In some countries, moreover, the resultant squeeze on profits has been intensified during the period of rapid inflation by the revenue authorities' use of historical rather than replacement values to calculate depreciation of fixed assets and appreciation of stock. The continued high rates of inflation in most countries and rapid changes in the international value of individual currencies have also helped to generate a sense of insecurity, which has been accentuated by the recession and, to some extent perhaps, by the altered energy situation.

In 1976 OECD estimates for satisfactory rates of growth up to 1980 required an increase in the share of gross fixed investment in GDP equivalent for the major countries in aggregate to between $2\frac{1}{4}$ and $2\frac{1}{2}$ per cent. In fact, however, though fixed investment fell much more steeply in 1974–5 than in previous recessions, its recovery has been slower than before in nearly all OECD countries. In 1977 it was still 3 per cent

[1] Commission of the European Communities, *Official Journal of the European Communities, Information and Notices* (English edn), vol. 20, no. C12, Brussels, 1977, p. 12.

below the 1973 level for the O E C D as a whole and as a percentage of G D P it was a little lower than it had been in 1974–5.

Most of the depressing influences seem likely to operate for some while yet and, for manufacturing industry at least, it seems that increases in the rate of investment may well make a smaller contribution to the growth of output in coming years than was the case in the 1960s and early 1970s.

Some GDP forecasts

The energy constraint is likely to be particularly important in Japan, where the Japan Economic Research Center envisages an annual rate of growth of GNP of 5.8 per cent over the five years from April 1979 to March 1984, compared with over 10 per cent from 1963 to 1973;[1] the official figure is also just under 6 per cent for the seven years to 1985.

In the United States, where GNP increased at an annual rate of just over 4 per cent from 1960 to 1973, the 1979 budget assumed annual growth rates averaging $4\frac{3}{4}$ per cent up to the end of 1983. But, even if these probably rather optimistic assumptions are fulfilled, a considerable slowing down is implied thereafter if the Council of Economic Advisers is right in believing that the long-term potential growth rate of the United States is now only about 3 per cent a year.

Early in 1977 the European Communities adopted a medium-term target of $4\frac{1}{2}$–5 per cent for annual growth of GDP for the period 1976–80. This is in line with actual performance from 1963 to 1973, but it assumed actual growth in 1977 and 1978 substantially in excess of longer-term potential growth and therefore implied some subsequent slowing down. While it was said to represent a minimum objective, it appears nevertheless to have been regarded from the outset as optimistic. Its achievement was said, in the foreword to the programme, to depend on a number of conditions, including a better social consensus and the creation of a climate of confidence such as would lead over the next few years to a faster growth of productive investment than of GDP. In practice the growth rates achieved in the first two years averaged only about $2\frac{1}{2}$ per cent. They were probably bettered in 1979, but it is now clear that the target was wholly unrealistic.

The Leontief study, considering prospects for the world economy up to the year 2000, adopted average annual growth rates for gross product in the developed countries ranging from 3.6 to 4.0 per cent from 1970 onwards. This assumed that rates per head of population would decline as wealth increased, from 4 per cent with annual increases per head at 1970 prices of $3000–$4000 to 2.5 per cent with increases in the range

---

[1] Japan Economic Research Center, *Five-Year Forecast 1979–1983*, Tokyo, 1979.

$5000–$6000.[1] The range 3.6–4.0 per cent from 1970 onwards implies about $\frac{1}{4}$ per cent more than this from 1975. The IBRD has suggested that from 1975 to 1985 a rate of 4.2 per cent for the industrialised countries collectively would be reasonable (4.3 per cent for North America, 5.6 per cent for Japan and Oceania, and 3.5 per cent for Western and Northern Europe).

Manufacturing

So far as the manufacturing sector is concerned, the annual rate of increase in output per man–year in OECD countries between 1963 and 1973 was about $4\frac{1}{2}$ per cent. Had the manufacturing labour force been constant this would have been sufficient, on a purely arithmetical calculation, to yield a growth in production of 50–55 per cent, or two thirds of the total rise of nearly 80 per cent actually achieved in these countries' manufacturing output. Of the remainder, about two thirds was attributable arithmetically to the growth of the labour force, including recruitment from agriculture, and the rest to the unallocated residual representing the combined effects of higher employment and higher productivity.

Because of the transfers of labour that have already taken place and the depletion of the agricultural labour force that has resulted, a return to former rates of growth of employment seems even more improbable for manufacturing industry than for the OECD countries' economies as a whole. Thus, if slower growth of output is to be avoided, there is even greater need in the manufacturing sector for a faster improvement in productivity, which, for reasons already discussed, appears unlikely to be forthcoming.

There are other grounds too for believing that the share of manufacturing in national economies will not rise for very much longer in the developed countries even if it regains its pre-recession level (it was still well short of this in 1978 after falling sharply in the recession). We have suggested in chapter 5 that this share may be expected to reach its peak when GDP per head of population is around $3800 at 1963 prices. The United States, which accounts for over a third of total OECD output, had already reached about $4100 by 1975, with Canada and Sweden between $3000 and $3500, and France, Switzerland, Denmark and Germany close to $2500, which was about the average for the OECD as a whole. If we adopt the ILO's forecast that the population will be rising by between 0.8 and 0.9 per cent a year from 1975,[2] then maintenance of the $4–4\frac{1}{2}$ per cent annual rate of increase in OECD

---

[1] Leontief *et al.*, *The Future of the World Economy*, p. 3.

[2] ILO, *Labour Force Estimates and Projections, 1950–2000.*

countries' aggregate GDP between 1975 and 1978 can be calculated to raise GDP per head to $3800 at 1963 prices over the area as a whole by 1988. A difference of $\frac{1}{4}$ per cent in the annual rate of GDP growth would advance or retard the date by about one year only.

It would obviously not be sensible to attach great weight to specific dates or specific levels of income. However, there seem to be grounds for believing that any return to the very rapid rates of growth of manufacturing output which were seen in the developed countries in the 1960s and early 1970s is unlikely to last for more than a few years, and perhaps for doubting whether it will be achieved at all in Japan or Western Europe. In the last two decades of the century an annual rate closer to 4 than to 6 per cent may be in prospect for OECD countries collectively.

THE GROWTH OF OUTPUT IN DEVELOPING COUNTRIES

Gross domestic product

The annual rate of increase in real GDP in all developing countries went up from 4.7 per cent between 1950 and 1960 to 5.6 per cent in the next thirteen years, but then declined slightly to 5.4 per cent between 1973 and 1977.[1] Per head of population the rate changed from 2.4 per cent to 3.0 per cent and then to 2.8 per cent. These figures compare with targets of 6 per cent a year in total, or $3\frac{1}{2}$ per cent per head, which the International Development Strategy for the Second Development Decade set at its outset and which were reaffirmed by the General Assembly of the United Nations in September 1975.

In both the 1950s and the 1960s, although total real GDP had grown faster in the developing than in the developed countries the difference was insufficient to compensate for the much faster rise in population in the former group. From 1970 to 1976, however, because of the recession in the developed countries in 1974 and 1975, output has increased less there than in the developing countries, per head as well as in aggregate. Thus a start has been made towards narrowing the income gap between developed and developing countries as called for by the 'Declaration on the establishment of a new international economic order', which the General Assembly of the United Nations adopted in May 1974.

The Leontief study considers various possible scenarios for the developing countries in the remainder of the century: one in which their gross product continues to increase at the 6 per cent annual rate envisaged for the Second Development Decade and others in which the

---

[1] This is according to figures published by UNCTAD in *Handbook of International Trade and Development Statistics 1976, Supplement 1977* and *Trade and Development*, no. 1, Spring 1979. Other publications of international organisations give rather different figures.

gap in incomes per head between the developed and the developing countries is approximately halved by the end of the century. On the assumptions outlined above about rates of growth in the developed countries, the latter target implies a growth rate of about 7 per cent a year for the developing countries and means that the developing regions' share in world gross product would approximately double between 1970 and 2000 from 11 to 22 per cent. Even so, their income per head at the end of the period is calculated at only a seventh of that of the developed countries; in most developing regions it would be within a range of some $1000–$2000 per annum at 1970 prices (which is about the current level in Greece, Ireland and Spain), but in the non-oil producing countries of Africa and Asia it would be only about $400 a year.[1]

Manufacturing

At the level of income calculated above the share of manufacturing production in total output must, of course, be expected to go on rising (even though the long-term plans of some developing countries suggest that they may now consider ill advised their relative neglect of agriculture in the past in favour of rapid industrialisation). If we are right in believing that manufacturing will not constitute a rising proportion of the developed countries' output, then the assumption that the developing countries will be increasing their share of total world output implies that their share of world manufacturing production will be rising even faster. According to the Leontief survey it could approximately treble between 1970 and 2000, with the actual percentage rising by the latter year to $17\frac{1}{2}$ per cent. This is on the basis of annual rates of rise in manufacturing production of 14 per cent in the oil-producing countries of Asia and Africa, $7\frac{1}{2}$–8 per cent and 6–7 per cent in the other developing countries of Asia and Africa respectively, and $8\frac{1}{2}$–9 per cent in Latin America.

Other scenarios are even more optimistic. The second general conference of UNIDO held at Lima in 1975 declared that by 2000 the share of the developing countries in world industrial production should if possible be increased to at least 25 per cent (more than double the 1977 figure) although this would mean a rate of industrial growth 'considerably higher than the 8 per cent recommended in the International Development Strategy for the Second United Nations Development Decade' (and even further above the $7\frac{1}{2}$ per cent actually achieved between 1955 and 1973). UNCTAD has calculated that the required annual rate of increase in the developing countries' manufacturing production would in fact be some $9\frac{1}{2}$ per cent from 1972 to

[1] Leontief, *The Future of the World Economy*, p. 32.

2000 (compared with $6\frac{1}{2}$ per cent between 1960 and 1972) on the assumption that the annual rate of rise in the rest of the world slowed down from about $6\frac{1}{4}$ to 5 per cent.[1] From 1972 to 1978 the rate was only about 3 per cent for the developed countries but continued at $6\frac{1}{2}$ per cent for the developing.

As we saw in chapter 5, achievement by the developing countries of accelerated growth in manufacturing output would probably necessitate even faster rates of increase in investment and hence in the development of heavy industry. According to UNCTAD, the annual rate of growth for heavy industry would have to be about $10\frac{1}{2}$ per cent. This would mean that by 2000 heavy industry would provide almost as big a share of total manufacturing output in the developing countries as it did in 1972 in Eastern Europe and the developed market economies.[2] The UNCTAD estimates are based on the view that the $9\frac{1}{2}$ per cent annual increase in the developing countries' manufactured output would correspond with a growth rate of about $7\frac{1}{2}$ per cent for GDP and would require an increase of at least 40 per cent in the ratio of investment to GDP. This assessment is broadly supported by the Leontief study, which further suggests, as in effect does the IBRD, that present ratios would be sufficient for GDP growth of only 4–6 per cent. [3]

Our cluster analysis showed that the achievement of high investment ratios tended to be confined to countries well endowed with mineral resources (and correspondingly well placed to attract private capital from abroad). The IBRD has drawn attention to a number of obstacles to high rates of domestic saving, including reliance on commodity taxation rather than progressive income taxes and value-added tax, the assignment to public enterprises of social objectives such as employment creation and price stabilisation, and the difficulties of restraining government expenditure on consumption.[4] Though the developing countries have nevertheless achieved substantial increases in domestic savings (which, as a percentage of GDP, rose between 1960 and 1975

---

[1] UNCTAD, *Restructuring of World Industry*, New York, 1978, p. 30.
[2] Ibid, p. 6.
[3] This apparent unanimity about the requisite changes in the investment ratio in developing countries does not, unfortunately, apply to the level of the ratio. The Leontief study puts it at 20 per cent in 1970 and the IBRD at 25.5 per cent in 1975, but UNCTAD estimates it at only 15.5 per cent (on the grounds that this was the median in 1966 for 82 countries) for the period 1960–72 (see Leontief *et al.*, *The Future of the World Economy*, p. 7; IBRD, *World Development Report*, p. 27; UNCTAD, *Restructuring of World Industry*, p. 4). The disparities in the figures seem to be too big to be explained by differences in the periods to which they relate. They may, however, be partly attributable to differences in country coverage and in the aggregates to which the ratio applies – final internal use for Leontief *et al.*, but GDP for the IBRD and UNCTAD. (Since the developing countries normally import more goods and services than they export, the ratio tends to be rather lower to final internal use than to GDP.) Also the IBRD figures of investment include changes in stocks, whereas Leontief *et al.* and UNCTAD include only fixed capital formation.
[4] IBRD, *World Development Report*, pp. 6–7.

from $11\frac{1}{2}$ to $15\frac{1}{2}$ per cent in low-income countries and from 18 to 22 per cent in middle-income countries), to raise investment ratios to the extent now envisaged seems likely to require not merely a high degree of domestic discipline but also a far wider measure of co-operation from the developed countries than has been forthcoming hitherto.

Current trends are not particularly encouraging in this respect. Though the proportion of industrial countries' direct foreign investment now going to developing countries rather than other industrial countries is increasing, it still appears to be only about a quarter for all direct investment and as low as a fifth for investment in manufacturing (even if southern European countries are classed as developing).[1] Private investors in advanced countries, and the big mining corporations in particular, have become increasingly reluctant to increase their stakes in the developing countries on account of doubts stemming from threats of nationalisation, participation by local interests, unexpected changes in taxation, and so on. Though a diminishing rate of return on investment in the developed countries might in itself tend to encourage investors to look elsewhere, success in attracting foreign capital is liable to be the prerogative of a very few small countries like Hong Kong and Singapore unless international safeguards can be worked out and implemented. Such arrangements would be a major innovation, but the survey suggests that if the 'old' economic order persists the developing countries will only be able to afford a rate of growth in real GDP of less than $5\frac{1}{2}$ per cent.

THE GROWTH OF TRADE IN MANUFACTURES

In chapter 4 we concluded that the most important factor tending to raise the ratio of imports of manufactures to supplies in the industrial countries during the 1960s was the reduction of tariffs resulting from the formation of the EEC and EFTA, from the United States–Canadian Automotive Agreement and from the Kennedy Round. Associated with this was the development of intra-industry trade, which was further boosted by the activities of multinational enterprises. Two contributory factors were the development of new tradeable products commanding a mass market and the emergence of Japan as the world's third largest industrial exporter. There were also major changes in competitiveness, which affected the ratio of imports to supplies, particularly in the United States, the United Kingdom and Germany.

During the 1970s there have been further major tariff reductions following the completion of the Kennedy Round, the introduction of the

[1] GATT, *Adjustment, Trade and Growth in Developed and Developing Countries* by R. Blackhurst, N. Marian and J. Tumlir, Geneva, 1978, p. 38.

Generalised System of Preferences (GSP), the admission of the United Kingdom, Ireland and Denmark to the EEC and the negotiation of what is virtually a free trade area for manufactures between the remaining members of EFTA and the enlarged EEC. To some extent these latter changes merely involved a redirection of trade previously diverted by the creation of the original EEC and EFTA, but over and above this there was a reduction in the general tariff level, inducing trade creation which helped to promote further increases in the ratio of imports of manufactures to supplies despite the contractionary influence of the oil price rise and the recession of the mid-1970s. For the developed countries as a group, the ratio of the increase in the volume of imports to the growth of manufacturing output was still over 2:1 between 1972 and 1977, as imports fell less than output in 1974 and 1975 and rebounded more strongly over the next two years.[1]

It seems unlikely that there will be any tariff reductions of comparable importance to those of the 1960s and early 1970s during the next ten to fifteen years. Although the Tokyo Round negotiations were brought to a reasonably successful conclusion, the effects will be less dramatic than those of the Kennedy Round simply because countries have fewer tariffs to abolish. There can be few if any prohibitive tariffs left in Europe, even if there are still some in the United States and Japan. So far as intra-European trade is concerned, the only real possibility lies in the further enlargement of the EEC to include Spain, Portugal and Greece, a move which clearly would have less effect than the original establishment of the Common Market or its enlargement in the 1970s. There will probably be some boost to trade from further tariff reductions, but nothing spectacular.

At the same time, however, the longer-term effects of tariff reductions may continue to encourage the growth of trade at a rate relative to domestic output that is high by historical standards, if not by those of the 1960s and 1970s. This is particularly so in Europe, where trade interdependence is still far below the level recorded between the different states of the United States; there is scope here for considerable further development of intra-industry trade and multinational enterprises (and others) seem less likely to fall foul of national governments in promoting it than they are in other areas of the world.

There is a further possibility. In making his projections of trade from 1959 to 1970–5, Maizels allowed for a return of the import ratio in large industrial countries other than the United States to what he

---

[1] This estimate is based on United Nations figures for the developed countries' index of manufacturing, adjusted to exclude the food, drink and tobacco industries, and for exports of SITC 5–8 at constant 1970 prices to the developed countries by developed and developing countries.

believed to be a '"normal" level ... when trade restrictions are minimal'.[1] In the event he underestimated this tendency in all the large industrial countries including the United States. In chapter 4 it was suggested that the rise in United States, United Kingdom and German import ratios from 1963 to 1971 could not wholly be accounted for in terms of tariff cuts and of competitive weakness (both price and non-price); there was an unexplained residual. It is possible that in consequence of the spread of industrialisation and the development of new technologies and new products the 'normal' import ratio for a large country is rising. If so this would be a factor making for faster growth of trade – especially if Japan began to exhibit a development pattern similar to that of other large mature industrial economies.

All these influences taken together give grounds for assuming that the growth of imports relative to output in the next ten to fifteen years, though lower than in the last 25 years, will still be above the historical level. As against this, however, there is a serious possibility that the development of overt non-tariff barriers will limit growth of trade as protectionism limited it in the 1930s. In recent years non-tariff barriers have been used by the industrial countries principally to limit imports of manufactures from non-industrial and semi-industrial countries (as well as Japan). How much this has retarded the growth of world trade as opposed to altering its pattern is unknown, but its effects have probably outweighed those of tariff concessions from developed to developing countries.

Neither the GSP nor the preferential system which the members of the European Communities established in favour of a narrower group of developing countries under the Yaoundé and Lomé Conventions seems to have had any great influence on trade as yet. In the case of the GSP an OECD estimate suggests that of total 1976 imports from beneficiaries by OECD countries participating in the scheme only 13.5 per cent qualified for the preference and only 7.1 per cent actually received it.[2] Similarly UNCTAD estimates that only about half the exports from the least developed countries actually received the preferences for which they were eligible in 1973, mainly because of failure to comply with documentary and other requirements of the system.[3] It remains to be seen whether, if the effects of these preferences became important, they would be found politically tolerable in the developed countries. Past experience and current trends seem to suggest that they would not, especially, of course, in labour-intensive industries

---

[1] Maizels, *Industrial Growth and World Trade*, p. 387.
[2] J. de Miramon and A. Kleitz, 'Tariff preferences for the developing world: operation and evolution of the generalised system of preferences', *OECD Observer*, no. 90, January 1978.
[3] UNCTAD, *Operation and Effects of the Generalized System of Preferences*, New York, 1974, p. 10.

such as textiles and clothing, in which lower wages can be expected to give the developing countries a continuing comparative advantage.

The Leontief survey's more optimistic scenario for economic growth in the developing countries has total world trade increasing at an annual rate of 6 per cent from 1970 to 2000, with trade in manufactures growing at 7 per cent, agricultural trade at 2.9 per cent and trade in mineral products at 5 per cent. Estimated at 1970 prices the share of manufactured products in total trade would increase from 62 per cent in 1970 to 79 per cent by the end of the century. This, however, is with the developing countries increasing their share of total world imports of goods from about a sixth in 1970 to nearly a third in 2000, which implies an annual rate of rise in the volume of their imports of some 8–8½ per cent, whereas the survey estimates that their share of world exports, also about a sixth in 1970, would rise relatively little. Thus their trade deficits excluding the surpluses of the oil producers would increase to very large amounts.

Inflation will no doubt continue to ease the real burden of debt service for the developing countries other than the oil producers. It can be shown that at the end of 1975, after two years in which the effects of world recession on their exports had been superimposed on those of higher oil prices on their import bills, the ratio of their external public debt to their current export earnings, though higher than it had been at the end of 1973, was considerably lower than at the end of 1970, and the ratio hardly changed at all in 1976. Such calculations can, however, be seriously misleading. The picture would probably be significantly less favourable if private borrowing, such as receipts of trade credit, were included and imports have been increasingly restricted by inability or unwillingness to borrow more. If the developing oil importers are now to increase the volume of their imports to the extent that Leontief envisages, while other trade in manufactures grows more slowly and trade in primary products more slowly still, then it is clear that at least one of three things must happen on a very substantial scale: the terms of trade must move in favour of the developing oil importers, the foreign aid and investment which they receive must be increased, or they must be permitted to supply a higher proportion of the developed countries' manufactured imports. Whether any of these conditions will be fulfilled is likely to depend at least as much on political decisions as on economic forces and at the time of writing it cannot be said that the prospects are favourable.

There are reasons for expecting *some* movement in the terms of trade in favour of the developing countries, partly because it will probably be necessary to extend production to areas less well endowed or harder to exploit, both above the ground and, more especially, below it.[1] Current international discussions on commodity prices are, however, directed mainly towards reducing fluctuations and stabilising the purchasing power of primary producers' exports in terms of their imports of manufactures through expanded and co-ordinated use of buffer stocks. To the extent that they are successful, therefore, the prospect of a *large* movement in the terms of trade in either direction seems likely to be diminished rather than increased.

Nor is there much sign that in other respects the adoption of the Declaration and the 'Programme of Action' on the establishment of a new international economic order will have much influence on actual policies. In the field of aid even the long-standing target for the developed countries each to devote at least 0.7 per cent of GNP to official development assistance has been achieved by none of the major countries and by only four of the smaller ones (Denmark, the Netherlands, Norway and Sweden). In 1978 the percentage (which is reckoned net of amortisation though not of interest payments) was 0.32 for the members of the Development Assistance Committee of OECD collectively. This was a marginal improvement over 1977, but still one of the lowest percentages recorded (in over twenty years) and it compared with 0.51 per cent in 1963. Aid is, however, much less important than trade. The developing countries' exports to the developed countries in 1977 were worth about fourteen times their receipts from them and from international agencies of grants and concessional loans. Thus it is even more disturbing that, under the pressure of rising unemployment, trade policies in the developed countries have tended to become more restrictive, particularly in respect of items which the developing countries are best fitted to supply.

Estimates by GATT suggest that between 1974 and 1977 3–5 per cent of world trade previously affected only by tariffs became subject to overt restriction or other disruption. The categories mainly affected are textiles and clothing (including shoes), steel, transport equipment (especially ships) and certain sectors of light engineering (notably electrical and electronic goods and ball-bearings). These are all areas in which there have recently been important shifts in comparative advantage towards countries which have become major exporters in the past decade or so. But even for textiles and clothing the IBRD estimates that imports from the developing countries accounted in 1974 for only 2 per cent of consumption in France, 4 per cent in the United States and Japan, 5 per cent in Canada, 6 per cent in the United Kingdom and 8 per cent in Germany. Moreover, even in Germany with its relatively

[1] See, for example, G. F. Ray, 'Primary products: prospects to 1985', *National Institute Economic Review*, no. 76, May 1976.

high penetration, it has been shown that in the clothing sector during the period 1962–75 growth of productivity displaced more than three times as many workers as imports from the developing countries; over the whole of German manufacturing industry the ratio was 48:1.[1] In the United States over the three years April 1975–March 1978 some 327,000 workers were certified involuntarily unemployed because of increased imports (from all sources) and hence eligible for special assistance under the Trade Act 1974; over the same period the labour force increased by over seven million and civilian employment by nine million.[2]

The apparent unwillingness of the traditional producing countries to adjust to changing competitive conditions is harmful not merely because of its immediate effect on the developing countries' exports. If these countries are denied the opportunity to make full use of the productive capacity which they have built up, further investment is bound to be discouraged and with it their demand for capital goods. Both on this account and because of the immediate loss of purchasing power by the developing countries, the exports of the industrial countries themselves will suffer. This applies particularly, perhaps, to trade with the newly industrialising countries. Between 1963 and 1977 OECD countries' exports of manufactures other than metals to the Far Eastern and Latin American developing countries rose in f.o.b. value from $2.6 billion to $28.4 billion, while their imports of the same commodities from these countries rose only from $0.6 billion to $22.9 billion, even valued c.i.f. for countries other than the United States and Canada. All these countries except Mexico (that is, Brazil, Hong Kong, Korea, Singapore and Taiwan) have increased their imports of manufactures faster than world trade (even though their exports of manufactures have risen faster still).[3] By restricting imports from them the developed countries are thus jeopardising important export markets. They also risk diverting developing countries' exports to other developing countries and so increasing the competition faced there by their own exporters.

UNCTAD has examined the restructuring of world manufacturing trade as well as world manufacturing output which would be required to enable the developing countries to achieve the Lima target for their share in the latter by the end of the century.[4] This involved the assumption, somewhat optimistic perhaps, that the developing countries will in fact be allowed to increase their share in developed countries' import markets slightly faster than in the past. Even so, the implied rate

[1] IBRD, *World Development Report*, p. 17.
[2] GATT, *Adjustment, Trade and Growth* by Blackhurst, Marian and Tumlir, p. 61.
[3] OECD, *The Impact of the Newly Industrialising Countries on Production and Trade in Manufactures*, Paris, 1979.
[4] UNCTAD, *Restructuring of World Industry*.

of rise in the developing countries' exports of manufactures to these markets ($9\frac{1}{2}$–10 per cent per annum in volume terms between 1972 and 2000) is rather slower than was actually achieved from 1960 to 1972, since the markets are expected to expand less rapidly. Trade in manufactures among the developing countries is taken as rising at about 12 per cent a year (to give them, by the turn of the century, a ratio of intra-trade to output in each sector of manufacturing industry about half that recorded by the industrial countries in 1972). But, since the Lima target involves their very rapid industrialisation, it is assumed that their propensity to import manufactures from the developed countries will be lower in relation to growth of GDP or manufacturing output than it was in 1972 (at least for intermediate goods and capital equipment) and these imports are taken as rising by only about $7\frac{1}{2}$ per

Table 8.3. *Patterns of manufacturing output in developed and developing countries, 1972, and projections to 2000 for developing countries*

Percentages

	Developed, market economies, 1972	Centrally planned countries,[a] 1972	Developing countries	
			1972	2000[b]
Food processing	10.8	13.3	21.8	*12.4*
Textiles	4.6	4.4	11.8	*7.8*
Clothing, leather, footwear	4.0	4.3	6.3	*5.4*
Wood products, furniture	4.2	3.4	3.3	*3.6*
Printing	4.4	1.2	3.1	*3.8*
Rubber and plastic products	3.1	1.9	3.2	*3.0*
Other light industry	2.1	2.7	1.6	*2.0*
Total light industry	(33.2)	(31.2)	(51.1)	*(38.0)*
Paper	3.4	1.2	1.8	*2.4*
Chemicals	9.8	7.2	9.4	*10.2*
Petroleum products	1.7	1.8	7.2	*4.1*
Non-metallic mineral products	4.1	6.4	5.2	*4.9*
Basic metals	8.0	7.7	6.2	*8.8*
Electrical equipment	8.7	9.9	4.2	*7.0*
Other machinery	21.0	23.9	8.9	*16.1*
Transport equipment	10.1	10.7	6.0	*8.5*
Total heavy industry	(66.8)	(68.8)	(48.9)	*(62.0)*
TOTAL MANUFACTURES	100.0	100.0	100.0	100.0

[a] Eastern Europe only.
[b] Projections based on regression analysis of the effects to be expected when a country moves from an annual GDP per head of $210 to one of $910 and from a population of 30 million to one of 50 million. (Income per head in developing countries averaged about $210 in 1970 and the greater part of their manufacturing output in 1972 was produced in countries with an average population of around 30 million. The implied increases in GDP per head and population correspond with the basic assumptions about the achievement of the Lima target.)
SOURCE: UNCTAD, *Restructuring of World Industry*, table 2.

Table 8.4. *Developing countries' manufacturing trade : actual and hypothetical patterns*

| | Actual, 1970 | | Hypothetical patterns, 2000 | | | |
| | | | Total | | With rest of world | |
	Imports	Exports	Imports[a]	Exports[b]	Imports[c]	Exports[d]
			(percentages)			
Food processing	9.4	22.4	6.4	12.3	5.9	15.3
Textiles	7.0	10.8	5.0	8.2	3.5	8.1
Clothing, leather, footwear	1.4	6.1	2.3	6.0	0.8	6.0
Wood products, furniture	1.3	3.5	1.7	3.2	1.3	3.6
Printing	0.7	0.7	0.6	0.5	0.5	0.4
Rubber and plastic products	0.9	0.5	1.1	1.4	0.4	0.6
Other light industry	4.8	5.8	1.2	2.1	0.8	2.2
Total light industry	(25.5)	(49.8)	(18.3)	(33.9)	(13.3)	(36.2)
Paper	3.3	0.7	3.7	2.9	4.1	3.0
Chemicals	14.0	4.1	13.8	9.7	14.8	8.7
Petroleum products	3.1	14.5	2.3	5.1	1.7	6.0
Non-metallic mineral products	1.9	1.0	1.6	1.5	1.3	1.0
Basic metals	11.1	19.1	14.4	13.6	16.0	15.5
Electrical equipment	8.0	3.2	8.7	7.0	9.4	7.0
Other machinery	21.5	4.4	26.1	15.7	29.4	14.1
Transport equipment	11.6	3.2	11.1	10.5	10.0	8.5
Total heavy industry	(74.5)	(50.2)	(81.7)	(66.1)	(86.7)	(63.8)
TOTAL MANUFACTURES	100.0	100.0	100.0	100.0	100.0	100.0
			($ billions, 1972 prices)			
Total value	61.6[e]	27.5	567.0	447.0	397.0	277.0

[a] Based on regression analysis of the effects on trade of the same changes as in note *b* to table 8.3, with the same assumptions.
[b] On the assumptions that the existing export pattern for developing countries' trade with developed countries will move half way towards the corresponding import pattern and, for their intra-trade, that the sectoral trading propensities with respect to gross output will be half of those in developed market economies' intra-trade in 1972.
[c] A residual, given the above assumptions.
[d] Based on the first assumption in note *b* above.
[e] For 1972.
SOURCE: UNCTAD, *Restructuring of World Industry*, pp. 9–12.

cent a year. On this basis the implied rates of volume increase for developing countries' total imports and exports of manufactures are 8–8½ and 10½ per cent respectively, which in turn would mean that the ratio of imports to exports at 1972 prices would fall from 2.2 to 1.3 (from 2.7 to 1.4 in trade with the developed countries).

Despite the declining import propensity assumed for the capital goods sector, its increasingly important role in the developing countries' economies is reflected in some degree in the structure of trade as well as output which UNCTAD envisages for the end of the century and which is shown in tables 8.3 and 8.4. The diminishing relative importance of food processing and of textiles and clothing also shows up clearly. The other main features of the trade projections are perhaps the emergence as a major element on the export side of chemicals (other than petroleum products, of which the relative importance is sharply reduced) and the contrasting changes in shares envisaged for basic metals (rising on the import side and falling rapidly on the other).

Nevertheless, as a proportion of the developed market economies' output in the sectors in question, UNCTAD envisages bigger surpluses in 2000 than in 1972 on their trade with the developing countries in both chemicals and basic metals, as well as in machinery and transport equipment; also in paper and printing and in non-metallic mineral products. At the same time their deficits on trade in food products, clothing, wood products and petroleum are expected to be higher in relation to output than they were before. There is, however, a big swing on the remaining products – textiles, rubber and plastic products, and miscellaneous light industry. Here the developed countries' existing surplus, which in 1972 was equivalent to 1.7 per cent of their gross output of these products, would change by 2000 to a deficit equivalent to about 2 per cent of output. This is in fact concentrated on textiles and miscellaneous light industry, approximate balance being envisaged for rubber and plastic products. Overall, though in the developing countries' trade in manufactures with the rest of the world the ratio of their imports to exports falls at unchanged prices from 2.7 in 1972 to less than 1.5 at the end of the century, the developed market economies' surplus on trade in manufactures with the developing countries remains roughly constant in relation to the gross manufacturing output of the former, at just under 2 per cent. They should not find this an intolerable prospect, but clearly they will not, if they can help it, allow the emergence of any more Japans with a high propensity to export and a low propensity to import manufactures.

It would be more serious if the United States and the EEC had recourse on a large scale to non-tariff measures in order to restrict imports from one another, which could well happen. Within Europe itself the risk is, of course, much smaller. Unfortunately this is not true of the more insidious form of non-tariff protection by way of subsidies to non-competitive industries, whether the subsidies are described as part of, say, industrial or regional policies, or take the form of straight subventions to loss-making enterprises in both private and public sectors. Some actions under these heads may subsidise trade (for example, tax holidays and other special inducements for firms believed to be potential exporters) and, since all industrial countries tend to assist similar industries, some may lead merely to a reshuffling of orders among suppliers. But the general thrust of such measures, if they are maintained over long periods rather than used as temporary palliatives, must be to restrict the growth of trade.

Whether the threat of increasing non-tariff protection materialises on a scale sufficient to counter the expansionary influences on world trade depends very much on the rate of economic growth sustained by the industrial countries. Demands for protection are stronger and harder to resist in bad times than in good, and hardest of all in periods of prolonged unemployment. In this connection the experience of the 1970s prompts a fairly optimistic forecast of the growth of world trade. So far as imports into the industrial countries are concerned, there is still sufficient impetus to keep trade growing at a rate above the historical average provided that output also continues to grow reasonably fast.

Appendix A

EXPORTS OF MANUFACTURES FROM MAJOR INDUSTRIAL COUNTRIES

by *R. L. Major*

In tables A.1–A.12 we carry on part of the analysis which Maizels provided in his appendix A of the major industrial countries' exports of manufactures at current and constant prices by destination and commodity group.[1] The correspondence between the two sets of tables is as follows:

Present book:	A.1	A.2	A.3	A.4	A.5–A.6	A.7–A.9	A.10–A.12
Previous book:	A.3	A.4	A.13	A.14	$\begin{Bmatrix} \text{A.46–A.65} \\ \text{A.68, A.69} \end{Bmatrix}$	A.70–A.72	A.75–A.77

The exporting countries that we cover are Belgium-Luxembourg, Canada, France, Germany (West), Italy, Japan, the Netherlands, Sweden, Switzerland, United Kingdom and United States (but not India, which Maizels included as an exporting country in some tables). In most of the tables Belgium-Luxembourg, Italy, the Netherlands, Sweden and Switzerland are grouped together as 'other Western Europe'.

The classification by destination follows the list on pages 5–6 (with Austria, Denmark, Finland, Greece, Ireland, Spain and Portugal included in 'rest of world'). Within the category of industrial countries 'EEC Six' comprises Belgium-Luxembourg, France, Germany, Italy and the Netherlands, while 'other Western Europe' comprises Norway, Sweden and Switzerland. (This sub-division of the group, which Maizels called 'continental Western Europe', was made for the earlier years with the help of his worksheets.)

The commodity classifications are given in appendix B. There are minor inconsistencies between the figures for years before and after 1960 because of the revision of the S I T C. 'Other manufactures' here include metal goods. Re-exports from the United Kingdom and exports of diamonds from the United Kingdom are included only for 1963, 1967 and 1971, as are certain United States exports which were removed in 1965 from the 'special category' for which destination by commodity is not disclosed. Other 'special category' exports from the United States are excluded throughout. The market distribution for United Kingdom

---

[1] Maizels, *Industrial Growth and World Trade*, pp. 419–505.

253

Table A.1. *Exports of manufactures at current prices by destination*

Exports to:		Industrial countries				
		United Kingdom	EEC Six	Other W. Europe	North America	Total[a]
Exports from:						
United Kingdom	1950	—	512	369	511	1,396
	1955	—	818	434	688	1,968
	1959	—	1,019	481	1,334	2,886
	1963	—	2,024	756	1,275	4,167
	1967	—	2,335	1,041	1,933	5,515
	1971	—	3,888	1,587	2,866	8,662.
France	1950	128	296	146	98	671
	1955	145	620	210	163	1,149
	1959	140	976	277	452	1,862
	1963	226	2,105	470	376	3,215
	1967	346	3,128	612	650	4,803
	1971	610	6,953	955	1,139	9,793
Germany	1950	53	435	204	96	795
	1955	219	1,309	815	395	2,777
	1959	362	2,088	1,241	992	4,769
	1963	498	4,501	1,889	1,119	8,198
	1967	792	6,745	2,280	2,099	12,221
	1971	1,454	13,279	3,824	4,050	23,101
Other Western	1950	297	1,192	326	369	2,190
Europe	1955	441	2,194	584	688	3,939
	1959	625	3,291	780	1,268	6,032
	1963	903	6,452	1,196	1,411	10,126
	1967	1,432	10,186	1,668	2,436	15,978
	1971	2,471	20,558	2,738	3,836	30,038
Canada	1950	105	29	11	905	1,051
	1955	292	80	21	1,384	1,782
	1959	305	116	30	1,601	2,064
	1963	361	158	34	1,792	2,372
	1967	477	179	38	4,428	5,215
	1971	635	308	60	8,278	9,385
United States	1950	179	568	171	1,161	2,121
	1955	333	838	254	2,331	3,896
	1959	323	999	297	2,774	4,699
	1963	676	2,290	481	3,152	7,246
	1967	1,158	3,220	677	5,836	11,888
	1971	1,631	5,197	939	8,398	18,069
Japan	1950	19	26	13	135	195
	1955	33	46	15	385	479
	1959	32	69	47	997	1,145
	1963	92	245	83	1,499	1,918
	1967	226	458	358	3,154	4,196
	1971	488	1,503	541	8,160	10,692
TOTAL	1950	781	3,057	1,241	3,275	8,419
	1955	1,462	5,900	2,332	6,037	15,987
	1959	1,787	8,558	3,153	9,417	23,457
	1963	2,756	17,775	4,908	10,623	37,241
	1967	4,431	26,252	6,673	20,535	59,815
	1971	7,290	51,686	10,645	36,727	109,742

[a] Includes Japan.

	Semi-industrial countries			Rest of world	World total
Oceania, S. Africa	India, Pakistan	Other	Total		

Oceania, S. Africa	India, Pakistan	Other	Total	Rest of world	World total
1,247	362	315	1,923	1,781	5,100
1,564	405	211	2,180	2,538	6,686
1,250	543	320	2,113	2,865	7,864
1,473	452	432	2,358	3,460	9,984
1,606	350	498	2,454	4,120	12,089
2,059	415	951	3,425	6,963	19,050
41	23	168	232	1,091	1,993
50	44	219	313	1,615	3,077
50	51	192	293	2,021	4,176
86	50	292	428	2,198	5,841
188	82	293	563	3,084	8,450
245	61	626	932	4,667	15,392
47	26	177	250	418	1,462
160	168	531	859	1,614	5,250
266	268	684	1,217	2,694	8,680
328	260	640	1,228	3,485	12,910
517	286	1,073	1,876	5,383	19,480
887	258	2,075	3,220	8,656	34,978
127	86	376	589	1,293	4,074
236	129	540	905	1,929	6,773
248	131	625	1,003	2,536	9,571
326	160	761	1,247	3,434	14,808
518	231	1,063	1,812	5,699	23,489
766	208	1,973	2,947	8,998	41,983
54	31	50	136	80	1,266
91	27	72	191	96	2,069
84	34	65	183	144	2,391
123	56	123	302	155	2,830
186	60	116	362	309	5,886
214	107	218	539	528	10,452
206	121	1,199	1,526	1,880	5,526
399	164	1,301	1,864	2,536	8,296
415	150	1,525	2,090	2,841	9,630
685	628	1,638	2,950	3,307	13,503
1,140	540	2,137	3,817	4,592	20,297
1,523	449	3,310	5,282	6,322	29,673
52	72	29	154	349	697
85	126	140	351	918	1,748
134	97	99	330	1,557	3,032
270	191	157	618	2,412	4,948
565	216	263	1,044	4,518	9,758
1,244	287	682	2,213	9,716	22,621
1,774	714	2,322	4,810	6,890	20,119
2,585	1,062	3,013	6,660	11,249	33,896
2,447	1,273	3,510	7,230	14,657	45,344
3,290	1,797	4,043	9,130	18,454	64,824
4,720	1,764	5,443	11,927	27,708	99,450
6,938	1,785	9,835	18,558	45,849	174,149

Table A.2. *Exports of manufactures at constant prices by destination*

Exports to:			United Kingdom	EEC Six	Other W. Europe	North America	Total[a]
					Industrial countries		
Exports from:							
United Kingdom		1950	—	663	453	657	1,776
	b	1955	—	818	434	688	1,968
		1959	—	944	445	1,235	2,672
		1963	—	*1,772*	*670*	*1,105*	*3,644*
	c	1963	—	2,024	756	1,275	4,167
		1967	—	2,144	960	1,770	5,064
		1971	—	3,263	1,348	2,401	7,287
France		1950	148	364	175	120	809
	b	1955	145	620	210	163	1,149
		1959	141	982	278	454	1,873
		1963	*218*	*1,990*	*451*	*366*	*3,064*
	c	1963	226	2,105	470	376	3,215
		1967	317	2,918	574	603	4,475
		1971	506	5,912	818	949	8,304
Germany		1950	63	535	256	119	980
	b	1955	219	1,309	815	395	2,777
		1959	355	2,047	1,217	972	4,675
		1963	*445*	*3,995*	*1,677*	*996*	*7,284*
	c	1963	498	4,501	1,889	1,119	8,198
		1967	770	6,555	2,211	2,019	11,854
		1971	1,190	10,914	3,103	3,346	18,949
Other Western Europe		1950	285	1,251	382	407	2,329
	b	1955	441	2,194	584	688	3,939
		1959	610	3,221	754	1,248	5,899
		1963	*870*	*6,186*	*1,140*	*1,378*	*9,733*
	c	1963	903	6,452	1,196	1,411	10,126
		1967	1,365	9,627	1,593	2,282	15,107
		1971	2,152	17,851	2,367	3,249	25,993
Canada		1950	133	33	14	1,055	1,236
	b	1955	292	80	21	1,384	1,782
		1959	299	113	29	1,569	2,023
		1963	*378*	*155*	*34*	*1,755*	*2,350*
	c	1963	361	158	33	1,792	2,372
		1967	426	164	35	4,210	4,918
		1971	496	240	48	6,929	7,795
United States		1950	225	704	208	1,432	2,619
	b	1955	333	838	254	2,331	3,896
		1959	281	869	259	2,413	4,088
		1963	*591*	*1,999*	*415*	*2,658*	*6,229*
	c	1963	676	2,290	481	3,152	7,246
		1967	1,084	3,030	635	5,435	11,124
		1971	1,350	4,341	784	6,754	14,817
Japan		1950	18	33	15	168	233
	b	1955	33	46	15	385	479
		1959	31	67	46	968	1,112
		1963	*99*	*260*	*84*	*1,540*	*1,983*
	c	1963	92	244	83	1,499	1,918
		1967	233	473	364	3,200	4,270
		1971	475	1,482	511	7,778	10,246
TOTAL		1950	870	3,586	1,502	3,957	9,984
	b	1955	1,462	5,900	2,332	6,037	15,987
		1959	1,717	8,243	3,028	8,859	22,342
		1963	*2,601*	*16,358*	*4,472*	*9,798*	*34,288*
	c	1963	2,756	17,775	4,908	10,623	37,241
		1967	4,195	24,911	6,372	19,520	56,813
		1971	6,169	44,001	8,979	31,405	93,390

[a] Includes Japan. [b] At 1955 prices. [c] At 1963 prices.

| | Semi-industrial countries | | | Rest of world | World total |
Oceania, S. Africa	India, Pakistan	Other	Total		
1,602	466	400	2,468	2,279	6,523
1,564	405	211	2,180	2,538	6,686
1,157	503	297	1,957	2,652	7,281
1,280	384	376	2,040	3,044	8,728
1,473	452	432	2,358	3,460	9,984
1,479	321	457	2,257	3,796	11,117
1,728	340	792	2,860	5,878	16,025
51	28	220	299	1,358	2,466
50	44	219	313	1,615	3,077
50	51	194	295	2,033	4,201
79	44	260	383	2,069	5,516
86	50	292	428	2,199	5,841
171	73	272	516	2,834	7,826
201	51	509	760	3,864	12,928
62	32	220	314	519	1,813
160	168	531	859	1,614	5,250
260	263	670	1,193	2,480	8,348
291	216	569	1,076	3,133	11,493
328	260	640	1,228	3,484	12,910
499	277	1,043	1,819	5,222	18,895
714	204	1,692	2,610	7,042	28,601
139	89	415	643	1,479	4,451
236	129	540	905	1,929	6,773
242	129	620	991	2,486	9,376
310	150	722	1,182	3,319	14,234
326	160	761	1,247	3,435	14,808
493	220	1,018	1,731	5,451	22,289
657	178	1,722	2,557	7,851	36,401
63	37	58	158	88	1,482
91	27	72	191	96	2,069
83	33	64	180	151	2,354
114	57	117	288	150	2,788
123	56	123	302	155	2,829
176	55	107	338	292	5,548
176	87	174	436	433	8,664
250	147	1,481	1,878	2,234	6,731
399	164	1,301	1,864	2,536	8,296
361	131	1,326	1,818	2,444	8,350
592	538	1,395	2,525	2,845	11,599
685	628	1,637	2,950	3,308	13,503
1,070	515	2,004	3,589	4,313	19,026
1,252	369	2,736	4,357	5,216	24,391
64	78	45	187	396	816
85	126	140	351	918	1,748
130	94	96	320	1,512	2,944
281	221	178	680	2,628	5,291
270	191	157	618	2,413	4,949
586	229	269	1,084	4,665	10,019
1,220	275	653	2,147	9,571	21,964
2,230	876	2,840	5,947	8,352	24,283
2,585	1,062	3,013	6,660	11,249	33,896
2,284	1,203	3,266	6,753	13,760	42,854
2,947	1,610	3,617	8,174	17,187	59,649
3,290	1,797	4,043	9,130	18,453	64,824
4,475	1,690	5,170	11,335	26,573	94,720
5,948	1,503	8,277	15,728	39,856	148,974

Table A.3. *Exports of manufactures at constant prices: totals by importing country*

$ *million*

	At 1955 prices				At 1963 prices		
	1950	1955	1959	*1963*	1963	1967	1971
INDUSTRIAL COUNTRIES							
United Kingdom	870	1,462	1,717	*2,601*	2,756	4,195	6,169
Belgium-Luxembourg	747	1,108	1,400	*2,513*	2,757	3,994	6,844
France	700	1,118	1,411	*3,347*	3,645	5,917	9,780
Germany	513	1,325	2,416	*4,445*	4,704	6,523	13,592
Italy	524	761	1,099	*2,911*	3,248	3,449	5,605
Netherlands	1,101	1,588	1,916	*3,143*	3,421	5,028	8,181
Sweden	599	977	1,194	*1,561*	1,722	2,142	2,811
Switzerland	498	750	1,113	*1,965*	2,135	2,626	4,275
Canada	1,892	2,853	3,299	*3,446*	4,020	6,734	9,038
United States	2,065	3,184	5,560	*6,352*	6,603	12,786	22,367
Japan	71	256	495	*1,059*	1,180	1,815	2,836
SEMI-INDUSTRIAL COUNTRIES							
Australia	1,190	1,204	1,068	*1,364*	1,522	2,196	2,771
New Zealand	353	473	331	*444*	493	473	591
South Africa	688	908	884	*1,139*	1,277	1,805	2,585
India	590	820	971	*1,150*	1,279	1,106	1,052
Pakistan	286	242	232	*459*	518	584	451
Argentina	607	539	663	*536*	600	597	990
Brazil	757	532	677	*622*	681	836	1,793
Chile	122	151	202	*250*	284	399	398
Colombia	312	456	253	*327*	363	300	492
Mexico	552	677	726	*817*	932	1,412	1,634
Israel	136	150	190	*329*	372	406	927
Turkey	228	327	306	*380*	431	471	596
Yugoslavia	125	180	249	*357*	382	749	1,447
USSR	124	155	359	*676*	698	940	1,651
OTHER SELECTED COUNTRIES							
Morocco	203	231	..	*228*	243	241	314
Nigeria	131	209	..	*326*	356	341	757
Peru	129	174	..	*326*	372	448	433
Philippines	242	349	..	*471*	498	791	791
Venezuela	486	732	..	*640*	721	850	1,172

Table A.4. *Exports of manufactures at constant prices: totals per head by
importing country*

$ *million*

	At 1955 prices				At 1963 prices		
	1950	1955	1959	*1963*	1963	1967	1971
INDUSTRIAL COUNTRIES							
United Kingdom	17	29	33	*48*	51	77	111
Belgium-Luxembourg	84	120	149	*261*	287	403	684
France	17	16	31	*70*	76	119	191
Germany	11	26	46	*80*	85	109	222
Italy	11	16	22	*57*	64	65	104
Netherlands	110	147	169	*263*	286	399	620
Sweden	86	134	160	*205*	227	272	347
Switzerland	95	150	212	*341*	370	433	676
Canada	138	182	188	*182*	212	330	418
United States	14	19	31	*34*	35	64	108
Japan	1	3	5	*11*	12	18	27
SEMI-INDUSTRIAL COUNTRIES							
Australia	145	131	106	*125*	139	186	217
New Zealand	186	225	142	*175*	194	174	207
South Africa	55	66	57	*67*	75	87	112
India	2	2	2	*2*	3	2	2
Pakistan	4	3	2	*4*	5	5	3
Argentina	35	28	33	*25*	28	26	41
Brazil	15	9	10	*8*	9	10	19
Chile	20	22	27	*30*	35	45	42
Colombia	28	36	17	*19*	21	16	23
Mexico	21	23	21	*20*	23	32	31
Israel	105	88	92	*138*	156	151	309
Turkey	11	14	11	*13*	14	14	17
Yugoslavia	8	10	14	*19*	20	38	70
USSR	1	1	2	*3*	3	4	7
OTHER SELECTED COUNTRIES							
Morocco	26	27	..	*18*	19	17	20
Nigeria	5	7	..	*7*	8	7	13
Peru	15	19	..	*30*	34	36	31
Philippines	12	16	..	*16*	17	23	21
Venezuela	97	126	..	*79*	89	91	109

Table A.5. *Total exports at current prices by commodity* $ million

	1950	1955	1959	1963	1967	1971
METALS from:						
United Kingdom	441	647	852	860	1,084	1,533
France	333	735	890	895	1,194	1,846
Germany	290	582	1,165	1,364	2,263	3,378
Other W. Europe	623	1,324	1,664	2,021	3,203	4,985
Canada	346	642	717	849	1,255	1,682
United States	508	894	634	937	1,078	1,388
Japan	129	328	280	745	1,376	3,748
Total	2,670	5,152	6,202	7,671	11,452	18,559
MACHINERY from:						
United Kingdom	1,018	1,605	2,229	2,911	3,334	5,507
France	234	428	594	1,102	1,832	3,687
Germany	344	1,516	2,570	4,213	6,280	11,284
Other W. Europe	748	1,213	1,859	3,484	5,799	10,493
Canada	119	166	294	369	810	1,306
United States	1,794	2,619	3,457	5,139	7,066	10,096
Japan	38	123	354	832	1,998	5,019
Total	4,295	7,670	11,356	18,050	27,119	47,392
TRANSPORT EQUIPMENT from:						
United Kingdom	1,152	1,428	1,769	2,233	2,644	3,909
France	213	358	778	1,058	1,471	3,214
Germany	133	941	1,712	2,604	3,502	7,215
Other W. Europe	286	623	1,105	1,848	2,742	5,382
Canada	84	118	120	275	2,020	4,759
United States	1,041	1,651	1,651	2,592	5,080	8,618
Japan	44	124	456	664	1,820	5,568
Total	2,953	5,242	7,591	11,274	19,279	38,665
CHEMICALS from:						
United Kingdom	390	652	821	1,042	1,382	2,155
France	218	360	472	756	1,244	1,960
Germany	227	681	1,105	1,646	2,705	4,538
Other W. Europe	445	768	1,158	1,692	2,925	5,515
Canada	114	246	243	219	372	593
United States	752	1,106	1,502	1,943	2,803	3,837
Japan	17	94	167	316	684	1,488
Total	2,163	3,907	5,466	7,614	12,115	20,087
TEXTILES AND CLOTHING from:						
United Kingdom	1,113	960	778	837	886	1,346
France	534	534	576	826	971	1,579
Germany	97	353	429	673	1,078	2,341
Other W. Europe	963	1,071	1,354	2,218	2,922	5,120
Canada	23	19	23	45	67	175
United States	477	539	542	581	692	822
Japan	352	693	964	1,126	1,565	2,529
Total	3,559	4,168	4,666	6,306	8,181	13,912
OTHER MANUFACTURES from:						
United Kingdom	986	1,393	1,415	2,101	2,760	4,600
France	460	662	866	1,204	1,738	3,107
Germany	371	1,177	1,699	2,410	3,651	6,223
Other W. Europe	1,009	1,774	2,431	3,545	5,898	10,487
Canada	581	879	996	1,073	1,362	1,937
United States	954	1,487	1,844	2,311	3,579	4,911
Japan	117	386	812	1,265	2,317	4,269
Total	4,478	7,758	10,063	13,909	21,305	35,534

Table A.6. *Total exports at constant prices by commodity* $ million

	At 1955 prices				At 1963 prices		
	1950	1955	1959	1963	1963	1967	1971
METALS from:							
United Kingdom	617	647	845	860	860	951	1,179
France	500	735	893	886	895	1,170	1,525
Germany	418	582	1,196	1,482	1,364	2,176	2,598
Other W. Europe	818	1,324	1,662	2,011	2,021	2,903	3,869
Canada	445	642	781	953	849	1,055	1,193
United States	676	894	558	844	937	989	1,059
Japan	219	328	264	827	745	1,336	3,150
Total	3,693	5,152	6,199	7,865	7,671	10,579	14,574
MACHINERY from:							
United Kingdom	1,364	1,605	1,836	2,156	2,911	2,977	4,441
France	337	428	519	828	1,102	1,466	2,491
Germany	427	1,516	2,218	2,988	4,213	5,658	7,676
Other W. Europe	807	1,213	1,714	2,888	3,484	5,422	8,720
Canada	139	166	240	290	369	764	1,045
United States	2,261	2,619	2,842	4,178	5,139	6,483	7,766
Japan	46	123	315	979	832	2,038	5,174
Total	5,381	7,670	9,684	14,308	18,050	24,807	37,313
TRANSPORT EQUIPMENT from:							
United Kingdom	1,423	1,428	1,681	2,068	2,233	2,494	3,231
France	298	358	742	928	1,058	1,338	2,551
Germany	188	941	1,601	2,264	2,604	3,368	5,865
Other W. Europe	357	623	1,059	1,685	1,848	2,657	4,391
Canada	98	118	100	222	275	2,020	4,174
United States	1,291	1,651	1,306	1,964	2,592	4,703	6,629
Japan	52	124	434	763	664	1,838	5,016
Total	3,707	5,242	6,923	9,894	11,274	18,418	31,858
CHEMICALS from:							
United Kingdom	433	652	841	1,197	1,042	1,373	1,983
France	196	360	524	911	756	1,383	2,305
Germany	223	681	1,196	1,937	1,646	3,049	4,685
Other W. Europe	413	768	1,219	1,982	1,692	2,957	5,539
Canada	125	246	245	229	219	378	567
United States	884	1,106	1,516	2,045	1,943	2,818	3,993
Japan	19	94	199	472	316	831	1,938
Total	2,293	3,907	5,740	8,772	7,614	12,790	21,009
TEXTILES AND CLOTHING from:							
United Kingdom	1,386	960	797	761	837	831	1,281
France	537	534	646	861	826	919	1,482
Germany	104	353	449	765	673	1,143	2,569
Other W. Europe	890	1,071	1,469	2,430	2,218	2,910	5,116
Canada	22	19	22	43	45	65	151
United States	461	539	568	605	581	705	798
Japan	337	693	956	1,063	1,126	1,654	2,790
Total	3,738	4,168	4,907	6,528	6,306	8,227	14,188
OTHER MANUFACTURES from:							
United Kingdom	1,300	1,393	1,281	1,685	2,101	2,492	3,909
France	598	662	877	1,102	1,204	1,550	2,575
Germany	453	1,177	1,688	2,057	2,410	3,501	5,207
Other W. Europe	1,166	1,774	2,253	3,238	3,545	5,441	8,766
Canada	653	879	966	1,050	1,073	1,265	1,534
United States	1,158	1,487	1,560	1,963	2,311	3,328	4,146
Japan	144	386	776	1,187	1,265	2,322	3,895
Total	5,472	7,758	9,401	12,282	13,909	19,900	30,032

Table A.7. *Exports of metals at constant prices by destination*

Exports to:		United Kingdom	EEC Six	Other W. Europe	North America	Total[a]
Exports from:						
United Kingdom[b]	1950	—	63	43	77	183
	1955	—	78	50	67	195
	1963	—	206	78	106	394
[c]	1963	—	206	78	106	394
	1967	—	208	99	155	484
	1971	—	231	134	216	590
France[b]	1950	25	86	41	44	196
	1955	37	234	73	37	381
	1963	16	414	81	73	585
[c]	1963	16	418	82	74	591
	1967	31	524	91	127	774
	1971	27	714	114	229	1,085
Germany[b]	1950	22	103	55	48	228
	1955	20	155	93	39	308
	1963	20	672	183	126	1,007
[c]	1963	18	618	168	116	927
	1967	52	842	185	313	1,428
	1971	48	1,081	245	327	1,705
Other Western Europe[b]	1950	60	224	88	112	485
	1955	71	575	139	112	902
	1963	86	987	159	212	1,451
[c]	1963	86	991	159	212	1,455
	1967	151	1,426	201	337	2,143
	1971	182	2,168	253	416	3,030
Canada[b]	1950	109	14	5	292	420
	1955	209	27	9	350	597
	1963	213	60	21	498	804
[c]	1963	190	53	18	443	715
	1967	213	58	10	599	930
	1971	206	96	12	697	1,045
United States[b]	1950	56	89	30	163	339
	1955	125	194	52	234	614
	1963	59	197	19	150	449
[c]	1963	66	218	21	167	498
	1967	70	182	19	274	610
	1971	59	214	19	309	634
Japan[b]	1950	—	14	3	53	72
	1955	13	15	1	31	60
	1963	3	54	2	269	327
[c]	1963	3	48	2	242	295
	1967	7	31	4	594	635
	1971	43	198	33	1,010	1,284
TOTAL[b]	1950	272	592	264	792	1,922
	1955	475	1,278	417	869	3,056
	1963	397	2,589	543	1,435	5,017
[c]	1963	378	2,553	530	1,360	4,875
	1967	523	3,271	609	2,400	7,005
	1971	566	4,702	810	3,204	9,374

[a] Includes Japan. [b] At 1955 prices. [c] At 1963 prices.

	Semi-industrial countries			Rest of world	World total
Oceania, S. Africa	India, Pakistan	Other	Total		
137	34	43	214	220	617
142	39	25	206	246	647
78	40	42	160	307	860
78	40	42	160	307	860
79	37	39	155	311	951
72	73	59	204	385	1,179
18	11	86	115	189	500
10	18	47	75	279	735
3	3	28	35	266	886
3	3	29	35	269	895
5	10	40	55	341	1,170
15	7	56	78	362	1,525
24	7	44	75	115	418
7	12	62	81	193	582
6	20	62	88	387	1,482
6	18	57	81	356	1,364
11	45	101	157	591	2,176
15	32	121	168	725	2,598
18	13	72	103	230	818
29	16	77	122	300	1,324
16	16	94	125	435	2,011
15	16	97	128	438	2,021
29	26	87	142	618	2,903
26	19	117	162	677	3,869
6	8	7	21	4	445
14	5	17	36	9	642
24	36	45	105	45	953
22	32	40	94	40	849
31	22	30	83	41	1,055
21	21	49	91	57	1,193
32	14	134	180	157	676
36	27	125	188	92	894
14	161	77	252	143	844
16	179	85	280	159	937
16	91	87	194	185	989
17	80	122	219	206	1,059
31	9	30	70	77	219
22	48	79	149	119	328
33	39	48	121	379	827
30	35	44	109	341	745
55	37	33	125	576	1,336
172	100	224	496	1,370	3,150
267	96	416	779	992	3,693
260	165	432	857	1,239	5,152
175	315	396	886	1,962	7,865
170	323	393	886	1,910	7,671
226	268	418	911	2,663	10,579
338	333	747	1,418	3,782	14,574

263

Table A.8. *Exports of machinery at constant prices by destination*

Exports to :		Industrial countries				
		United Kingdom	EEC Six	Other W. Europe	North America	Total[a]
Exports from :						
United Kingdom	1950	—	185	82	57	324
	b 1955	—	208	83	113	411
	1963	—	*424*	*133*	*201*	*787*
	c 1963	—	572	180	271	1,062
	1967	—	541	197	366	1,145
	1971	—	922	293	496	1,782
France	1950	6	41	10	1	58
	b 1955	11	71	15	9	107
	1963	*31*	*285*	*46*	*21*	*390*
	c 1963	42	379	61	28	519
	1967	82	477	76	70	721
	1971	108	938	112	135	1,321
Germany	1950	8	145	56	9	219
	b 1955	69	453	202	64	800
	1963	*131*	*1,089*	*392*	*141*	*1,822*
	c 1963	185	1,536	552	199	2,570
	1967	294	1,881	622	414	3,308
	1971	352	2,770	860	523	4,674
Other Western Europe	1950	26	214	52	19	311
	b 1955	71	383	84	64	611
	1963	*144*	*1,123*	*206*	*176*	*1,702*
	c 1963	174	1,363	250	213	2,064
	1967	319	1,939	341	494	3,167
	1971	473	3,518	543	627	5,284
Canada	1950	2	4	2	90	98
	b 1955	4	6	1	109	120
	1963	*12*	*18*	*3*	*190*	*227*
	c 1963	16	22	4	242	289
	1967	33	27	6	575	652
	1971	58	43	9	748	869
United States	1950	81	330	70	503	993
	b 1955	86	236	63	805	1,253
	1963	*215*	*754*	*135*	*960*	*2,286*
	c 1963	264	928	166	1,181	2,811
	1967	441	1,042	205	1,654	3,681
	1971	481	1,478	226	1,757	4,475
Japan	1950	—	—	—	8	8
	b 1955	—	1	—	19	20
	1963	*10*	*48*	*20*	*294*	*372*
	c 1963	9	41	17	250	316
	1967	31	100	28	723	883
	1971	117	416	96	1,930	2,559
TOTAL	1950	123	920	272	688	2,013
	b 1955	240	1,358	448	1,183	3,321
	1963	*544*	*3,741*	*935*	*1,983*	*7,586*
	c 1963	689	4,842	1,231	2,383	9,631
	1967	1,199	6,008	1,476	4,297	13,556
	1971	1,590	10,084	2,139	6,216	20,964

[a] Includes Japan. [b] At 1955 prices. [c] At 1963 prices.

Oceania, S. Africa	Semi-industrial countries			Rest of world	World total
	India, Pakistan	Other	Total		
322	162	109	593	447	1,364
382	161	71	614	580	1,605
336	156	107	599	771	2,156
454	211	144	809	1,040	2,911
481	121	141	743	1,089	2,977
586	114	295	995	1,664	4,440
2	2	31	35	244	337
3	5	68	76	245	428
15	16	74	105	333	828
20	22	98	140	443	1,102
31	29	69	129	616	1,466
49	15	175	239	931	2,491
11	8	60	79	129	427
38	63	211	312	404	1,516
72	100	187	358	807	2,988
101	141	264	505	1,138	4,213
183	102	370	655	1,694	5,658
244	73	604	922	2,080	7,676
21	12.	119	152	344	807
39	24	168	231	371	1,213
94	52	249	395	791	2,888
114	63	295	472	948	3,483
179	87	395	661	1,594	5,422
259	72	695	1,026	2,410	8,720
4	2	20	26	15	139
6	5	17	28	18	166
15	8	19	42	21	290
19	10	24	53	27	369
26	13	16	55	57	764
39	19	30	88	89	1,045
100	58	555	713	555	2,261
130	46	459	635	731	2,619
213	182	555	950	942	4,178
262	224	683	1,169	1,159	5,139
368	130	733	1,231	1,571	6,483
369	73	994	1,436	1,855	7,766
1	13	2	16	22	46
1	19	24	44	59	123
30	70	56	156	451	979
26	59	48	133	383	832
88	76	89	253	902	2,038
229	66	194	489	2,126	5,174
461	256	896	1,613	1,755	5,381
598	321	1,016	1,935	2,414	7,670
775	585	1,246	2,606	4,116	14,308
995	730	1,555	3,280	5,139	18,050
1,355	558	1,814	3,727	7,523	24,807
1,774	433	2,986	5,194	11,155	37,313

Table A.9. *Exports of transport equipment at constant prices by destination*

Exports to:		Industrial countries				
		United Kingdom	E E C Six	Other W. Europe	North America	Total[a]
Exports from:						
United Kingdom	b 1950	—	133	135	146	415
	1955	—	152	130	130	417
	1963	—	382	175	268	837
	c 1963	—	412	189	290	904
	1967	—	442	211	475	1,154
	1971	—	667	222	606	1,514
France	b 1950	9	44	27	3	83
	1955	7	53	17	7	86
	1963	31	325	81	47	485
	c 1963	36	370	92	54	553
	1967	49	467	94	91	703
	1971	149	1,180	140	130	1,602
Germany	b 1950	1	58	45	1	105
	1955	21	182	170	67	441
	1963	49	658	383	386	1,484
	c 1963	56	756	441	444	1,706
	1967	95	987	417	723	2,239
	1971	290	1,865	560	1,485	4,223
Other Western Europe	b 1950	7	59	108	6	180
	1955	22	139	114	23	298
	1963	113	729	234	104	1,187
	c 1963	125	794	264	114	1,305
	1967	163	1,065	323	242	1,800
	1971	416	1,926	417	517	3,284
Canada	b 1950	1	1	1	7	10
	1955	2	7	2	41	52
	1963	5	19	2	122	149
	c 1963	6	24	2	152	185
	1967	8	18	7	1,796	1,830
	1971	30	26	10	3,862	3,930
United States	b 1950	13	99	31	244	392
	1955	24	126	44	454	657
	1963	46	217	66	557	967
	c 1963	60	287	87	735	1,276
	1967	111	565	154	1,977	2,930
	1971	253	814	187	2,765	4,355
Japan	b 1950	—	2	3	—	5
	1955	—	1	—	—	1
	1963	34	7	—	59	100
	c 1963	30	6	—	51	87
	1967	97	56	227	221	601
	1971	149	161	229	1,922	2,461
TOTAL	b 1950	30	398	350	407	1,191
	1955	75	658	476	723	1,949
	1963	278	2,336	941	1,544	5,209
	c 1963	312	2,650	1,076	1,840	6,017
	1967	522	3,602	1,434	5,526	11,257
	1971	1,287	6,639	1,764	11,287	21,369

[a] Includes Japan.   [b] At 1955 prices.   [c] At 1963 prices.

Oceania, S. Africa	India, Pakistan	Other	Total	Rest of world	World total
		Semi-industrial countries			
387	104	106	597	411	1,423
357	64	37	458	553	1,428
366	*93*	*91*	*550*	*681*	*2,068*
395	101	98	594	735	2,233
368	83	101	552	789	2,494
423	73	124	619	1,097	3,231
5	1	11	17	198	298
9	5	33	47	225	358
24	*11*	*67*	*101*	*342*	*928*
27	12	76	115	389	1,058
79	13	60	152	482	1,338
66	9	96	170	778	2,551
7	2	25	34	49	188
32	43	91	166	334	941
77	*40*	*81*	*198*	*582*	*2,264*
88	47	93	228	670	2,604
112	52	145	308	821	3,368
169	34	221	424	1,219	5,865
2	2	72	76	101	357
7	13	88	108	217	623
21	*17*	*91*	*129*	*369*	*1,685*
23	19	94	136	407	1,848
59	20	99	178	679	2,657
78	9	135	222	885	4,391
34	18	16	68	20	98
37	14	2	53	13	118
28	*3*	*24*	*55*	*18*	*222*
34	4	29	68	22	275
60	6	28	94	96	2,020
50	8	40	98	146	4,174
43	27	340	410	489	1,291
99	53	302	454	540	1,651
104	*85*	*277*	*466*	*531*	*1,964*
137	112	365	615	701	2,592
310	75	529	914	860	4,703
411	102	641	1,154	1,120	6,629
—	1	—	1	46	52
—	19	11	30	93	124
33	*52*	*33*	*118*	*545*	*763*
29	45	29	103	474	664
111	24	77	212	1,024	1,838
282	40	49	371	2,183	5,016
478	156	574	1,208	1,308	3,707
542	211	561	1,314	1,979	5,242
653	*302*	*663*	*1,618*	*3,068*	*9,894*
734	340	785	1,859	3,398	11,274
1,098	273	1,038	2,409	4,752	18,418
1,479	274	1,306	3,060	7,429	31,858

Table A.10. *Exports of chemicals at constant prices by destination*

Exports to :		Industrial countries				
		United Kingdom	EEC Six	Other W. Europe	North America	Tota
Exports from :						
United Kingdom	*b* 1950	—	41	23	34	9
	1955	—	89	34	43	17
	1963	—	*240*	*86*	*76*	*41*
	c 1963	—	209	75	66	36
	1967	—	266	128	94	52
	1971	—	400	184	123	76
France	*b* 1950	20	34	16	10	8
	1955	31	56	28	20	14
	1963	*53*	*265*	*78*	*57*	*47*
	c 1963	44	220	65	47	39
	1967	62	488	115	75	76
	1971	92	1,006	166	114	1,4
Germany	*b* 1950	16	63	25	14	12
	1955	43	160	81	39	34
	1963	*121*	*550*	*221*	*92*	*1,0*
	c 1963	103	468	187	78	8
	1967	157	977	319	154	1,7
	1971	222	1,691	499	265	2,8
Other Western Europe	*b* 1950	36	118	24	25	2
	1955	58	216	43	61	3
	1963	*128*	*696*	*112*	*118*	*1,1*
	c 1963	112	601	96	100	9
	1967	209	1,203	163	142	1,7
	1971	323	2,686	305	238	3,6
Canada	*b* 1950	10	10	4	69	
	1955	26	26	8	142	2
	1963	*23*	*12*	*2*	*148*	*1*
	c 1963	22	12	2	142	1
	1967	38	26	4	246	3
	1971	57	26	5	368	4
United States	*b* 1950	48	97	28	149	3
	1955	57	169	35	219	5
	1963	*122*	*439*	*72*	*318*	*1,1*
	c 1963	116	417	68	302	1,0
	1967	170	595	71	423	1,4
	1971	222	953	144	619	2,2
Japan	*b* 1950	—	1	1	2	
	1955	3	4	—	7	
	1963	*11*	*30*	*4*	*54*	
	c 1963	7	20	3	36	
	1967	20	54	12	92	1
	1971	48	196	22	275	5
TOTAL	*b* 1950	131	363	120	303	9
	1955	217	720	228	530	1,7
	1963	*457*	*2,233*	*574*	*863*	*4,4*
	c 1963	404	1,947	496	772	3,9
	1967	657	3,609	812	1,226	6,7
	1971	964	6,958	1,325	2,002	11,9

[a] Includes Japan. [b] At 1955 prices. [c] At 1963 prices.

	Semi-industrial countries			Rest of world	World total
Oceania, S. Africa	India, Pakistan	Other	Total		
63	42	41	146	189	433
109	58	31	198	284	652
155	45	54	255	523	1,197
135	40	47	222	455	1,042
182	38	63	283	568	1,373
203	28	103	334	887	1,983
3	5	16	24	89	196
4	7	25	36	180	360
11	9	47	67	370	911
9	8	39	56	307	756
18	13	57	88	530	1,383
25	13	97	135	749	2,305
3	7	22	32	67	223
20	25	61	106	233	681
61	32	156	249	636	1,937
52	27	133	212	540	1,646
83	51	232	365	973	3,049
114	41	370	525	1,360	4,685
7	15	37	59	147	413
22	24	65	111	267	768
44	30	149	223	647	1,982
39	25	125	189	543	1,692
68	46	203	316	860	2,957
91	35	354	480	1,402	5,539
3	6	3	12	20	125
5	1	16	22	20	246
10	3	5	18	18	229
10	3	4	17	17	219
15	7	6	28	23	378
18	24	12	54	36	567
20	28	188	236	301	884
37	23	208	268	317	1,106
99	66	272	436	489	2,045
94	63	258	415	465	1,943
140	185	351	677	654	2,818
193	80	554	827	893	3,993
—	1	2	3	12	19
3	4	5	12	68	94
26	33	15	74	299	472
18	22	10	50	200	316
55	61	21	137	516	831
121	38	74	233	1,164	1,938
99	104	310	513	825	2,293
199	143	408	750	1,375	3,907
407	218	698	1,323	2,981	8,772
356	187	617	1,160	2,527	7,614
561	399	934	1,894	4,124	12,790
765	261	1,563	2,588	6,490	21,009

269

Table A.11. *Exports of textiles and clothing at constant prices by destination*

Exports to :		United Kingdom	EEC Six	Industrial countries Other W. Europe	North America	Total[a]
Exports from :						
United Kingdom	b 1950	—	105	104	179	390
	1955	—	88	56	156	309
	1963	—	129	80	123	348
	c 1963	—	142	87	136	383
	1967	—	124	116	117	378
	1971	—	189	196	212	630
France	b 1950	48	80	43	31	202
	1955	22	100	41	36	199
	1963	33	340	66	52	495
	c 1963	31	327	63	50	475
	1967	27	390	75	61	562
	1971	32	869	97	95	1,115
Germany	b 1950	9	32	19	7	67
	1955	11	56	91	18	176
	1963	33	273	151	40	501
	c 1963	29	240	133	35	441
	1967	36	495	151	55	747
	1971	82	1,176	224	292	1,788
Other Western Europe	b 1950	79	363	62	63	567
	1955	69	380	104	98	651
	1963	151	1,232	204	292	1,889
	c 1963	137	1,154	185	252	1,737
	1967	148	1,585	212	261	2,223
	1971	230	3,176	287	354	4,088
Canada	b 1950	1	1	—	13	15
	1955	1	3	—	9	13
	1963	10	4	1	12	27
	c 1963	10	4	1	13	28
	1967	14	3	1	29	48
	1971	25	8	2	90	126
United States	b 1950	2	23	18	55	100
	1955	2	23	17	108	151
	1963	22	90	26	125	271
	c 1963	21	86	25	120	260
	1967	30	107	37	147	333
	1971	45	127	37	184	420
Japan	b 1950	17	11	8	43	79
	1955	10	17	6	154	187
	1963	8	39	18	279	344
	c 1963	8	42	19	295	364
	1967	18	54	21	458	550
	1971	31	94	21	864	1,010
TOTAL	b 1950	155	614	254	388	1,416
	1955	115	665	316	578	1,685
	1963	255	2,107	546	924	3,875
	c 1963	237	1,994	514	901	3,688
	1967	273	2,759	614	1,128	4,841
	1971	444	5,638	865	2,091	9,177

[a] Includes Japan. [b] At 1955 prices. [c] At 1963 prices.

$ million

Oceania, S. Africa	Semi-industrial countries			Rest of world	World total
	India, Pakistan	Other	Total		
417	47	38	502	494	1,386
280	21	11	313	337	960
130	7	5	142	271	761
143	8	5	156	298	837
106	3	7	116	337	831
116	6	17	139	512	1,281
10	5	23	38	297	537
16	5	13	34	301	534
13	1	6	20	345	861
13	1	6	20	331	826
14	1	13	28	329	919
20	1	20	40	326	1,482
2	1	10	13	24	104
21	6	34	62	115	353
26	5	12	43	221	765
23	5	10	38	195	673
32	6	45	83	313	1,143
66	3	167	236	544	2,569
42	28	36	106	217	890
73	20	35	128	292	1,071
68	8	30	105	436	2,430
61	7	25	93	388	2,218
62	4	50	115	571	2,910
73	5	91	169	859	5,116
4	—	1	4	3	22
1	—	1	2	4	19
5	—	1	6	10	43
5	—	1	7	10	45
6	1	1	8	9	65
6	1	2	9	16	151
26	5	38	69	292	461
48	1	33	82	306	539
62	9	35	107	228	605
60	9	34	102	219	581
72	5	45	121	250	705
56	6	75	137	241	798
29	51	2	83	175	337
44	26	10	80	426	693
111	7	6	124	594	1,063
118	8	7	132	630	1,126
168	8	8	184	920	1,654
228	10	30	268	1,512	2,790
529	136	150	815	1,507	3,738
484	79	137	700	1,783	4,168
414	38	96	548	2,105	6,528
421	37	89	547	2,071	6,306
460	28	168	656	2,730	8,227
565	32	402	999	4,011	14,188

Table A.12. *Exports of other manufactures at constant prices by destination*

Exports to:			United Kingdom	EEC Six	Other W. Europe	North America	Total
					Industrial countries		
Exports from:							
United Kingdom	b	1950	—	135	66	165	367
		1955	—	203	78	179	463
		1963	—	392	117	330	859
	c	1963	—	483	146	406	1,059
		1967	—	562	210	563	1,383
		1971	—	854	319	749	2,009
France	b	1950	37	61	30	25	153
		1955	38	103	38	54	234
		1963	55	360	100	116	635
	c	1963	58	390	107	123	683
		1967	67	571	122	179	950
		1971	98	1,205	189	246	1,760
Germany	b	1950	7	136	54	40	237
		1955	55	303	177	169	710
		1963	92	753	348	211	1,416
	c	1963	107	882	408	246	1,660
		1967	135	1,373	517	359	2,421
		1971	195	2,331	715	454	3,758
Other Western Europe	b	1950	75	274	48	182	580
		1955	150	499	99	332	1,085
		1963	248	1,420	225	475	2,393
	c	1963	269	1,547	241	520	2,605
		1967	375	2,409	352	805	3,993
		1971	527	4,377	563	1,096	6,650
Canada	b	1950	10	4	2	583	599
		1955	50	11	2	733	797
		1963	115	43	4	784	949
	c	1963	117	44	5	800	969
		1967	120	32	7	965	1,130
		1971	120	42	11	1,164	1,348
United States	b	1950	26	64	32	318	449
		1955	39	89	43	511	699
		1963	127	302	97	548	1,137
	c	1963	148	354	113	647	1,336
		1967	264	537	147	960	2,083
		1971	290	755	171	1,119	2,659
Japan	b	1950	—	4	1	59	64
		1955	7	10	6	174	197
		1963	33	83	40	586	742
	c	1963	35	88	42	625	790
		1967	60	177	73	1,112	1,422
		1971	89	417	108	1,777	2,391
TOTAL	b	1950	156	678	233	1,372	2,449
		1955	341	1,218	444	2,152	4,186
		1963	670	3,352	932	3,049	8,133
	c	1963	735	3,788	1,062	3,367	9,102
		1967	1,021	5,662	1,427	4,943	13,382
		1971	1,320	9,980	2,075	6,605	20,575

[a] Includes Japan.   [b] At 1955 prices.   [c] At 1963 prices.

	Semi-industrial countries			Rest of	World total
Oceania, S. Africa	India, Pakistan	Other	Total		

276	77	63	416	517	1,300
294	63	35	392	538	1,393
214	42	78	334	492	1,685
268	53	96	417	625	2,101
263	38	106	407	702	2,492
328	45	195	567	1,333	3,909
10	3	41	54	391	598
7	5	33	45	383	662
12	4	38	54	413	1,102
13	5	44	62	459	1,204
24	8	32	64	536	1,550
26	7	65	98	717	2,575
15	7	58	80	136	453
42	20	71	133	334	1,177
50	19	71	139	500	2,057
58	22	83	163	586	2,410
79	21	151	251	829	3,501
107	20	208	335	1,114	5,207
49	18	81	148	438	1,166
64	31	109	204	485	1,774
67	27	110	204	641	3,238
74	31	124	229	711	3,545
98	37	185	319	1,129	5,441
130	37	331	498	1,618	8,766
12	2	11	25	29	653
29	3	19	51	31	879
33	6	24	63	38	1,050
34	6	25	65	39	1,073
38	6	26	70	65	1,265
43	13	41	97	90	1,534
29	16	227	272	437	1,158
50	14	173	237	551	1,487
100	34	180	313	512	1,963
117	41	212	370	605	2,311
164	30	258	452	792	3,328
206	27	351	584	903	4,146
4	4	7	15	65	144
14	9	12	35	154	386
47	19	19	86	360	1,187
50	21	20	91	384	1,265
110	23	40	173	727	2,322
187	20	83	290	1,214	3,895
394	128	486	1,008	2,015	5,472
502	145	454	1,101	2,471	7,758
523	152	519	1,194	2,955	12,282
614	179	604	1,397	3,409	13,909
775	164	797	1,737	4,781	19,900
1,027	169	1,273	2,469	6,988	30,032

diamond exports in 1963 was estimated by reference to import data for major markets and the distribution of exports in 1964. The United States 'special category' exports included in our totals were estimated by reference to the distribution of other exports in the same four-digit SITC heading or, for aircraft parts, to import data for major markets and the distribution of exports of complete aircraft.

Sources of current price data and constant price data for 1950 to 1959 are: Maizels, *Industrial Growth and World Trade*; OECD, *Statistics of Foreign Trade*; United Nations Statistical Office, *Commodity Trade Statistics* and NIESR estimates. The calculation of the price indices used to obtain the other constant price series is described in appendix D. As indicated there, the valuation of 1963 exports at 1955 prices is not reliable owing to deficiencies in the data. It is given (in italics) merely to provide some link between the series at 1955 prices and those at 1963 prices.

Appendix B

COMMODITY CLASSIFICATIONS OF TRADE DATA
by *R. A. Batchelor* and *A. D. Morgan*

The commodity classifications used by Maizels for the years 1950, 1955 and 1959 and by ourselves for the years 1963, 1967 and 1971 were in general as shown in table B.1.

A separate classification based on rates of growth of trade between 1963 and 1971 was also used in our chapter 4. Table B.2 shows the numerical relationship between the two classifications in each of the two years.

Table B.1. *Commodity groups defined in terms of the Standard International Trade Classification*

Heading no.

	1950, 1955, 1959	1963, 1967, 1971 [a]
Metals	68	67; 68 *less* 681
Metal goods	69	69
Machinery	71 *less* 711–04, 711–05; 72 *less* 721–07	71 *less* 711.4, 711.5; 72 *less* 729.4
Transport equipment	711–04, 711–05; 721–07; 73	711.4, 711.5; 729.4; 73
Chemicals		
Intermediate	51; 52; 531, 532, 533–01; 551; 599 *less* 599–02	51 *less* 515; 52; 53 *less* 533.1; 59 *less* 599.2
Finished	Rest of 5	Rest of 5
Textiles and clothing		
Intermediate	651	651
Finished	Rest of 65; 841	Rest of 65; 841
Other manufactures		
Intermediate	611, 613; 621; 631–01, 631–09; 641; 663, 664; 671, 672	611, 613; 621; 631 *less* 631.2; 641; 663, 664, 667; 681
Finished	Rest of 6 and 8	Rest of 6 and 8

[a] Heading numbers in revised SITC.

275

Table B.2. *Cross-classification of manufactures by commodity group and product group, 1963 and 1971*

$ *million*

	Product groups[a]					
	1	2	3	4	5	Total
1963						
Metals	894	—	376	2,357	4,044	7,671
Metal goods	273	—	—	—	2,071	2,344
Machinery	5,309	—	—	6,329	6,412	18,050
Transport equipment	7,097	—	3,396	—	781	11,274
Chemicals						
Intermediate	1,582	341	160	613	2,437	5,133
Finished	43	114	110	1,023	1,191	2,481
Textiles and clothing						
Intermediate	492	—	—	—	833	1,325
Finished	1,201	576	—	—	3,205	4,982
Other manufactures						
Intermediate	181	—	142	628	2,834	3,785
Finished	927	424	673	1,696	4,060	7,780
TOTAL	17,999	1,455	4,857	12,646	27,868	64,825
1971						
Metals	3,398	—	1,276	5,218	8,667	18,559
Metal goods	864	—	—	—	5,049	5,913
Machinery	18,244	—	—	14,852	14,296	47,392
Transport equipment	27,073	—	9,922	—	1,670	38,665
Chemicals						
Intermediate	6,152	970	516	1,398	5,231	14,267
Finished	134	361	321	2,385	2,619	5,820
Textiles and clothing						
Intermediate	2,048	—	—	—	1,026	3,074
Finished	5,156	1,675	—	—	4,007	10,838
Other manufactures						
Intermediate	657	—	607	1,548	5,557	8,369
Finished	4,041	1,134	2,186	3,933	9,958	21,252
TOTAL	67,767	4,140	14,828	29,334	58,080	174,149

[a] Groups 1, 2 and 3 = growth products, group 4 = competitive shift products, group 5 = other products (see also pp. 63–4 and table 4.8).

Appendix C

GDP AND MANUFACTURING OUTPUT AND CONSUMPTION

by *R. A. Batchelor* and *R. L. Major*

In chapter 3 international trade in manufactured goods is related in real terms to output per head, and to production and apparent consumption of manufactures per head, in a number of countries. This appendix explains how the relationships were calculated.

EXCHANGE RATES

So far as trade is concerned, official rates of exchange have normally been used where conversion to United States dollars of figures expressed in other currencies was needed. When national outputs are being compared however, use of official exchange rates is inappropriate. As Maizels put it:

For every country, by far the largest portion of its total output does not enter international trade and is not subject to the same pressures of the world market as are goods which are exported. Consequently, considerable price differences ... emerge between similar goods sold on the home markets of different countries. Such differences must be taken into account if genuine 'volume' comparisons are attempted of the output of different countries, and this can most conveniently be done by the calculation of 'purchasing power parity' rates of exchange. Such rates are, in principle, what the rates of exchange would have to be if the same bundle of commodities produced in different countries were to cost the same in terms of the currency of any one of them.[1]

Maizels therefore calculated rates of exchange, designed to represent an approximation to relative purchasing power in 1955,[2] which he used for calculating United States dollar values at 1955 prices of GDP and manufacturing production in countries other than the United States. The method is described by him as follows:

It was assumed that the official mean rate in 1938 correctly reflected the relative purchasing power of the different currencies; the 1955 rate was then estimated by multiplying the 1938 rate by the ratio of the change in United States prices between the two years to the corresponding price change in the country in question. Wherever possible, the (implicit) price change used for

[1] Maizels, *Industrial Growth and World Trade*, p. 543.
[2] Ibid, p. 546.

277

estimating the real gross domestic product was taken as the indicator of changes in internal purchasing power. Where such indices were not available wholesale or retail prices were used, as seemed most appropriate.[1]

We have taken over the estimates which Maizels made of United States dollar values of other countries' output in 1955,[2] and thus implicitly his estimates of purchasing power parities in that year. It should, however, be re-emphasised that, as he wrote: 'The results of such a calculation cannot pretend to provide more than "orders of magnitude", and they are subject also to the inherent limitations included in comparisons between countries at different levels of economic development.'[3] A similar process of working back from the parities for more recent years which have been calculated in detailed studies of certain countries, for example by Braithwaite for 1960 and by Kravis and others for 1970 and 1973, would give very different rates for 1955 in some cases.[4] Nevertheless the rates which Maizels used were, as he showed, reasonably consistent for the most part with estimates of purchasing power parities made at about the same time by the United Nations and OECD. Not surprisingly, the most important disparities arise in the cases of Japan, where rapid changes in the composition of output aggravated the weighting problems inherent in this type of exercise, and some Latin American countries (Argentina, Brazil, Colombia and Peru), where exceptionally rapid price inflation has been endemic. The figures for these countries should be regarded as correspondingly suspect.

APPARENT CONSUMPTION OF MANUFACTURES

Output

The calculation of dollar values of GDP and manufacturing output in 1955 is described above. Similar estimates at 1955 prices for other years were derived by extrapolation based on officially published constant price data. But a number of adjustments were necessary before the figures for output of manufactures could be combined with the trade data to give the estimates of consumption of manufactures in total and per head which are shown in tables C.1 and C.2 respectively and used in chapter 3. The figures for trade in manufactures exclude products of the

---

[1] Ibid, p. 544.
[2] Ibid, pp. 531–2 and 535–6.
[3] Ibid, p. 544.
[4] S. N. Braithwaite, 'Real income levels in Latin America', *Review of Income and Wealth*, series 14, June 1968; I. B. Kravis, Z. Kenessey, A. Heston and R. Summers, *A System of International Comparisons of Gross Product and Purchasing Power*, Baltimore, Johns Hopkins University Press, 1975; I. B. Kravis, A. Heston and R. Summers, *International Comparisons of Real Product and Purchasing Power*, Baltimore, Johns Hopkins University Press, 1978.

Table C.1. *Total consumption of non-food manufactures, 1950–71*

$ billion, 1955 prices

	Original basis				Revised basis		
	1950	1955	1959	1963	1963	1967	1971
INDUSTRIAL COUNTRIES							
United Kingdom	20.90	27.40	28.90	32.70	37.00	43.80	46.60
Austria	..	2.40	..	4.46	4.82	5.65	7.92
Belgium-Luxembourg	4.64	6.01	6.37	8.21	7.78	9.54	12.62
Denmark	..	2.01	..	3.45	3.98	5.11	6.20
Finland	..	1.28	..	1.79	2.27	2.78	3.87
France	8.18	13.80	18.90	25.60	27.30	35.30	45.40
Germany	11.80	21.90	26.70	37.50	45.90	51.90	73.80
Italy	6.27	10.60	13.60	20.70	21.90	26.00	30.80
Netherlands	3.01	4.26	4.76	6.48	7.05	8.82	11.62
Norway	1.31	1.78	1.91	2.41	2.67	3.53	4.15
Sweden	4.83	5.71	6.41	8.11	9.20	12.08	13.94
Canada	11.60	14.10	16.00	17.80	16.30	21.90	25.80
United States	129.30	167.40	184.00	218.20	236.40	310.00	340.90
Japan	1.92	4.89	9.57	17.73	28.45	45.47	65.77
SEMI-INDUSTRIAL COUNTRIES							
Greece	..	1.09	..	1.92	1.90	2.57	4.32
Ireland	..	0.59	..	0.89	0.86	1.02	1.25
Portugal	..	1.47	..	2.65	2.53	3.69	5.54
Spain	..	4.55	..	10.17	10.37	14.67	19.17
Yugoslavia	1.85	2.67	4.29	5.61	9.48	12.19	16.15
Australia	5.10	6.35	7.98	9.18	9.66	11.87	13.82
New Zealand	1.20	1.66	1.91	2.39	2.25	3.03	3.73
South Africa	2.20	3.25	3.30	4.35	4.81	7.19	9.30
India	2.62	3.95	4.82	6.12	6.47	7.22	8.19
Pakistan	0.44	0.80	1.04	1.53	2.02	2.39	2.76
Argentina	4.16	4.45	4.28	4.48	5.50	7.47	10.30
Brazil	3.90	4.80	7.50	9.99	9.14	10.23	16.56
Chile	0.34	0.55	0.79	0.93	0.83	0.86	1.27
Colombia	0.70	0.98	0.93	1.03	1.10	1.24	1.77
Mexico	2.03	2.75	3.61	4.74	3.96	6.47	8.52
Israel	..	0.50	0.63	1.07	1.26	1.47	2.73
Turkey	0.75	1.23	1.43	1.58	1.48	2.41	3.74
OTHER SELECTED COUNTRIES							
Morocco	..	0.46	..	0.65	..	0.50	0.59
Nigeria	..	..	..	0.59	0.50	0.47	1.01
Peru	..	0.43	..	0.68	0.66	..	0.81
Philippines	..	0.67	..	1.08	0.89	1.44	1.70
Venezuela	..	1.29	..	2.01	1.70	2.34	3.60

Table C.2. *Consumption per head of non-food manufactures, 1950–71*

$, *1955 prices*

	Original basis				Revised basis		
	1950	1955	1959	1963	1963	1967	1971
INDUSTRIAL COUNTRIES							
United Kingdom	415	535	555	610	685	800	840
Austria	..	345	..	620	670	770	1060
Belgium-Luxembourg	520	655	675	855	810	960	1260
Denmark	..	470	..	735	850	1055	1250
Finland	..	300	..	395	500	605	840
France	195	320	420	535	570	710	885
Germany	250	435	505	675	830	865	1205
Italy	135	220	275	410	430	495	570
Netherlands	300	395	420	540	590	700	880
Norway	395	525	540	655	730	930	1065
Sweden	690	780	860	1065	1210	1535	1720
Canada	850	895	915	940	860	1075	1195
United States	855	1015	1035	1150	1250	1560	1645
Japan	25	55	105	185	295	450	625
SEMI-INDUSTRIAL COUNTRIES							
Greece	..	135	..	225	225	295	490
Ireland	..	200	..	310	300	350	420
Portugal	..	165	..	295	280	395	595
Spain	..	155	..	325	330	450	560
Yugoslavia	115	150	235	295	495	615	785
Australia	620	690	795	840	885	1005	1085
New Zealand	630	790	820	940	885	1115	1310
South Africa	175	235	210	255	280	345	405
India	7	10	10	15	15	15	15
Pakistan	6	10	10	20	20	20	20
Argentina	240	235	210	205	255	330	430
Brazil	75	80	110	130	120	120	175
Chile	55	80	105	115	100	95	135
Colombia	60	75	60	60	65	65	85
Mexico	80	95	105	120	100	145	160
Israel	..	295	305	450	530	550	910
Turkey	35	50	55	55	50	75	105
OTHER SELECTED COUNTRIES							
Morocco	..	45	..	50	..	35	40
Nigeria	..	..	..	15	10	9	20
Peru	..	45	..	60	60	..	60
Philippines	..	30	..	35	30	45	45
Venezuela	..	225	..	245	210	250	335

food, beverage and tobacco industries, although their processing is defined as manufacturing for purposes of the output statistics. The latter have, therefore, been adjusted to make them comparable with the trade statistics in this respect.[1]

A more important difficulty arises from the fact that, whereas the production figures are on a 'net' (value-added) basis, the trade figures are 'gross', that is to say they include the cost of materials and services used in their production and transport. Attempts were therefore made, both here and by Maizels, to inflate the production data by the ratio to net output of gross output (excluding taxation and items sold by one part of the manufacturing sector as inputs to another part), both valued at factor cost. Unfortunately, however, the data on intra-manufacturing purchases and sales which are needed for computing this ratio are available only for a limited number of countries in individual years.

Maizels based his calculations partly on the ratios which he had been able to compute for individual countries (mainly relating to the early 1950s) and partly on a 'rule of thumb'. He ascribed ratios of 1.75 to industrial countries, 2.0 to semi-industrial countries and 2.25 to non-industrial countries (other than Pakistan, for which a ratio computed for India provided a guide). The 1.75 ratio was applied only to Western European industrial countries, for which the average of available ratios was 1.8. The few ratios available for semi-industrial and non-industrial countries were for the most part higher and Maizels reasoned that less developed countries tended to have relatively low wage costs per unit of output, and to produce manufactures embodying less fabrication per unit of materials, than countries which were more advanced. These are both factors which would tend to reduce value added and hence to result in a high gross–net ratio. Data available to us for later years, mainly around 1960, suggested, however, that the relationship between the gross–net ratio and the level of industrialisation was not strong; indeed it is not even clear that the correlation is negative.

In the belief that other factors such as size, natural resource-endowments and the ratio of investment to GDP might also be important, we tried to capture the underlying multivariate relationship by computing a regression of available gross–net output ratios on the share of manufactures in GDP, population size, population density and the ratio of investment to GDP in the same countries. The result was as follows, with all dependent variables based on data for 1963, where G is

---

[1] For this purpose we used data published in United Nations Statistical Office, *Patterns of Industrial Growth, 1938–1958*, New York, 1960, *Yearbook of National Accounts Statistics* and *The Growth of World Industry*. A similar adjustment should in theory have been made in respect of oil refining and the processing of solid fuels. This, however, was not done because of the practical difficulties involved and because the amounts included are small in relation to the margin of error in the adjustment from gross to net figures (see below).

the gross–net ratio, Ym/Y the percentage share of manufacturing in GDP, N the population, N/A its density (used as a proxy for natural resource-endowment) and I/Y the investment ratio:

$$G = 0.7743 - 0.0229(Ym/Y) + 0.0030N + 0.001(N/A)$$
$$(1.10) \qquad\qquad (1.07) \qquad (0.81)$$
$$+ 0.0752(I/Y) \qquad (\bar{R}^2 = 0.35)$$
$$(2.38)$$

The regression as a whole explained only one third of the observed variation and attributed most of that to the influence of investment, presumably in raising productivity, with the coefficient on the manufacturing ratio significant only at the 85 per cent level. We concluded that the investment ratio provided a better basis for estimation than the degree of industrialisation, and used the equation

$$G = 1.0973 + 0.045 (I/Y)$$
$$(2.10)$$

to estimate gross–net ratios where these could not be calculated directly. We also used it for Austria, where direct calculation (from input–output data described as 'experimental') gave a ratio of 2.92. This seemed too high in itself and would have yielded even more implausible estimates of consumption.

The ratios which we have used are shown in table C.3, together with those which Maizels calculated for certain periods. Some disagreement may be considered inevitable for purely statistical reasons as the quality of national input–output tables improves and international standards of classification and presentation are adopted. Moreover, some of the differences may be presumed to represent genuine changes in ratios during the 1950s. The most striking case is that of Japan, where the ratio rose by 1.35, but the increase for Yugoslavia was almost as big at 1.17 and it was over 0.25 for Belgium and France. The apparent instability of the ratios suggests that, even where our estimates of the gross value of manufacturing production are based on direct information, very wide margins of error open up as the years to which this information relates recede into the past. The calculations into which such estimates enter must, therefore, be regarded as unreliable. This applies to consumption of manufactures in total and per head, and also to supplies of manufactures and the share of imports in supplies.

Imports

Since the estimates of manufacturing production are on a gross basis, they include in principle the value of all materials and components used, both home-produced and imported. To avoid double counting,

Table C.3. *Gross–net output ratios in manufacturing*

	Computed by Maizels		Revised basis[a]	
	Value	Date	Value	Date
INDUSTRIAL COUNTRIES				
United Kingdom	1.58	*1954*	1.63	*1963*
Austria	..	n.a.	2.17*	n.a.
Belgium-Luxembourg	1.84	*1953*	2.14	*1954*
Denmark	..	n.a.	1.99*	n.a.
Finland	..	n.a.	2.11*	n.a.
France	1.32	*1951*	1.59	*1959*
Germany	..	n.a.	1.76	*1959*
Italy	1.90	*1950*	1.79	*1959*
Netherlands	2.27	*1950*	2.12	*1959*
Norway	1.93	*1954*	1.87	*1959*
Sweden	..	n.a.	2.15*	n.a.
Canada	2.40	*1949*	2.05*	n.a.
United States	1.72	*1947*	1.87	*1963*
Japan	1.73	*1951*	3.08	*1960*
SEMI-INDUSTRIAL COUNTRIES				
Greece	..	n.a.	1.98*	n.a.
Ireland	..	n.a.	1.93*	n.a.
Portugal	..	n.a.	1.92	*1959*
Spain	..	n.a.	2.04*	n.a.
Yugoslavia	1.79	*1955*	2.96	*1962*
Australia	2.12	*1955–6*	2.02	*1963*
New Zealand	{ 2.42 { 2.32	*1952–3* } *1954–5* }	2.30	*1959–60*
South Africa	..	n.a.	1.97*	n.a.
India	1.66	*1953–4*	1.82*	n.a.
Pakistan	..	n.a.	3.12	*1954*
Turkey	..	n.a.	1.75*	n.a.
Argentina	2.02	*1950*	1.92*	n.a.
Brazil	..	n.a.	1.89*	n.a.
Chile	..	n.a.	1.87*	n.a.
Colombia	1.79	*1953*	1.84*	n.a.
Mexico	1.86	*1950*	1.74*	n.a.
OTHER SELECTED COUNTRIES				
Morocco	..	n.a.	1.63*	n.a.
Nigeria	..	n.a.	1.24	*1959–60*
Peru	2.02	*1955*	1.94*	n.a.
Philippines	..	n.a.	1.87*	n.a.
Venezuela	..	n.a.	1.84*	n.a.

[a] All values marked * computed from equation on p. 282; other revised values from input–output data.

therefore, only imports of *finished* manufactures can be added to the gross value of production to arrive at total supplies.

Maizels derived his 'import' figures from export data. Thus, for all importing countries an addition in respect of freight and insurance was necessary to make the values comparable with gross production. For this purpose he used data published in the I M F *Balance of Payments Yearbook* on the freight and insurance element in the c.i.f. values of the total imports of certain countries, assuming that this element would be the same proportion for imports of manufactures as for total imports. On our basis such adjustments were necessary only where the import data used were not already on a c.i.f. basis. The percentages which we added on this account were: United States, 8 per cent; Canada, 9 per cent; South Africa, 10 per cent; Australia, 12 per cent; Philippines $8\frac{1}{4}$ per cent in 1963 and $10\frac{1}{2}$ per cent in 1967. They are slightly lower than Maizels' percentages, partly because there are grounds for believing that freight and insurance costs are on the whole lower in relation to c.i.f. values for finished manufactures than for imports in total.

The deflator which we used for converting current price import data to 1955 prices were calculated from our current and 1955 price data for total exports of manufactures to the country in question from the eleven major exporting countries. Shares of finished manufactures in total imports of manufactures were also calculated from the eleven-country export data.

Exports

While most countries value their exports f.o.b., the United States uses an f.a.s. (free alongside ship) basis for goods exported by vessel and Canada the value at the inland point of consignment for export. To maintain comparability with the production estimates, which generally relate to values 'ex works', a deduction must be made from f.o.b. or f.a.s. values of exports to allow for transport, merchanting and other costs incurred between factory and port.

On the basis of official census data for the United States and the United Kingdom, Maizels estimated that appropriate deductions in the case of these two countries lay between 8 and 9 per cent and between 7 and 8 per cent respectively. He therefore used a figure of 8 per cent for other industrial countries (apart from Canada, for which he made no deduction) and of 5 per cent for India, on the basis of a comparison made in 1957 of unit values of output and exports of cotton and piece goods. We have taken 8 per cent in all cases, since Maizels' deductions differed so little for the industrial countries, more recent data for the United States point to a rather smaller deduction for that country than before and textiles now constitute a substantially smaller proportion of Indian exports.

POPULATION

The population series used to produce our estimates per head for GDP and for output and consumption of manufactures are derived from official publications. Some of the series have been revised significantly since Maizels was writing. For the calculation on the 'original basis' of consumption of manufactures per head in 1963, adjustments have been made to give figures comparable with his in table 3.2. and, for India and Pakistan (the countries mainly affected), in table C.2.

Appendix D

EXPORT UNIT VALUES

by *A. D. Morgan*

In *Industrial Growth and World Trade*, Maizels used specially computed unit value indices covering selected years in the period 1899–1959. The change in unit values for successive pairs of years was calculated using the values of the later years as weights and the resulting indices were chained to give a continuing series. Covering a much shorter period, and with more comprehensive data available, we have used conventional Paasche (current-weighted) indices, derived where possible from official export unit value indices and adjusted to a dollar basis. For a number of countries, however, no current-weighted index existed and new indices were computed from export or wholesale price indices using current trade values as weights. Export and wholesale price series were also used to supplement official unit value indices in certain commodity groups and, where important commodities were not covered by the official index, the movement of unit values was estimated from the trade returns. Although the index numbers for some commodity groups in some countries look implausible, we believe that for most countries the index for all manufactures is reasonably reliable. However, it was not possible to calculate comprehensive indices using current weights for two countries, Italy and the Netherlands, which published export unit value indices calculated according to Fisher's ideal formula for all or part of the period covered. In these cases it is possible that the index numbers used in the text, especially in 1971, are biased upwards in comparison with those used for other countries. United Kingdom indices may also be biased upwards (see below). For these three countries, therefore, there may be a corresponding downward bias in the value of trade estimated at constant prices.

The index numbers shown in this appendix (table D.1) and used in chapter 4 were calculated with 1963 as a reference year; they were linked to Maizels' indices at 1959 and the reference year shifted to 1955 for the calculations in chapters 2 and 3. Indices for 1959 (both those estimated by Maizels based on 1955 and the backward link based on 1963) are less reliable than those for subsequent years.

A comparison of our calculated index numbers with those published by the United Nations shows considerable divergences in absolute values and also in the ranking of countries in terms of the rate of increase in export unit values, as may be seen from table D.2. The differences in the two series are largely due to the use of base-weighted (or Fisher's ideal) indices for certain countries by the United Nations and to differences in coverage. In a period when trade is expanding rapidly and its commodity structure is changing, base-weighted and Fisher indices will generally run higher than current-weighted indices, even though the price series used for individual commodities are identical. Thus the United Nations overstates the rise in British, Canadian, Swedish and Swiss prices by quoting base-weighted indices and in American and Japanese prices by quoting Fisher's ideal indices. (Japanese price and unit value indices are particularly susceptible to changes in weights.) Differences in coverage account for the discrepancies between the two series for Belgium-Luxembourg and for Italy.

The sources and methods used in computing the NIESR indices were as follows:

United States: derived from wholesale price indices, published by the Department of Labor in *Wholesale Prices and Price Indexes.* Published data were matched to trade figures at the three-digit and four-digit levels of the SITC.

United Kingdom: derived from official average value indices published by the Central Statistical Office in the *Annual Abstract of Statistics.* Information from the wholesale price index was used to supplement the unit value indices for certain commodity groups. The old average value index (1961 = 100) was nominally current-weighted, but in fact parts of it were base-weighted, imparting an upward bias to the average value index. Incomplete coverage, especially of new products, had the same effect. The new average value index (1970 = 100) is more comprehensive and is current-weighted throughout.

Japan: derived from official export price indices published by the Bank of Japan in *Export and Import Price Indexes.* Published data were matched to trade figures at the three- and four-digit levels of the SITC.

France: derived from official indices of export unit values (current-weighted) and volume and value data, published by the Institut National de la Statistique et des Études Économiques in *Annuaire Statistique de la France* and *Bulletin Mensuel de Statistique,* and regrouped. Indices for ships and aircraft were derived from figures on the volume and value of trade.

Germany: derived from official export unit value indices (current-weighted) and from volume and value data published by the Statistisches Bundesamt in *Aussenhandel,* Fachserie G, Reihe 1 and 5, and *Statistisches Jahrbuch für die Bundesrepublik Deutschland.* The published series were regrouped.

Table D.1. *Export unit values, 1967 and 1971*

	United States	United Kingdom	Japan	France
1967				
Metals				
Intermediate	109	114	103	102
Finished	109	117	100	112
Machinery	109	112	98	125
Transport equipment	108	106	99	110
Chemicals				
Intermediate	100	100	79	85
Finished	98	102	96	100
Textiles				
Intermediate	94	99	92	94
Finished	99	109	95	110
Other manufactures				
Intermediate	108	112	107	109
Finished	107	108	99	113
TOTAL MANUFACTURES	107	109	97	108
1971				
Metals				
Intermediate	131	130	119	121
Finished	130	119	122	121
Machinery	130	124	97	148
Transport equipment	130	121	111	126
Chemicals				
Intermediate	95	108	73	76
Finished	99	110	110	104
Textiles				
Intermediate	94	99	80	87
Finished	105	107	94	114
Other manufactures				
Intermediate	121	118	107	109
Finished	115	117	107	124
TOTAL MANUFACTURES	122	119	103	119

[a] In terms of US dollars.

Indices, 1963 = 100[a]

rmany	Italy	Belgium-Luxembourg	Nether-lands	Canada	Sweden	Switzer-land	Total
104	102	113	116	119	105	108	108
101	109	101	114	107	107	113	107
111	99	115	107	106	112	115	109
104	107	107	93	100	100	111	105
83	93	100	97	97	90	94	91
109	109	104	100	100	100	121	103
86	100	95	92	96	100	87	93
97	101	103	102	103	105	105	101
99	92	119	101	107	104	106	107
107	106	106	122	111	108	109	107
103	102	109	105	106	105	108	105
130	120	134	129	141	123	118	127
129	100	128	126	136	122	126	123
147	112	133	111	125	126	138	127
123	131	119	114	114	120	138	121
91	93	99	94	102	82	98	91
121	131	113	103	107	100	119	110
70	84	90	88	96	97	74	82
103	107	100	107	119	103	109	104
110	97	122	118	122	112	109	116
119	117	121	136	137	112	134	119
122	112	119	111	121	117	121	117

Table D.2. *A comparison with United Nations export unit value indices for 1971*

	UN index		NIESR index	
	Value (1963 = 100)	Rank of country	Value (1963 = 100)	Rank of country
United States	127 ⎫	(7), (8)	122	(10), (11)
United Kingdom	127 ⎭		119	(5), (6), (7)
Japan	116	(3)	103	(1)
France	120	(5)	119	(5), (6), (7)
Germany	125	(6)	122	(10), (11)
Italy	117	(4)	112	(3)
Belgium-Luxembourg	114	(2)	119	(5), (6), (7)
Netherlands	113	(1)	111	(2)
Canada	130	(9)	121	(8), (9)
Sweden	131	(10)	117	(4)
Switzerland	138	(11)	121	(8), (9)

Italy: derived from official export unit value, volume and value indices published by the Istituto Centrale di Statistica in *Statistica Annuale del Commercio con l'Estero.* The unit value indices are calculated according to Fisher's ideal formula from 1966 onwards, but are current-weighted prior to that year. Information from the wholesale price index was used to supplement unit value indices for certain commodity groups.

Belgium-Luxembourg: derived from current-weighted unit value indices calculated by the National Bank of Belgium and published in their *Bulletin de la Banque Nationale de Belgique* (the Bank computes its indices from information supplied by the Institut National de Statistique, though their results differ). The published series were regrouped to conform to the commodity classification used in the present study, which involved some estimation of unit value changes in certain groups. Estimates for diamonds, which are not covered in the Bank's index, were included.

Netherlands: derived for all manufactures from the official Dutch export unit value index for 'manufactured goods', calculated according to Fisher's ideal formula and published by the Central Bureau of Statistics in the *Statistical Yearbook of the Netherlands,* adjusted to exclude food manufactures and petroleum; for commodity groups, estimated from detailed export price indices published by the Central Bureau of Statistics in *Maandstatistiek van de Binnenlandse Handel.*

Canada: derived from Statistics Canada's 'Industry selling price indexes' published in the *Bank of Canada Review* (various issues). Published data were matched to trade figures at the three-digit and four-digit levels of the SITC.

Sweden: derived from official indices published by the Central Bureau of Statistics in *Statistiska Meddelanden,* series H (both the base-weighted export unit value index, usually taken as 'the' Swedish index, and a current-weighted index are published in this source). Information from the producer price index was used to supplement unit value indices for certain commodity groups.

Switzerland: derived from base-weighted volume indices and data on values published by the Département Fédéral de l'Économie Publique in *La Vie Économique;* the resulting indices were regrouped.

Appendix E

MULTINATIONAL ENTERPRISES: STATISTICS AND SOURCES

by *A. D. Morgan*

CLASSIFICATION PROBLEMS

Firms are generally classified as being 'enterprises with foreign ownership' by reference to the proportion of assets owned abroad, but different sources adopt different criteria ranging from as little as 1 per cent of foreign ownership of assets to 50 per cent or over. It is true that most foreign direct investment in manufacturing and almost all investment undertaken in recent years is in enterprises where the foreign investor has a majority interest (frequently 100 per cent). Nonetheless, there are sizeable differences between the value of sales, for example, by all overseas affiliates and by majority owned affiliates only in respect of most investing and host countries. In the case of United States investment abroad, the value of sales was 15.5 per cent greater in 1966 and 18.9 per cent greater in 1970 if transactions by affiliates in which United States investors had a minority interest were included. Where possible data have been adjusted to exclude enterprises with minority foreign ownership, but this is by no means always practicable.

A related problem is that some host countries exclude indirect foreign investment, that is, investment by a foreign owned or controlled subsidiary in another enterprise (sub-subsidiary) when collecting data on foreign owned enterprises, thus understating the extent of foreign influence. For example, much of the data available for Germany refers only to enterprises where the foreign interest is direct, although by 1970 over 13 per cent of foreign owned nominal capital was held indirectly.

So far as manufacturing is concerned there is a further classification problem because of differences in the definition of 'industry' or 'manufacturing'. Ideally, the figures used in chapter 4 should refer only to manufacturing industries producing goods classified in trade statistics under SITC 5–8. In practice much of the available information covers a wider range of industries, including food manufacturing and/or oil refining. Our figures have been adjusted to exclude these two activities, since their inclusion would seriously falsify the results, but industries producing goods not classified in SITC 5–8 still remain in the statistics.

The geographical classification of data also leaves a good deal to be

292

desired. In particular, American investments via Swiss holding companies may be classified as Swiss rather than American owned by host countries. Similar problems arise in relation to investments made through Canada, the United Kingdom, and tax-havens such as Panama.

Finally, there are wide differences from one country to another, in methods of valuation, in timing and in the exchange rates used, which seriously impair the comparability of estimates between countries. Thus the statistics used in chapter 4 to illustrate the activities of foreign owned enterprises can provide only very crude indicators of their size and importance. Minor differences in, for example, rates of asset growth between countries may be solely due to differences in definition. Absolute figures from different sources are not comparable at all.

Additional statistics on trade in manufactures by foreign owned firms on various definitions are given in tables E.1–E.3.

SOURCES AND COVERAGE OF DATA IN TABLES 4.14 AND 4.15

United States

Department of Commerce, *Survey of Current Business*, September 1965, October 1969 and September 1973. Data are derived from sample surveys, grossed up by reference to the 1957 benchmark survey in respect of United States investment overseas and the 1959 benchmark survey in respect of overseas investment in the United States. The former covers investments of $2 million or more where the United States share in assets exceeds 10 per cent if directly held, or a larger proportion if indirectly held. The latter covers in principle all firms where 25 per cent or more of the voting stock or 'an equivalent interest' is foreign owned. Book values include parent companies' net equity and outstanding loans to affiliates.

United Kingdom

Board of Trade Journal, 7 August 1964, 26 January 1968 and 23 September 1970; *Trade and Industry*, 15 November 1973. Data in this source are grossed up from a survey of companies' direct investment abroad and those companies in which there was a direct investment from overseas. Direct investment is defined as investment by companies in branches, subsidiaries and affiliates, and includes minority holdings. Book values include parent companies' share of the book value of fixed assets and net current assets less long-term liabilities other than those to the parent company, except in respect of investments in associates, which include only the book value of the investment as shown in the investing company's accounts. Figures for 1963 and 1967 have been

Table E.1. *Exports of manufactures by American owned[a] firms and all firms,* 1963–71

$million

	Machinery	Transport equipment	Chemicals	Other[b]	Total[b]
1963 EXPORTS FROM:					
Canada					
By US firms (A)	181	121	160	1,214	1,676
Total	369	275	219	2,849	3,712
United Kingdom[c]	2,911	2,233	1,042	3,920	10,106
EEC Six[c]	7,444	4,995	3,526	13,661	29,626
Total Europe[d]					
By US firms (A)	932	1,093	465	658	3,148
Total	12,578	8,097	5,482	23,464	49,621
Japan[c]	832	664	316	3,207	5,019
1967 EXPORTS FROM:					
Canada					
By US firms (A)	362	1,804	134	1,804	4,104
By US firms (B)	294	1,727	161	770	2,952
Total	810	2,020	372	3,733	6,935
United Kingdom[c]					
By US firms (B)	684	546[e]	272	589[e]	2,091
Total	3,334	2,644	1,382	4,901	12,261
EEC Six					
By US firms (A)	1,241	649	590	574	3,053
By US firms (B)	1,251	650[e]	588	577[e]	3,066
Total	11,888	7,008	6,000	20,690	45,586
Total Europe[d]					
By US firms (A)	1,980	1,240	942	1,355	5,517
By US firms (B)	2,076	1,270[e]	943	1,412[e]	5,700
Total	18,691	10,982	8,934	34,306	72,913
Japan[c]					
By US firms (B)	60	—	54	11	125
Total	1,997	1,820	684	5,409	9,910
1971 EXPORTS FROM:					
Canada					
By US firms (B)	594	3,960	244	1,151	5,949
Total	1,307	4,759	593	5,503	12,162
United Kingdom					
By US firms (B)	1,400	766	490	821	3,477
Total	5,507	3,909	2,155	7,754	19,325
EEC Six					
By US firms (B)	2,533	1,924	1,564	1,103	7,124
Total	21,855	14,422	10,496	35,670	82,443
Total Europe[d]					
By US firms (B)	4,319	2,788	2,198	2,535	11,840
Total	33,814	20,823	15,296	57,802	127,735
Japan					
By US firms (B)	85	—	106	28	219
Total	5,019	5,568	1,488	10,867	22,942

[a] By US firms (A) = exports by firms where direct ownership was 25 per cent or more; by US firms (B) = exports by firms where ownership, direct or indirect, was 50 per cent or more.
[b] Includes tobacco manufactures, synthetic rubber, pulp and waste paper, timber, man-made fibres.
[c] No separate figures available for US firms (A).
[d] Includes EEC, EFTA, Cyprus, Gibraltar, Greece, Iceland, Ireland, Malta, Spain, Turkey and Yugoslavia.   [e] Estimated.
SOURCES: United States Department of Commerce, *Survey of Current Business*; OECD, *Statistics of Foreign Trade*; United Nations Statistical Office, *Commodity Trade Statistics*; NIESR estimates.

Table E.2. *Trade in manufactures of United States multinational companies (MNCs) and their majority owned foreign affiliates (MOFAs)*

Percentages

	Machinery	Transport equipment	Chemicals	Other[a]	Total[a]
1966					
Exports from United States					
MNC-associated[b]	62	82	73	46	63
(of which related trade)[c]	(19)	(31)	(22)	(10)	(19)
Total	100	100	100	100	100
Total value ($ million)	*6,551*	*4,610*	*2,676*	*6,830*	*20,667*
Imports into United States					
MNC-associated[d]	40	54	67	26	35
(of which related trade)[e]	(17)	(39)	(11)	(6)	(13)
Total	100	100	100	100	100
Total value ($ million)	*2,358*	*2,470*	*957*	*9,437*	*15,222*
Exports by MOFAs					
(of which related trade)[f]	(65)	(79)	(44)	(50)	(63)
Total	100	100	100	100	100
Total value ($ million)	*2,463*	*2,718*	*1,017*	*1,985*	*8,183*
1970					
Exports from United States					
MNC-associated[b]	58	86	61	58	66
(of which related trade)[c]	(21)	(27)	(21)	(14)	(21)
Total	100	100	100	100	100
Total value ($ million)	*10,050*	*7,832*	*3,826*	*9,814*	*31,522*
Imports into United States					
MNC-associated[d]	36	57	56	28	38
(of which related trade)[e]	(18)	(41)	(14)	(7)	(18)
Total	100	100	100	100	100
Total value ($ million)	*4,527*	*6,645*	*1,450*	*13,450*	*26,072*
Exports by MOFAs					
(of which related trade)[f]	(65)	(84)	(45)	(48)	(65)
Total	100	100	100	100	100
Total value ($ million)	*4,284*	*5,648*	*2,170*	*4,205*	*16,307*

[a] Includes tobacco manufactures, synthetic rubber, pulp and waste paper, timber, man-made fibres.
[b] Transactions by and for the account of US MNCs, including exports to MOFAs of products of other US firms.
[c] Products of parent companies exported to own MOFAs.
[d] All imports by US MNCs and by non-related US firms from MOFAs of MNCs.
[e] Products of own MOFAs imported by US parents.
[f] Exports to US parents and to affiliates in third countries.
SOURCES: United States Senate, *Implications of Multinational Firms*; OECD, *Statistics of Foreign Trade, 1966 and 1970.*

estimated or partly estimated by reference to the value of total direct investment in the years in question and the share of manufacturing in total investment by country in 1962, 1965 and 1968.

Table E.3. *Exports of manufactures from the United Kingdom by enterprises with foreign ownership (E F Os) and United Kingdom firms with investments overseas*

Percentages

	Machinery	Transport equipment	Chemicals	Other	Total
1966 exports from U K					
By E F Os					
U S owned	17	29	13	4	14
Other	4	6	6	5	5
Associates	4	—	7	1	2
Total	25	35	26	10	21
(of which related)	(8)	(24)	(11)	(3)	(10)
By U K overseas investors	46	49	63	37	45
(of which related)	(15)	(13)	(22)	(7)	(12)
Total	100	100	100	100	100
Total value ($ million)	*3,444*	*2,798*	*1,343*	*4,708*	*12,293*
1970 exports from U K					
By E F Os					
U S owned	26	30	14	5	17
Other	10	—	8	5	5
Associates	3	—	8	2	3
Total	39	30	30	12	25
(of which related)	(16)	(21)	(15)	(3)	(12)
By U K overseas investors	48	50	65	41	47
(of which related)	(13)	(17)	(24)	(8)	(12)
Total	100	100	100	100	100
Total value ($ million)	*4,649*	*3,273*	*1,883*	*6,530*	*16,335*

Note: Figures for E F Os and U K overseas investors refer to direct exports only; related exports are exports to overseas affiliates.

SOURCES: Department of Trade, *Board of Trade Journal*, 16 August 1968 and *Trade and Industry*, 13 April 1972; Customs and Excise, *Annual Statement of Trade of the United Kingdom, 1966* and *1970*, London, H M S O.

Germany as investor

Monatsberichte der Deutschen Bundesbank, December 1965; Bundes-ministerium für Wirtschaft, *Leistung im Zahlen 1975*; H. E. Scharrer (ed.), *Förderung privater Direktinvestitionen*, Hamburg, Verlag Weltarchiv, 1972. Data refer to the transaction values of 'asset-increasing' expenditure (cumulative since 1952), reported under the provisions of the Foreign Trade and Payments Order. According to the Bundes-bank this corresponds approximately to the 'initial value' of German direct investment abroad including investment in minority holdings; it excludes reinvested profits, short-term credits from parent companies, valuation adjustments and outstanding prewar investments. It has been estimated that the inclusion of reinvested profits and prewar investments would raise the German total at the end of 1969 by 25 per cent and that the disparity between recorded and actual investments is increasing over time (see H. Krägenau, 'Wie hoch sind die deutschen Auslandsinvestitionen?', *Wirtschaftsdienst*, vol. 50, November 1970). Investments are classified by industry according to the activity of the parent company rather than the affiliate. Figures in the tables were estimated from data for total recorded investment by major industries in 1963, 1967 and 1971; the area distribution was estimated by reference to the share of manufacturing in total investment by country in 1964 and 1976, the only years for which such a breakdown is available.

Germany as host

Monatsberichte der Deutschen Bundesbank, May 1965, May 1969, January 1972 and November 1974. Data by country of origin and industry refer only to the direct foreign share in nominal capital, including minority interests. They understate the true foreign share, since the parent companies' share in reserves is excluded, as are indirect holdings (holdings of foreign owned enterprises in other companies domiciled in Germany). In recent years information on the total value of these two items has been published; from this it is possible to estimate that by 1971 the book value of all foreign owned assets was some 50 per cent greater than the value in terms of 'nominal capital' directly held. Data for the value of investment in manufacturing in 1963, 1967 and 1971 shown in table 4.15 were estimated from data on investment in manufacturing in 1964, 1968 and 1970 and total investment in 1963, 1967 and 1971.

Canada

Statistics Canada, *Canada's International Investment Position 1926 to 1967, 1968 to 1970* and *1971 to 1973*, Ottawa, Information Canada, 1971, 1975 and 1977. Data refer to direct investment (equity, retained earnings and long-term debt) in branches, subsidiaries and controlled companies. Canadian investments in 1963 include merchandising activities.

Sweden

Swedenborg, *Den Svenska Industrins Investeringar i Utlandet 1965–1970* and EFTA, *EFTA Foreign Investment* (undated). Data are derived from a survey of companies in Sweden with more than 50 employees and cover the 'Swedish stake' (Swedish parent share of equity plus long-term liabilities to parent) in subsidiaries with more than 50 per cent Swedish ownership. Original data relate to 1960, 1965 and 1970; estimates for 1963, 1967 and 1971 have been interpolated.

SOURCES USED IN COMPILING ESTIMATES IN THE TEXT AND
IN TABLES 4.16 AND 4.17

General

United Nations, Department of Economics and Social Affairs, *Multinational Corporations in World Development*, New York, 1973; OECD, *Interim Report of the Industry Committee on International Enterprises*, Paris, 1974; Scharrer (ed.), *Förderung privater Direktinvestitionen*.

United States

Department of Commerce, *Survey of Current Business* and *Foreign Direct Investment in the United States*, Washington (DC), US Government Printing Office, 1976.

United Kingdom

Department of Trade, *Board of Trade Journal* and *Trade and Industry*.

Japan

Japan External Trade Organization, *Japan: into the multinationalization era*, Tokyo, 1973.

France

'Les investissements français à l'étranger', *Journal Officiel de la République Française*, 5 November 1970; 'Balance des payements entre la France et l'Extérieur' and 'Les participations étrangères dans l'industrie française au 1er Janvier 1973', *Statistiques et Études Financières*, vol. 14 (1962)–vol. 24 (1972) and vol. 27, September 1975.

Germany

Monatsberichte der Deutschen Bundesbank; Bundesministerium für Wirtschaft, *Leistung im Zahlen 1975*.

Italy

'La partecipazione straniera nelle società italiane', *Vita Italiana*, vol. 24, June 1974.

Belgium-Luxembourg

'Les investissements étrangers dans des entreprises industrielles en Belgique', *Bulletin d'Information et de Documentation*, vol. 45, October 1970; Ministère des Affaires Économiques, *Rapport* (various issues).

Netherlands

F. Stubenitsky, *American Direct Investment in the Netherlands Industry*, Rotterdam University Press, 1970.

Sweden

Swedenborg, *Den Svenska Industrins Investeringar i Utlandet 1965–1970*; EFTA, *EFTA Foreign Investment*.

Switzerland

M. Iklé, *Switzerland: an international banking and finance centre*, London, Academic Press, 1972.

Appendix F

THE DEVELOPMENT PROCESS:
AN APPLICATION OF CLUSTER ANALYSIS

by *R. A. Batchelor*

INTRODUCTION

Standardised statistics on the behaviour of national accounting aggregates have accumulated rapidly during the 1960s, with coverage gradually extended to most developing economies. This should help to free investigation of the process of economic growth and development from the narrow basis of industrial revolutions in Western Europe and North America. There are, however, limits to the kind of generalisation which can be based on this new data. Some problems arise from arguments over whether certain events are unique to individual countries; some arise from the failure of measurable economic variables to reflect key social and institutional factors; some arise from the inevitable discrepancies between published statistics and their images in economic theory.

In the study of industrialisation these negative views have some force but, while it may be futile to search for a single set of laws of growth applicable to all parts of the world economy, nonetheless groups of countries may exist for which valid generalisations can be framed and distinctive growth models formulated. This viewpoint lies between the universality proposed initially by Chenery[1] and the particularist approach to which Kuznets was driven. Thus the latter could write:

The variability over time and diversity in space in the empirical coefficients of modern economic growth have been demonstrated . . . While all countries showed fairly similar trends in the share of agriculture versus that of the industry sectors the trends were not of the same magnitude; and even currently there are fairly notable diversities among the developed countries in the sectoral structure of output, not closely related to the level of economic development, at least as measured by per capita income.[2]

This argument implies that analysis of growth requires case studies and that its proper subject is individual development problems rather than global development patterns.

[1] Chenery, 'Patterns of industrial growth'.
[2] Kuznets, *Modern Economic Growth*, p. 504.

300

CONVERGENT AND DIVERGENT FORCES IN DEVELOPMENT

The classification of countries into discrete groups for purposes of building models can be represented schematically as in the top section (A) of chart F.1. This shows a mapping of countries from a diffuse distribution with respect to their initial *state* into classes which are distinct and homogeneous with respect to economic *structure*. Both lines are uni-dimensional representations of multi-dimensional concepts. The *state* variable summarises the geographic, demographic, economic and social characteristics of a country at a single point in time, whereas *structure* may embrace static features, such as the composition of national income, or dynamic features, such as the relationship between income growth and the nature of demand and productive activity. The two lower sections of the chart illustrate the logical extremes which have been attributed to Chenery (B) and Kuznets (C). In the first, one model suffices to explain the experience of all countries; in the other, each country is so distinctive that any general statements on the growth process are precluded.

The wide range of countries' *states* is generally acknowledged; the Secretary General of the United Nations has taken it as fundamental that 'the development spectrum ... is a continuum with countries spread across its whole length, whatever criterion of development is applied'.[1] What is questioned is whether or not differences in indicators like national income per head and population size can be continuously related to the structural characteristics which determine growth potential and policy requirements.

Chenery's argument rests on the probability that 'universal factors' in economic growth will dominate 'particular factors' tending to cause divergences. Similarities in the evolution of tastes as income rises, a stable sequence of industrial development as population growth permits plants to be of optimum size and the parallel progress of human and physical capital formation are the principal universal factors producing convergence of countries to a simple model relating sectoral shares in value added to income and size. The normal pattern is in fact an increase in the shares of manufacturing in total economic activity and of capital-intensive sectors like heavy engineering and industrial chemicals in manufacturing. The chief disruptive force endogenous to Chenery's general equilibrium framework is the influence of specific resource-endowments on production techniques – that is, sharp differences between the initial *state* of certain economies and the rest, as with the third group in chart F.1(A). However, he believes that countervailing

---

[1] United Nations, Department of Economic and Social Affairs, *The International Development Strategy: first overall review and appraisal of issues and policies*, New York, 1973, pp. 4–5.

Chart F.1. *Alternative methods of analysing the development process*

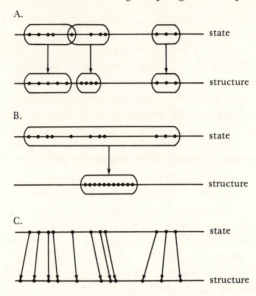

mechanisms exist to bring into line eccentric patterns falling outside the usual relationships.[1] This is offered as a purely empirical proposition – based on studies in Japan and Latin America – but it is not hard to rationalise in terms of the profitability incentives to ancillary industries offered by unbalanced growth. The point to note is that, in principle, within a general equilibrium model the 'growth elasticities' of sector shares with respect to income and size are functionally dependent on *all* of the arguments of the production function, including specific natural resources.[2] So the paradigm by which Chenery sought to analyse the process of growth admits as a logical possibility the non-existence of general laws, with each country's experience determined entirely by its initial *state*.

The differences between the above and the particularist approach arise from different opinions on:

(a) what elements in the model can be treated as parameters rather than variables;

---

[1] Chenery, 'Patterns of industrial growth', p. 651.

[2] The level of production X_i in sector i is given in Chenery's model as $X_i = [1 - \mu_i(K, S, R, N, R_i)]$ $[\dot{W}_i(Y, N) + D_i(Y) + E_i(K, S, R, R_i) + \Delta W_i(\Delta X_1, \Delta X_2, \ldots, \Delta X_n)]$, where K, S, R are capital, labour skills and raw materials, the arguments of the production function; $Y =$ income per head; $N =$ population size; $\dot{W}_i$ and ΔW_i are normal and incremental intermediate demands on sector i and R_i its sector-specific resources; D_i and E_i are home and export demands for, and μ_i is the import content in consumption of, the ith good (Chenery, 'Patterns of industrial growth', p. 629).

(b) whether the relations in the model are indeed stable or continuous;
(c) the value of the purely economic definition of the *state* variable implicit in the Walrasian framework.

The parametric treatment of the partial elasticities of value added with respect to income and size implies a number of subsidiary hypotheses. One is the invariance of *structure* with respect to resource-endowments; another is the requirement that export expansion and import substitution be similarly determined by universal factors such as wealth and scale (otherwise in the commodity balance equation $X = D + W + E - M$ no direct connection would exist between domestic output X and intermediate and final demands W and D). The existence of patterns in import substitution has been disputed on empirical grounds by Steuer and Voivodas,[1] and it is clear that *a priori* these subsidiary hypotheses are more plausible for certain types of economy than for others. To be precise, they become more likely the larger, richer, or more closed to trade a particular country is, since size guarantees a balanced set of resources, wealth a low natural resource content in final consumption, and self-sufficiency a close correspondence between demand and home output. Considerations of this sort led Chenery in a later exercise to partition countries by size and by resource-bias of exports.[2]

Problems over the stability of structural relationships can arise from tastes or technology. Technical progress can have profound effects on *state*, since distinctive resources or comparative advantages are defined against the prevailing state of the arts. Its general tendency over time to lower unit costs in manufacturing by large-scale capital-intensive processes not only expands the choice of techniques available to countries at early stages of industrialisation but also changes the appropriate investment policy for such countries. Gerschenkron has pointed out that it is quite rational for developing countries to adopt current best-practice methods however capital-intensive, since this is their only hope of competing against advanced economies with older capital stocks and their only means of circumventing shortages of local skilled labour.[3] However, as Kuznets observes, 'technological innovation is selective and its economic impact shifts over time from one branch of production to another', thus the pattern of industrialisation

---

[1] Steuer and Voivodas, 'Import substitution and Chenery's patterns of industrial growth: a further study'.

[2] Chenery and Taylor, 'Development patterns: among countries and over time'; see also, IBRD, *The International Division of Labor* by Chenery and Hughes.

[3] Gerschenkron, *Economic Backwardness in Historical Perspective*, chap. 1. Rationality can of course be defined only against given objectives. In Gerschenkron's thesis output or labour productivity is maximised rather than employment, a capitalist notion appropriate mainly to advanced economies.

undertaken is critically dependent on its timing. Technical progress increases not only the optimal plant size for individual industries but often the *minimum* scale at which operations are viable, so that over time it becomes progressively more difficult for small countries to support a broad industry-mix.

Whereas technological change can destroy the stability of development patterns by causing the *state* variables of countries to diverge according to the date of their industrialisation, divergences due to taste differences stem from interactions between *state* and *structure* at one point in time. The self-validating nature of production is central to Kuznets' case. He writes: 'Although changes in the production side do not necessarily affect the basic structure of human wants ... they do affect the relative costs and varieties of specific goods that are comprised in these wants.'[1] Not only does availability stimulate consumption through the price mechanism and perpetuate consumption through habit formation, but the social environment created generates particular kinds of secondary activities (urbanisation, for example, increases demand for services and construction). The character and location of these derived demands may emphasise any initial peculiarities in *structure* caused by eccentric tastes or technologies and they may be strong enough to prevent major changes in industrial structure by encouraging expansion of existing industries and exacerbating frictional unemployment.

These considerations are also relevant to another problem with the general equilibrium account of growth patterns – its failure to take into account non-economic forces causing divergent evolution of otherwise similar economies. Catastrophes have obvious, but not necessarily deleterious, effects on industrialisation – the world wars actually promoted development in many countries, as Maizels argues, through the encouragement of self-sufficiency and the diversion of resources into heavy industries.[2] More sustained institutional pressures are also important: the existence of banks and efficient capital markets has influenced not only the rate at which savings are transformed into investment but also the sectoral distribution of capital formation. The effects of political and territorial status of nations on growth patterns have been explored empirically. The United Nations, after running regressions of value added per head in thirteen industries on income per head, population size and a general measure of industrialisation, inspected the deviations from normal levels in centrally planned economies; their capital goods sectors were found to be substantially larger than those in other countries, although there were great

---

[1] Kuznets, *Modern Economic Growth*, p. 102.
[2] Maizels, *Industrial Growth and World Trade*, chap. 1.

variations among the seven countries studied.[1] This method assumes that the effects of planning on sector shares are additive, but subsequently Gregory showed that for centrally planned Eastern European economies the whole concept of growth patterns breaks down.[2]

The opposing convictions of Chenery and Kuznets with respect to the impact of all these disturbing factors – economic, technological and political – on the stability of the relationship between sector shares and national income per head can be traced to the empirical material with which they operate. Chenery is concerned primarily with cross-sectional regressions on a large sample of countries, Kuznets with historical data on the productive structure of about a dozen developed countries. There is in principle no reason why the results of time-series and cross-sectional analysis should agree, since the points making up the cross-section may lie on distinct growth paths. However, both authors check their findings against each sort of data base, with conflicting results. Chenery and Taylor plot time-series on sector shares in some developed countries alongside the path predicted by their regressions for large countries and find general conformity, with some tendency for the share of agriculture to fall more rapidly than expected;[3] Temin, whose data they use, had earlier shown that the relations between bi-decennial changes in these shares and national income per head did not differ significantly among the nine countries.[4] Kuznets, however, points out first that the decline in primary production is not confined to growing economies but was also a feature of the recent (postwar) history of some underdeveloped countries – Egypt, the Philippines, Honduras – and must have been present in the pre-industrial phase of advanced countries; secondly, that the rate of industrialisation implied by cross-sectional analyses understates the actual rate achieved in developed countries by about 40 per cent on average, a bias which is far from constant over time or systematically distributed across countries.[5]

In an attempt to resolve these inconsistencies, Gregory and Griffin tested formally for inter-temporal and inter-country stability in simple logarithmic regressions on GNP per head of the shares in GNP of manufacturing and of metal production and food processing using constant price data for ten countries from each decade since 1910.[6] Their results suggest that over the period as a whole there is little

---

[1] United Nations, Department of Economic and Social Affairs, *A Study of Industrial Growth.*
[2] Gregory, 'Cross section comparisons of the structure of GNP by sector of origin'.
[3] Chenery and Taylor, 'Development patterns', pp. 400–2.
[4] P. Temin, 'A time-series test of patterns of industrial growth', *Economic Development and Cultural Change*, vol. 15, January 1967.
[5] Kuznets, *The Economic Growth of Nations*, pp. 152–5.
[6] Gregory and Griffin, 'Secular and cross-sectional industrialization patterns'.

Chart F.2. *Cross-sections and time-series for growth of the manufacturing share*

GDP per head

conflict between time-series and cross-sectional elasticity estimates, but a tendency for the estimates from successive cross-sections to fall over time could explain the disparity between Kuznets' inferences from historical statistics and Chenery's from postwar data. This trend is attributable partly to genuine non-linearities in the equations, but mainly to non-homogeneity among the individual country regressions. If their interpretation of the evidence is correct, it indicates a source of confusion in the debate over growth patterns of a statistical rather than methodological kind, since cross-sectional instability is then possible even without changes in tastes, technology or institutional factors which disrupt the general equilibrium model. An example of this problem is illustrated in chart F.2. The time paths of the manufacturing share in GDP in three countries are shown as TS_1, TS_2 and TS_3, and a cross-section observed for period t could give the relation CS_t. If between periods t and $t+1$ income per head increases faster in country 3 than in country 2, and faster in country 2 than in country 1 – as is quite likely since countries with larger manufacturing sectors tend to grow faster – then a cross-sectional relation like CS_{t+1} will emerge. Indeed, with the non-linear time path shown, the cross-sectional relation will tend to flatten over time even if income growth is everywhere equal. So stability in such regressions is necessary but not sufficient to establish time-series stability in situations where the sample is not homogeneous.

This demonstration of the impossibility of validating growth patterns from cross-sectional data has serious implications for studies which attempt to extend the analysis of industrialisation to less developed countries lacking historical data. Direct testing for homogeneity in the time path of growth is then ruled out and only by indirect assessment – with reference to the factors shown earlier to influence the pattern of development – can observations be assigned to particular expansion paths. We now turn to this problem of classification.

THE CLASSIFICATION OF NATIONAL ECONOMIC STRUCTURES

Cluster analysis is an umbrella term for a battery of statistical techniques designed to group entities according to their similarity with respect to certain measured characteristics.[1] Here the sample to be classified consists of 116 countries and their characteristics are those *economic* variables discussed above which could alter the terms in which the growth process of particular countries is best described.

This exercise is subject at all points to theoretical as well as statistical considerations. The only computational requirement for the choice of variables is that there should be sufficient to avoid the spurious bunching effect which could be produced by a purely random scatter of observations on a single variable. Seven economic and demographic features have been collected for the basic cluster analysis – the level of income per head, Y/N, the size of population, N, and its density, N/A, the investment ratio, I/Y, and the foreign trade ratio, $(E+M)/Y$, the share of manufactures in total exports E_m/E and the proportion of the economically active population engaged in agriculture, N_a.[2]

Before these variables can be used to define similarities or differences between countries they must be adjusted by subtracting from each its mean in the whole sample and dividing by its standard deviation, otherwise variables which happen to take large numerical values because of the units in which they are measured would dominate in the assessment of distances. There are then many ways in which the

---

[1] A survey of these techniques is provided in B. Everitt, *Cluster Analysis*, London, Heinemann, 1974.
[2] Details of the raw data and its sources are available on request from the NIESR, 2 Dean Trench Street, Smith Square, London S.W.1.

standardised matrix $[X_{ij}]$ for 116 countries (i) and seven variables (j) can be manipulated to give a matrix of distances $[d_{ik}]$ between the economic structures of countries i and k.[1] The most natural measure of d_{ik} is defined simply by $d_{ik}{}^2 = (\mathbf{X}_i - \mathbf{X}_k)'(\mathbf{X}_i - \mathbf{X}_k)$, where $\mathbf{X}_i$ is the column vector $(X_{i1} X_{i2} \ldots X_{i7})$. Alternative definitions have generally been advanced to meet the needs of particular disciplines – notably botany and astronomy. In economic literature the measure most frequently adopted is the cosine of the angle subtended at the origin by the vectors $\mathbf{X}_i$ and $\mathbf{X}_k$, following the pioneering work of Linneman on trade patterns.[2] This procedure, and methods based on analogues to it such as the simple correlation between $\mathbf{X}_i$ and $\mathbf{X}_k$, have been shown by Wishart to be unreliable because the results depend heavily on where the origin lies after standardisation.[3] Thus, in the analysis below the difference between the economic structures of any two individual countries is measured by the squared distance between the vectors of their characteristics and the difference between any two groups of countries by the same measure applied to their centroids.

The aggregation of countries into clusters sharing broadly similar characteristics is determined by their closeness to one another on this criterion. There are two methodologically distinct approaches to this problem.[4] The first – hierarchical fusion – gradually builds up clusters from the scatter of standardised data by combining at each stage those two countries, or clusters of countries formed at an earlier stage, which are closest together. Thus the classification is reduced from 116 clusters, each containing one country, to 115 – made up of 114 one-country clusters and a cluster consisting of the two most similar countries in the sample – to 114, and so on until some optimal number of terminal clusters is reached. The second method – mode analysis – is more complicated. It involves scanning the data for observations which have a large number of neighbours lying within some prescribed distance D. These 'dense points' are adopted as the nuclei of clusters consisting of all their near neighbours. As D is then increased, either more points come within the ambit of these initial groups or new dense regions appear elsewhere in the data and form separate clusters. Because at each value of D the estimated clusters may overlap, certain rules on the allocation of shared observations between clusters, and on the complete fusion of

---

[1] Eight basic families are discussed in R. M. Cormack, 'A review of classification', *Journal of the Royal Statistical Society* (series A), vol. 134, part 3, 1971.

[2] See H. Linneman, *An Econometric Study of International Trade Flows*, Amsterdam, North-Holland, 1966. Other applications can be found in Hufbauer, 'The impact of national characteristics and technology' and Girgis, 'Development and trade patterns in the Arab world'.

[3] D. Wishart, 'An algorithm for hierarchical classifications', *Biometrics*, vol. 25, March 1969.

[4] Strictly speaking the methods discussed are merely representative members of larger families of clustering techniques (see Everitt, *Cluster Analysis*, chap. 2).

adjacent clusters, have to be continuously invoked. The result is that the number and composition of classes fluctuates as the parameter D increases.

The properties of the two methods are quite different. There are two technical problems with hierarchical fusion. The first is that individual observations, once fused, remain in the same group throughout the process, although subsequent switching of some observations between clusters can be shown to reduce the total sum of squares of distances between all observations and their cluster centroids. The second problem is that the phenomenon of 'chaining' may crop up with certain data sets, so that the new observations introduced into any particular group may become progressively further away from the original cluster members. Both difficulties can be reduced by sensible relocation in conjunction with the fusion process or, in other words, by looking for improvements in the separation of groups by switching borderline cases into the nearest alternative clusters. The difficulty with mode analysis is in a sense the obverse of chaining – namely, that all clusters are assumed spherical and within classes the possibility of a stretch of observations along any characteristics dimension is ruled out *ab initio*. The method is thus more appropriate to the determination of very distinct 'natural' groups than to classifying the economic structures of countries with very diverse living standards.

A final technical question in both cases is the selection of the optimal number of clusters. In the case of mode analysis the most significant classification is taken by convention to be that in which the number of clusters is a maximum. In the fusion method, it is possible to check the information lost in merging the nearest two clusters from the resultant increase in the sum of squares of distances from the new cluster centroids, but more important is the economic interpretation of the classification; if a meaningful distinction is eliminated by the next fusion, then it is desirable to halt the process at that point.

The remainder of this section deals with the results of some clustering experiments. All classifications are described in 'characterisation tables' showing for each grouping of countries the mean values taken by the original variables within the cluster, and two statistics (a t-statistic and an F-statistic) associated with those means. The first is the distance between the group mean and the mean value of the variable in the sample as a whole divided by its standard deviation in the whole sample; this helps to identify formally what characteristics distinguish any particular group from the rest of the population. The second measures the internal homogeneity of the group with respect to each variable as the ratio of the standard deviation of the variable in a cluster to its standard deviation in the whole sample. These tables are designed to facilitate comparisons of one cluster with another. To help compare whole classifications with each other 'concordance tables' are constructed showing the distribution of the members of each cluster in one classification among the clusters of a second classification. Clusters are designated throughout by roman numerals, higher numbers being assigned to clusters with higher mean GDP per head. In this sense clusters labelled V and VI can be considered 'more developed' than those labelled I and II.

The characterisation statistics of the classification obtained by hierarchical fusion from the 1963 data are shown in text table 5.7 and the countries comprising the seven clusters involved are listed in text table 5.6. The concordance comparing the outcome of a mode analysis with the solution produced by hierarchical fusion is shown in table F.1, and the characterisation for the former in table F.2.

Table F.1. *Concordance of clusters formed by hierarchical fusion and mode analysis on 1963 data*

		Clusters from mode analysis				
	I	II	III	IV	V	VI
Hierarchical fusion:						
Cluster I (All 47 countries from table 5.6)						
II (All 11 countries from table 5.6)						
III		(All 7 countries from table 5.6)				
IV (All 22 countries from table 5.6)						
V			Barbados Malta Puerto Rico Singapore Trinidad & Tobago	Luxembourg		Netherlands
VI Chile				Austria Israel Finland Norway Switzerland	France Germany Italy Japan UK	Australia Belgium Denmark Iceland N. Zealand Sweden
VII					USA	Canada Kuwait

Table F.2. *Economic characteristics of clusters formed by mode analysis, 1963 cross-section*

	Income per head	Population		Propn. in agri-culture[a]	Ratio to GDP of:		Share of manufac-tures in total exports
		Size	Density		Invest-ment	Foreign trade[b]	
	($)	(millions)	(ooo/Mha)	(%)	(percentages)		
Mean value							
Cluster I	249.06	11.95	491.62	66.21	14.56	45.48	12.91
II	257.14	7.32	136.14	74.46	35.00	83.43	53.27
III	602.50	1.54	9517.17	16.30	21.50	152.33	31.23
IV	1328.17	3.98	784.83	20.17	28.67	76.83	77.82
V	1538.14	136.51	1602.29	26.49	22.00	24.57	77.56
VI	2149.56	7.40	875.56	12.92	22.00	62.89	40.73
t-statistic							
Cluster I	−0.38	−0.12	−0.16	0.40	−0.43	−0.26	−0.43
II	−0.37	−0.22	−0.27	0.69	2.20	0.78	0.92
III	0.06	−0.34	2.48	−1.40	0.46	2.69	0.18
IV	1.00	−0.29	−0.77	−1.26	1.39	0.60	1.74
V	1.27	2.43	0.16	−1.04	0.53	−0.84	1.74
VI	2.05	−0.22	−0.05	−1.53	0.53	0.22	0.50
F-statistic							
Cluster I	0.07	0.16	0.04	0.53	0.36	0.37	0.37
II	0.05	0.02	0.01	0.22	1.77	0.54	0.93
III	0.07	—	11.87	0.08	0.36	1.73	1.15
IV	0.12	—	0.02	0.09	0.08	1.18	0.09
V	2.93	8.36	0.05	0.63	0.49	0.09	0.22
VI	2.29	0.01	0.13	0.05	0.22	0.38	0.89

[a] Of economically active population.
[b] Total trade in goods and services.

Six groups of countries were isolated by the mode analysis. The most striking features are that all the less developed countries belonging to Clusters I, II and IV as determined by hierarchical fusion have been assimilated into one very large bloc, that the satellite clusters – the mineral exporters (Cluster III) and the island economies (Cluster V) – have preserved their separate identities, and that the advanced countries have been fragmented into three subgroups each with five to eight members. Luxembourg and the Netherlands are alone in two of these clusters and Chile is demoted from an advanced to a less developed economy.

The impression given by table F.2 is that the criteria applied in the mode analysis are more stringent than in the hierarchical fusion, but that less weight is given to the general structural homogeneity of each cluster. Thus the t-statistics of Clusters II–VI are on average higher than those in text table 5.7, but homogeneity within groups is one-dimensional only, concerned mainly with population size, and the F-statistics on some other variables are much higher than would be tolerated in the fusion table.

The most interesting aspect of the mode analysis classification is the separation of advanced economies into Clusters IV, V and VI. The distinction between the first two is largely a matter of size, but it also reflects the very open nature of the smaller European economies – Luxembourg, Norway and Switzerland in particular – compared with France, Germany and the United Kingdom. Cluster VI resembles Cluster IV in many ways, but it is distinguished by the somewhat paradoxical co-existence of abundant land and primary exports with

Table F.3. *Economic characteristics of clusters formed by hierarchical fusion, 1971 cross-section*

| | Income per head | Population | | | Ratio to G D P of: | | Share of manufactures in total exports |
		Size	Density	Propn. in agriculture[a]	Investment	Foreign trade[b]	
	($)	(millions)	(ooo/Mha)	(%)	(percentages)		
Mean value							
Cluster I	110.42	16.73	484.13	80.79	11.46	31.79	7.51
II	291.29	17.84	407.29	60.31	16.43	47.00	17.61
III	380.18	5.73	293.55	61.97	29.45	78.82	26.87
IV	817.79	9.07	1197.26	34.50	21.32	64.42	24.01
V	1472.00	1.17	4427.80	12.44	27.40	144.40	47.54
VI	2834.67	88.86	1747.33	12.08	23.83	31.67	80.05
VII	2962.36	7.12	913.14	10.84	24.50	66.93	49.16
t-statistic							
Cluster I	−0.67	−0.08	−0.18	1.13	−1.11	−0.72	−0.68
II	−0.51	−0.06	−0.20	0.39	−0.41	−0.27	−0.32
III	−0.43	−0.27	−0.23	0.45	1.43	0.68	0.01
IV	−0.03	−0.21	−0.01	−0.54	0.28	0.25	−0.09
V	0.56	−0.35	0.78	−1.34	1.14	2.63	0.75
VI	1.79	1.17	0.13	−1.36	0.64	−0.73	1.91
VII	1.90	−0.24	−0.07	−1.40	0.73	0.32	0.81
F-statistic							
Cluster I	—	0.25	0.02	0.12	0.18	0.14	0.07
II	0.02	0.21	0.01	0.30	0.22	0.32	0.21
III	0.04	0.02	0.01	0.34	0.85	0.36	1.43
IV	0.16	0.03	0.10	0.15	0.29	0.78	0.69
V	0.54	—	0.84	0.04	0.13	1.41	0.98
VI	1.04	0.94	0.05	0.07	0.79	0.12	0.08
VII	0.64	0.01	0.08	0.04	0.48	0.34	1.17

Note: see notes *a* and *b* to table F.2.

extremely small agricultural labour forces – a paradox resolved by the highly mechanised nature of farming and mining in those countries.

Table F.3 gives the characterisation statistics for a grouping of countries by hierarchical fusion on data for 1971 and table F.4 compares these groups with those obtained from data for 1963. The mineral exporters and the island economies have remained stable, though by 1971 the first had gained new members in Botswana, Fiji, Guadeloupe and Panama, and the second had lost the Netherlands and Trinidad and Tobago. Other minor changes took place between the two years – Greece, Korea, Spain and Portugal moved up to the intermediate Cluster IV and Chile was demoted to the same cluster from Cluster VI; Iraq, Jordan, Malaysia, Peru, Rhodesia and Uruguay also dropped back. However, the most striking changes between 1963 and 1971 concern the clusters at each extreme of the development spectrum. The least developed Cluster I in 1963 was effectively merged by 1971 with the slightly more successful Cluster II and the whole split into two new groups which differ mainly in their level of income and industrialisation. There is a strong regional flavour to this new division – whereas Cluster I in 1963 contained ten Latin American states and 37 countries from Africa and Asia, in 1971 it consisted almost entirely of African countries; half the Latin American countries in the whole sample were then in the more prosperous Cluster II. The classification of advanced economies in 1971 is very similar to that produced by mode analysis of the 1963 data, except that the differences between the mode analysis Clusters IV and VI with respect to agricultural productivity have been discounted and the two merged to form the 1971 fusion Cluster VII. The main factor separating this group from the other advanced economies, such as France, Germany and Japan, is its small average population.

As a final test of the sensitivity of the classification, the number of characteristics was reduced from seven to three – population size, the share of manufactures in total exports and the size of the agricultural labour force. These are essentially the features on which Chenery and Taylor based their sample separation. Table F.6 shows the characterisation statistics for this grouping, which is compared with that based on all seven variables in table F.5. Cluster II is distinguished from Cluster I by its inward-looking industrialisation, which shows up in its modest level of manufacturing exports relative to the labour resources devoted to industry as a whole. Cluster III contains most of the mineral exporters identified earlier, with the proper addition of Sierra Leone and the improper addition of South Korea – a country with high manufacturing exports based on abundant labour and imported technology rather than any natural advantages. Similarly, Cluster V

Table F.4. *Concordance of clusters formed by hierarchical fusion on 1963 and 1971*

	I	II			Clus
1963 data:					
Cluster I	(47 countries from table 5.6 *less* 23 in 1971 Cluster II and one in 1971 Cluster III)	Bolivia C. Africa Republic Colombia Dahomey Dominican Republic Ecuador El Salvador	Gambia Guatemala Honduras Iran Ivory Coast Kenya Liberia Morocco	Nicaragua Paraguay Philip- pines Sri Lanka Syria Tanzania Togo Turkey	Bot
II	Pakistan	Brazil Egypt Indonesia	Mexico Sierra Leone	Thailand	
III					Alg Co Ga Ma Yu Zai Zar
IV		Iraq Jordan	Malaysia Peru	Rhodesia Uruguay	Fiji Gu Par
V					
VI					
VII					

1971 data

	IV	V	VI		VII	

Greece
Korea, S.

Portugal
Spain

Argentina	Libya					
Costa Rica	Martinique					
Cyprus	Mauritius					
Guyana	S. Africa					
Ireland	Tunisia					
Jamaica	Venezuela					
Lebanon						
Trinidad & Tobago		Barbados Luxembourg Malta Puerto Rico Singapore		Nether- lands		
Chile		France Germany Italy Japan U K	Australia Austria Belgium Denmark Finland Iceland	Israel New Zealand Norway Sweden Switzerland	
		U S A	Canada	Kuwait	

Table F.5. *Concordance of clusters formed using seven and three variables, 1963 cross-sections*

		I		II	
Complete matrix:					
Cluster	I	(47 countries from table 5.6 *less* 19 in Cluster II from reduced matrix)	Bolivia Burma Colombia Dahomey Dominican Republic Ecuador	El Salvador Ghana Guatemala Honduras Iran Morocco Nicaragua	Nig Par Phi p Sri Syr Tur
	II	Thailand	Brazil		
	III	Gabon	Algeria		
	IV		Costa Rica Fiji Guadeloupe	Iraq Libya Panama	Tur
	V				
	VI				
	VII				

Note: Indonesia, Pakistan and the United States also remained unclassified when clusters from the reduced matrix emerged.

usters from reduced matrix

	III	IV	V				VI	VII
.	Sierra Leone	Greece Egypt Mexico					Portugal	Spain
nia via	Zaire Zambia	Congo						
		Ireland Lebanon Malaysia Peru Rhodesia S. Africa		Argentina Cyprus Guyana Jamaica Jordan	Martinique Mauritius Uruguay Venezuela			
			Barbados Puerto Rico	Trinidad & Tobago		Malta Nether- lands Singapore	Luxem- bourg	
			Iceland	New Zealand		Australia Denmark Israel	Austria Belgium Chile Finland France Germany Italy	Japan Norway Sweden Switzerland U K
			Kuwait			Canada		

Table F.6. *Economic characteristics of clusters formed using three variables only,*
1963 cross-section

| | Population | | Share of manufactures in total exports |
	Size	Proportion in agriculture[a]	
	(millions)	(%)	(%)
Mean value			
Cluster I	6.50	88.08	6.16
II	12.04	60.00	4.80
III	11.29	79.92	74.07
IV	12.19	52.69	32.91
V	3.04	27.95	5.81
VI	7.29	12.37	46.53
VII	24.66	22.29	80.11
t-statistic			
Cluster I	−0.23	1.19	−0.65
II	−0.12	0.17	−0.70
III	−0.14	0.78	1.62
IV	−0.12	−0.09	0.24
V	−0.30	−0.98	−0.67
VI	−0.22	−1.55	0.70
VII	0.14	−1.19	1.82
F-statistic			
Cluster I	0.02	0.03	0.04
II	0.12	0.08	0.02
III	0.04	0.12	0.15
IV	0.06	0.14	0.10
V	0.01	0.16	0.03
VI	0.02	0.01	0.17
VII	0.31	0.19	0.10

Note: see note *a* to table F.2.

resembles the small industrialised 'island economies' in the main analysis. The two high-income Clusters VI and VII are distinguished mainly by their participation in trade in manufactures. The former consists of primary exporters with an efficient domestic agriculture and a large industrial labour force producing goods mainly for domestic consumption; the latter relies much more on exports of manufactures.

The concordance table indicates that in general the reduction of the data matrix has not significantly altered the shape of the classification – an interesting point, since it suggests that much of the variation in income per head and other such indices can be accounted for by three structural characteristics alone. However, these similarities are most evident at the extremes of the income scale and the reduced number of criteria gives a rather different picture for countries at intermediate levels of development; for such countries the rate of growth (investment), access to foreign markets and factor-endowments are clearly necessary considerations when analysing patterns of growth.

Appendix G

THE CALCULATION OF MEDIAN PLANT SIZES
by *R. A. Batchelor*

Data on employees and numbers of plants operating in particular industries are recorded for many countries in the United Nations series, *The Growth of World Industry*, vol. I: *General Industrial Statistics*. Direct international comparisons are, however, hampered by variations in basic definitions of which employees should be counted and exactly what constitutes a plant, also by differing sampling practices in the national industrial censuses from which the figures are taken. Little can be done about the first problem, but in a study in which comparisons are to be made between economies at widely different stages of development such definitional problems are probably unimportant. The elimination from the censuses of plants below some minimum size is, however, often a major distorting influence and some means must be found to adjust the data for these differences in coverage.

Our approach is to start with a general theoretical distribution of firm sizes; to express this as parameters for ten industry groups on the basis of size distributions for these groups in some easily accessible complete census; then, using these results, to apply a correction factor to the average figure for employees per plant obtained from the incomplete United Nations data to obtain a better estimate of the median plant size in each industry for some forty countries.

A Pareto distribution function $p_i(s)$ is used to describe the variety of firm sizes, s, found in industry i. This function gives the proportion of plants with less than s_0 persons engaged as

$$\int_0^{s_0} p_i(s)\,.\,ds = 1 - (k_i/s_0)^{a_i} \tag{G.1}$$

where a_i and k_i are industry-specific parameters. The minimum plant size is k_i, and the median plant size is $m_i = k_i \,.\, 2^{b_i}$, where $b_i = 1/a_i$ (see chart G.1).

If we have a complete census of all firms down to the very smallest, and an incomplete census giving the average firm size $\hat{n}_i$ of firms above some cut-off size l_i, it is fairly easy to estimate both a_i and k_i from

$$2^{b_i} = \hat{n}_i/l_i,\, k_i = l_i \hat{m}_i/\hat{n}_i \tag{G.2}$$

320

Chart G.1. *Pareto distribution of plant sizes in an industry*

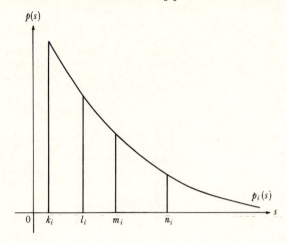

Table G.1. *Estimates of minimum plant sizes in manufacturing*

Persons engaged per plant

	France	Germany	Italy	Belgium	Luxem-bourg	Nether-lands	Average ($\bar{s}$)
Food	2.03	1.79	1.43	1.09	1.44	1.79	1.60
Beverages	1.03	3.82	2.69	4.67	8.75	4.20	4.19
Tobacco	1.00	7.29	3.02	2.11	..	4.07	3.84
Basic metals	4.04	7.08	4.85	6.36	6.67	5.22	5.70
Machinery							
Non-electrical	3.14	5.44	4.29	3.78	5.84	4.39	4.48
Electrical	2.05	4.55	2.34•	1.33	2.65	1.71	2.44
Transport equipment	0.32	1.84	0.64	0.82	2.75	1.45	1.30
Other metal products	1.79	2.17	1.52	1.69	1.70	1.83	1.78
Chemicals	3.36	4.43	3.79	3.85	6.03	5.08	4.42
Plastics, etc.	2.49	5.12	2.52	4.65	10.00	4.00	4.80
Textiles	2.54	3.89	1.52	3.46	..	4.38	3.16
Leather	0.82	2.29	2.36	1.66	..	3.42	2.11
Clothing, etc.	0.80	0.89	0.70	1.16	1.00	1.24	0.97
Wood	0.77	1.77	1.10	1.99	3.13	3.05	1.96
Furniture	1.04	1.83	1.69	1.76	2.89	2.35	1.93
Paper, printing, etc.	4.16	7.01	5.04	5.62	..	7.11	5.79
Mineral products	1.85	5.36	3.36	0.99	3.90	4.25	3.29
Other manufactures	1.25	2.20	1.71	0.82	1.47	1.19	1.44
TOTAL	1.11	1.93	1.27	1.49	1.28	1.96	1.51

Table G.2. *Estimates of median plant sizes in manufacturing*

	Food, beverages, tobacco	Basic metals	Metal products	Chem
Germany	15.0	129.6	18.5	104
Italy	8.9	58.4	11.2	42
Luxembourg	32.4	2431.4	90.1	75
Netherlands	13.4	2115.2	..	70
Denmark	26.8	253.8	34.8	61
Finland	12.3	129.6	53.0	70
Greece	4.8	118.0	4.0	12
Ireland	29.6	56.9	92.7	41
Norway	9.0	183.6	26.5	75
Portugal	9.6	400.0	60.5	27
Spain	7.1	79.8	45.0	27
Sweden	13.7	291.6	52.2	91
Australia	8.8	74.0	18.1	36
New Zealand	46.1	13.6	24.1	28
Japan	10.9	65.1	28.7	6
Ghana	8.8	16.8	24.6	2
Kenya	13.8	..	23.9	147
Libya	2.6	285.0	1.7	
Nigeria	17.2	79.8	23.4	66
South Africa	69.9	324.0	64.4	117
Tunisia	28.9	62.4	27.6	41
Uganda	11.0	33.1	7.7	2
Burma	9.7	655.5	8.8	35
Iran	1.7	2.6	1.0	
Iraq	13.9	..	15.8	62
Israel	21.8	39.8	15.2	3
Korea, South	15.4	40.7	20.3	2
Malaysia	21.1	24.1	110.7	3
Pakistan	24.1	59.5	21.8	4
Philippines	11.3	79.7	25.3	6
Singapore	8.7	50.2	10.4	4
Sri Lanka	29.9	..	108.9	12
Thailand	7.7	23.9	7.7	2
Turkey	15.9	187.2	29.3	3
Brazil	11.6	80.5	44.8	5
Colombia	7.4	100.0	13.0	4
Costa Rica	6.9	3.0	4.0	1
Ecuador	13.5	814.3	11.3	3
El Salvador	12.6	75.5	10.3	2
Guatemala	16.9	..	9.8	3
Honduras	13.2	..	13.5	3
Jamaica	51.4	..	..	4
Peru	38.9	426.5	30.9	4

Persons engaged per plant

	Leather, clothing, footwear	Wood and furniture	Paper, printing, etc.	Mineral products	Total
3	12.0	7.4	21.5	27.1	20.3
2	5.5	5.7	5.7	17.5	9.4
3	55.3	21.1	21.1	114.3	155.1
7	10.4	9.5	9.5	24.3	15.8
4	10.4	11.7	35.1	21.2	14.7
)	17.4	28.1	70.2	27.6	18.1
7	2.6	2.6	2.6	6.8	4.3
)	30.2	23.3	34.9	58.8	27.2
)	9.7	9.6	24.0	14.9	10.6
3	4.8	15.8	31.7	51.3	15.8
	10.6	5.9	5.9	12.7	14.1
	16.7	19.1	47.7	27.6	20.3
)	7.7	6.2	12.4	17.1	8.9
3	20.6	15.3	15.3	13.3	18.6
	11.1	10.3	10.3	17.3	17.3
	4.7	14.9	43.3	6.2	9.1
4	5.4	6.6	166.0	9.1	7.9
5	0.5	1.1	3.1	3.1	1.5
	9.0	19.6	56.9	39.2	15.7
	57.3	59.6	59.6	83.7	71.6
	37.5	36.5	36.6	51.8	34.8
3	..	12.8	37.0	31.3	9.2
)	3.8	13.2	38.2	22.4	7.8
	0.5	0.7	2.2	3.2	0.8
2	15.8	16.3	47.1	27.6	12.8
)	9.2	10.3	10.3	23.2	16.9
7	12.9	15.3	15.3	12.5	22.0
	..	23.7	23.7	22.9	27.1
	8.7	26.6	77.1	66.4	22.9
)	4.1	16.4	41.0	31.6	10.2
	4.8	7.9	22.9	29.9	7.1
	40.7	40.0	100.0	770.0	37.4
	3.4	8.3	24.0	17.3	6.5
7	7.9	18.0	52.3	48.3	15.2
7	9.1	9.3	23.2	19.6	13.7
5	4.4	7.5	18.7	15.7	7.6
2	3.5	5.5	5.5	7.8	6.2
	6.8	11.3	32.7	22.1	10.7
	4.5	5.1	12.7	11.5	9.2
	6.4	11.6	29.1	20.3	9.9
	5.6	24.4	61.0	10.3	9.9
	693.0	28.1	70.1	..	44.7
	28.8	24.9	24.9	42.6	39.3

where hatted variables are estimated mean sizes from the census data. Having obtained these, estimates of the true median of other incomplete samples with minimum size l_i' and mean $\hat{n}_i'$ can be calculated as

$$\hat{m}_i = k_i \hat{n}_i / l_i' \tag{G.3}$$

In this study, the key parameter k_i has been estimated in the first place using data for E E C countries in 1963 for all firms in each industry and for firms with over ten persons engaged. These data are published by the Statistical Office of the European Communities in *Industriezensus von 1963*, Luxembourg, 1969. The results for eighteen branches of manufacturing industry are shown in table G.1. When equation G.3 was applied to data for other countries from the United Nations statistics, the estimates of median plant sizes shown in table G.2 were obtained for nine broader industry groups.

In spite of the great variety of data bases used, there is considerable agreement over the ranking of industries by plant size: leather, clothing and footwear plants are generally very small and plants in basic metal manufacturing very large. Textiles and chemicals also tend to be produced in large plants. As a summary measure of agreement of industry rankings by plant size among the 43 countries, Kendall's coefficient of concordance was computed for the data in table G.2 at 0.62, a highly significant result.

LIST OF WORKS CITED

I. BOOKS, ARTICLES AND PERIODICALS

ADAMS, N. A. 'Import structure and economic growth: a comparison of cross-section and time-series data', *Economic Development and Cultural Change*, vol. 15, January 1967.

ADELMAN, I. and CHENERY, H. B. 'Foreign aid and economic development: the case of Greece', *Review of Economics and Statistics*, vol. 48, February 1966.

ADELMAN, I. and MORRIS, C. T. *Society, Politics and Economic Development: a quantitative approach*, Baltimore, Johns Hopkins University Press, 1967.

ALECKO, S. A. 'How many Nigerians?', *Modern African Studies*, vol. 3, October 1965.

ARROW, K. J., CHENERY, H. B., MINHAS, B. S. and SOLOW, R. M. 'Capital–labor substitution and economic efficiency', *Review of Economics and Statistics*, vol. 43, August 1961.

BACON, R. W. and ELTIS, W. A. *Britain's Economic Problem: too few producers*, London, Macmillan, 1976.

BALASSA, B. 'Trade liberalisation and "revealed" comparative advantage', *Manchester School of Economic and Social Studies*, vol. 33, May 1965.

– 'Trade creation and diversion in the European Common Market: an appraisal of the evidence' in B. Balassa (ed.), *European Economic Integration*, Amsterdam, North-Holland, 1975.

BALDWIN, R. E. 'Export technology and development from a subsistence level', *Economic Journal*, vol. 73, March 1963.

– *Economic Development and Export Growth: a study of Northern Rhodesia 1920–1960*, Berkeley, University of California Press, 1966.

– *Nontariff Distortions of International Trade*, Washington (DC), Brookings Institution, 1970.

– 'Determinants of the commodity structure of US trade', *American Economic Review*, vol. 61, March 1971.

BANERJI, R. 'Major determinants of the share of manufactures in exports: a cross-section analysis and case study on India', *Weltwirtschaftliches Archiv*, vol. 108, no. 3, 1972.

BATCHELOR, R. A. and BOWE, C. 'Forecasting UK international trade: a general equilibrium approach', *Applied Economics*, vol. 6, June 1974.

BECKERMAN, W. 'Projecting Europe's growth', *Economic Journal*, vol. 72, December 1962.

BERGSMAN, J. *Brazil: industrialization and trade policies*, London, Oxford University Press, 1970.

BHAGWATI, J. 'The pure theory of international trade: a survey', *Economic Journal*, vol. 74, March 1964.

BHAGWATI, J. and CHEH, J. 'LDC exports: a cross-sectional analysis' in L. E. di Marco (ed.), *International Economics and Development*, New York, Academic Press, 1973.

BRAITHWAITE, S. N. 'Real income levels in Latin America', *Review of Income and Wealth*, series 14, June 1968.

BRANSON, W. H. and JUNZ, H. B. 'Trends in US trade and comparative advantage', *Brookings Papers in Economic Activity*, no. 2, 1971.

CAVES, R. E. 'Export-led growth and the new economic history' in J. Bhagwati, R. W. Jones, R. A. Mundell and J. Vanek (eds.), *Trade, Balance of Payments and Growth*, Amsterdam, North-Holland, 1971.

CHAMBERS, E. J. and GORDON, D. F. 'Primary products and economic growth: an empirical measurement', *Journal of Political Economy*, vol. 74, August 1966.

CHENERY, H. B. 'Patterns of industrial growth', *American Economic Review*, vol. 50, September 1960.

CHENERY, H. B. and BRUNO, M. 'Development alternatives in an open economy: the case of Israel', *Economic Journal*, vol. 72, March 1962.

CHENERY, H. B. and STROUT, A. M. 'Foreign assistance and economic development', *American Economic Review*, vol. 56, September 1966.

CHENERY, H. B. and SYRQUIN, M. *Patterns of Development 1950–70*, London, Oxford University Press, 1975.

CHENERY, H. B. and TAYLOR, L. 'Development patterns: among countries and over time', *Review of Economics and Statistics*, vol. 50, November 1968.

CLAGUE, C. 'An international comparison of industrial efficiency: Peru and the United States', *Review of Economics and Statistics*, vol. 49, November 1967.

CLARK, C. 'Is international commerce necessary?', *Bulletin d'Information et de Documentation*, vol. 32, July 1953.

– *The Conditions of Economic Progress* (3rd edn), London, Macmillan, 1975.

COOPER, R. N. 'Growth and trade: some hypotheses about long-term trends', *Journal of Economic History*, vol. 24, December 1964.

COPPOCK, J. D. *International Economic Instability: the experience after World War II*, New York, McGraw-Hill, 1962.

CORMACK, R. M. 'A review of classification', *Journal of the Royal Statistical Society* (series A), vol. 134, part 3, 1971.

CRIPPS, T. F. and TARLING, R. J. *Growth in Advanced Capitalist Economies 1950–1970*, Cambridge University Press, 1973.

DENISON, E. F. *The Sources of Economic Growth in the United States and the Alternatives before Us*, New York, Committee for Economic Development, 1962.

DEUTSCH, K. W., BLISS, C. J. and ECKSTEIN, A. 'Population, sovereignty, and the share of foreign trade', *Economic Development and Cultural Change*, vol. 10, October 1961.

DEUTSCH, K. W. and ECKSTEIN, A. 'National industrialization and the declining share of the international economic sector 1890–1959', *World Politics*, vol. 13, January 1961.

DIAB, M. A. *The United States Capital Position and the Structure of its Foreign Trade*, Amsterdam, North-Holland, 1956.

DIAZ ALEJANDRO, C. F. 'Industrialization and labor productivity differentials', *Review of Economics and Statistics*, vol. 47, May 1965.

DIWAN, R. K. 'A test of the two gap theory of economic development', *Journal of Development Studies*, vol. 4, July 1968.

DRÈZE, J. H. 'Quelques réflexions sereines sur l'adaptation de l'industrie belge au Marché Commun', *Comptes rendus des Travaux de la Société Royale d'Économie Politique de Belgique*, no. 275, December 1960.

– 'Les exportations entre CEE en 1958 et la position belge', *Recherches Économiques de Louvain*, vol. 27, December 1961.

EMERY, R. F. 'The relation of exports and economic growth', *Kyklos*, vol. 20, no. 2, 1967.

EVERITT, B. *Cluster Analysis*, London, Heinemann, 1974.

FELS, G., SCHATZ, K.-W. and WOLTER, F. 'Der Zusammenhang zwischen Produktionstruktur und Entwicklungsniveau', *Weltwirtschaftliches Archiv*, vol. 106, no. 2, 1971.

FINGER, J. M. 'Factor intensity and "Leontief type" tests of the factor proportions theory', *Economia Internazionale*, vol. 22, August 1969.

FRANKEL, H. 'Industrialisation of agricultural countries and the possibilities of a new international division of labour', *Economic Journal*, vol. 53, June/September 1943.

FRIED, E. R. and SCHULTZE, C. L. (eds.), *Higher Oil Prices and the World Economy*, Washington (DC), Brookings Institution, 1975.

FRIEND, I. and SCHOR, S. 'Who saves?', *Review of Economics and Statistics*, vol. 41, May 1959.

GEHRELS, F. 'Factor efficiency, substitution and the basis for trade: some empirical evidence', *Kyklos*, vol. 23, no. 2, 1970.

GERSCHENKRON, A. *Economic Backwardness in Historical Perspective: a book of essays*, Cambridge (Mass.), Harvard University Press, 1962.

GIERSCH, H. (ed.) *The International Division of Labour: problems and perspectives*, Tübingen, Mohr, 1974.

GIRGIS, M. 'Development and trade patterns in the Arab world', *Weltwirtschaftliches Archiv*, vol. 109, no. 1, 1973.

GLEJSER, H. 'An explanation of differences in trade–product ratios among countries', *Cahiers Économiques de Bruxelles*, no. 37, February 1968.

– 'The respective impacts of relative income, price and technology changes, US foreign investment, the EEC and EFTA on the American balance of trade' in H. Glejser (ed.), *Quantitative Studies of International Economic Relations*, Amsterdam, North-Holland, 1976.

GLEZAKOS, C. 'Export instability and economic growth: a statistical verification', *Economic Development and Cultural Change*, vol. 21, July 1973.

GRAY, H. P. 'A tripartite model of international trade', *Economia Internazionale*, vol. 27, May 1974.

GREEN, R. H. *Stages in Economic Development: changes in the structure of production, demand and international trade*, New Haven (Conn.), Yale University Economic Growth Center, 1969.

GREGORY, P. R. 'Cross section comparisons of the structure of GNP by sector of origin: socialist and western countries', *Kyklos*, vol. 24, no. 3, 1971.

GREGORY, P. R. and GRIFFIN, J. M. 'Secular and cross-sectional industrialization patterns: some further evidence on the Kuznets–Chenery controversy', *Review of Economics and Statistics*, vol. 56, August 1974.

GRUBEL, H. G. and LLOYD, P. J. *Intra-Industry Trade: theory and measurement of international trade in differential products*, London, Macmillan, 1975.

GUPTA, K. L. 'Development patterns: an interregional study', *Quarterly Journal of Economics*, vol. 85, November 1971.

HAHN, F. H. and MATTHEWS, R. C. O. 'The theory of economic growth: a survey', *Economic Journal*, vol. 74, December 1964.

HEGEL, G. W. F. *Philosophy of Right* (tr. W. T. M. Knox), London, Oxford University Press, 1942.

HELLEINER, G. K. 'Manufactured exports from less-developed countries and multinational firms', *Economic Journal*, vol. 83, March 1973.

HICKS, J. R. 'An inaugural lecture: II, the long-run dollar problem', *Oxford Economic Papers*, vol. 5, June 1953.

HIRSCH, S. 'Hypotheses regarding trade between developing and industrial countries' in Giersch (ed.), 1974, q.v.

HIRSCHMAN, A. O. *National Power and the Structure of Foreign Trade*, Berkeley, University of California Press, 1945.

HOBSON, J. A. *Imperialism: a study*, London, Nisbet, 1902.

HOFFMANN, W. G. *The Growth of Industrial Economies*, Manchester University Press, 1958.

HONG, W. 'Industrialization and trade in manufactures: the East Asian experience' in P. B. Kenen and R. Lawrence (eds.) *The Open Economy: essays on international trade and finance*, New York, Columbia University Press, 1968.

HORVAT, B. 'The relation between rate of growth and level of development', *Journal of Development Studies*, vol. 10, April/July 1974.

HOSELITZ, B. F. 'Some problems in the quantitative study of industrialization', *Economic Development and Cultural Change*, vol. 9, April 1961.

HOUTHAKKER, H. S. and MAGEE, S. P. 'Income and price elasticities in world trade', *Review of Economics and Statistics*, vol. 51, May 1969.

HUFBAUER, G. C. *Synthetic Materials and the Theory of International Trade*, London, Duckworth, 1966.

– 'The impact of national characteristics and technology on the commodity composition of trade in manufactured goods' in R. Vernon (ed.), *The Technology Factor in International Trade*, New York, National Bureau of Economic Research, 1970.

HUFBAUER, G. C. and CHILAS, J. G. 'Specialization by industrial countries: extent and consequences' in Giersch (ed.), 1974, q.v.

IKLÉ, M. *Switzerland: an international banking and finance centre*, London, Academic Press, 1972.

ISSAWI, C. 'Egypt since 1800: a study in lop-sided development', *Journal of Economic History*, vol. 21, March 1961.

Japan Economic Research Center. *Five-Year Forecast 1979–1983*, Tokyo, 1979.

JOHNSON, H. G. 'Mercantilism: past, present and future', *Manchester School of Economic and Social Studies*, vol. 42, March 1974.

JONES, R. F. 'Factor proportions and the Heckscher–Ohlin theorem', *Review of Economic Studies*, vol. 24, no. 1, 1956–7.

JUNZ, H. B. and RHOMBERG, R. R. 'Prices and export performance of industrial countries, 1953–63', *IMF Staff Papers*, vol. 12, July 1965.

– 'Price competitiveness in export trade among industrial countries', *American Economic Review*, vol. 63, May 1973.

KALDOR, N. *Causes of the Slow Rate of Economic Growth of the United Kingdom*, Cambridge University Press, 1966.

– *Strategic Factors in Economic Development*, Ithaca (NY), Cornell University Press, 1967.

– 'The irrelevance of equilibrium economics', *Economic Journal*, vol. 82, December 1972.

KANAMORI, H. *Economic Growth: the Japanese experience since the Meiji era*, Homewood (Ill.), Irwin, 1968.

KEESING, D. B. and SHERK, D. R. 'Population density in patterns of trade and development', *American Economic Review*, vol. 61, December 1971.

KENEN, P. B. (ed.) *International Trade and Finance: frontiers for research*, Cambridge University Press, 1975.

KENEN, P. B. and VOIVODAS, C. S. 'Export instability and economic growth', *Kyklos*, vol. 25, no. 4, 1972.

KEYNES, J. M. 'National self-sufficiency', *Yale Review*, vol. 23, June 1933.

KINDLEBERGER, C. P. 'Foreign trade and economic growth: lessons from Britain and France 1850 to 1913', *Economic History Review*, vol. 14 (second series), December 1961.

– *Europe's Postwar Growth: the role of labor supply*, London, Oxford University Press, 1967.

KLEIMAN, E. 'Trade and the decline of colonialism', *Economic Journal*, vol. 86, September 1976.

KNAPP, J. 'Pragmatism and the British *malaise*', *Lloyds Bank Review*, no. 90, October 1968.

KRÄGENAU, H. 'Wie hoch sind die deutschen Auslandsinvestitionen?', *Wirtschaftsdienst*, vol. 50, November 1970.

KRAUSE, L. B. 'United States imports, 1947–1958', *Econometrica*, vol. 30, April 1962.

KRAUSE, L. B. and SEKIGUCHI, S. 'Japan and the world economy' in H. Patrick and H. Rosovsky (eds.), *Asia's New Giant: how the Japanese economy works*, Washington (DC), Brookings Institution, 1975.

KRAVIS, I. B. 'Trade as a handmaiden of growth: similarities between the nineteenth and twentieth centuries', *Economic Journal*, vol. 80, December 1970.

KRAVIS, I. B., HESTON, A. and SUMMERS, R. *International Comparisons of Real Product and Purchasing Power*, Baltimore, Johns Hopkins University Press, 1978.

KRAVIS, I. B., KENESSEY, Z., HESTON, A. and SUMMERS, R. *A System of International Comparisons of Gross Product and Purchasing Power*, Baltimore, Johns Hopkins University Press, 1975.

KREININ, M. E. 'Effects of the EEC on imports of manufactures', *Economic Journal*, vol. 82, September 1972.

KUZNETS, S. *Uses of National Income in Peace and War*, New York, National Bureau of Economic Research, 1942.

– 'Level and structure of foreign trade: comparisons for recent years', *Economic Development and Cultural Change*, vol. 13, October 1964.

– 'Level and structure of foreign trade: long-term trends', *Economic Development and Cultural Change*, vol. 15, January 1967.

– *Modern Economic Growth*, New Haven (Conn.), Yale University Press, 1966.

– *The Economic Growth of Nations: total output and production structure*, Cambridge (Mass.), Harvard University Press, 1971.

LAGO, A. M. 'The Hoffmann industrial growth development path: an international comparison', *Weltwirtschaftliches Archiv*, vol. 103, no. 1, 1969.

LALL, S. 'Transfer pricing by multinational manufacturing firms', *Oxford University Bulletin of Economics and Statistics*, vol. 35, August 1973.

LAMFALUSSY, A. 'Contribution à un théorie de la croissance en économie ouverte', *Recherches Économiques de Louvain*, vol. 29, December 1963.

– *The United Kingdom and the Six: an essay on economic growth in Western Europe*, London, Macmillan, 1963.

LEAMER, E. E. 'The commodity composition of international trade in manufactures: an empirical analysis', *Oxford Economic Papers*, vol. 26, November 1974.

LEONTIEF, W. W. 'Domestic production and foreign trade: the American capital position re-examined', *Economia Internazionale*, vol. 7, February 1954.

LEONTIEF, W. W. *et al.* *The Future of the World Economy*, New York, Oxford University Press, 1977.

LEVIN, J. V. *The Export Economies: their pattern of development in historical perspective*, Cambridge (Mass.), Harvard University Press, 1960.

LEWIS, W. A. 'World production, prices and trade 1870–1960', *Manchester School of Economic and Social Studies*, vol. 20, May 1952.

– *The Theory of Economic Growth*, London, Allen & Unwin, 1955.

LINDER, S. B. *An Essay on Trade and Transformation*, Stockholm, Almqvist & Wiksell, 1961.

LINNEMAN, H. *An Econometric Study of International Trade Flows*, Amsterdam, North-Holland, 1966.

LIPSEY, R. E. *Price and Quantity Trends in the Foreign Trade of the United States*, Princeton (NJ), National Bureau of Economic Research, 1963.

LITTLE, I. M. D., SCITOVSKY, T. and SCOTT, M. FG. *Industry and Trade in Some Developing Countries: a comparative study*, London, Oxford University Press, 1970.

LUBITZ, R. 'Export-led growth in industrial economies', *Kyklos*, vol. 26, no. 2, 1973.

MACBEAN, A. *Export Instability and Economic Development*, London, Allen & Unwin, 1966.

MACDOUGALL, G. D. A. 'British and American exports: a study suggested by the theory of comparative costs – Part I', *Economic Journal*, vol. 61, December 1951.

MAGEE, S. P. 'Prices, incomes and foreign trade' in Kenen (ed.), 1975, q.v.

MAIZELS, A. *Industrial Growth and World Trade*, Cambridge University Press, 1963.

– *Exports and Economic Growth of Developing Countries*, Cambridge University Press, 1968.

MAJOR, R. L. and HAYS, S. 'Another look at the Common Market', *National Institute Economic Review*, no. 54, November 1970.

MAMALAKIS, M. and REYNOLDS, C. W. (eds.), *Essays on the Chilean Economy*, Homewood (Ill.), Irwin, 1965.

Massachusetts Institute of Technology, Workshop on Alternative Energy Strategies. *Energy: global prospects 1985–2000*, New York, McGraw-Hill, 1977.

MASSELL, B. F., PEARSON, S. R. and FITCH, J. B. 'Foreign exchange and economic development: an empirical study of selected Latin American countries', *Review of Economics and Statistics*, vol. 54, May 1972.

MEYER, J. R. 'An input–output approach to evaluating the influence of exports on British industrial production in the late 19th century', *Explorations in Entrepreneurial History*, no. 8, October 1955.

MICHALOPOULOS, C. 'Production and substitution in two-gap models', *Journal of Development Studies*, vol. 11, July 1975.

MIRAMON, J. de and KLEITZ, A. 'Tariff preferences for the developing world: operation and evolution of the generalised system of preferences', *OECD Observer*, no. 90, January 1978.

MORGAN, A. D. 'Tariff reductions and UK imports of manufactures: 1955–1971', *National Institute Economic Review*, no. 72, May 1975.

– 'Commercial policy' in F. T. Blackaby (ed.), *British Economic Policy 1960–74*, Cambridge University Press, 1978.

MYINT, H. *South-East Asia's Economy: development policies in the 1970's*, Harmondsworth, Penguin Books, 1972.

NAYA, S. 'Fluctuations in export earnings and economic patterns of Asian countries', *Economic Development and Cultural Change*, vol. 21, July 1973.

NELSON, R. R. 'A "diffusion" model of international productivity differences in manufacturing industry', *American Economic Review*, vol. 58, December 1968.

NURKSE, R. *Patterns of Trade and Development*, New York, Oxford University Press, 1961.

OHLIN, G. 'Trade in a non-*laissez-faire* world' in P. A. Samuelson (ed.), *International Economic Relations*, London, Macmillan, 1969.

ONIKI, H. and UZAWA, H. 'Patterns of trade and investment in a dynamic model of international trade', *Review of Economic Studies*, vol. 32, January 1965.

POSNER, M. V. 'International trade and technical change', *Oxford Economic Papers*, vol. 13 (new series), October 1961.

PREEG, E. H. *Traders and Diplomats*, Washington (DC), Brookings Institution, 1970.

PRYOR, F. L. 'The size of production establishments in manufacturing', *Economic Journal*, vol. 82, June 1972.

RAY, G. F. 'Primary products: prospects to 1985', *National Institute Economic Review*, no. 76, May 1976.

REDDAWAY, W. B. *et al. Effects of UK Direct Investment Overseas: final report*, Cambridge University Press, 1968.

ROBERTSON, D. H. 'The future of international trade', *Economic Journal*, vol. 48, March 1938.

ROBINSON, J. *The New Mercantilism*, Cambridge University Press, 1966.

SCAPERLANDA, A. E. and MAUER, L. J. 'The determinants of U.S. direct investment in the E.E.C.', *American Economic Review*, vol. 59, September 1969.

SCHARRER, H. E. (ed.), *Förderung privater Direktinvestitionen*, Hamburg, Verlag Weltarchiv, 1972.

SEVERN, A. K. 'Exports and economic growth: comment', *Kyklos*, vol. 21, no. 3, 1968.

SOLOW, R. M. 'Technical change and the aggregate production function', *Review of Economics and Statistics*, vol. 39, August 1957.

SOMBART, W. *Die deutsche Volkwirtschaft im neunzehnten Jahrhundert* (3rd edn), Berlin, G. Bondi, 1913.

STERN, R. M. *Foreign Trade and Economic Growth in Italy*, New York, Praeger, 1967.

– 'Testing trade theories' in Kenen (ed.), 1975, q.v.

STEUER, M. D. and VOIVODAS, C. S. 'Import substitution and Chenery's patterns of industrial growth: a further study', *Economia Internazionale*, vol. 18, February 1965.

STUBENITSKY, F. *American Direct Investment in the Netherlands Industry: a survey of the year 1966*, Rotterdam University Press, 1970.

SWEDENBORG, B. *Den Svenska Industrins Investeringar i Utlandet 1965–1970*, Uppsala, Almqvist & Wiksell, 1973.

SYRON, R. F. and WALSH, B. M. 'The relation of exports and economic growth: a note', *Kyklos*, vol. 21, no. 3, 1968.

TEMIN, P. 'A time-series test of patterns of industrial growth', *Economic Development and Cultural Change*, vol. 15, January 1967.

TINBERGEN, J. *Shaping the World Economy: suggestions for an international economic policy*, New York, Twentieth Century Fund, 1962.

TORRENS, R. *Essay on the Production of Wealth*, London, 1821 (new imprint, Kelley, USA, 1970).

TRAVIS, W. P. 'Production, trade and protection when there are many commodities and two factors', *American Economic Review*, vol. 62, March 1972.

VACIAGO, G. 'Increasing returns and growth in advanced economies: a re-evaluation', *Oxford Economic Papers*, vol. 27, July 1975.

VERDOORN, P. J. 'Fattori che regolano lo sviluppo della produttività del lavoro', *L'Industria*, no. 1, 1949.

VERDOORN, P. J. and SCHWARTZ, A. N. R. 'Two alternative estimates of the effects of EEC and EFTA on the pattern of trade', *European Economic Review*, vol. 3, October 1972.

VERNON, R. 'International investment and international trade in the product cycle', *Quarterly Journal of Economics*, vol. 80, May 1966.

VOIVODAS, C. S. 'Exports, foreign capital inflow and economic growth', *Journal of International Economics*, vol. 3, November 1973.

WEISSKOPF, T. E. 'An econometric test of alternative constraints on the growth of underdeveloped countries', *Review of Economics and Statistics*, vol. 54, February 1972.

WELLS, L. T. (ed.), *The Product Life Cycle and International Trade*, Boston (Mass.), Harvard Business School, 1972.

WILLIAMSON, J. and BOTTRILL, A. 'The impact of customs unions on trade in manufactures', *Oxford Economic Papers*, vol. 23 (new series), November 1971.

WISHART, D. 'An algorithm for hierarchical classifications', *Biometrics*, vol. 25, March 1969.

YAMAZAWA, I. 'Structural changes in world trade flows', *Hitotsubashi Journal of Economics*, vol. 11, February 1971.

2. OFFICIAL PUBLICATIONS

(a) United Kingdom
Central Statistical Office. *Annual Abstract of Statistics*.
Customs and Excise. *Annual Statement of Trade of the United Kingdom*.
National Economic Development Office. *Product Changes in Industrial Countries' Trade: 1955–1968* by M. Panić and A. H. Rajan, 1971.
Department of Trade. *Trade and Industry* [formerly *Board of Trade Journal*] (monthly).

(b) Belgium
Ministère des Affaires Économiques. *Rapport* (annual).
Banque Nationale de Belgique. 'Les investissements étrangers dans des entreprises industrielles en Belgique', *Bulletin d'Information et de Documentation*, vol. 45, October 1970.
– *Bulletin de la Banque Nationale de Belgique* (monthly).

(c) Canada
Bank of Canada. *Bank of Canada Review* (monthly).
Economic Council of Canada. *An Econometric Analysis of the Canada, United States Automotive Agreement* by D. A. Wilton, 1976.
Statistics Canada. *Canada's International Investment Position, 1926 to 1967, 1968 to 1970* and *1971 to 1973*, 1971, 1975 and 1977.

(d) France
'Les investissements français à l'étranger', *Journal Officiel de la République Française*, 5 November 1970.
Ministère de l'Économie et des Finances. 'Balance des payements entre la France et l'Extérieur', *Statistiques et Études Financières*, vol. 14, 1962–vol. 24, 1972.
– 'Les participations étrangères dans l'industrie française au 1er Janvier 1973', *Statistiques et Études Financières*, vol. 27, September 1975.
Institut National de la Statistique et des Études Économiques. *Annuaire Statistique de la France*.
– *Bulletin Mensuel de Statistique*.

(*e*) *Germany*
Bundesministerium für Wirtschaft. *Leistung im Zahlen, 1975* (annual).
Deutsche Bundesbank. *Monatsberichte der Deutschen Bundesbank.*
Statistisches Bundesamt. *Aussenhandel,* Fachserie G, Reihe 1 and 5.
– *Statistisches Jahrbuch für die Bundesrepublik Deutschland.*

(*f*) *Italy*
Istituto Centrale di Statistica. *Statistica Annuale del Commercio con l'Estero.*
Servizi Informazioni. 'La partecipazione straniera nelle società italiane', *Vita Italiana,* June 1974.

(*g*) *Japan*
Bank of Japan. *Export and Import Price Indexes* (annual).
Japan External Trade Organization. *Japan: into the multinationalization era,* 1973.

(*h*) *Netherlands*
Central Bureau of Statistics. *Maandstatistiek van de Binnenlandse Handel* (monthly).
– *Statistical Yearbook of the Netherlands.*

(*i*) *Sweden*
Central Bureau of Statistics. *Statistiska Meddelanden,* series H.

(*j*) *Switzerland*
Département Fédéral de l'Économie Publique. *La Vie Économique* (monthly).

(*k*) *United States*
Central Intelligence Agency. *The International Energy Situation: outlook to 1985,* 1977.
Department of Commerce. *Foreign Direct Investment in the United States,* 1976.
– *Survey of Current Business* (monthly).
Department of Energy. *A Technical Analysis of the International Oil Market* by Petroleum Economics Ltd, 1978.
Department of Labor. *Wholesale Prices and Price Indexes* (monthly).
Senate Committee on Finance. *Implications of Multinational Firms for World Trade and Investment and for U.S. Trade and Labor,* 1973.
Treasury. *Overseas Manufacturing Investment and the Balance of Payments* by G. C. Hufbauer and F. M. Adler, 1968.

(*l*) *International*
Bank for International Settlements. *48th Annual Report 1977–78,* Basle, 1978.
Commission of the European Communities. *Official Journal of the European Communities, Information and Notices* (English edition), vol. 20, no. C.12, Brussels, 1977.
– Statistical Office. *Industriezensus von 1963,* Luxembourg, 1969.
European Free Trade Association. *EFTA Foreign Investment: changes in the pattern of EFTA foreign direct investment,* Geneva (undated).
– Secretariat. *The Trade Effects of EFTA and the EEC 1959–1967,* Geneva, 1972.
General Agreement on Tariffs and Trade [GATT]. *Adjustment, Trade and*

Growth in Developed and Developing Countries by R. Blackhurst, N. Marian and J. Tumlir, Geneva, 1978.
– *International Trade*, Geneva (annual).
International Bank for Reconstruction and Development [IBRD]. *The International Division of Labor: the case of industry* by H. B. Chenery and H. Hughes, Paris, 1972.
– *World Development Report*, Washington (DC), 1978.
International Labour Office [ILO]. *The Quality of Labour and Economic Development in Certain Countries: a preliminary study* by W. Galenson and G. Pyatt, Geneva, 1964.
– *Labour Force Estimates and Projections, 1950–2000*, Geneva, 1977.
International Monetary Fund [IMF]. *Balance of Payments Yearbook*, Washington (DC).
League of Nations. *Europe's Trade*, Geneva, 1941.
– *The Network of World Trade*, Geneva, 1942.
– *Industrialization and Foreign Trade*, Geneva, 1945.
Organisation for Economic Co-operation and Development [OECD]. *Energy Prospects to 1985*, Paris, 1974.
– *Interim Report of the Industry Committee on International Enterprises*, Paris, 1974.
– *Labour Force Statistics 1962–1973*, Paris, 1975.
– *Towards Full Employment and Price Stability* by P. McCracken *et al.*, Paris, 1977.
– *World Energy Outlook*, Paris, 1977.
– *The Impact of the Newly Industrialising Countries on Production and Trade in Manufactures*, Paris, 1979.
– *Economic Outlook*, Paris (twice yearly).
– *National Accounts of OECD Countries*, Paris (annual).
– *Statistics of Foreign Trade*, Paris (series A: monthly, series B: quarterly and series C: annual).
United Nations
   Conference on Trade and Development [UNCTAD]. *Handbook of International Trade and Development Statistics, 1972, 1976* and *Supplement 1977*, New York, 1972, 1976 and 1977.
   – *Operation and Effects of the Generalized System of Preferences*, New York, 1974.
   – *Restructuring of World Industry*, New York, 1978.
   – *Trade and Development*, no. 1, Spring 1979.
   – *Trade in Manufactures of Developing Countries and Territories*, New York (annual).
   Department of Economic and Social Affairs. *A Study of Industrial Growth*, New York, 1963.
   – *The Growth of World Industry 1938–61*, New York, 1963–5.
   – *The Growth of World Industry* (1969 and 1972 edns), New York, 1971 and 1974.
   – *The International Development Strategy: first overall review and appraisal of issues and policies*, New York, 1973.
   – *Multinational Corporations in World Development*, New York, 1973.
   Economic Commission for Africa. *A Survey of Economic Conditions in Africa, 1972*, New York, 1973.

Economic Commission for Europe. *Economic Survey of Europe in 1971.* Part I: *The European Economy from the 1950s to the 1970s,* New York, 1972.
– *Factors and Conditions of Long-Term Growth,* New York, 1974.
Food and Agriculture Organization. *Production Yearbook 1972,* Rome, 1973.
Industrial Development Organization [UNIDO]. 'The role of the industrial sector in economic development', *Industrialization and Productivity Bulletin,* no. 14, 1969.
– *Industrial Development Survey,* New York (annual).
Statistical Office. *Patterns of Industrial Growth 1938–1958,* New York, 1960.
– *Commodity Trade Statistics,* New York (annual).
– *Monthly Bulletin of Statistics,* New York.
– *Statistical Yearbook,* New York.
– *Yearbook of International Trade Statistics,* New York.
– *Yearbook of National Accounts Statistics,* New York.

INDEX

Adams, N. A., 176, 178, 182
Adelman, I., 110n, 224
Adler, F. M., 77–8
aero-industry, 65
Africa
    growth rates, 198, 201
    share of world manufacturing production, 241
    shares of production, by sector, 95, 96
    structure classification, 111
agriculture
    in growth theory, 211
    labour productivity in, 98–100, 232–3
    population share in, 307, 313–18
    recruitment from, 236, 239
    share of national output, 9–10, 140, 241
    transformation trends, 121–2, 133–4
    variations in sector share, 95, 96
aircraft industry, 55, 64, 65, 274
Alaskan oil, 229
Alecko, S. A., 100
Algeria, current account deficit, 231
Argentina
    balance of payments, 39
    exchange rates, 278
    exports, 41, 199
    import substitution, 225
    labour, 102, 137
    manufacturing, growth rates, 98; share in GDP, 125
    tariffs, 152
    trade ratio, 162
Arrow, K. J., 134–5, 141
Asia
    exports, 199, 202, 220
    share of world manufacturing production, 241
    shares of production, by sector, 95, 96
assets, foreign
    growth in host countries, 84–5
    in manufacturing, 82–3, 85–8
Association of Southeast Asian Nations, 167
Australia
    consumption of manufactures, 27, 34, 35
    export ratio, 41
    growth patterns, 162, 165, 212

import data, 284
intra-industry trade, 155
shares of production, by sector, 95, 131
structure classification, 115
vertical trade, 165, 187
Austria, output ratio, 282, 283
autarky, 122, 169
Automotive Agreement (Canada–United States, 1965), 8, 27, 53–5, 60, 63, 65–6, 69, 73, 82, 88, 243

Bacon, R. W., 1n.
Balassa, B., 69, 70, 71n, 155
Baldwin, R. E., 155, 169n, 214
Banerji, R., 177
Bangladesh, 37
    halts to industrialisation, 108
Bank of England, 231
Batchelor, R. A., 217
bauxite, 213
Beckerman, W., 215–17
Belgium
    commodity effect, 52
    competitiveness, 58, 60, 65, 75–6
    export, flexibility, 62–3; ratio, 41; share of US owned enterprises, 90
    growth rates, 202–3
    output ratios, 236, 282
    price indices, 287, 288–90
    protection, 72
    source material, 290, 298
    structure classification, 114
Bergsman, J., 214n
beverages, 97, 281
    tropical, 23
Bhagwati, J., 157n, 177, 214n
Blackaby, F. T., 75n
Blackhurst, R., 243n, 248n
Bliss, C. J., 159n, 161, 169
Botswana, characterisation statistics, 313
Bottrill, A., 69, 70, 71n, 72
Bowe, C., 217
Braithwaite, S. N., 278
Branson, W. H., 155
Brazil
    balance of payments, 39

337

PUBLICATIONS OF THE
NATIONAL INSTITUTE OF ECONOMIC
AND SOCIAL RESEARCH

published by

THE CAMBRIDGE UNIVERSITY PRESS

Books published for the Institute by the Cambridge University Press are available through the ordinary booksellers. They appear in the five series below:

ECONOMIC & SOCIAL STUDIES

*I   *Studies in the National Income, 1924–1938*
Edited by A. L. BOWLEY. Reprinted with corrections, 1944. pp. 256.

*II   *The Burden of British Taxation*
By G. FINDLAY SHIRRAS and L. ROSTAS. 1942. pp. 140.

*III   *Trade Regulations and Commercial Policy of the United Kingdom*
By THE RESEARCH STAFF OF THE NATIONAL INSTITUTE OF ECONOMIC AND SOCIAL RESEARCH. 1943. pp. 275.

*IV   *National Health Insurance: A Critical Study*
By HERMAN LEVY. 1944. pp. 356.

*V   *The Development of the Soviet Economic System: An Essay on the Experience of Planning in the U.S.S.R.*
By ALEXANDER BAYKOV. 1946. pp. 520.
(Out of print in this series, but reprinted 1970 in Cambridge University Press Library Edition, £7.50 net.)

*VI   *Studies in Financial Organization.*
By T. BALOGH. 1948. pp. 328.

*VII   *Investment, Location, and Size of Plant: A Realistic Inquiry into the Structure of British and American Industries*
By P. SARGANT FLORENCE, assisted by W. BALDAMUS. 1948. pp. 230.

*VIII   *A Statistical Analysis of Advertising Expenditure and of the Revenue of the Press*
By NICHOLAS KALDOR and RODNEY SILVERMAN. 1948. pp. 200.

*IX   *The Distribution of Consumer Goods*
By JAMES B. JEFFERYS, assisted by MARGARET MACCOLL and G. L. LEVETT. 1950. pp. 430.

*X   *Lessons of the British War Economy*
Edited by D. N. CHESTER. 1951. pp. 260.

*XI   *Colonial Social Accounting*
By PHYLLIS DEANE. 1953. pp. 360.

*XII   *Migration and Economic Growth*
By BRINLEY THOMAS. 1954. pp. 384.

*XIII   *Retail Trading in Britain, 1850–1950*
By JAMES B. JEFFERYS. 1954. pp. 490.

*XIV   *British Economic Statistics*
By CHARLES CARTER and A. D. ROY. 1954. pp. 192.

*XV   *The Structure of British Industry: A Symposium*
Edited by DUNCAN BURN. 1958. Vol. I. pp. 403. Vol. II. pp. 499.

*XVI   *Concentration in British Industry*
By RICHARD EVELY and L. M. D. LITTLE. 1960. pp. 357.

*XVII   *Studies in Company Finance*
Edited by BRIAN TEW and R. F. HENDERSON. 1959. pp. 301.

* At present out of print.

OCCASIONAL PAPERS

* At present out of print.

STUDIES IN THE NATIONAL INCOME AND EXPENDITURE OF THE UNITED KINGDOM

Published under the joint auspices of the National Institute and the Department of Applied Economics, Cambridge.

* At present out of print.

* At present out of print.

THE NATIONAL INSTITUTE OF ECONOMIC AND
SOCIAL RESEARCH

publishes regularly

THE NATIONAL INSTITUTE ECONOMIC REVIEW

A quarterly analysis of the general economic situation in the United Kingdom and overseas, with forecasts eighteen months ahead. The last issue each year usually contains an assessment of medium-term prospects. There are also in most issues special articles on subjects of interest to academic and business economists.

Annual subscriptions, £25.00 (home), and £35.00 or $75 (abroad), also single issues for the current year, £7.00 (home) and £10.00 or $22 (abroad), are available direct from NIESR, 2 Dean Trench Street, Smith Square, London, SW1P 3EH.

Subscriptions at the special reduced price of £10.00 p.a. are available to students in the United Kingdom and Irish Republic on application to the Secretary of the Institute.

Back numbers and reprints of issues which have gone out of stock are distributed by Wm. Dawson and Sons Ltd., Cannon House, Park Farm Road, Folkestone. Microfiche copies for the years 1959–79 are available from EP Microform Ltd., Bradford Road, East Ardsley, Wakefield, Yorks.

Published by
HEINEMANN EDUCATIONAL BOOKS
and available from booksellers

AN INCOMES POLICY FOR BRITAIN
Edited by FRANK BLACKABY. 1972. pp. 260. £4.00 net.

*THE MEDIUM TERM: MODELS OF THE BRITISH ECONOMY
Edited by G. D. N. WORSWICK and FRANK BLACKABY. 1974. pp. 256.

THE UNITED KINGDOM ECONOMY
By the NIESR. 4th edn. 1979. pp. 128. £1.80 net.

DEMAND MANAGEMENT
Edited by MICHAEL POSNER. 1978. pp. 256. £9.50 (hardback), £4.50 (paperback) net.

DE-INDUSTRIALISATION
Edited by FRANK BLACKABY. 1979. pp. 282. £9.50 (hardback),
£5.50 (paperback) net.

BRITAIN'S TRADE AND EXCHANGE-RATE POLICY
Edited by ROBIN MAJOR. 1979. pp. 240. £9.75 (hardback),
£5.50 (paperback) net.

* At present out of print.